PRECEDENTS IN ARCHITECTURE

Analytic Diagrams, Formative Ideas, and Partis

Third Edition

Roger H. Clark
Michael Pause

WILEY

JOHN WILEY & SONS, INC.

To Judy and Kathy

CONTENTS

PREFACES

PREFACE TO THE FIRST EDITION

This book is about architecture.

In particular, it focuses on a way of thinking about architecture that emphasizes what is in essence the same, rather than different. Our concern is for a continuous tradition that makes the past part of the present. We do not wish to aid the repetition or revival of style whether in whole or part. Rather, by a conscious sense of precedent that identifies patterns and themes, we hope to pursue archetypal ideas that might aid in the generation of architectural form.

While architecture embodies many realms, we concentrate on built form. Without apology, we make no attempt to discuss the social, political, economic, or technical aspects of architecture. The domain of design ideas lies within the formal and spatial realm of architecture, and thus it is this arena that is explored in this book.

Obviously, a sound architectural idea will not, as a tool for design, inevitably lead to a good design. One can imagine many undesirable buildings which might originate with formative ideas. To be sensitive to the potential of archetypal pattern in design does not lessen the importance of concern for other issues or for the building itself. However, one commonality shared by the great buildings of this era with those of the past, is a demonstrated understanding of basic architectural ideas which are recognizable as formative patterns.

Our analysis and interpretations are of built form and, therefore, may not necessarily coincide with the architect's intentions or the interpretations of others. The analysis is not all-inclusive in that it is limited to characteristics which can be diagrammed.

The intentions of this study are to assist the understanding of architectural history, to examine basic similarities of architects' designs over time, to identify generic solutions to design problems which transcend time, and to develop analysis as a tool for design. Of importance is the development of a vehicle for the discussion of ideas through the use of example. The understanding of history derived from this kind of investigation can only be obtained by far greater labor than that involved in acquiring a knowledge of history that focuses on names and dates. The reward for this effort is a design vocabulary that has evolved and been tested over time. We believe designers benefit from a comprehensive understanding of formative ideas, organizational concepts, and partis.

As a resource, this book offers factual graphic information on 64 buildings, a detailed analysis of each of these buildings, a range of designs by individual architects, a compilation of formative ideas for design generation, a collection of architectural images, and a reference for a technique of analysis. Some of this information is not readily available in other sources.

We are indebted to the Graham Foundation for Advanced Studies in the Fine Arts for support to make this study possible.

Any effort of this nature is the fruit of many encounters with individuals and ideas, but one debt in particular stands out as significant. Through a series of conversations with George E. Hartman, Jr., several years ago, some of our thoughts and ideas about architecture and history were focused. Since that time, he has continuously and enthusiastically offered support and encouragement. James L. Nagel, Ludwig Glaser, William N. Morgan, and the late William

Caudill each generously sponsored our efforts to secure assistance from the Graham Foundation. Roger Cannon, Robert Humenn, and Debbie Buffalin provided valuable help in locating material and information. For their assistance and support we thank several persons in the School of Design: Dean Claude E. McKinney, Winifred Hodge, the secretaries, and the librarians. The students in our classes have enriched, stimulated, and challenged our ideas, and encouraged us to record them in this volume. We fully acknowledge our debt to them.

A special acknowledgment is reserved for Rebecca H. Mentz and Michael A. Nieminen, whose considerable talents were used to draw the sheets reproduced in this volume. Without their skill, patience, diligence, and dedication this volume would not have been possible.

Our gratitude is extended to our families who have aided our efforts through sacrifice, devotion, and understanding.

To all other persons who have encouraged or in some way contributed to this study we collectively give thanks.

By making available the information that is presented in this volume, we hope to expand the understanding of precedents in architecture; to illustrate an educational technique that is useful to students, educators, and practitioners; and to demonstrate an analytic technique that can have impact on architectural form and space decisions.

PREFACE TO THE SECOND EDITION

The success of the first edition indicated that there was a need for conceptual and analytic information about architecture. Our experience with the first edition over the past decade demonstrated that the material has been useful as a tool for teaching architecture. It has provided a vocabulary for analysis that helps students and architects understand the works of others and aids them in creating their own designs. This approach continues to be useful and there was no apparent need to revise the information. Instead, the second edition gave us the opportunity to enrich the content of the analysis section by adding the works of seven architects. They were chosen initially to augment the content of the original sixteen architects. Some were selected for historical significance, some for lack of widespread documentation of their work. Others were picked because of emerging reputations and the production of a meaningful body of work since the publication of the first edition. All were selected because of the strength, quality, and interest of their designs. It is our intent to continue to show that design ideas transcend culture and time. Keeping the same format, we have added factual and analytic information on two or four buildings by each of the seven new architects.

While some may find this book useful for information about a particular architect or building, it is not our primary purpose to present any one building or architect exhaustively (e.g., photographs, written descriptions, or contract documents). Rather, our intention is to continue to explore the commonality of design ideas through comparison. To achieve this we have used the diagrammatic technique that was developed in the original study. While some of the architects and architectural authors have used diagrams to explain or inform others about the buildings included in this volume, the diagrams in this book are our own creation.

In addition to the acknowledgments cited in the preface of the first edition the following have helped make this edition a reality. The Graham Foundation for Advanced Studies in the Fine Arts supported our work for a second time; for this we are grateful. Van Nostrand Reinhold also contributed grant money to make this edition possible. Both of these sources aided our research and allowed for the production of the drawings.

While difficult to acknowledge all individuals who have contributed to or influenced our ideas, certain people's efforts deserve recognition. We are indebted to Wendy Lochner for persuading us to attempt a second edition. Her support and encouragement were critical. The editorial staff at Van Nostrand Reinhold provided us with willing and valuable assistance. James L. Nagle, Victor Reigner, and Mark Simon supported our efforts through encouragement, suggestions, and recommendations. Peter Bohlin and Carole Rusche generously contributed valuable information on the works of some of the architects. Collectively, we thank the staff of the School of Design for their willing assistance.

Special recognition goes to Mara Murdoch who single-handedly, with great skill, dedication, and patience, drew all of the new pages.

Finally, we wish to acknowledge all of our students, who have shown us that the study of precedents is a valuable tool for learning to design, and who continue to challenge us.

PREFACE TO THE THIRD EDITION

We commend to the reader the Prefaces to the first and second editions of this volume. Much of what is included in those Prefaces remains pertinent to us and our feelings about this work. The approach to understanding architecture presented herein continues to be useful and this edition again gave us the opportunity to enrich the Analysis section by adding factual and analytic information on two buildings by each of eight architects.

As with the previous editions, we have chosen to continue to present the buildings as a series of analytical diagrams that examine archetypal ideas. Our intention is to continue to explore the commonality of design ideas for comparison. We, of course, are aware that the architects examined herein may not have embraced the subjects of the diagrams nor, if they did consider the issues, approached them in the same way we have interpreted them. Thus, the diagrams are our own interpretations and some are more interpretive than others. Obviously these diagrams are then abstractions that focus on an issue that we have identified. For a particular architect or building a single diagram may be clearer or more revealing, which might suggest the identification of an issue of interest to the architect involved. By examining the buildings through the same issues it is possible to see relationships and nuances of development between architects and their buildings. We also understand that architecture has many manifestations—social, technical, economical, cultural, legal, and political. Any or all of these areas can impact the final form of the building, as can an individual architect's or client's personal predilection or whim.

Of those architects, for instance, that have been added for this edition, we know of Sigurd Lewerentz's interest in not doing things the conventional way. He is perhaps not as well known as some of the other architects in this volume, probably because he did not write about his work and did not teach. Fortunately, some publications have appeared in recent years that have chronicled his life and his work. We found it interesting that while he began with a refined, yet original, Classical language (at the Chapel of the Resurrection, for instance), his later work, represented here by the St. John's Church in Klippan, rejected that language. Yet there are similarities between the earlier and later work, as revealed by the analytical diagrams. His work demonstrates a subdued and restrained imagination that resulted in uncompromising and mysterious buildings.

Steven Holl seems to borrow from concepts of biology and geology in making sculpturally fluid spaces. While his buildings gesture toward their context, he has an obvious interest in the introduction and manipulation of natural light for the interior spaces of his buildings. Much has been written about the importance of his sketches and watercolors in capturing the feelings he desires for a building, yet his early interest in geometries is still demonstrated in his recent buildings.

Rafael Moneo's work included in this edition shows his intense use of the site, resulting in a building that is compact and basically fills the site. Through this compactness, Moneo reacts to the urban context while providing an autonomous and animated inner world. Herzog and de Meuron, on the other hand, give obvious priority in their work to the skin, the surface, of their buildings. Perhaps their desire is to create a visual and tactile surface that will create the perception that the built form has disappeared.

The common thread is that each of these architects has, regardless of their interest or considerations, produced built forms that include the physical and spatial realms of architecture. Architecture is not formless. In the end the built form may outlast the current fascinations and considerations. The issues we examine here may not be part of those considerations. Our analytical diagrams afford a way to understand buildings. In some cases they may help build a formal vocabulary. The issues examined could be the means for ordering or organizing an idea, or they may possibly be a way to generate a design. In any case, we can diagram what has been done, but not necessarily why it has been done.

The work that has been used for this third edition is in the same format as the previous editions. The new pages have been seamlessly inserted into the Analysis section in alphabetical order. This section now includes the work of thirty-one architects. Collectively they represent architects of historic importance and those who have produced meaningful work recently. All were selected not only because of the quality and strength of their work, but also because they afford the opportunity to explore buildings, their organizations and ordering ideas, through comparison.

We began exploring the analysis of architectural precedents in the 1970s and first published such work in a student publication of the School (now College) of Design at North Carolina State University. That volume, titled *Analysis of Precedent*, appeared in 1978. Van Nostrand Reinhold published the original edition of *Precedents in Architecture* in 1985 and the second edition followed in 1996. Both editions have been through several printings, and each has been translated into Spanish and Japanese. We are also aware that these editions have been translated on an ad-hoc basis into Korean and Chinese. The second edition received an International Architecture Book Award from the American Institute of Architects. The jury for this awards program, which included books from publishers worldwide, commented that "*Precedents in Architecture* provides a vocabulary for architectural analysis that helps architects understand the works of others and aids in creating original ideas. Whether a novice or professional, this work enriches the reader's design vocabulary."

The success and longevity of this work suggests there is a need for this information about architecture. As we started to produce the material for this third edition, we were keenly aware of the initial premise for the study—the commonality and significance of design ideas that transcend time and place. As the work progressed, these assumptions have been reinforced. Architectural ideas are the underpinnings of architecture upon which other concerns—social, technical, economical, cultural, legal, and political—are layered.

In addition to the acknowledgements cited in the prefaces to the first and second editions, we wish to recognize some people directly related to this edition. It is always difficult to thank adequately all of the individuals who have had an influence on this work or have contributed to its development. We are indebted to each of them whether they knew they had an influence or not. Certain people, however, deserve to be mentioned specifically. This edition would not have existed at all without the efforts of Margaret Cummins of John Wiley and Sons. She approached us about considering a third edition, and she made it all possible by securing for us a grant from John Wiley to support our work. Her powers of persuasion, suggestions, and encouragement were critical. The other members of the editorial, art, and production staff at Wiley were also helpful. Peter Q. Bohlin, James L. Nagle, and Victor Reignier encouraged us through suggestions and recommendations. We also thank the College of Design, its administration and staff, for their willing assistance.

As with previous editions all of the pages in this edition are from original drawings. While we are responsible for the content of the drawings, Jason Miller has with diligence, patience, and great skill interpreted our sketches to create these thirty-two new pages. We owe him a special thank you.

Finally, as we have done previously, we wish to thank our students, who reinforce, challenge, and question constantly while demonstrating that analytical processes are valuable as a tool for design. They make each day an interesting pleasure.

Roger H. Clark and Michael Pause

INTRODUCTION

The renewed and growing interest in architectural history and historic architectural example has focused the need to clarify the link between history and design. History studied in the academic sense of seeing our place within a continuum, or in the strictly scholarly sense of knowing the past, can limit our knowledge as architects to little more than names, dates, and style recognition. Seeing between and beyond the layers of historical styles, within which architecture is generally categorized and presented, can make history a source of enrichment for architectural design.

The search, in this study, is for theory which transcends the moment and reveals an architectural idea. The technique for this search is the careful examination and analysis of buildings. The desired result is the development of theory to generate ideas with which to design architecture.

This volume is organized into two parts. The first concentrates on the analysis of 104 buildings which are presented in both conventional drawings—site plan, plan, and elevation—and diagrams. The second identifies and delineates formal archetypal patterns or formative ideas from which architecture might evolve. It can be observed that certain patterns persist through time, with no apparent relationship to place.

Buildings that represent a range of time, function, and style, and architects who exemplify seemingly different approaches to architecture, were selected. This selection was tempered by availability of information; some architects and some buildings were not included because the material available did not permit thorough analysis.

Preference was given to built buildings in lieu of projects, which are included in the second part only when they represent pertinent examples of an idea. While the analytic technique utilized in this volume is applicable to groups of buildings, this study is limited to single works of architecture.

The information available for the selected buildings contained inconsistencies in some areas. When discrepancies did occur, every effort was made to verify the accuracy of the information. If it could not be totally verified, then reasonable assumptions were made. For example, a site plan was never drawn by Robert Venturi for the Tucker House; therefore, the site plan indicated in this volume is inferred from other information.

In some instances, particular buildings are cited in the literature by more than one name. For example, La Rotonda by Andrea Palladio is often referred to as Villa Capra. Less frequently it is called Villa Almerico, after the name of the family for whom it was originally built. In cases where such multiplicity occurs, buildings are identified in the body of this study by the most frequently used name and in the index by the several names used.

Opinion also differs about dates attributed to several buildings. Because of the length of time it takes to complete a building or because of the imprecision of recorded history, it is often difficult to establish an exact date or series of dates for a building. The significance of the date is simply to place the work in a chronological context. When conflict did occur between sources, the date that is ascribed most often is the one used.

Undoubtedly, the complexity of architecture often makes it difficult to attribute a building to a single person. It is clear that buildings, regardless of when executed, are the products of partnerships or collaborations and the result of inputs from several persons. However, for the sake of clarity, the buildings in this study are assigned to the person who is normally recognized as the designer. For instance, Charles

Moore is listed rather than the several associations which might be included for each building. Similarly, Romaldo Giurgola is acknowledged instead of the firm in which he is a partner.

In the analysis part of the study, the plan, elevation, and section for any individual building are drawn at the same scale. However, the scale between any two buildings varies depending upon building size and presentation format. Site plans are oriented to correspond generally to the orientation of the floor plan, and north is indicated where known.

To communicate the analysis of the buildings and the formative ideas in this study, a diagram or a set of diagrams is utilized. The diagrams are drawings that, as abstractions, are intended to convey essential characteristics and relationships in a building. As such, the diagrams focus on specific physical attributes which allow for the comparison of that attribute between buildings independent of style, type, function, or time. The diagrams are developed from the three-dimensional form and space configurations of the building. They take into account more information than is normally apparent in a plan, an elevation, or a section. To

reduce the building to its essentials, the diagrams have been intentionally simplified. This elimination of all but the most important considerations makes those that remain both dominant and memorable.

For the analysis, it was necessary to establish a graphic standard so that comparison could be made between the diagrams. In general, heavy lines are used in each diagram to accent a particular issue. In the formative idea part of the study, the plan, elevation, or section of the building is drawn lightly for orientation purposes, while the issue being analyzed and compared is indicated by heavy lines or shading. The legend on page xiii indicates the specific graphic standard used for the diagrams in the analysis section.

This study is not exhaustive; rather, examples are included to illustrate the nuances of the idea. It is rare to find a building configuration which embodies a single formal theme in absolute purity. More normal is a variety of patterns layered upon one another—the consequence of which is the potential for the richness that can evolve from multiple interpretations. In this study dominant patterns have been identified, but this is not to suggest that others do not exist.

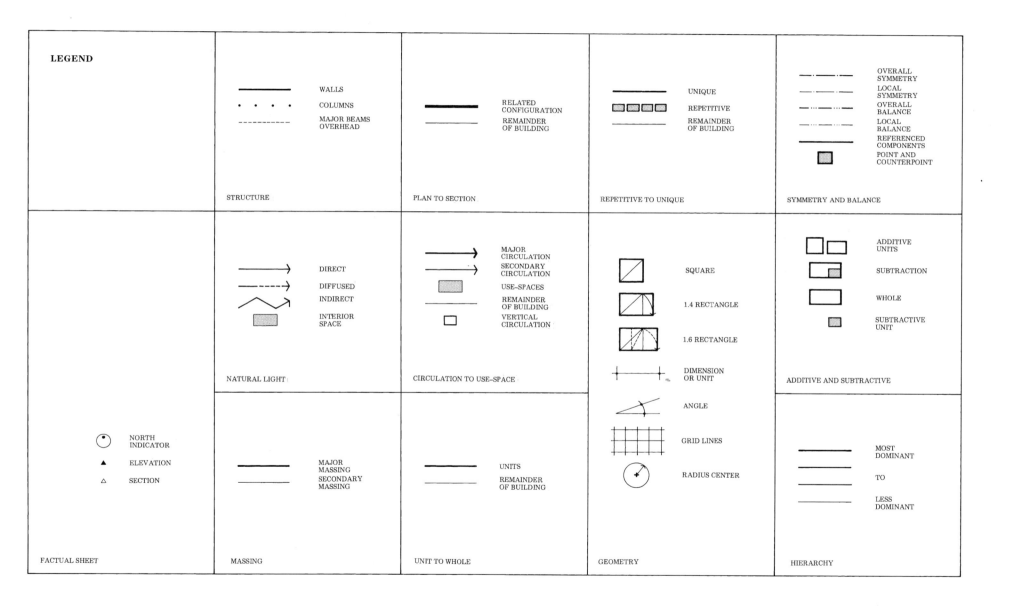

LEGEND

STRUCTURE
- ———— WALLS
- · · · · COLUMNS
- – – – – MAJOR BEAMS OVERHEAD

PLAN TO SECTION
- ▬▬▬ RELATED CONFIGURATION
- ———— REMAINDER OF BUILDING

REPETITIVE TO UNIQUE
- ———— UNIQUE
- ▫▫▫▫ REPETITIVE
- ———— REMAINDER OF BUILDING

SYMMETRY AND BALANCE
- —·—·— OVERALL SYMMETRY
- —··—··— LOCAL SYMMETRY
- —·—·— OVERALL BALANCE
- —··—··— LOCAL BALANCE
- ———— REFERENCED COMPONENTS
- ▫ POINT AND COUNTERPOINT

NATURAL LIGHT
- —→ DIRECT
- – –→ DIFFUSED
- ∿→ INDIRECT
- ▭ INTERIOR SPACE

CIRCULATION TO USE-SPACE
- ——→ MAJOR CIRCULATION
- ——→ SECONDARY CIRCULATION
- ▭ USE-SPACES
- ———— REMAINDER OF BUILDING
- ▭ VERTICAL CIRCULATION

GEOMETRY
- ▱ SQUARE
- ▱ 1.4 RECTANGLE
- ▱ 1.6 RECTANGLE
- ┼ DIMENSION OR UNIT
- ∠ ANGLE
- ▦ GRID LINES
- ⊙ RADIUS CENTER

ADDITIVE AND SUBTRACTIVE
- ▭▭ ADDITIVE UNITS
- ▭▪ SUBTRACTION
- ▭ WHOLE
- ▪ SUBTRACTIVE UNIT

FACTUAL SHEET
- ⊙ NORTH INDICATOR
- ▲ ELEVATION
- △ SECTION

MASSING
- ———— MAJOR MASSING
- ———— SECONDARY MASSING

UNIT TO WHOLE
- ———— UNITS
- ———— REMAINDER OF BUILDING

HIERARCHY
- ———— MOST DOMINANT
- ———— TO
- ———— LESS DOMINANT

ANALYSIS

ANALYSIS

In this section, 104 works of architecture are documented. The buildings are the designs of 31 architects. For most architects, four buildings are presented which are representative of that person's work. The material is ordered with the architects arranged alphabetically and the buildings for each architect presented chronologically and successively.

Each building is recorded on two adjacent pages; the left-hand page documents the building with name, date, and location as well as drawings of the site plan, floor plans, elevations, and sections; illustrated on the right-hand page is a series of eleven analysis diagrams and the parti diagram which culminates and summarizes the analysis for the building. The parti is seen as the dominant idea of a building which embodies the salient characteristics of that building. It encapsulates the essential minimum of the design, without which the scheme would not exist, but from which the architecture can be generated.

A major concern of the analysis is to investigate the formal and spatial characteristics of each work in such a way that the building parti can be understood. To accomplish this, 11 issues were selected from the widest range of characteristics: fundamental elements which are common to all buildings, relationships among attributes, and formative ideas. Each issue is first explored in isolation and then in relationship to the other issues. This information is studied to discern reinforcement and to identify the dominant underlying idea. From the analysis and the resulting parti for each building, similarities and differences among the designs can be identified.

The issues selected for the analysis are: structure; natural light; massing; and the relationships of plan to section, circulation to use-space, unit to whole, and repetitive to unique. Also included are symmetry and balance, geometry, additive and subtractive, and hierarchy.

STRUCTURE

At a basic level, structure is synonymous with support, and therefore exists in all buildings. At a more germane level, structure is columnar, planar, or a combination of these, all of which a designer can intentionally use to reinforce or realize ideas. In this context, columns, walls, and beams can be thought of in terms of the concepts of frequency, pattern, simplicity, regularity, randomness, and complexity. As such, structure can be used to define space, create units, articulate circulation, suggest movement, or develop composition and modulations. In this way, it becomes inextricably linked to the very elements which create architecture, its quality and excitement. This analysis issue has the potential to reinforce the issues of natural light, unit to whole relationships, and geometry. It can also strengthen the relationship of circulation to use-space and the definition of symmetry, balance, and hierarchy.

NATURAL LIGHT

Natural light focuses on the manner in which, and the locations where, daylight enters a building. Light is a vehicle for the rendering of form and space, and the quantity, quality, and color of the light affect the perceptions of mass and volume. The introduction of natural light may be the consequence of design decisions made about the elevation and section of a building. Daylight can be considered in terms of qualitative differences which result from filtering, screening, and reflecting. Light which enters a space from the side, after modification by a screen, is different from light which enters directly overhead. Both examples are quite different from light which is reflected within the envelope of the building before entering the space. The concepts of size, location, shape, and frequency of opening; surface material, texture, and color; and modification before, during, or after entering the building envelope are all relevant to light as a design idea. Natural light can reinforce structure, geometry, hierarchy, and the relationships of unit to whole, repetitive to unique, and circulation to use-space.

MASSING

As a design issue, massing constitutes the perceptually dominant or most commonly encountered three-dimensional configuration of a building. Massing is more than the silhouette or elevation of a building. It is the perceptual image of the building as a totality. While massing may embody, approximate, or at times parallel either the outline or the elevation, it is too limiting to view it as only this. For example, on the elevation of a building the fenestration may in no way affect the perception of the volume of the building. Similarly, the silhouette may be too general and not reflect productive distinctions in form.

Massing, seen as a consequence of designing, can result from decisions made about issues other than the three-dimensional configuration. Viewed as a design idea, massing may be considered relative to concepts of context, collections and patterns of units, single and multiple masses, and primary and secondary elements. Massing has the potential to define and articulate exterior spaces, accommodate site, identify entrance, express circulation, and emphasize importance in architecture. As an issue in the analysis, massing can strength-

en the ideas of unit to whole, repetitive to unique, plan to section, geometry, additive and subtractive, and hierarchy.

PLAN TO SECTION OR ELEVATION

Plan, section, and elevation are conventions common to the simulation of the horizontal and vertical configurations of all buildings. As with any of the design ideas in this analysis, the relationship of plan configuration to vertical information may result from decisions made about other issues. The plan can be the device to organize activities and can, therefore, be viewed as the generator of form. It may serve to inform about many issues such as the distinction between passage and rest. The elevation and section are often considered to be more closely related to perception since these notations are similar to encountering a building frontally. However, the use of plan or section notations presumes volumetric understanding; that is, a line in either has a third dimension. The reciprocity and the dependence of one on the other can be a vehicle for making design decisions, and can be used as a strategy for design. Considerations in plan, section, or elevation can influence the configuration of the others through the concepts of equality, similarity, proportion, and difference or opposition.

It is possible for the plan to relate to the section or elevation at a number of scales: a room, a part, or the whole building. As an issue for analysis, the plan to section relationship reinforces the ideas of massing, balance, geometry, hierarchy, additive, subtractive, and the relationships of unit to whole and repetitive to unique.

CIRCULATION TO USE-SPACE

Fundamentally, circulation and use-space represent the significant dynamic and static components in all buildings. Use-space is the primary focus of architectural decision making relative to function, and circulation is the means by which that design effort is engaged. Together, the articulation of the conditions of movement and stability form the essence of a building. Since circulation determines how a person experiences a building, it can be the vehicle for understanding issues like structure, natural light, unit definition, repetitive and unique elements, geometry, balance, and hierarchy. Circulation may be defined within a space that is for movement only, or implied within a use-space. Thus, it can be separate from, through, or terminate in the use-spaces; and it may establish locations of entry, center, terminus, and importance.

Use-space can be implied as part or all of a free or open plan. It can also be discrete, as in a room. Implicit in the analysis of this issue is the pattern created by the relationship between the major use-spaces. These patterns might suggest centralized, linear, or clustered organizations. The relationship of circulation and use-space can also indicate the conditions of privacy and connection. Basic to employing this issue as a design tool is the understanding that the configuration given to either circulation or use directly affects the manner in which the relationship to the other takes place.

UNIT TO WHOLE

The relationship of unit to whole examines architecture as units which can be related to create buildings. A unit is an identified entity which is part of a building. Buildings may comprise only one unit, where the unit is equal to the whole, or aggregations of units. Units may be spatial or formal entities which correspond to use-spaces, structural components, massing, volume, or collections of these elements. Units may also be created independently of these issues.

The nature, identity, expression, and relationship of units to other units and to the whole are relevant considerations in the use of this idea as a design strategy. In this context, units are considered as adjoining, separate, overlapping, or less than the whole. The relationship of unit to whole can be reinforced by structure, massing, and geometry. It can support the issues of symmetry, balance, geometry, additive, subtractive, hierarchy, and the relationship of repetitive to unique.

REPETITIVE TO UNIQUE

The relationship of repetitive to unique elements entails the exploration of spatial and formal components for attributes which render these components as multiple or singular entities. If unique is understood to be a difference within a class or a kind, then the comparison of elements within a class can result in the identification of the attributes which make the unique element different. This distinction links the realms of the repetitive and the unique through the common reference frame of the class or kind. Essentially, the definition of one is determined by the realm of the other. In this context, components are determined to be repetitive or unique through the absence or presence of attributes. Concepts of size, orientation, location, shape, configuration, color, material, and texture are useful in making distinctions between repetitive and unique. While repetitive and unique elements occur in numerous ways and at several scales within buildings, the analysis focuses on the dominant relationship. In the analysis, this issue generates information which strengthens or is reinforced by the concepts of structure, massing, units related to whole, plan related to section, geometry, and symmetry or balance.

SYMMETRY AND BALANCE

The concepts of symmetry and balance have been in use since the beginning of architecture. As a fundamental issue of composition, balance in architecture occurs through the use of spatial or formal components. Balance is the state of perceptual or conceptual equilibrium. Symmetry is a specialized form of balance. Compositional balance in terms of equilibrium implies a parallel to the balance of weights, where so many units of "A" are equal to a dissimilar number of units of "B." Balance of components establishes that a relationship between the two exists, and that an implied line of balance can be identified. For balance to exist, the basic nature of the relationship between two elements must be determined; that is, some element of a building must be equivalent in a knowable way to another part of the building. The equivalency is determined by the perception of identifiable attributes within the parts. Conceptual balance can occur when a component is given additional value or meaning by an individual or group. For example, a smaller sacred space can be balanced by a much larger support or secondary space.

Whereas balance is developed through differences in attributes, symmetry exists when the same unit occurs on both sides of the balance line. In architecture this can happen in three precise ways: reflected, rotated about a point, and translated or moved along a line.

Both symmetry and balance can exist at the building, component, or room level. As scales change, a distinction is made between overall and local symmetry or balance. Consideration of size, orientation, location, articulation, configuration, and value is involved in its use as a formative idea. Balance and symmetry may have an impact on all of the other analysis issues.

GEOMETRY

Geometry is a formative idea in architecture that embodies the tenets of both plane and solid geometry to determine built form. Within this issue, grids are identified as being developed from the repetition of the basic geometries through multiplication, combination, subdivision, and manipulation.

Geometry has been used as a design tool since the very beginnings of architectural history. Geometry is the single most common determinant or characteristic in buildings. It can be utilized on a broad range of spatial or formal levels that includes the use of simple geometric shapes, varied form languages, systems of proportions, and complex form generated by intricate manipulations of geometries. The realm of geometry as an architectural form generator is a relative one of measurement and quantification. As a focus for this analysis, it centers on the concepts of size, location, shape, form, and proportion. It also concentrates on the consistent changes in geometries and form languages that result from the combination, derivation, and manipulation of basic geometric configurations. In the analysis, grids are observed for frequency, configuration, complexity, consistency, and variation. As the pervasive attribute of buildings, geometry can reinforce all of the issues used in the analysis.

ADDITIVE AND SUBTRACTIVE

The formative ideas of additive and subtractive are developed from the processes of adding, or aggregating, and subtracting built form to create architecture. Both require the perceptual understanding of the building. Additive, when used to generate built form, renders the parts of the building as dominant. The perception of a person engaging an additive design is that the building is an aggregation of identifiable units or parts. Subtractive, when utilized in designing, results in a building in which the whole is dominant. A person viewing a subtractive scheme understands the building as a recognizable whole from which pieces have been subtracted. Generally, additive and subtractive are formal considerations which can have spatial consequences.

Richness can occur when both ideas are employed simultaneously to develop built form. For example, it is possible to add units together to form a whole from which pieces are subtracted. It is also possible to subtract pieces from an identifiable whole and then to add the subtracted parts back to create the building.

The manner in which the building whole was articulated, and the ways in which the forms were rendered, was important to the analysis. This was achieved by observing massing, volumes, color, and material changes. Additive and subtractive, as ideas, can strengthen or be reinforced by massing, geometry, balance, hierarchy, and the relationships of unit to whole, repetitive to unique, and plan to section.

HIERARCHY

As a formative idea, hierarchy in the design of buildings is the physical manifestation of the rank ordering of an attribute or attributes. Embodied in this concept is the assignment of relative value to a range of characteristics. This entails the understanding that qualitative differences within a progression can be identified for a selected attribute. Hierarchy implies a rank ordered change from one condition to another, where ranges such as major-minor, open-closed, simple-complex, public-private, sacred-profane, served-servant, and individual-group are utilized. With these ranges, the rank ordering can occur in the realm of the formal, spatial, or both.

In the analysis, hierarchy was explored relative to dominance and importance within the built form through examination of patterns, scale, configuration, geometry, and articulation. Quality, richness, detail, ornament, and special materials were used as indicators of importance. Hierarchy, as a design idea, can be related to and support any of the other issues explored in the analysis.

ALVAR AALTO

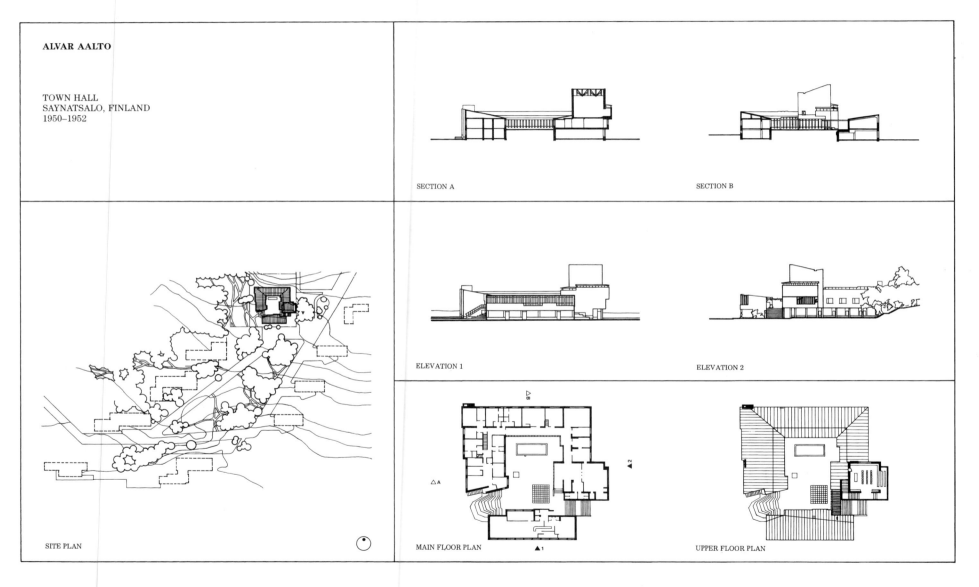

ALVAR AALTO

TOWN HALL
SAYNATSALO, FINLAND
1950–1952

SECTION A

SECTION B

ELEVATION 1

ELEVATION 2

SITE PLAN

MAIN FLOOR PLAN

UPPER FLOOR PLAN

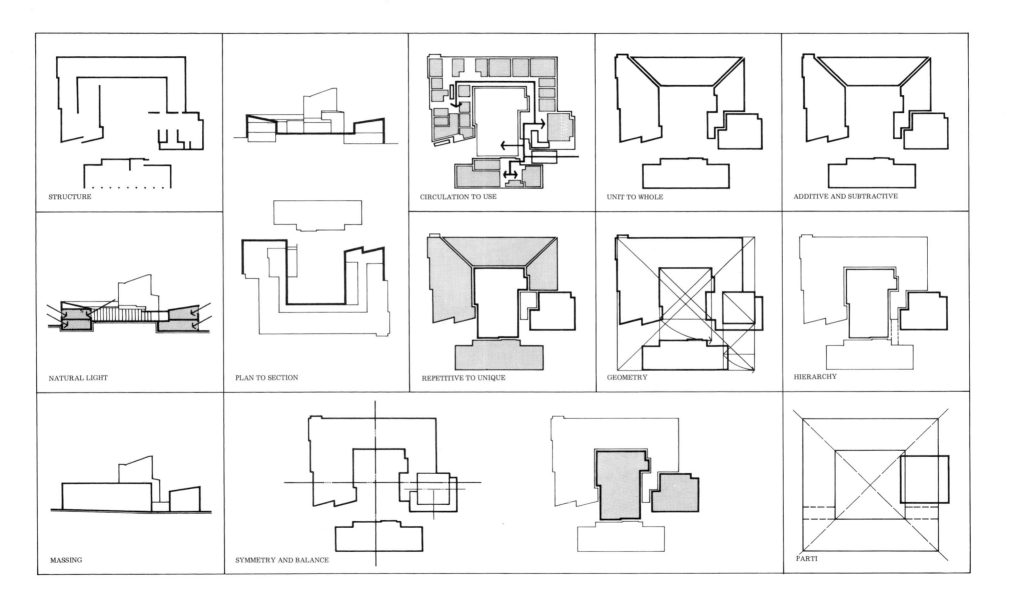

STRUCTURE

CIRCULATION TO USE

UNIT TO WHOLE

ADDITIVE AND SUBTRACTIVE

NATURAL LIGHT

PLAN TO SECTION

REPETITIVE TO UNIQUE

GEOMETRY

HIERARCHY

MASSING

SYMMETRY AND BALANCE

PARTI

9

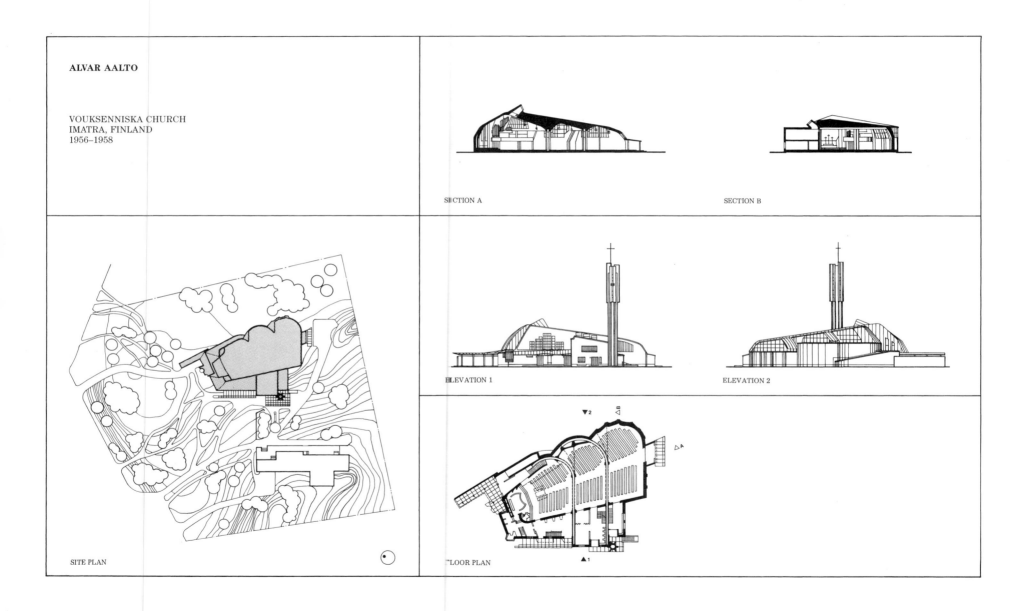

ALVAR AALTO

VOUKSENNISKA CHURCH
IMATRA, FINLAND
1956–1958

SECTION A

SECTION B

ELEVATION 1

ELEVATION 2

SITE PLAN

FLOOR PLAN

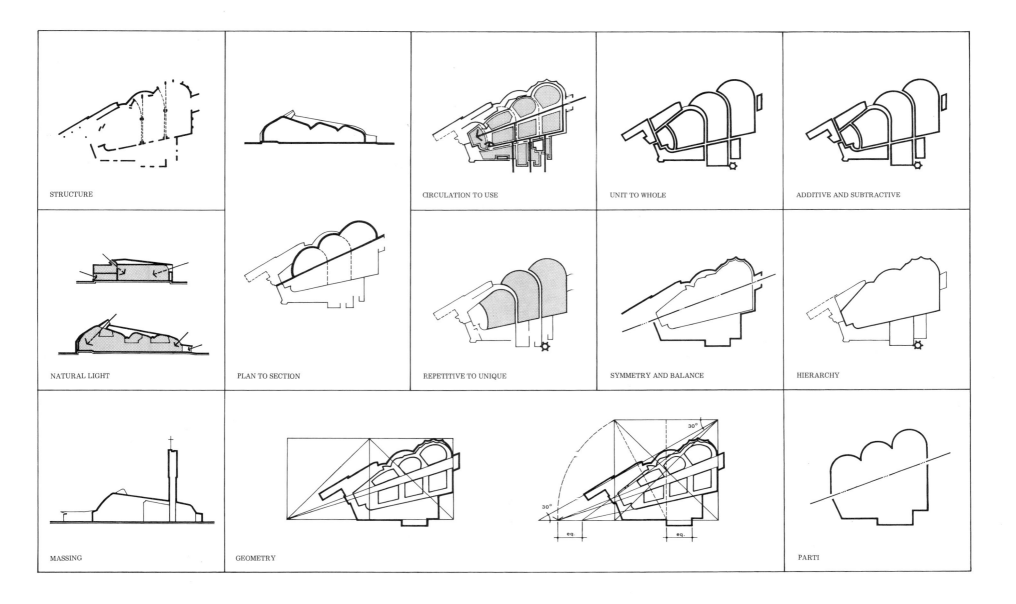

STRUCTURE

CIRCULATION TO USE

UNIT TO WHOLE

ADDITIVE AND SUBTRACTIVE

NATURAL LIGHT

PLAN TO SECTION

REPETITIVE TO UNIQUE

SYMMETRY AND BALANCE

HIERARCHY

MASSING

GEOMETRY

PARTI

11

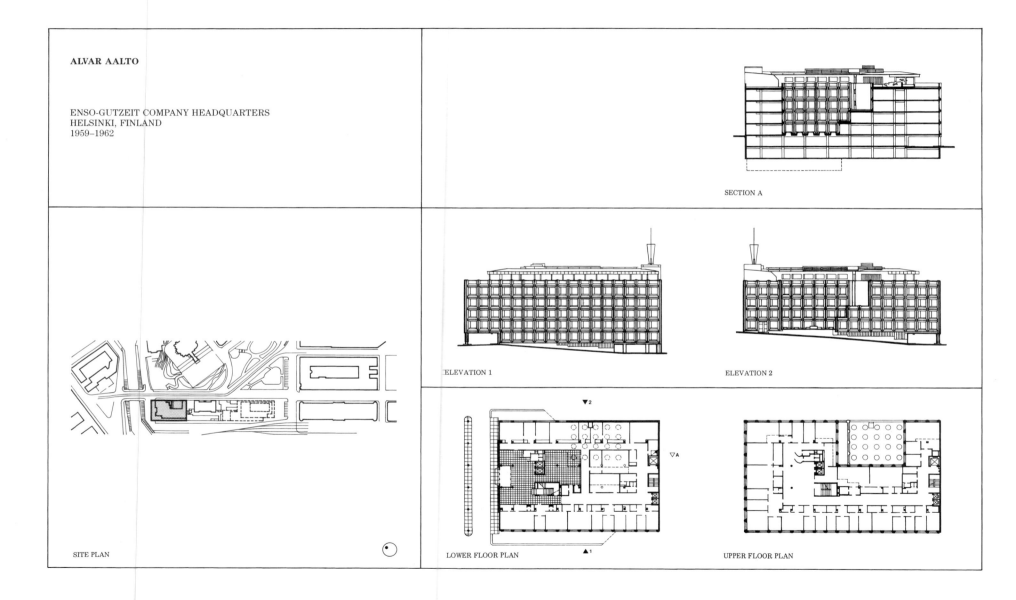

ALVAR AALTO

ENSO-GUTZEIT COMPANY HEADQUARTERS
HELSINKI, FINLAND
1959–1962

SECTION A

ELEVATION 1

ELEVATION 2

SITE PLAN

LOWER FLOOR PLAN

UPPER FLOOR PLAN

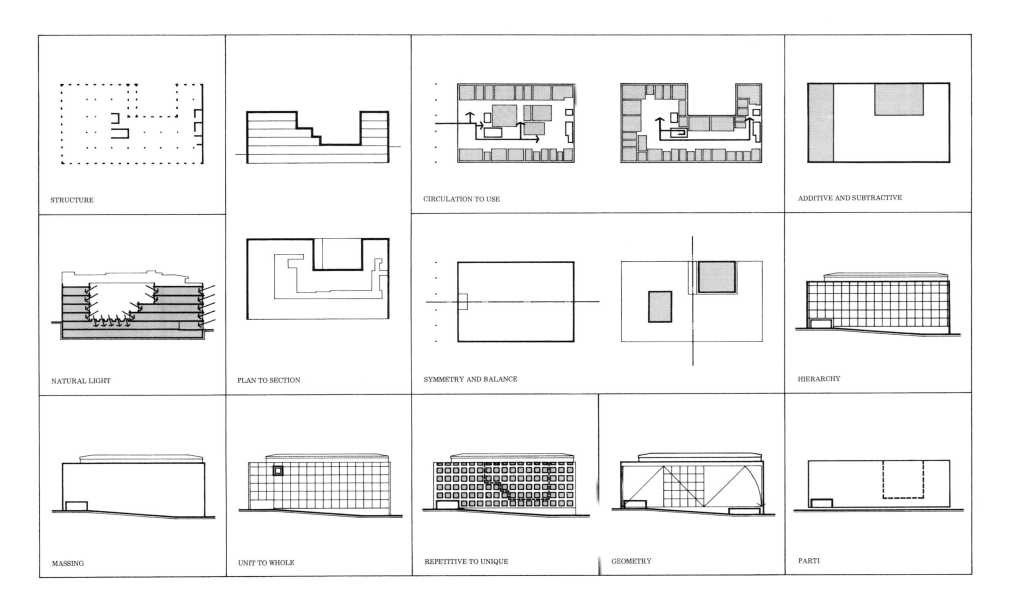

STRUCTURE

CIRCULATION TO USE

ADDITIVE AND SUBTRACTIVE

NATURAL LIGHT

PLAN TO SECTION

SYMMETRY AND BALANCE

HIERARCHY

MASSING

UNIT TO WHOLE

REPETITIVE TO UNIQUE

GEOMETRY

PARTI

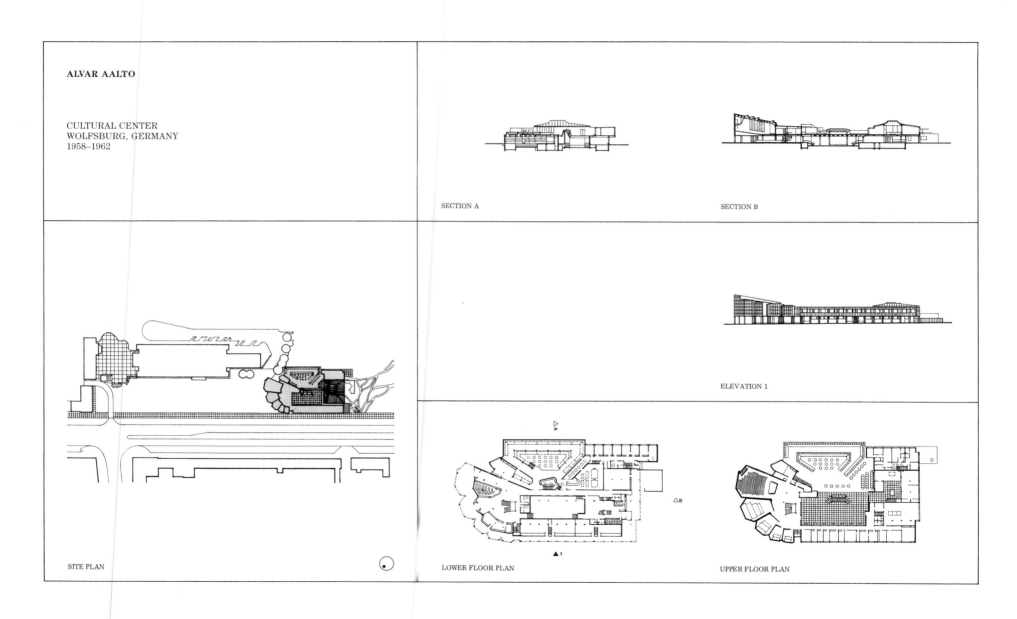

ALVAR AALTO

CULTURAL CENTER
WOLFSBURG, GERMANY
1958–1962

SECTION A

SECTION B

ELEVATION 1

SITE PLAN

LOWER FLOOR PLAN

UPPER FLOOR PLAN

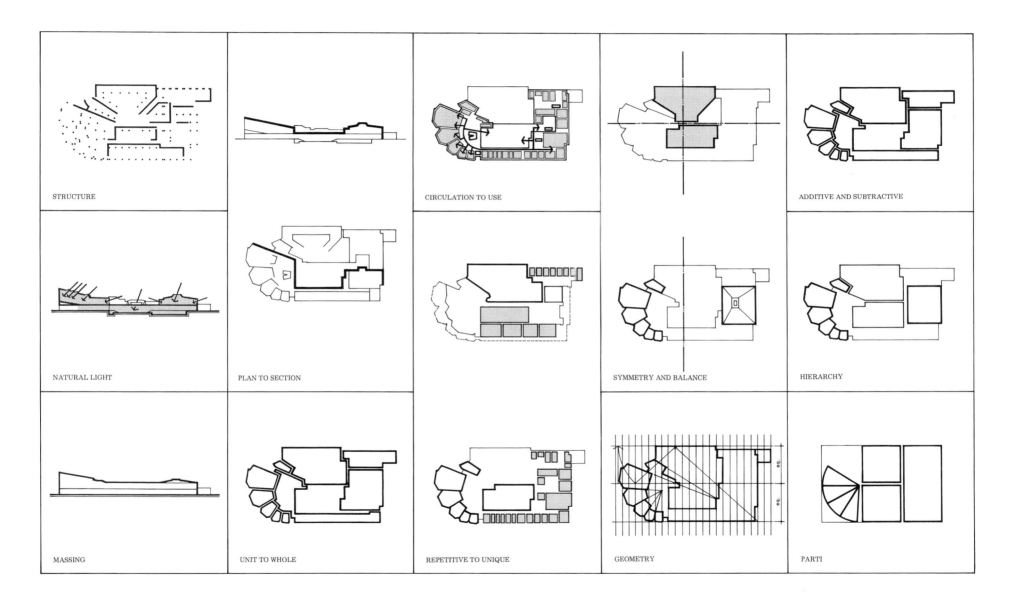

STRUCTURE

CIRCULATION TO USE

ADDITIVE AND SUBTRACTIVE

NATURAL LIGHT

PLAN TO SECTION

SYMMETRY AND BALANCE

HIERARCHY

MASSING

UNIT TO WHOLE

REPETITIVE TO UNIQUE

GEOMETRY

PARTI

15

TADAO ANDO

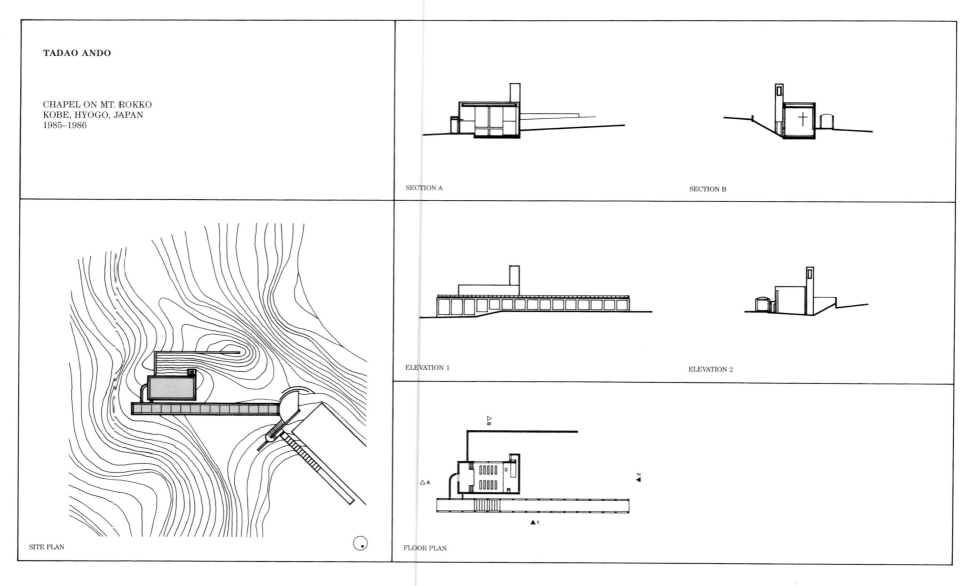

TADAO ANDO

CHAPEL ON MT. ROKKO
KOBE, HYOGO, JAPAN
1985–1986

SECTION A

SECTION B

ELEVATION 1

ELEVATION 2

SITE PLAN

FLOOR PLAN

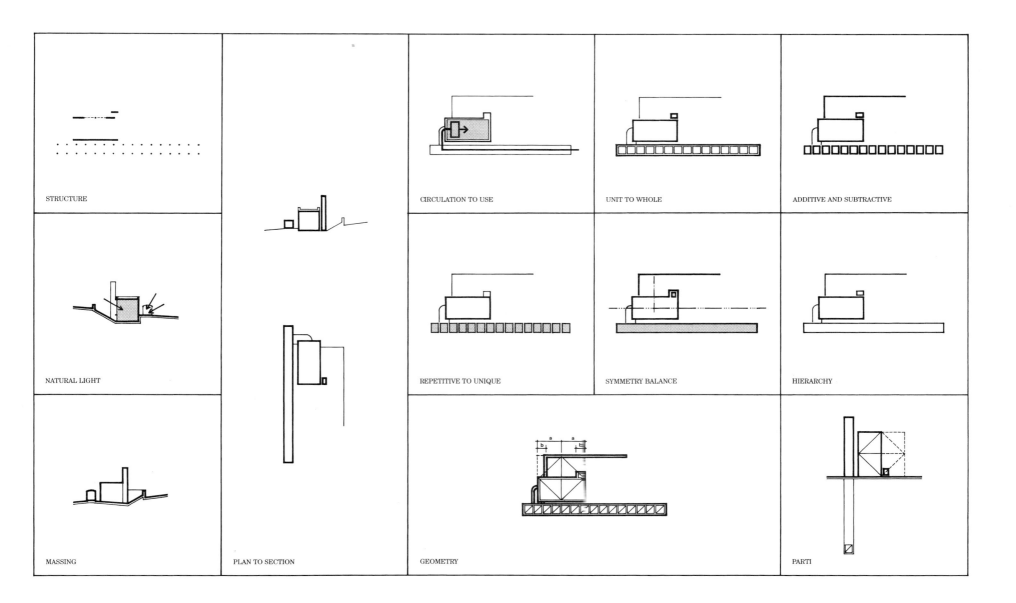

STRUCTURE

CIRCULATION TO USE

UNIT TO WHOLE

ADDITIVE AND SUBTRACTIVE

NATURAL LIGHT

REPETITIVE TO UNIQUE

SYMMETRY BALANCE

HIERARCHY

MASSING

PLAN TO SECTION

GEOMETRY

PARTI

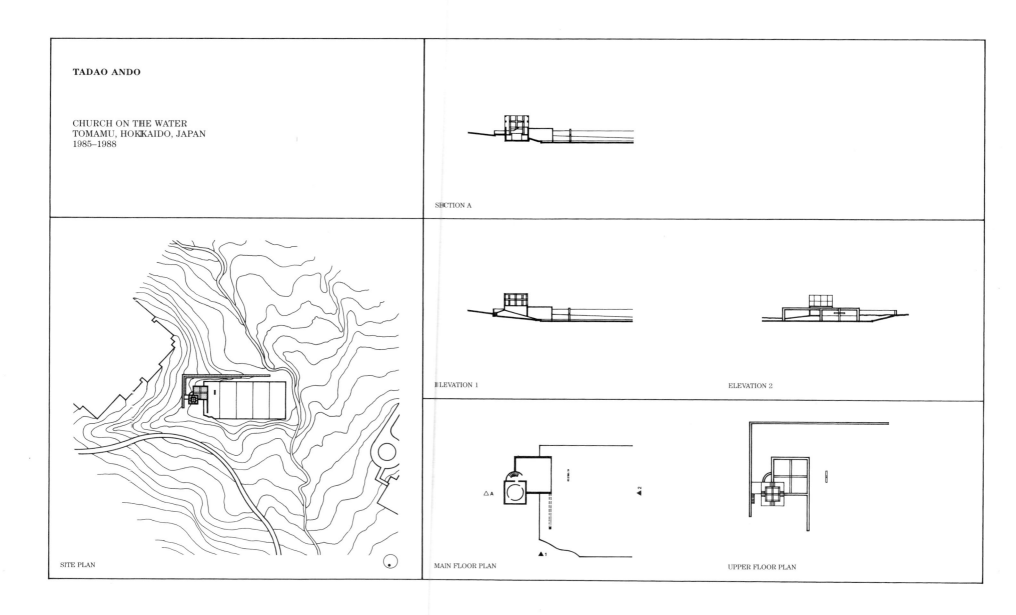

TADAO ANDO

CHURCH ON THE WATER
TOMAMU, HOKKAIDO, JAPAN
1985–1988

SECTION A

ELEVATION 1

ELEVATION 2

SITE PLAN

MAIN FLOOR PLAN

UPPER FLOOR PLAN

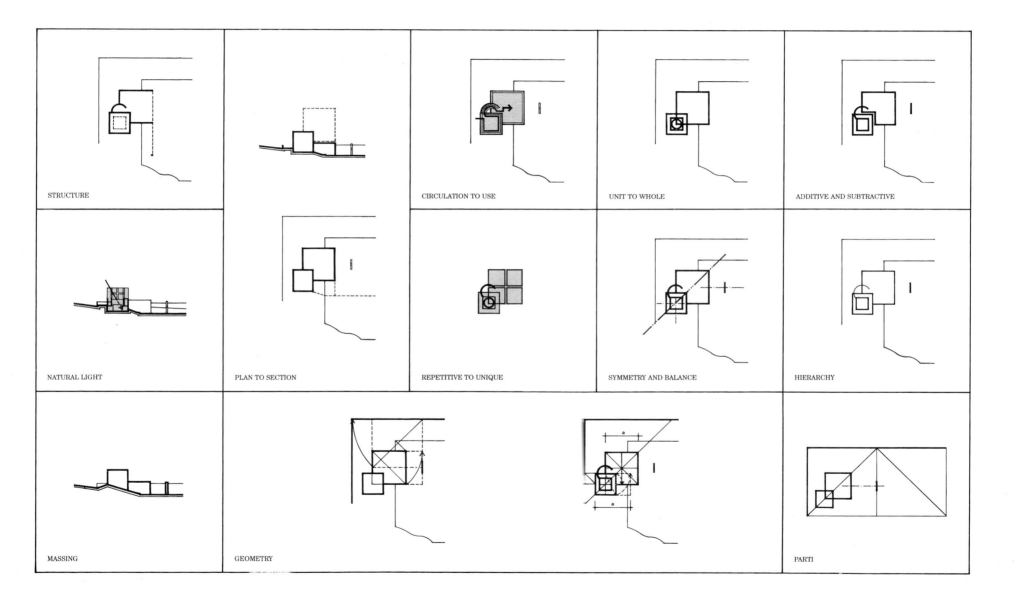

STRUCTURE

CIRCULATION TO USE

UNIT TO WHOLE

ADDITIVE AND SUBTRACTIVE

NATURAL LIGHT

PLAN TO SECTION

REPETITIVE TO UNIQUE

SYMMETRY AND BALANCE

HIERARCHY

MASSING

GEOMETRY

PARTI

19

ERIK GUNNAR ASPLUND

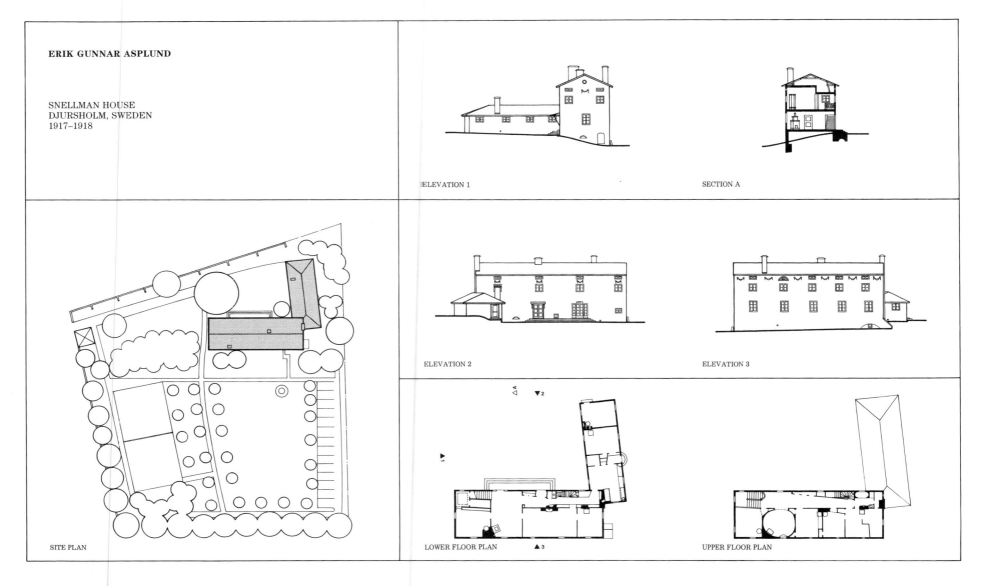

ERIK GUNNAR ASPLUND

SNELLMAN HOUSE
DJURSHOLM, SWEDEN
1917–1918

ELEVATION 1

SECTION A

ELEVATION 2

ELEVATION 3

SITE PLAN

LOWER FLOOR PLAN

UPPER FLOOR PLAN

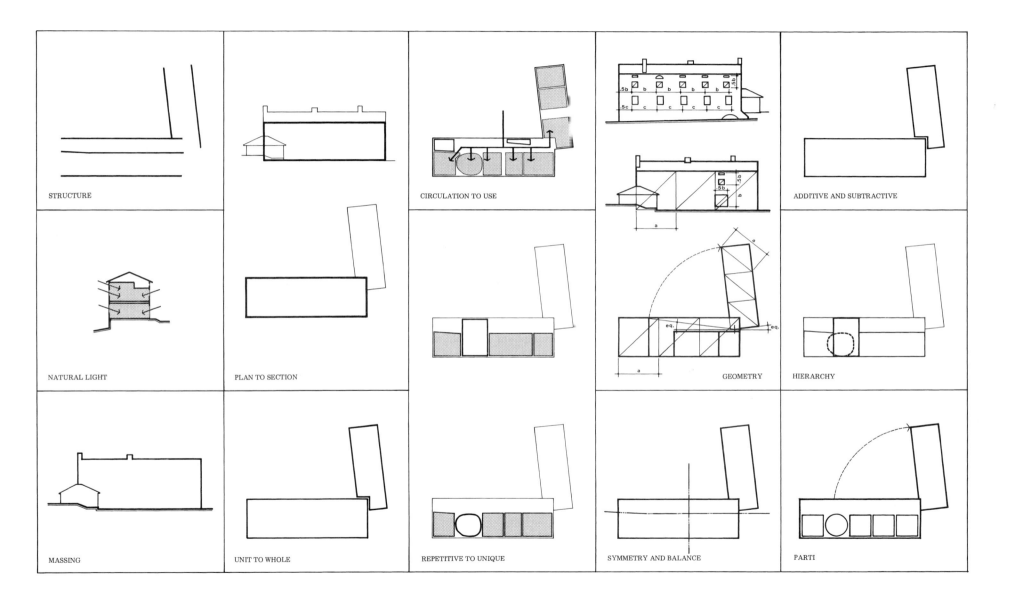

STRUCTURE

CIRCULATION TO USE

ADDITIVE AND SUBTRACTIVE

NATURAL LIGHT

PLAN TO SECTION

GEOMETRY

HIERARCHY

MASSING

UNIT TO WHOLE

REPETITIVE TO UNIQUE

SYMMETRY AND BALANCE

PARTI

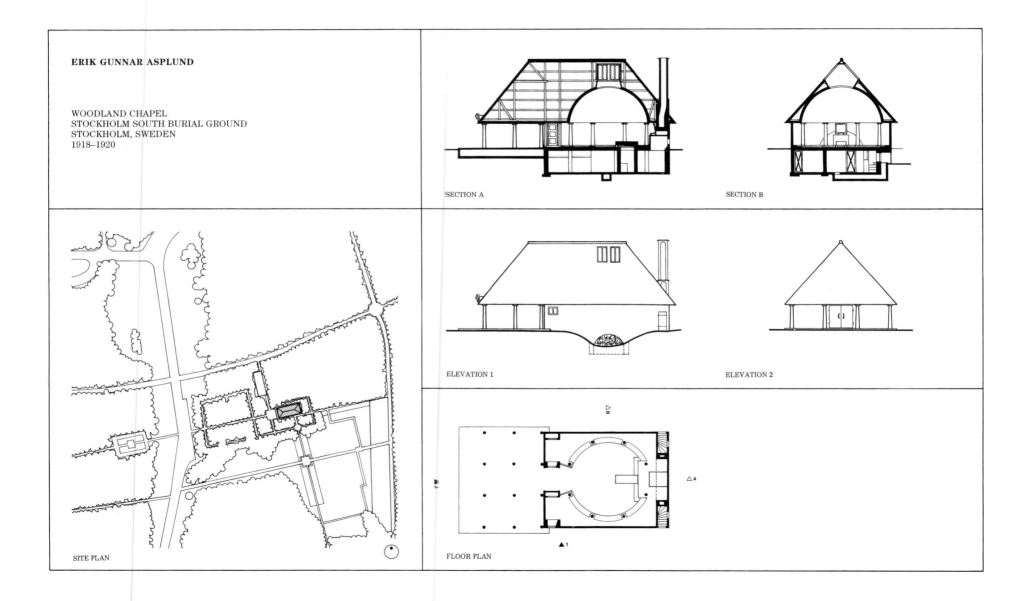

ERIK GUNNAR ASPLUND

WOODLAND CHAPEL
STOCKHOLM SOUTH BURIAL GROUND
STOCKHOLM, SWEDEN
1918–1920

SECTION A

SECTION B

ELEVATION 1

ELEVATION 2

SITE PLAN

FLOOR PLAN

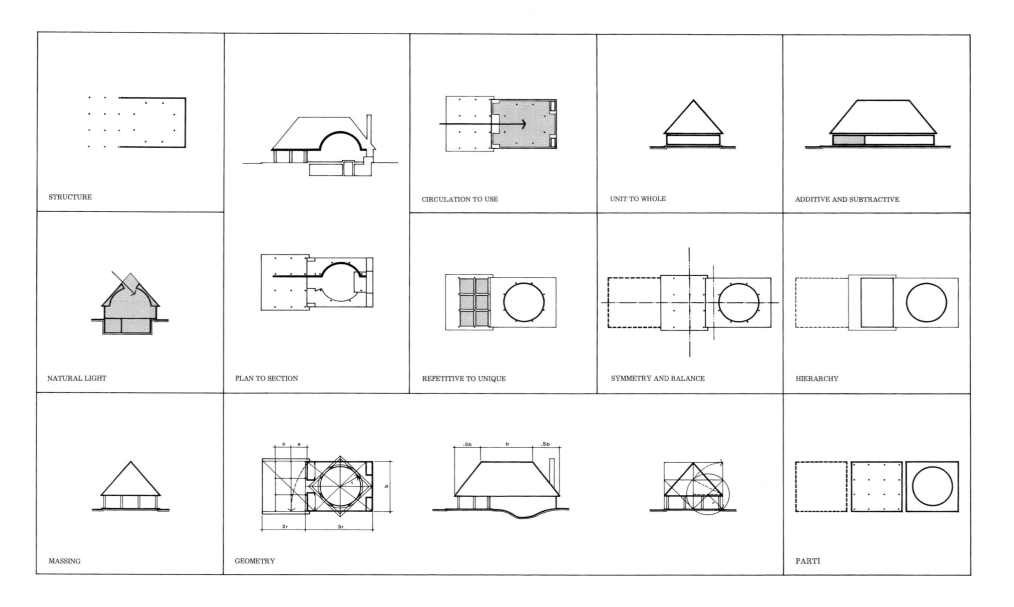

STRUCTURE

CIRCULATION TO USE

UNIT TO WHOLE

ADDITIVE AND SUBTRACTIVE

NATURAL LIGHT

PLAN TO SECTION

REPETITIVE TO UNIQUE

SYMMETRY AND BALANCE

HIERARCHY

MASSING

GEOMETRY

PARTI

23

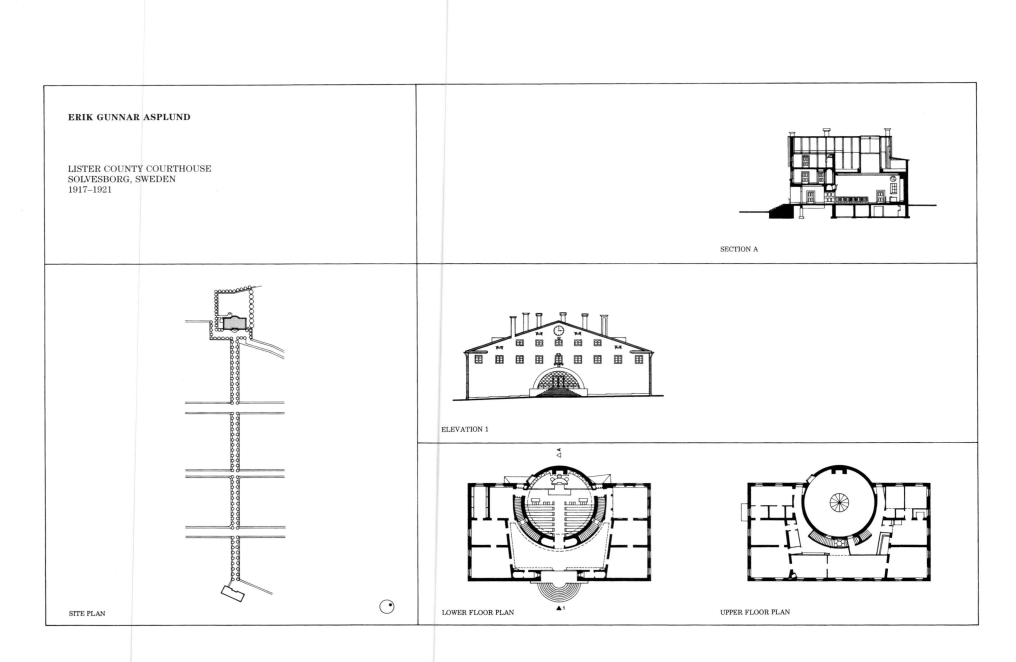

ERIK GUNNAR ASPLUND

LISTER COUNTY COURTHOUSE
SOLVESBORG, SWEDEN
1917–1921

SECTION A

ELEVATION 1

SITE PLAN

LOWER FLOOR PLAN

UPPER FLOOR PLAN

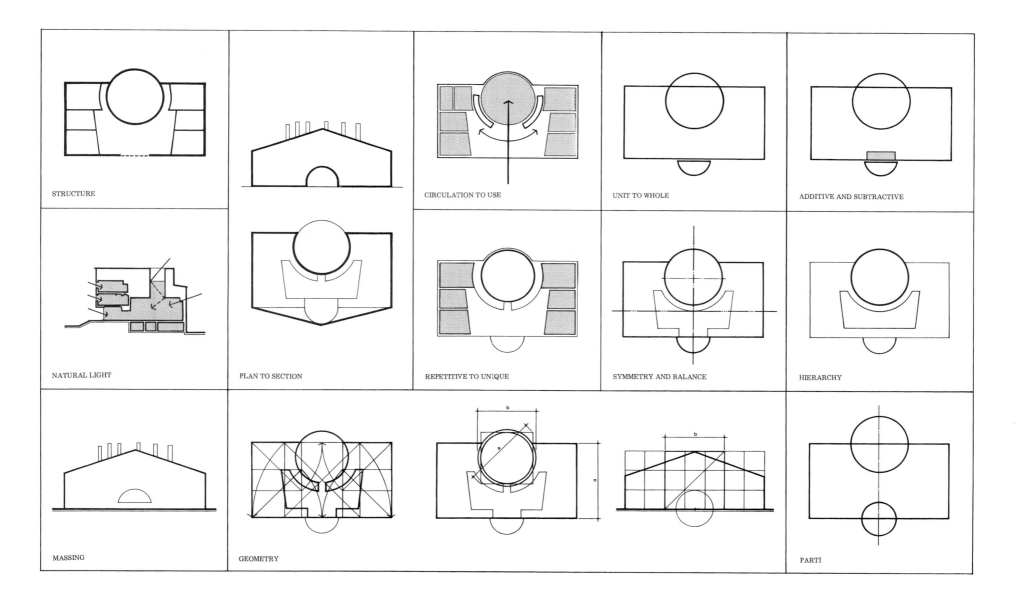

STRUCTURE

CIRCULATION TO USE

UNIT TO WHOLE

ADDITIVE AND SUBTRACTIVE

NATURAL LIGHT

PLAN TO SECTION

REPETITIVE TO UNIQUE

SYMMETRY AND BALANCE

HIERARCHY

MASSING

GEOMETRY

PARTI

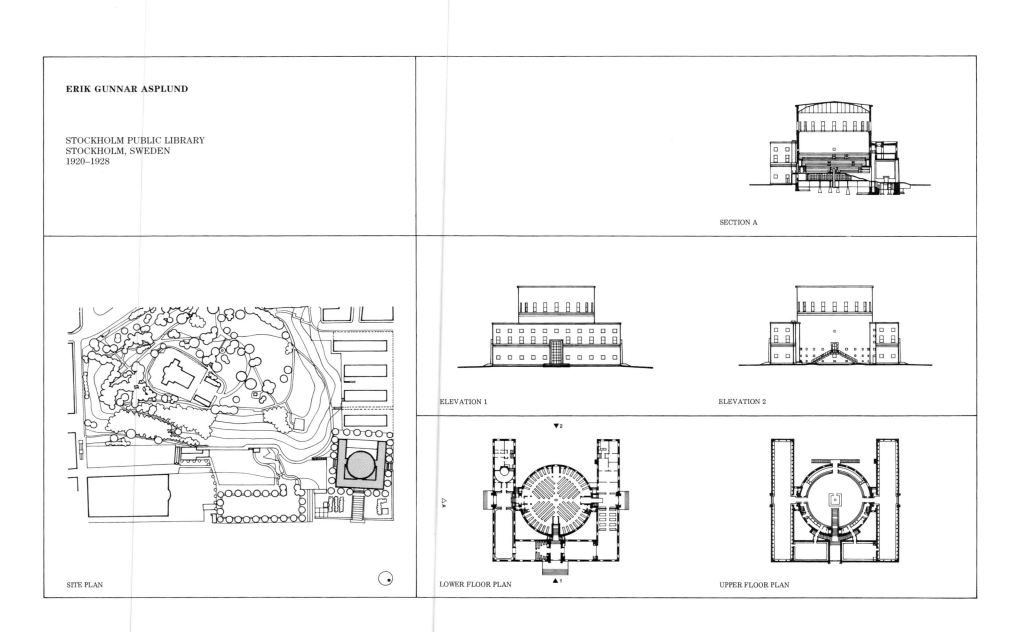

ERIK GUNNAR ASPLUND

STOCKHOLM PUBLIC LIBRARY
STOCKHOLM, SWEDEN
1920–1928

SECTION A

ELEVATION 1

ELEVATION 2

SITE PLAN

LOWER FLOOR PLAN

UPPER FLOOR PLAN

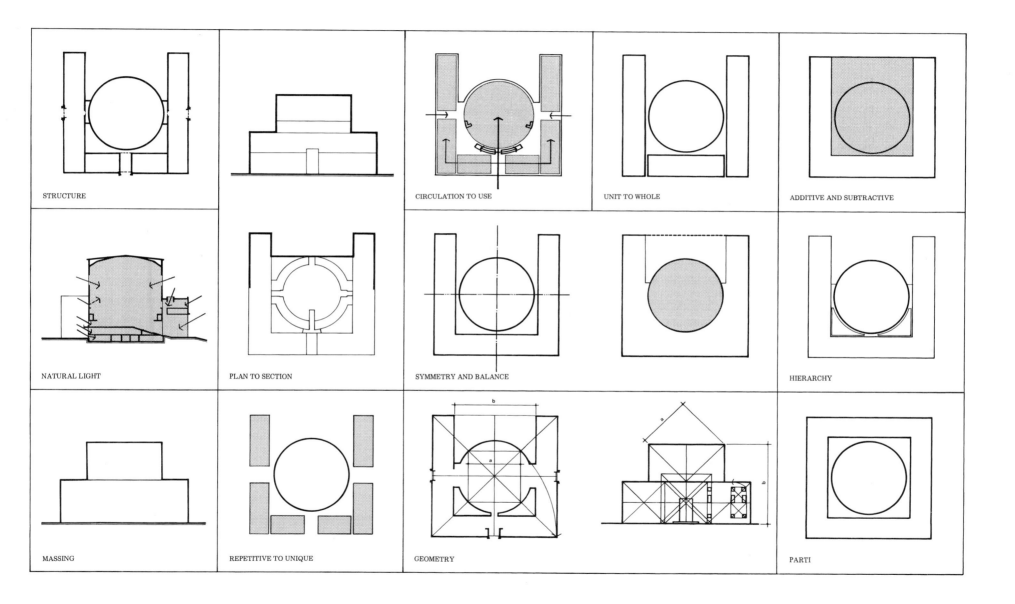

STRUCTURE

CIRCULATION TO USE

UNIT TO WHOLE

ADDITIVE AND SUBTRACTIVE

NATURAL LIGHT

PLAN TO SECTION

SYMMETRY AND BALANCE

HIERARCHY

MASSING

REPETITIVE TO UNIQUE

GEOMETRY

PARTI

PETER Q. BOHLIN

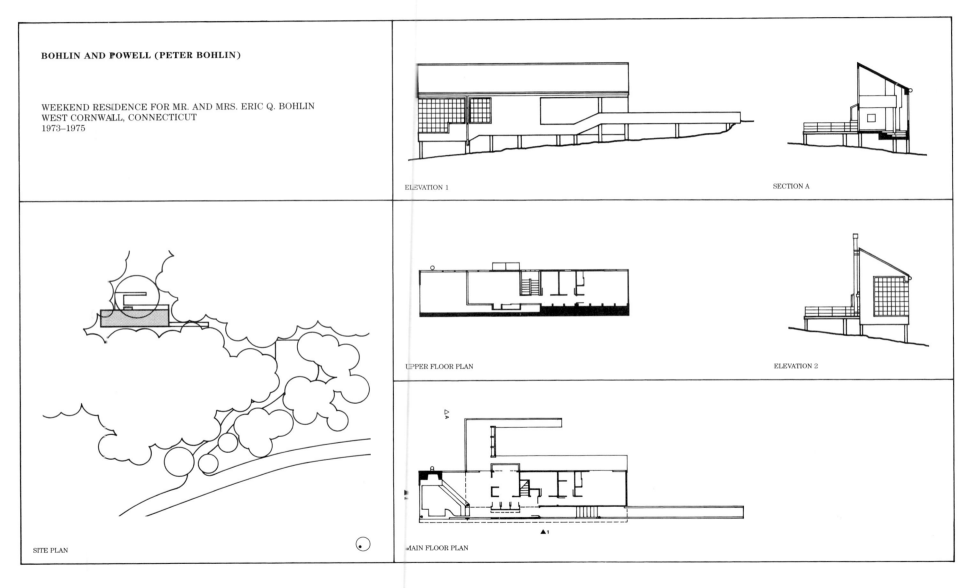

BOHLIN AND POWELL (PETER BOHLIN)

WEEKEND RESIDENCE FOR MR. AND MRS. ERIC Q. BOHLIN
WEST CORNWALL, CONNECTICUT
1973–1975

ELEVATION 1

SECTION A

UPPER FLOOR PLAN

ELEVATION 2

SITE PLAN

MAIN FLOOR PLAN

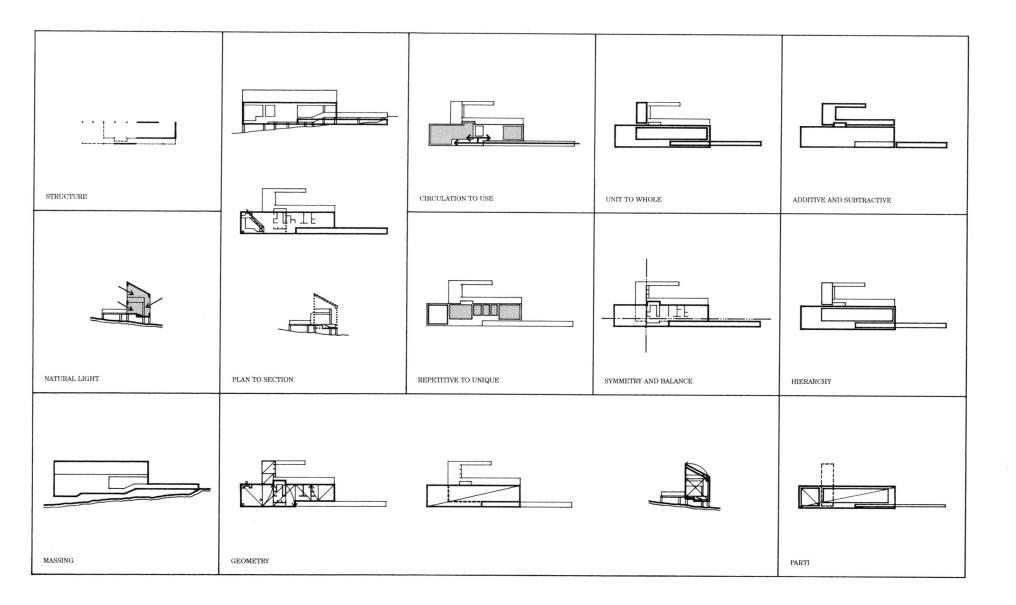

STRUCTURE

CIRCULATION TO USE

UNIT TO WHOLE

ADDITIVE AND SUBTRACTIVE

NATURAL LIGHT

PLAN TO SECTION

REPETITIVE TO UNIQUE

SYMMETRY AND BALANCE

HIERARCHY

MASSING

GEOMETRY

PARTI

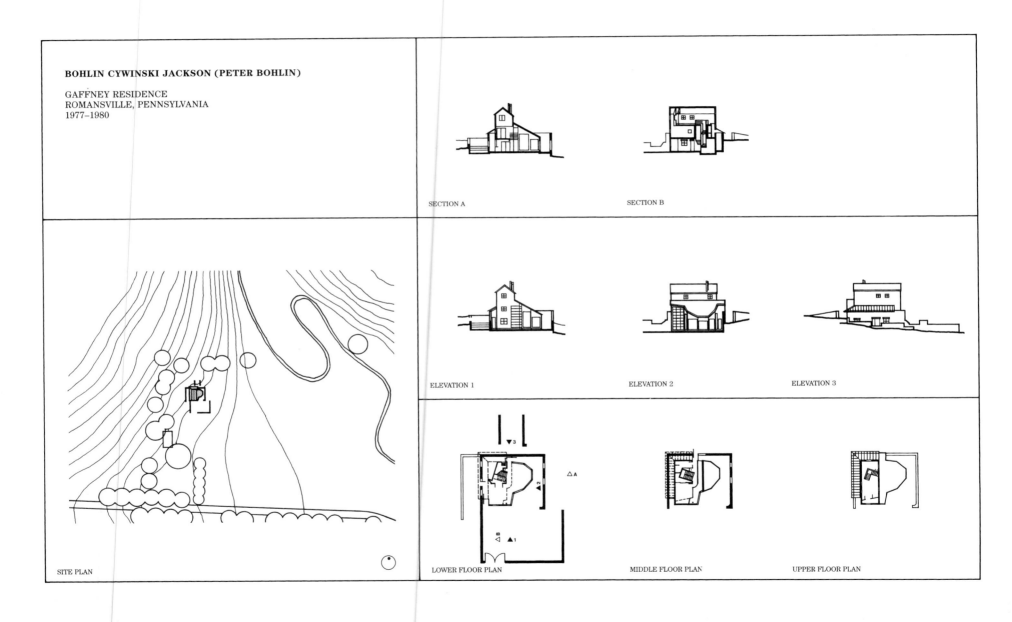

BOHLIN CYWINSKI JACKSON (PETER BOHLIN)

GAFFNEY RESIDENCE
ROMANSVILLE, PENNSYLVANIA
1977–1980

SECTION A

SECTION B

ELEVATION 1

ELEVATION 2

ELEVATION 3

SITE PLAN

LOWER FLOOR PLAN

MIDDLE FLOOR PLAN

UPPER FLOOR PLAN

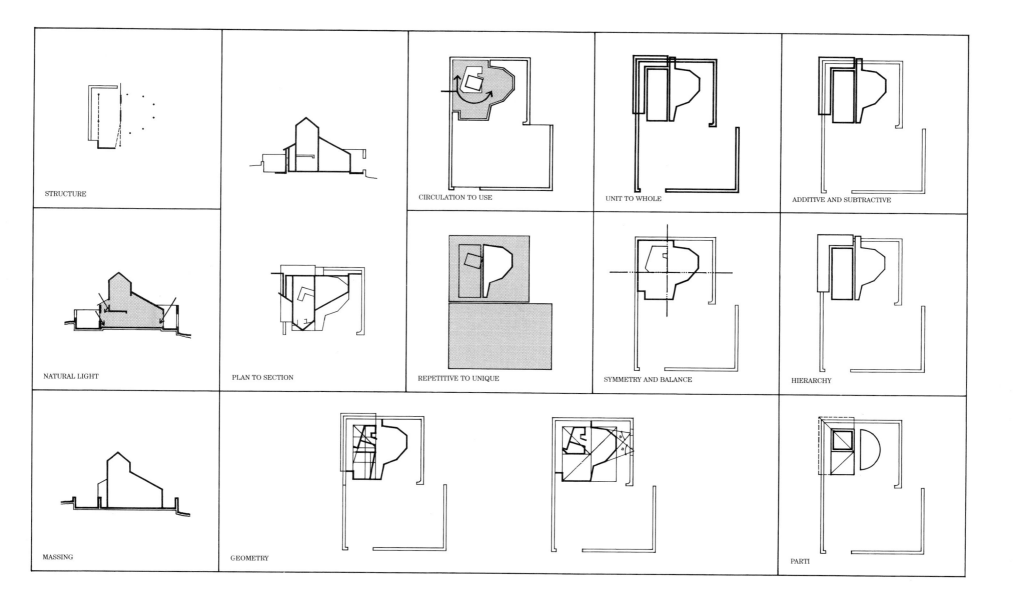

STRUCTURE

CIRCULATION TO USE

UNIT TO WHOLE

ADDITIVE AND SUBTRACTIVE

NATURAL LIGHT

PLAN TO SECTION

REPETITIVE TO UNIQUE

SYMMETRY AND BALANCE

HIERARCHY

MASSING

GEOMETRY

PARTI

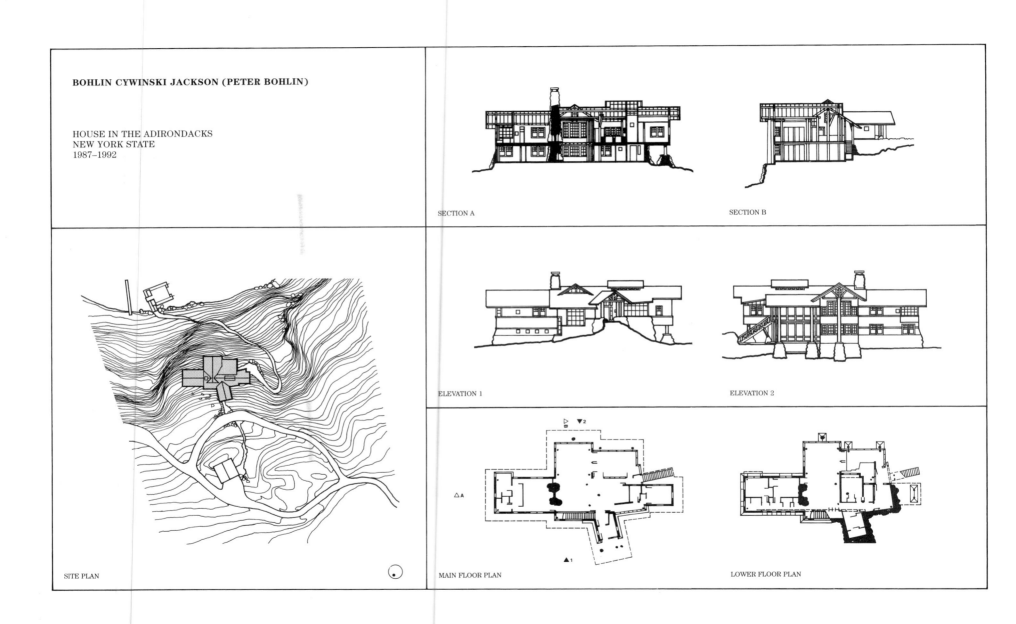

BOHLIN CYWINSKI JACKSON (PETER BOHLIN)

HOUSE IN THE ADIRONDACKS
NEW YORK STATE
1987–1992

SECTION A

SECTION B

ELEVATION 1

ELEVATION 2

SITE PLAN

MAIN FLOOR PLAN

LOWER FLOOR PLAN

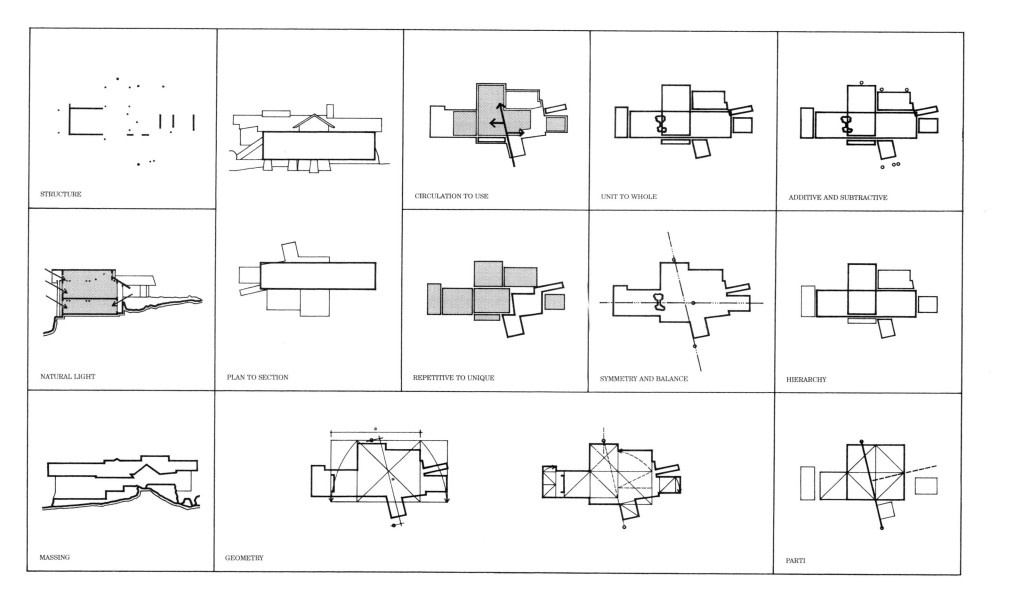

STRUCTURE

CIRCULATION TO USE

UNIT TO WHOLE

ADDITIVE AND SUBTRACTIVE

NATURAL LIGHT

PLAN TO SECTION

REPETITIVE TO UNIQUE

SYMMETRY AND BALANCE

HIERARCHY

MASSING

GEOMETRY

PARTI

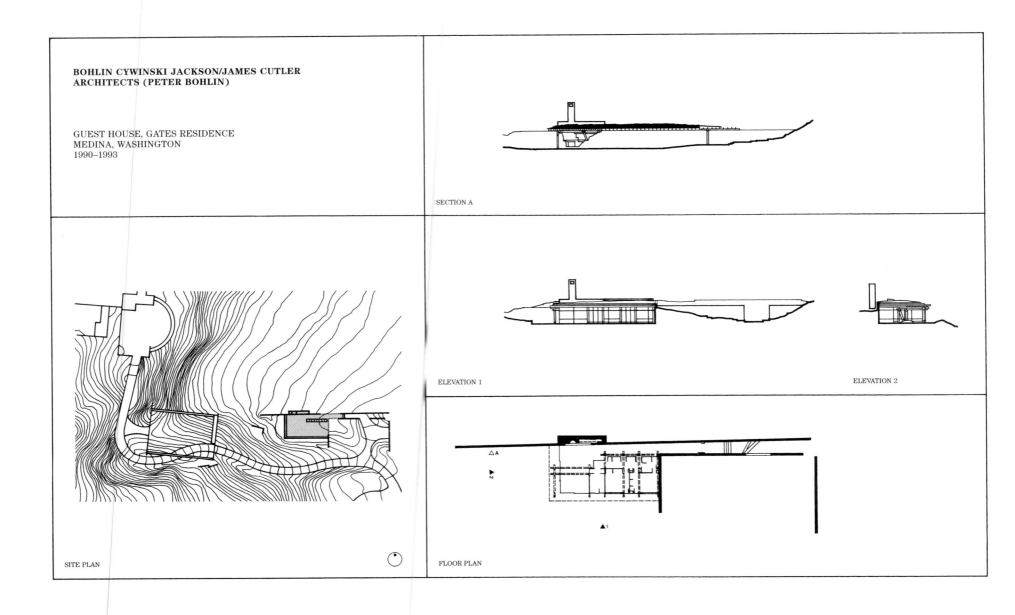

BOHLIN CYWINSKI JACKSON/JAMES CUTLER ARCHITECTS (PETER BOHLIN)

GUEST HOUSE, GATES RESIDENCE
MEDINA, WASHINGTON
1990–1993

SECTION A

ELEVATION 1

ELEVATION 2

SITE PLAN

FLOOR PLAN

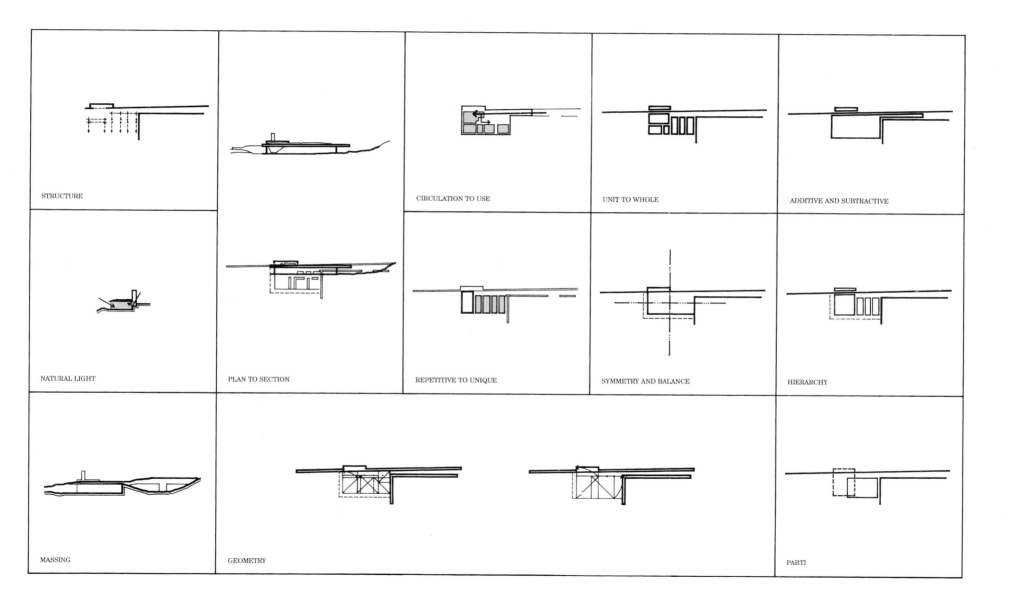

STRUCTURE

CIRCULATION TO USE

UNIT TO WHOLE

ADDITIVE AND SUBTRACTIVE

NATURAL LIGHT

PLAN TO SECTION

REPETITIVE TO UNIQUE

SYMMETRY AND BALANCE

HIERARCHY

MASSING

GEOMETRY

PARTI

MARIO BOTTA

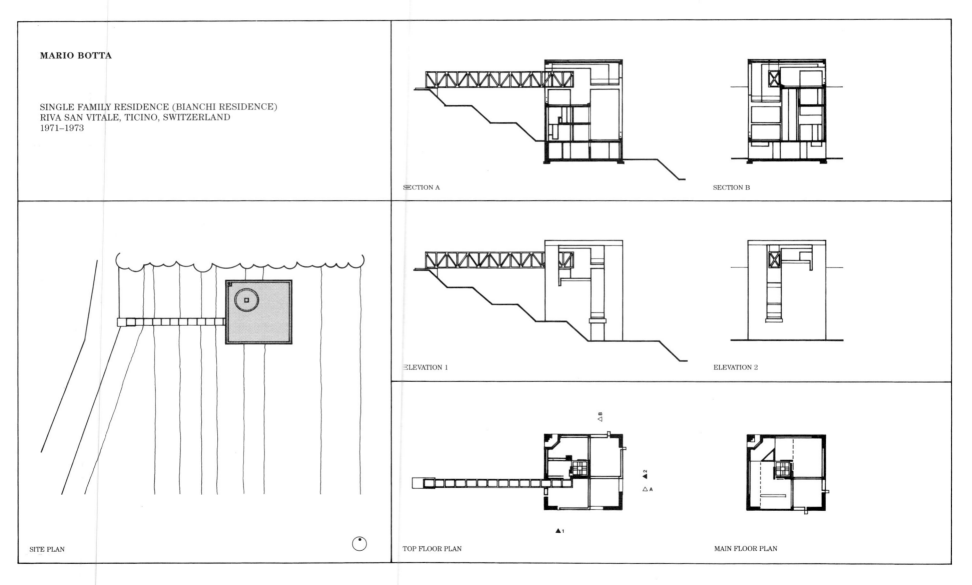

MARIO BOTTA

SINGLE FAMILY RESIDENCE (BIANCHI RESIDENCE)
RIVA SAN VITALE, TICINO, SWITZERLAND
1971–1973

SECTION A

SECTION B

ELEVATION 1

ELEVATION 2

SITE PLAN

TOP FLOOR PLAN

MAIN FLOOR PLAN

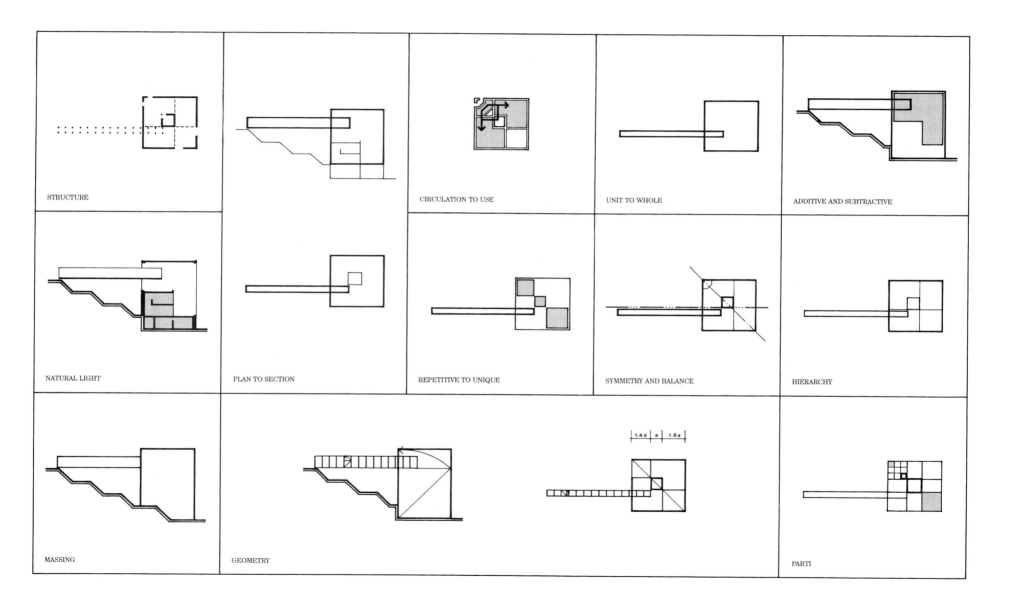

STRUCTURE

CIRCULATION TO USE

UNIT TO WHOLE

ADDITIVE AND SUBTRACTIVE

NATURAL LIGHT

PLAN TO SECTION

REPETITIVE TO UNIQUE

SYMMETRY AND BALANCE

HIERARCHY

MASSING

GEOMETRY

1.4 a | a | 1.6 a

PARTI

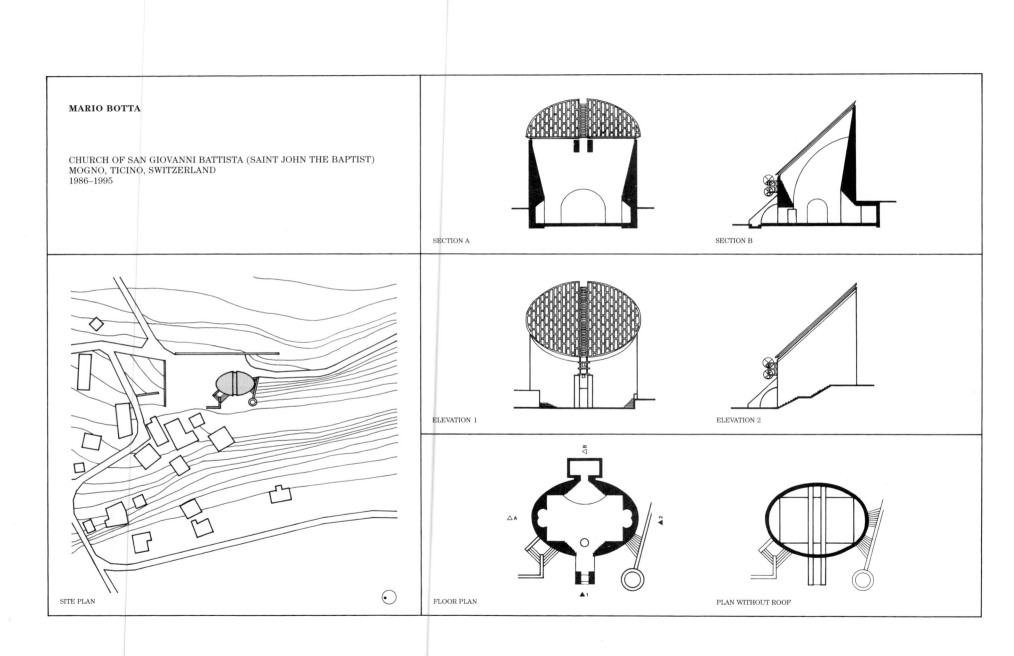

MARIO BOTTA

CHURCH OF SAN GIOVANNI BATTISTA (SAINT JOHN THE BAPTIST)
MOGNO, TICINO, SWITZERLAND
1986–1995

SECTION A

SECTION B

ELEVATION 1

ELEVATION 2

SITE PLAN

FLOOR PLAN

PLAN WITHOUT ROOF

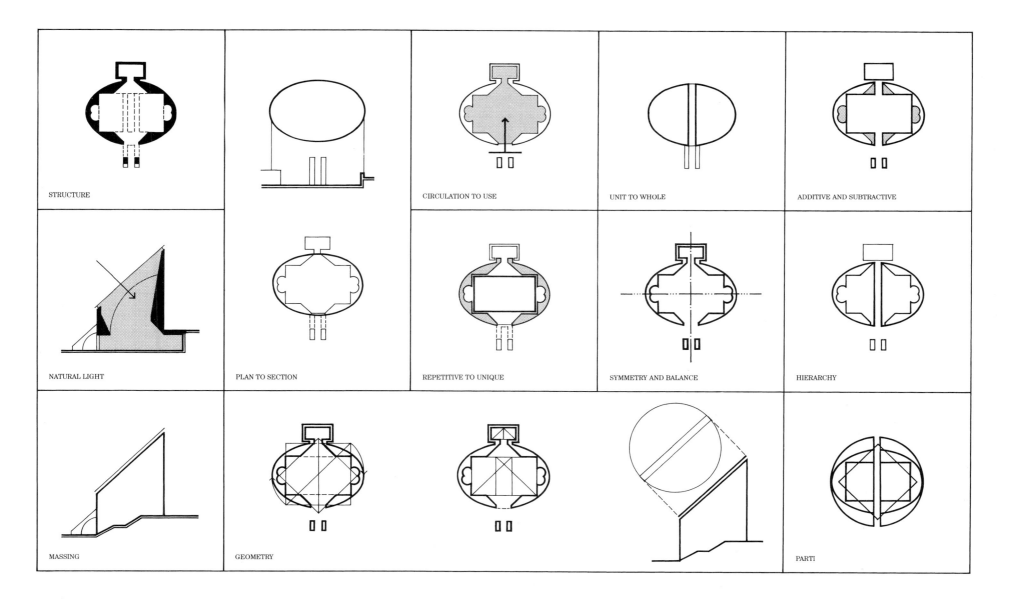

STRUCTURE

CIRCULATION TO USE

UNIT TO WHOLE

ADDITIVE AND SUBTRACTIVE

NATURAL LIGHT

PLAN TO SECTION

REPETITIVE TO UNIQUE

SYMMETRY AND BALANCE

HIERARCHY

MASSING

GEOMETRY

PARTI

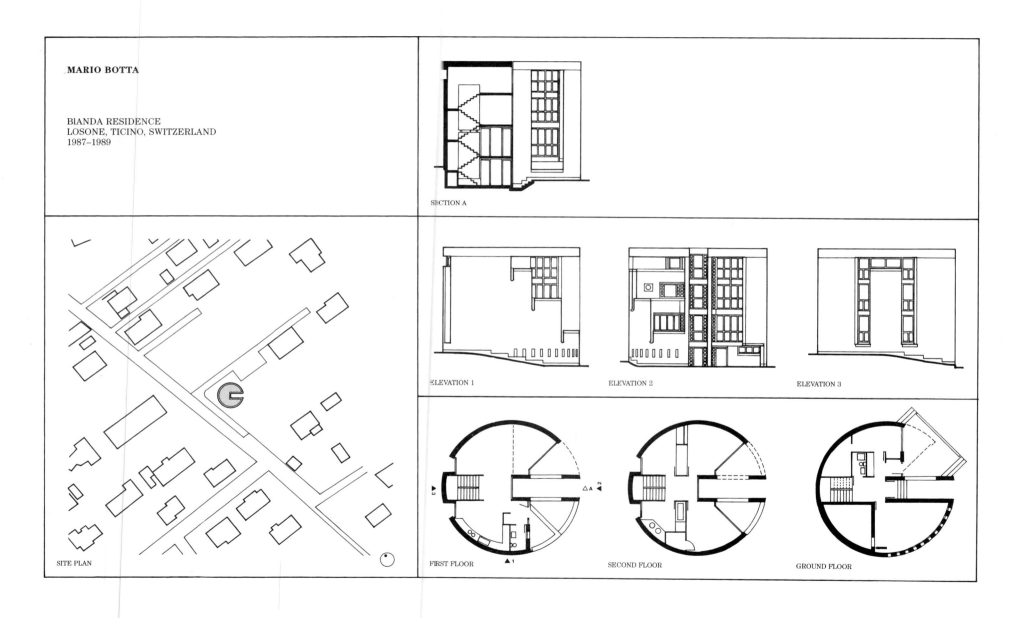

MARIO BOTTA

BIANDA RESIDENCE
LOSONE, TICINO, SWITZERLAND
1987–1989

SECTION A

SITE PLAN

ELEVATION 1

ELEVATION 2

ELEVATION 3

FIRST FLOOR

SECOND FLOOR

GROUND FLOOR

40

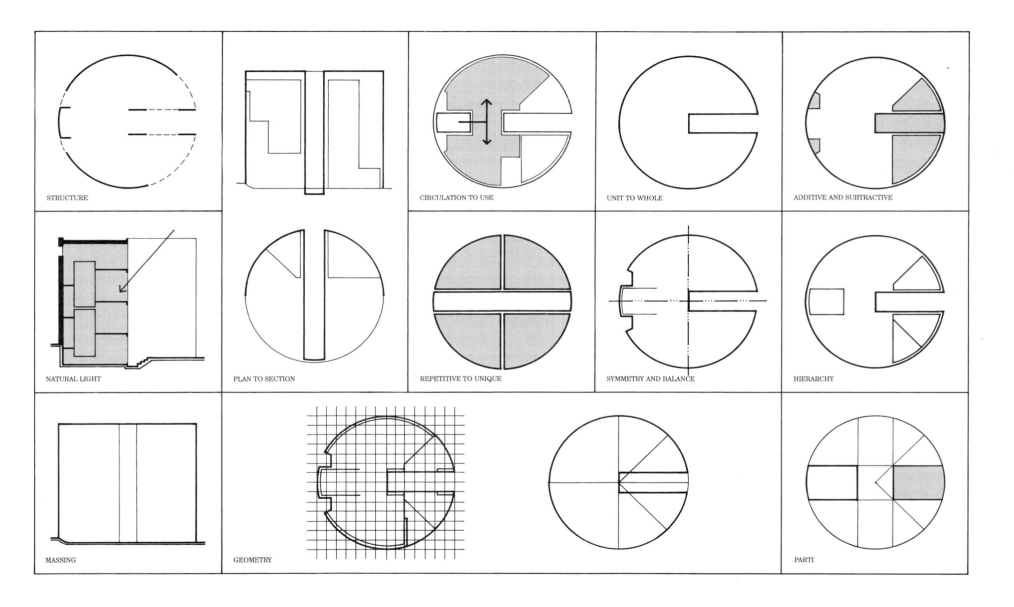

STRUCTURE

CIRCULATION TO USE

UNIT TO WHOLE

ADDITIVE AND SUBTRACTIVE

NATURAL LIGHT

PLAN TO SECTION

REPETITIVE TO UNIQUE

SYMMETRY AND BALANCE

HIERARCHY

MASSING

GEOMETRY

PARTI

41

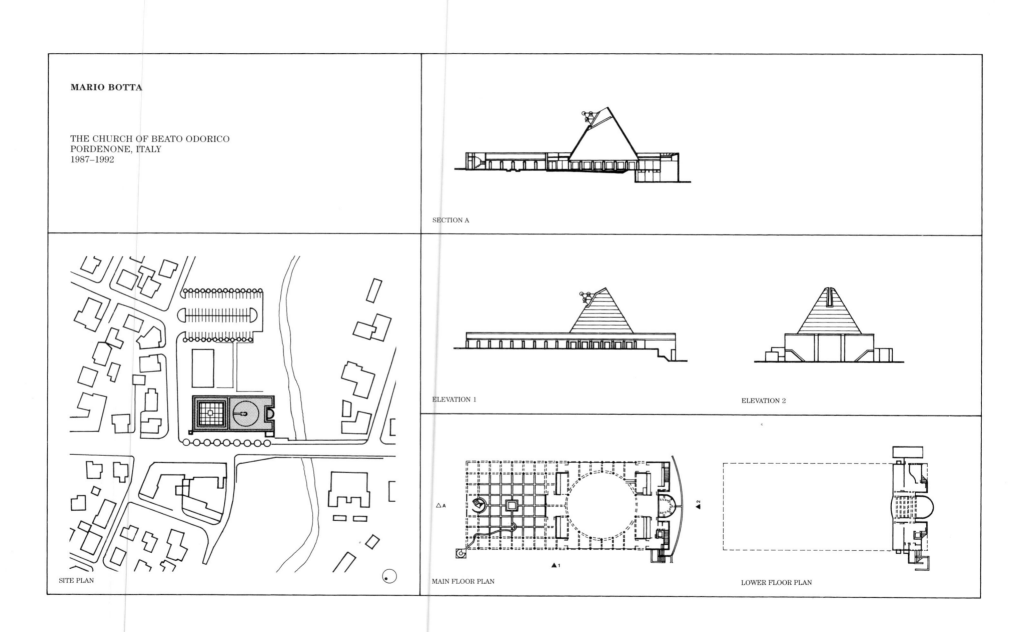

MARIO BOTTA

THE CHURCH OF BEATO ODORICO
PORDENONE, ITALY
1987–1992

SECTION A

SITE PLAN

ELEVATION 1

ELEVATION 2

MAIN FLOOR PLAN

LOWER FLOOR PLAN

42

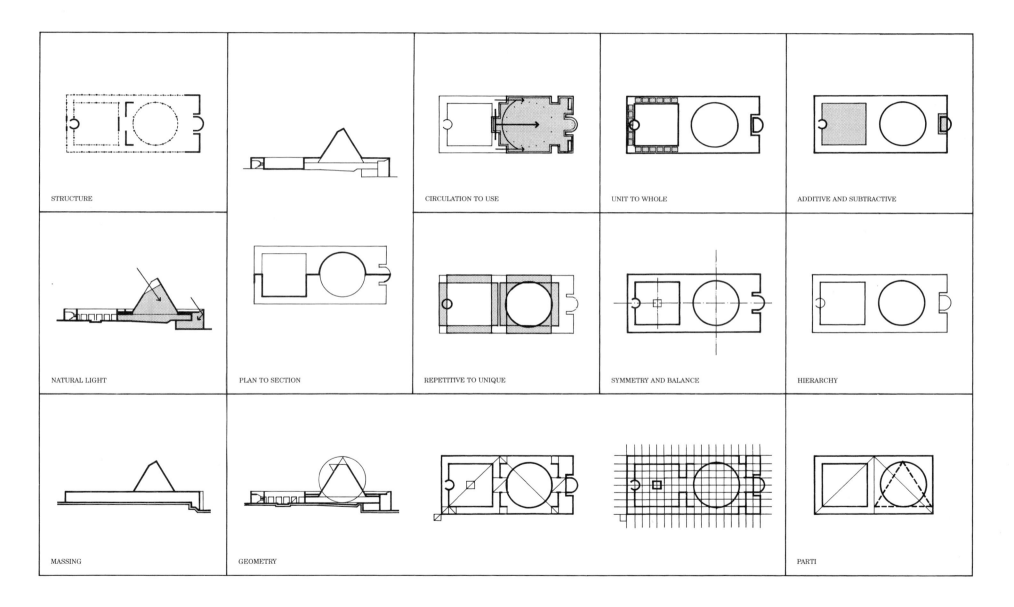

STRUCTURE

NATURAL LIGHT

MASSING

CIRCULATION TO USE

PLAN TO SECTION

GEOMETRY

UNIT TO WHOLE

REPETITIVE TO UNIQUE

ADDITIVE AND SUBTRACTIVE

SYMMETRY AND BALANCE

HIERARCHY

PARTI

FILIPPO BRUNELLESCHI

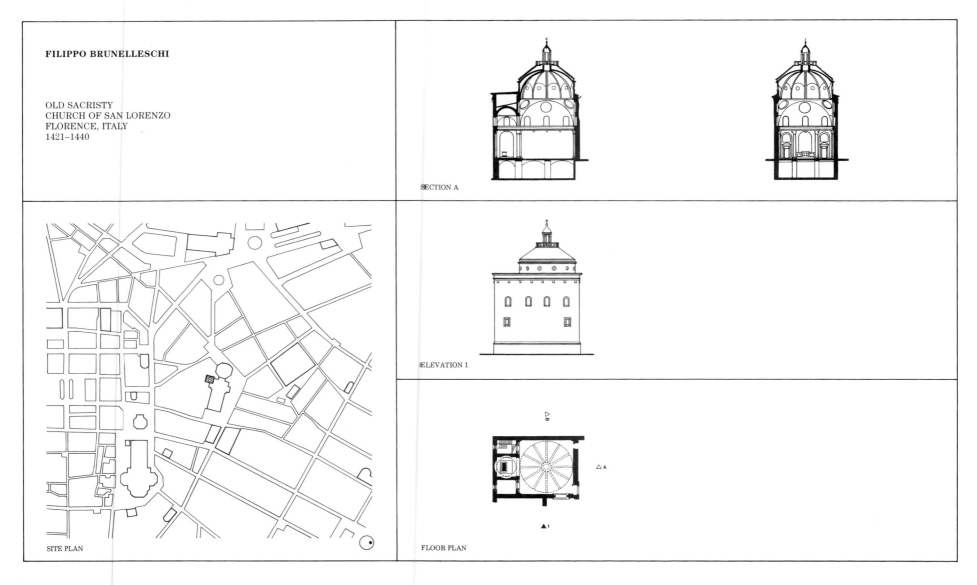

FILIPPO BRUNELLESCHI

OLD SACRISTY
CHURCH OF SAN LORENZO
FLORENCE, ITALY
1421–1440

SECTION A

ELEVATION 1

FLOOR PLAN

SITE PLAN

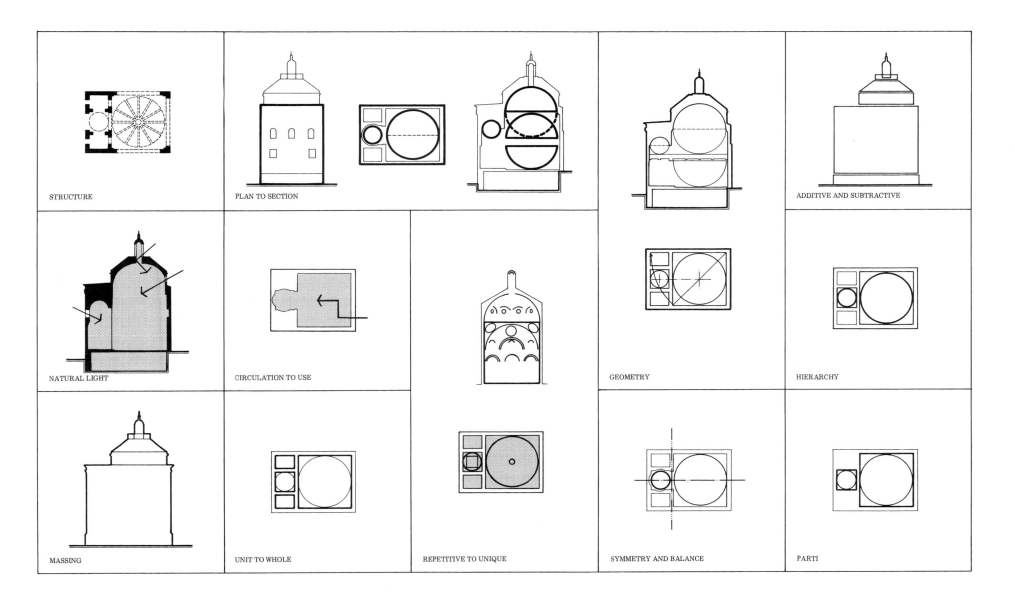

STRUCTURE

PLAN TO SECTION

ADDITIVE AND SUBTRACTIVE

NATURAL LIGHT

CIRCULATION TO USE

GEOMETRY

HIERARCHY

MASSING

UNIT TO WHOLE

REPETITIVE TO UNIQUE

SYMMETRY AND BALANCE

PARTI

FILIPPO BRUNELLESCHI

OSPEDALE DEGLI INNOCENTI
FLORENCE, ITALY
1421–1445

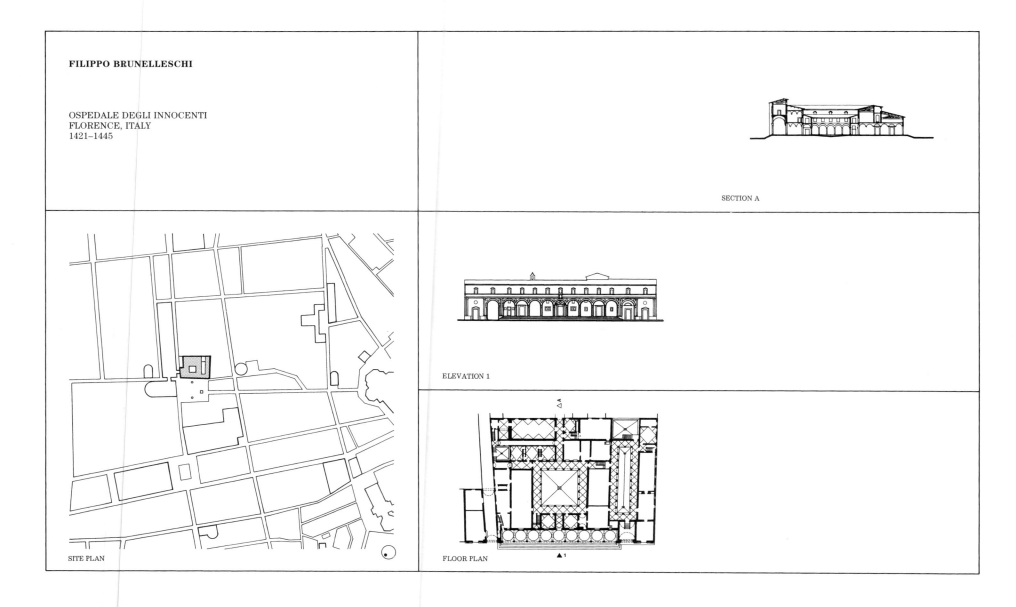

SECTION A

ELEVATION 1

SITE PLAN

FLOOR PLAN

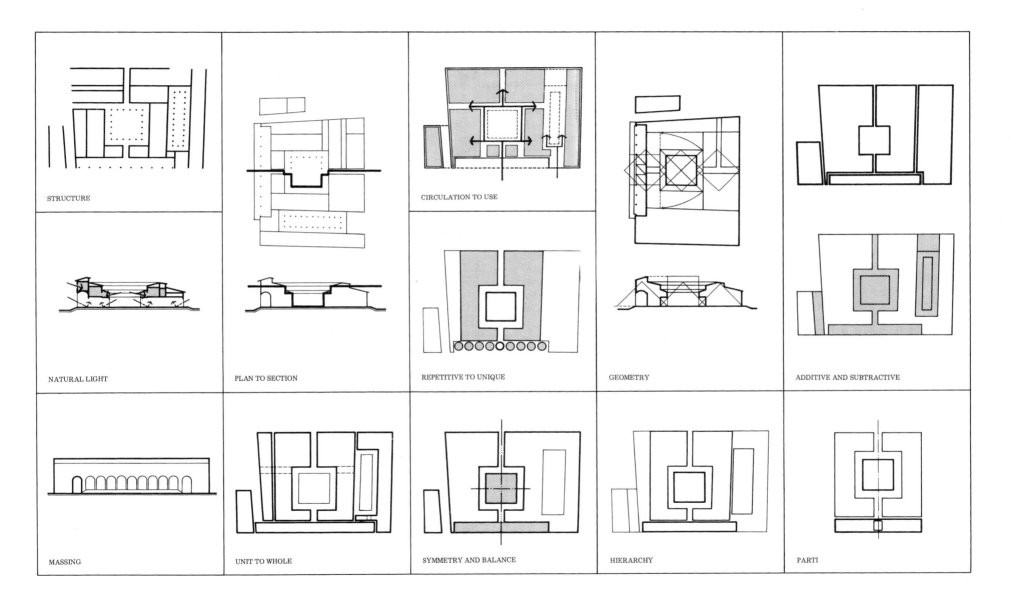

STRUCTURE

NATURAL LIGHT

MASSING

PLAN TO SECTION

UNIT TO WHOLE

CIRCULATION TO USE

REPETITIVE TO UNIQUE

SYMMETRY AND BALANCE

GEOMETRY

HIERARCHY

ADDITIVE AND SUBTRACTIVE

PARTI

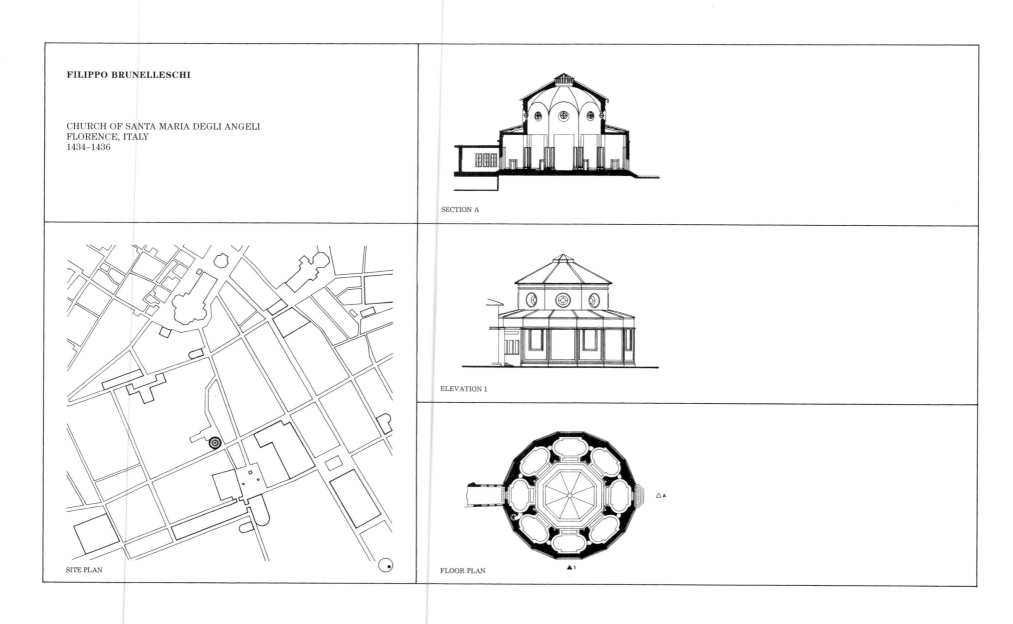

FILIPPO BRUNELLESCHI

CHURCH OF SANTA MARIA DEGLI ANGELI
FLORENCE, ITALY
1434–1436

SECTION A

ELEVATION 1

SITE PLAN

FLOOR PLAN

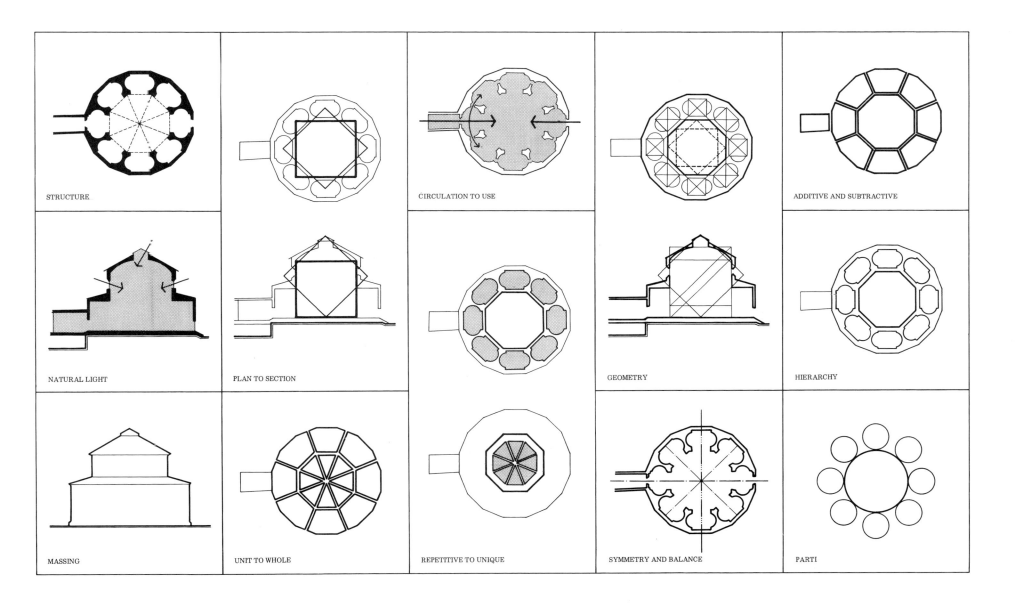

STRUCTURE

CIRCULATION TO USE

ADDITIVE AND SUBTRACTIVE

NATURAL LIGHT

PLAN TO SECTION

GEOMETRY

HIERARCHY

MASSING

UNIT TO WHOLE

REPETITIVE TO UNIQUE

SYMMETRY AND BALANCE

PARTI

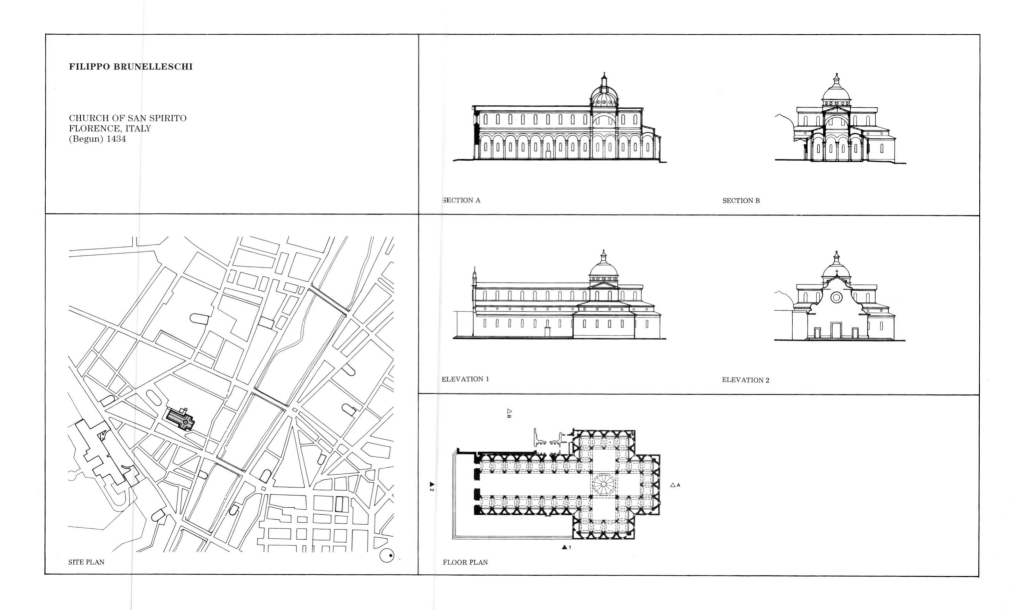

FILIPPO BRUNELLESCHI

CHURCH OF SAN SPIRITO
FLORENCE, ITALY
(Begun) 1434

SECTION A

SECTION B

ELEVATION 1

ELEVATION 2

SITE PLAN

FLOOR PLAN

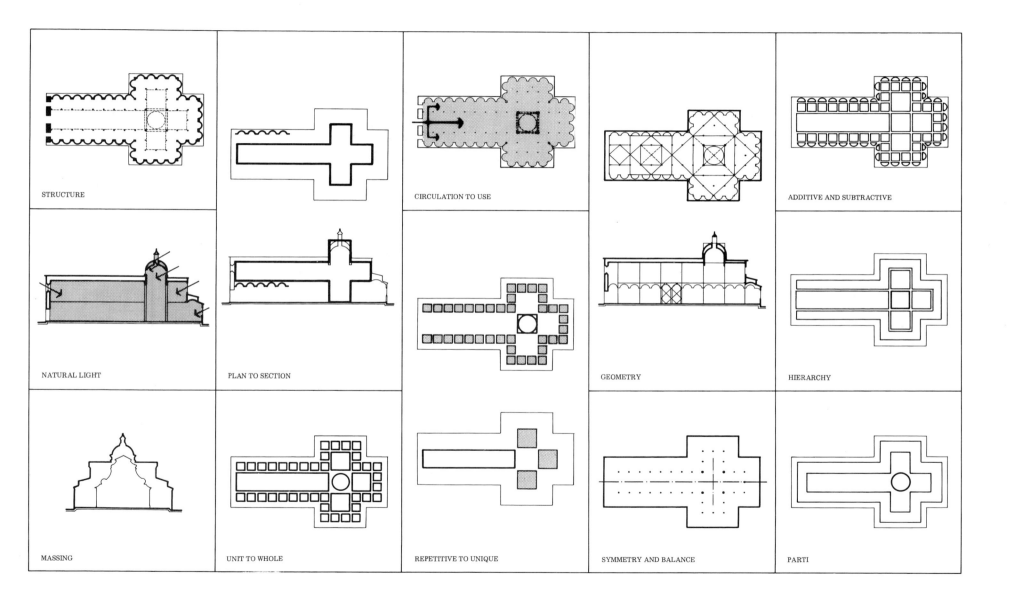

STRUCTURE

CIRCULATION TO USE

ADDITIVE AND SUBTRACTIVE

NATURAL LIGHT

PLAN TO SECTION

GEOMETRY

HIERARCHY

MASSING

UNIT TO WHOLE

REPETITIVE TO UNIQUE

SYMMETRY AND BALANCE

PARTI

51

SVERRE FEHN

SVERRE FEHN

VILLA BUSK
BAMBLE, TELEMARK, NORWAY
1990

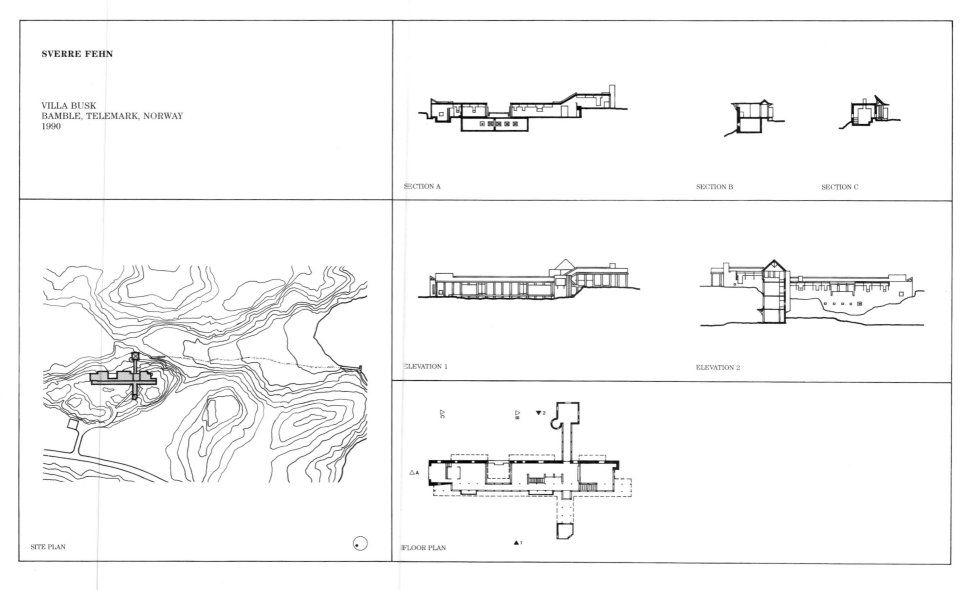

SECTION A

SECTION B

SECTION C

ELEVATION 1

ELEVATION 2

SITE PLAN

FLOOR PLAN

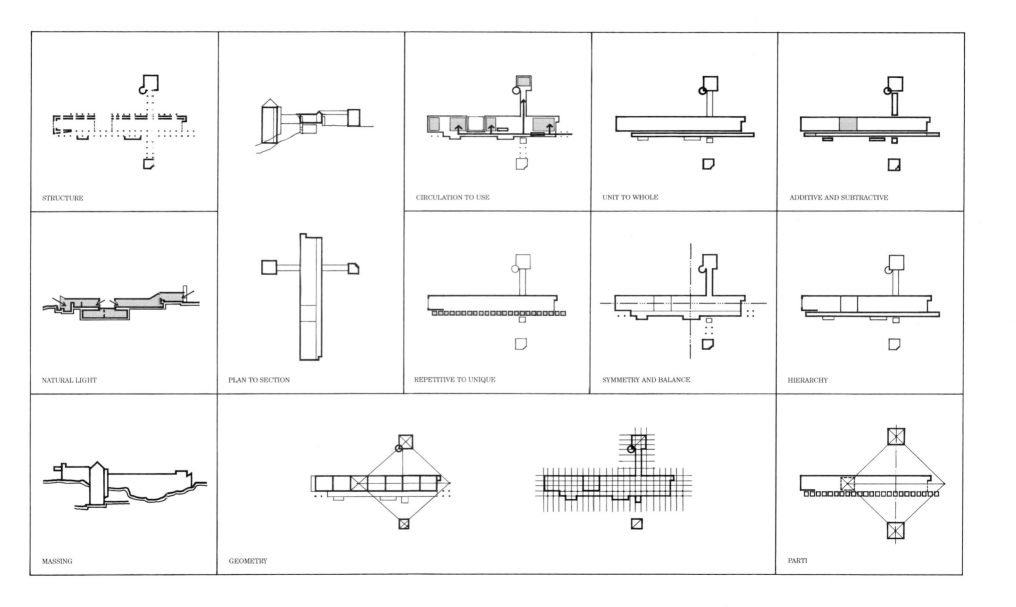

STRUCTURE

CIRCULATION TO USE

UNIT TO WHOLE

ADDITIVE AND SUBTRACTIVE

NATURAL LIGHT

PLAN TO SECTION

REPETITIVE TO UNIQUE

SYMMETRY AND BALANCE

HIERARCHY

MASSING

GEOMETRY

PARTI

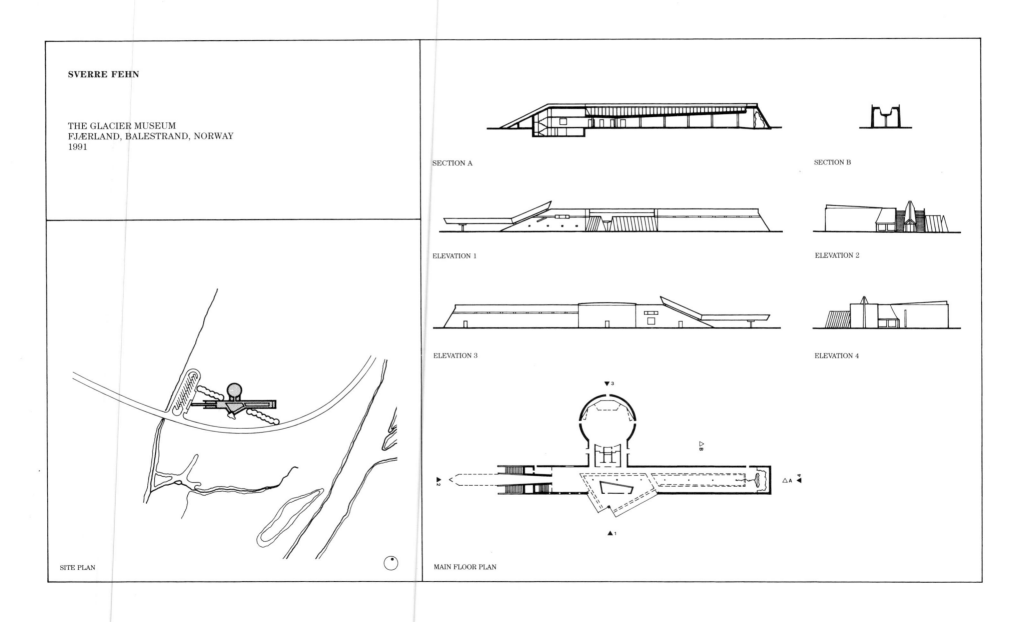

SVERRE FEHN

THE GLACIER MUSEUM
FJÆRLAND, BALESTRAND, NORWAY
1991

SITE PLAN

SECTION A

SECTION B

ELEVATION 1

ELEVATION 2

ELEVATION 3

ELEVATION 4

MAIN FLOOR PLAN

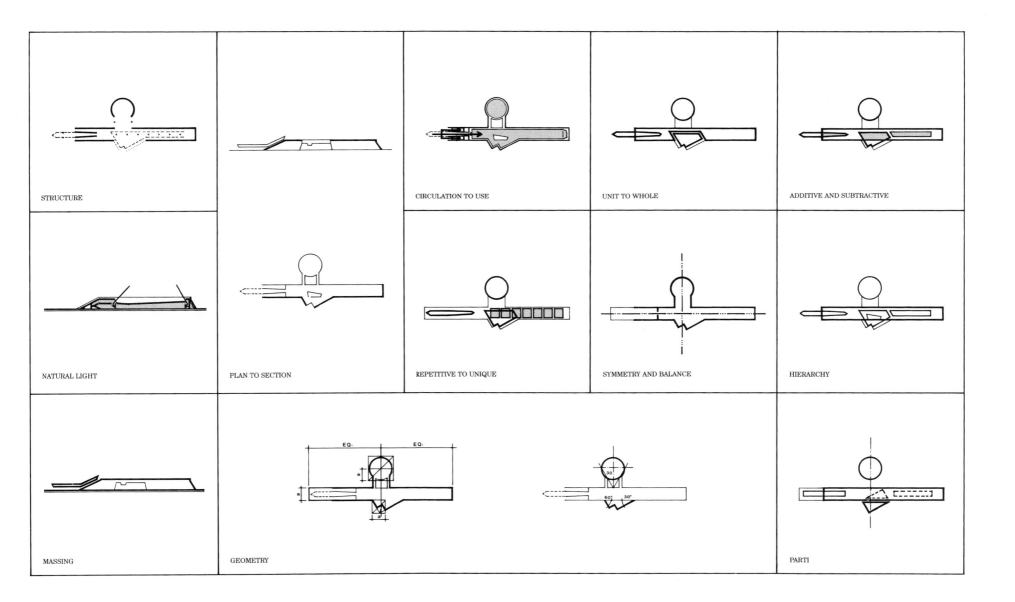

STRUCTURE

CIRCULATION TO USE

UNIT TO WHOLE

ADDITIVE AND SUBTRACTIVE

NATURAL LIGHT

PLAN TO SECTION

REPETITIVE TO UNIQUE

SYMMETRY AND BALANCE

HIERARCHY

MASSING

GEOMETRY

PARTI

ROMALDO GIURGOLA

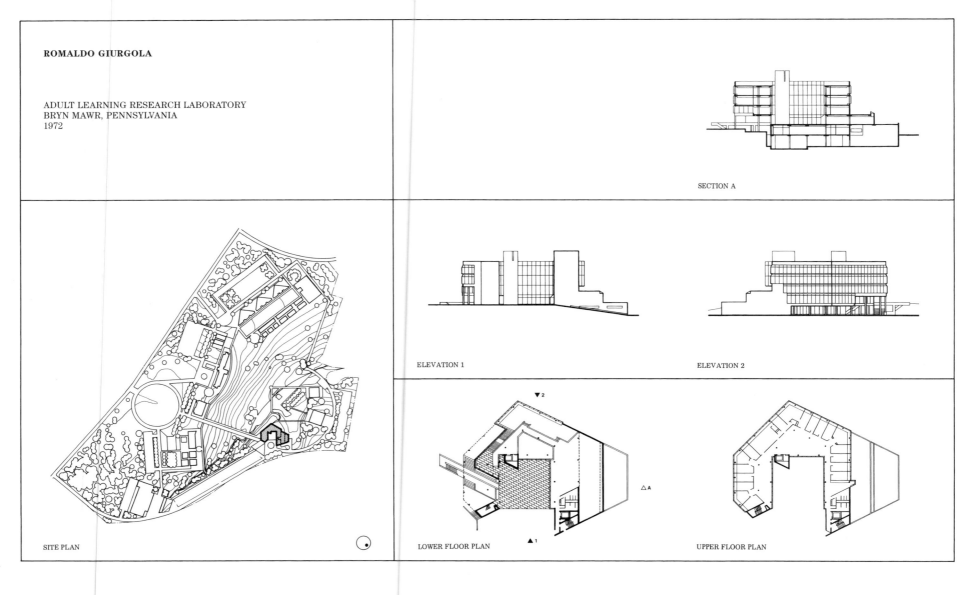

ROMALDO GIURGOLA

ADULT LEARNING RESEARCH LABORATORY
BRYN MAWR, PENNSYLVANIA
1972

SECTION A

ELEVATION 1

ELEVATION 2

SITE PLAN

LOWER FLOOR PLAN

UPPER FLOOR PLAN

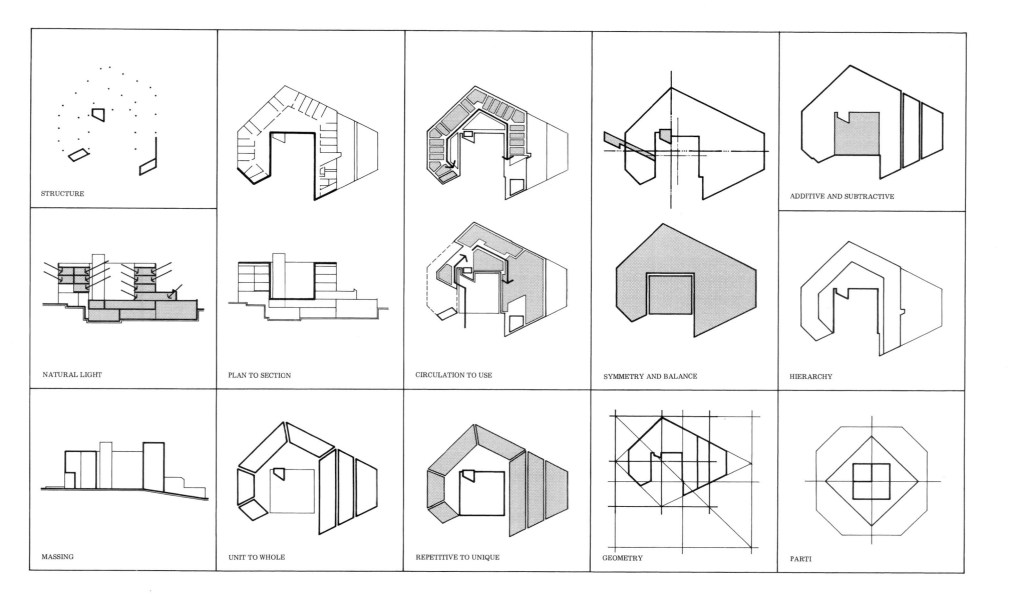

STRUCTURE

ADDITIVE AND SUBTRACTIVE

NATURAL LIGHT

PLAN TO SECTION

CIRCULATION TO USE

SYMMETRY AND BALANCE

HIERARCHY

MASSING

UNIT TO WHOLE

REPETITIVE TO UNIQUE

GEOMETRY

PARTI

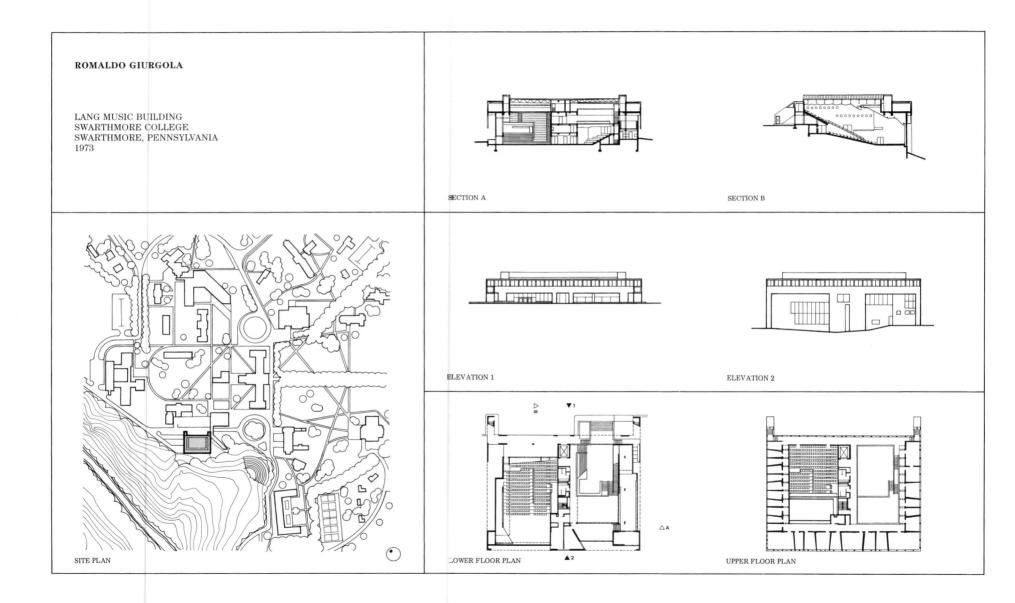

ROMALDO GIURGOLA

LANG MUSIC BUILDING
SWARTHMORE COLLEGE
SWARTHMORE, PENNSYLVANIA
1973

SECTION A

SECTION B

ELEVATION 1

ELEVATION 2

SITE PLAN

LOWER FLOOR PLAN

UPPER FLOOR PLAN

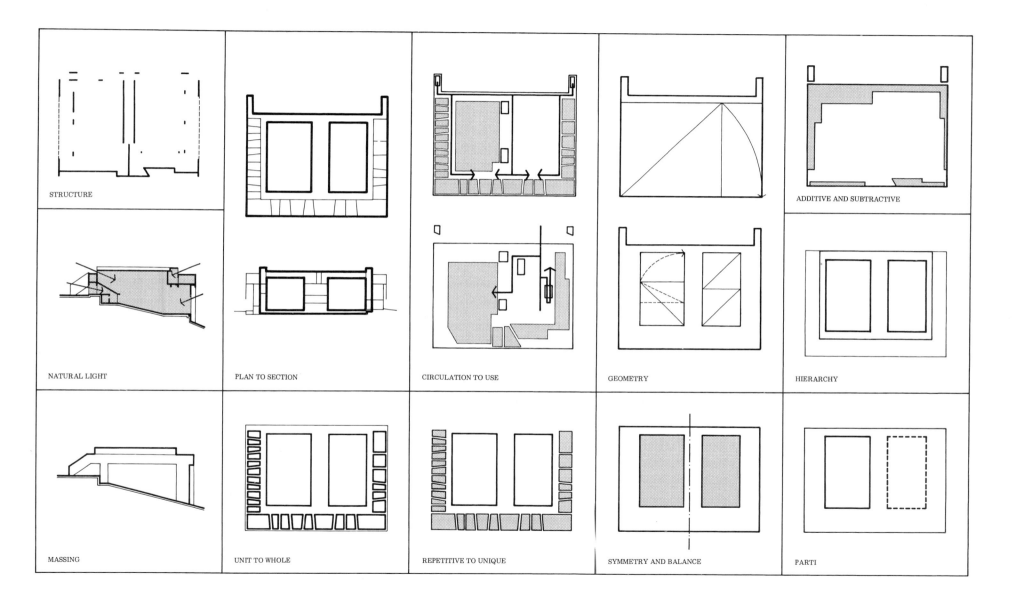

STRUCTURE

NATURAL LIGHT

MASSING

PLAN TO SECTION

UNIT TO WHOLE

CIRCULATION TO USE

REPETITIVE TO UNIQUE

GEOMETRY

SYMMETRY AND BALANCE

ADDITIVE AND SUBTRACTIVE

HIERARCHY

PARTI

ROMALDO GIURGOLA

STUDENT UNION
STATE UNIVERSITY COLLEGE OF NEW YORK
PLATTSBURGH, NEW YORK
1974

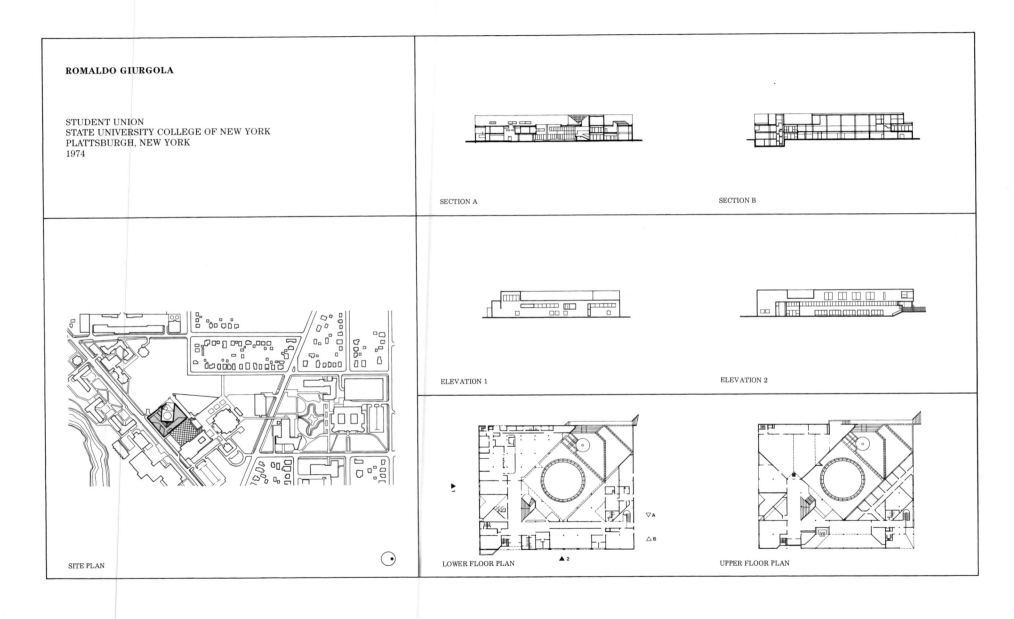

SECTION A

SECTION B

ELEVATION 1

ELEVATION 2

SITE PLAN

LOWER FLOOR PLAN

UPPER FLOOR PLAN

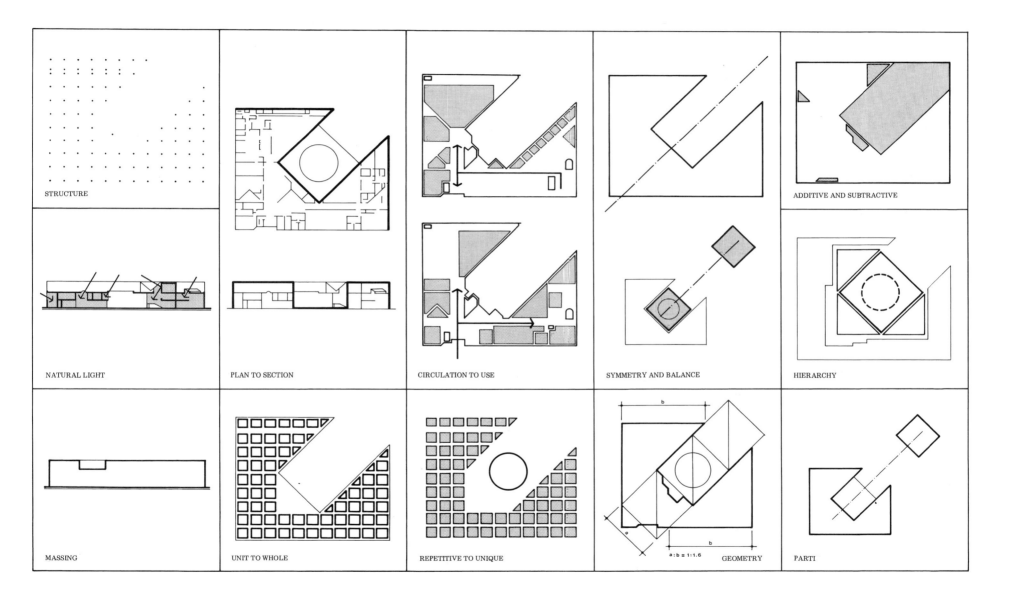

STRUCTURE

NATURAL LIGHT

MASSING

PLAN TO SECTION

UNIT TO WHOLE

CIRCULATION TO USE

REPETITIVE TO UNIQUE

SYMMETRY AND BALANCE

a : b = 1:1.6   GEOMETRY

ADDITIVE AND SUBTRACTIVE

HIERARCHY

PARTI

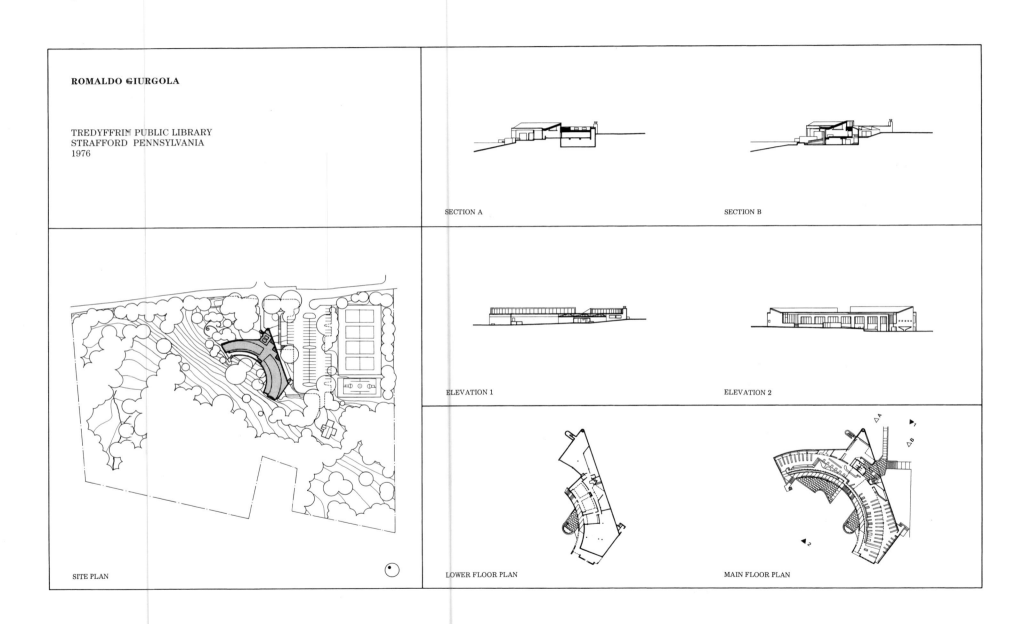

ROMALDO GIURGOLA

TREDYFFRIN PUBLIC LIBRARY
STRAFFORD PENNSYLVANIA
1976

SECTION A

SECTION B

ELEVATION 1

ELEVATION 2

SITE PLAN

LOWER FLOOR PLAN

MAIN FLOOR PLAN

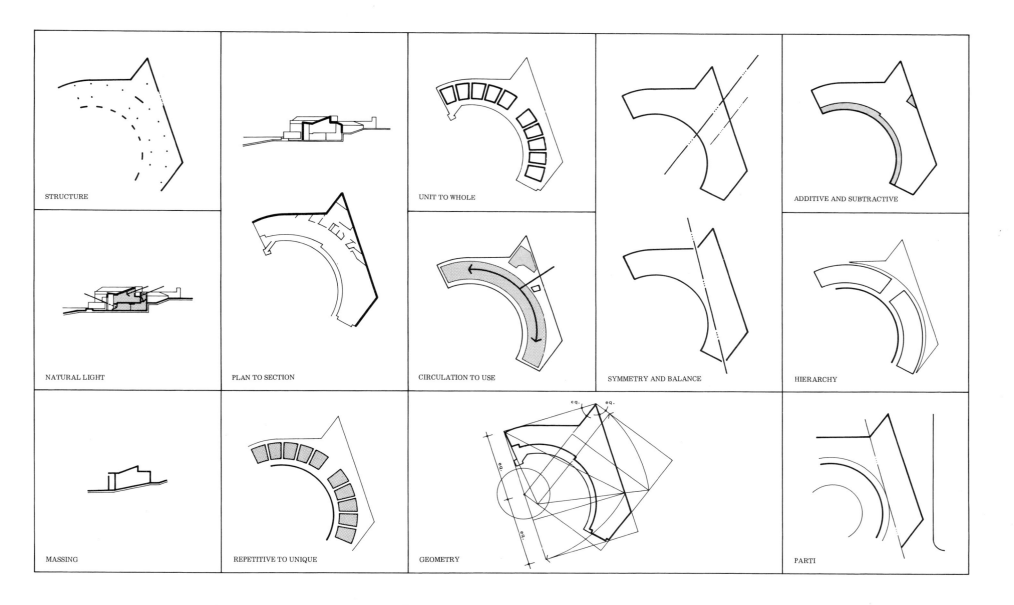

STRUCTURE

UNIT TO WHOLE

ADDITIVE AND SUBTRACTIVE

NATURAL LIGHT

PLAN TO SECTION

CIRCULATION TO USE

SYMMETRY AND BALANCE

HIERARCHY

MASSING

REPETITIVE TO UNIQUE

GEOMETRY

PARTI

NICHOLAS HAWKSMOOR

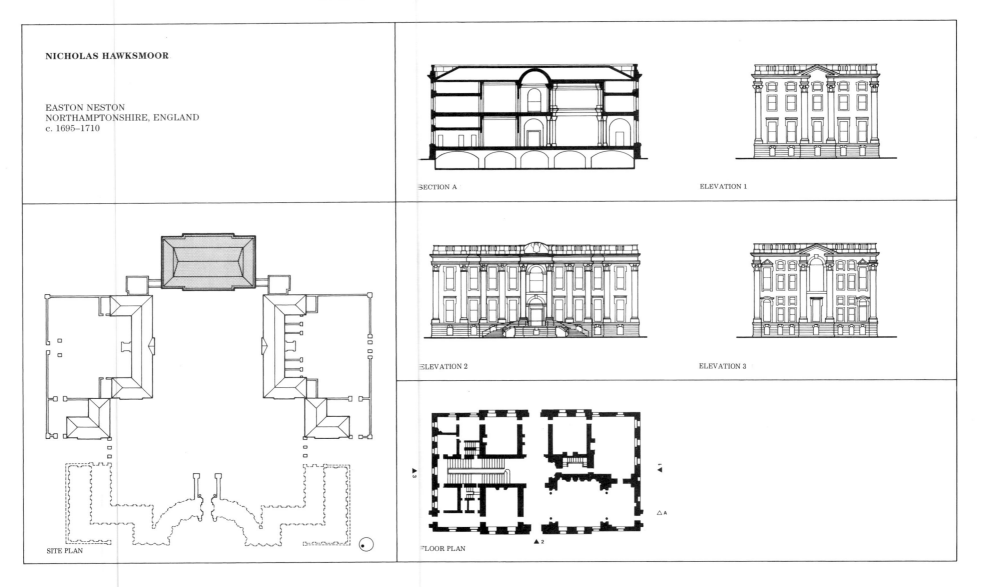

NICHOLAS HAWKSMOOR

EASTON NESTON
NORTHAMPTONSHIRE, ENGLAND
c. 1695–1710

SECTION A

ELEVATION 1

ELEVATION 2

ELEVATION 3

SITE PLAN

FLOOR PLAN

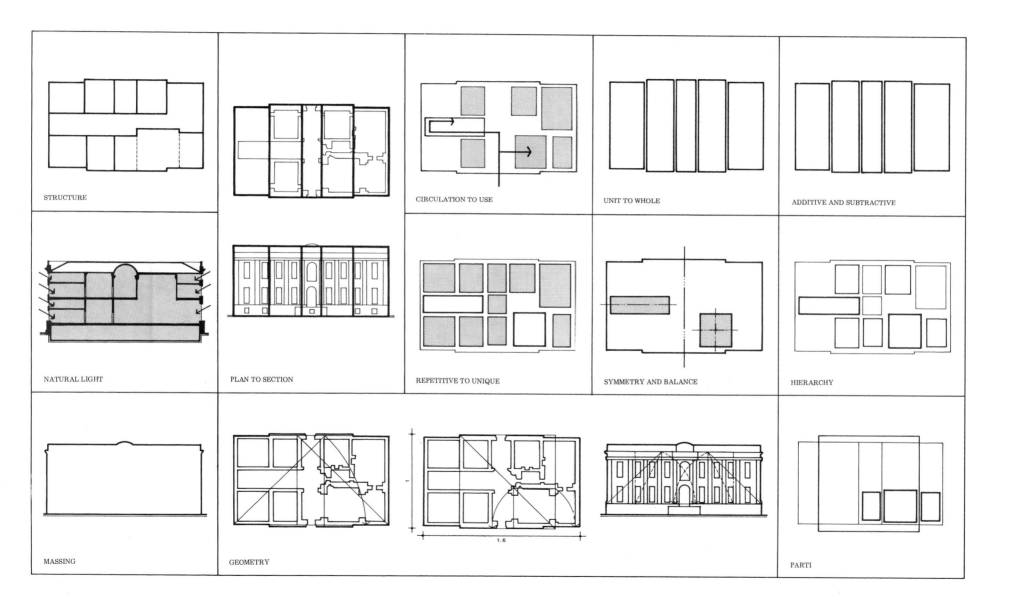

STRUCTURE

CIRCULATION TO USE

UNIT TO WHOLE

ADDITIVE AND SUBTRACTIVE

NATURAL LIGHT

PLAN TO SECTION

REPETITIVE TO UNIQUE

SYMMETRY AND BALANCE

HIERARCHY

MASSING

GEOMETRY

PARTI

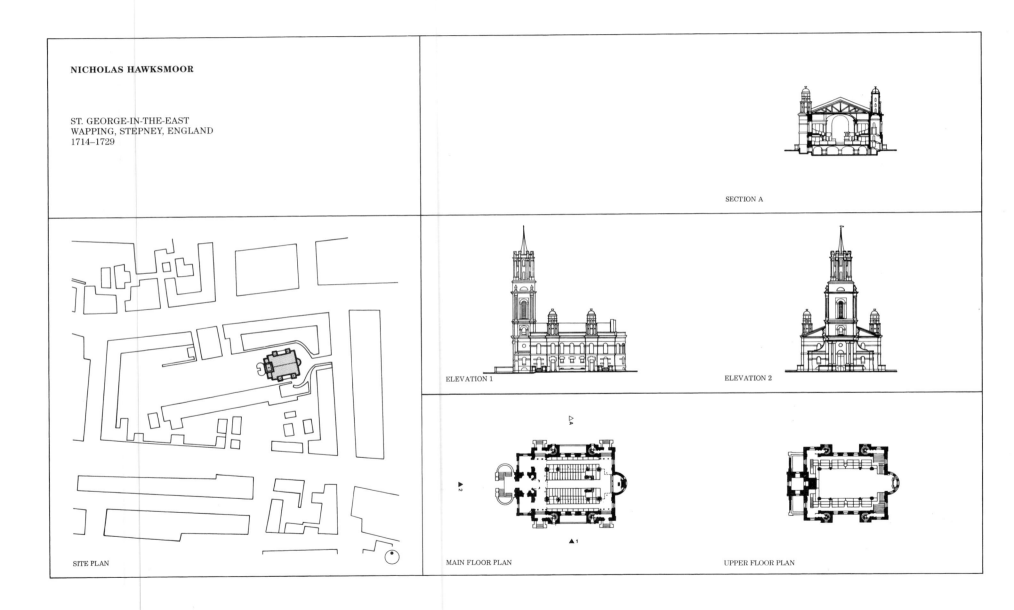

NICHOLAS HAWKSMOOR

ST. GEORGE-IN-THE-EAST
WAPPING, STEPNEY, ENGLAND
1714–1729

SECTION A

SITE PLAN

ELEVATION 1

ELEVATION 2

MAIN FLOOR PLAN

UPPER FLOOR PLAN

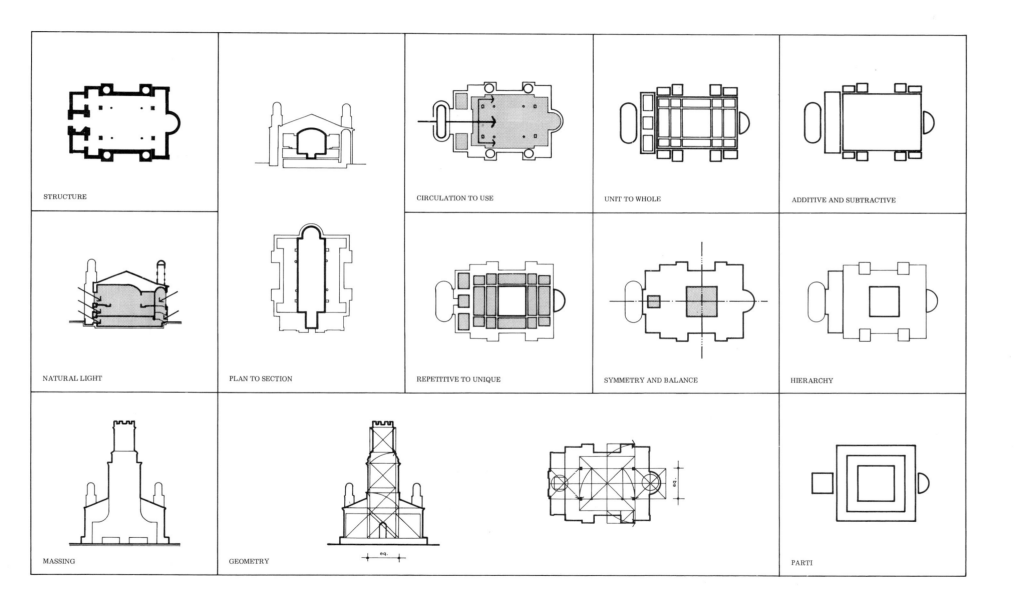

STRUCTURE

CIRCULATION TO USE

UNIT TO WHOLE

ADDITIVE AND SUBTRACTIVE

NATURAL LIGHT

PLAN TO SECTION

REPETITIVE TO UNIQUE

SYMMETRY AND BALANCE

HIERARCHY

MASSING

GEOMETRY

PARTI

67

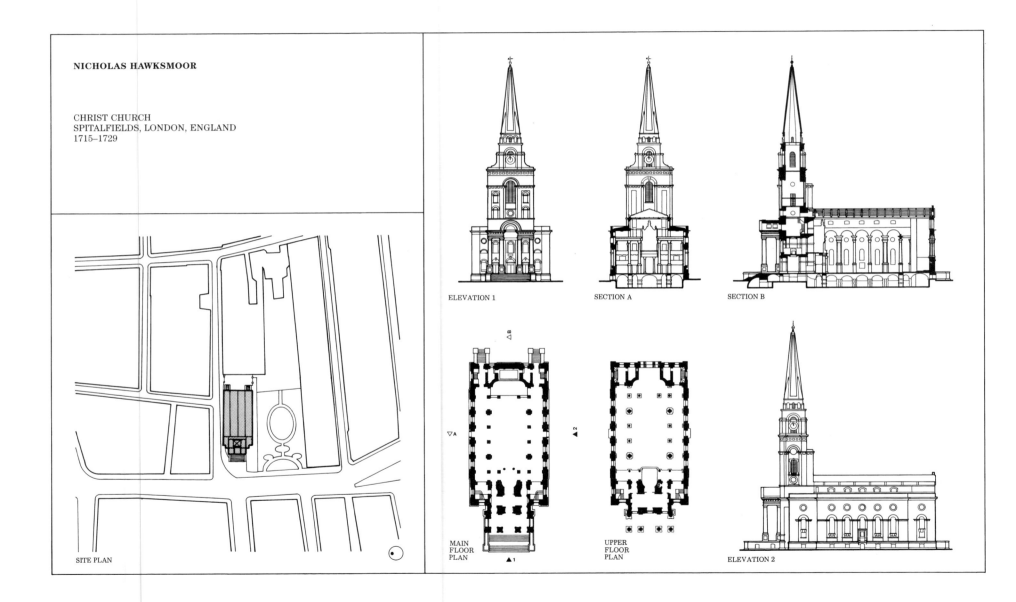

NICHOLAS HAWKSMOOR

CHRIST CHURCH
SPITALFIELDS, LONDON, ENGLAND
1715–1729

SITE PLAN

ELEVATION 1

SECTION A

SECTION B

MAIN
FLOOR
PLAN

UPPER
FLOOR
PLAN

ELEVATION 2

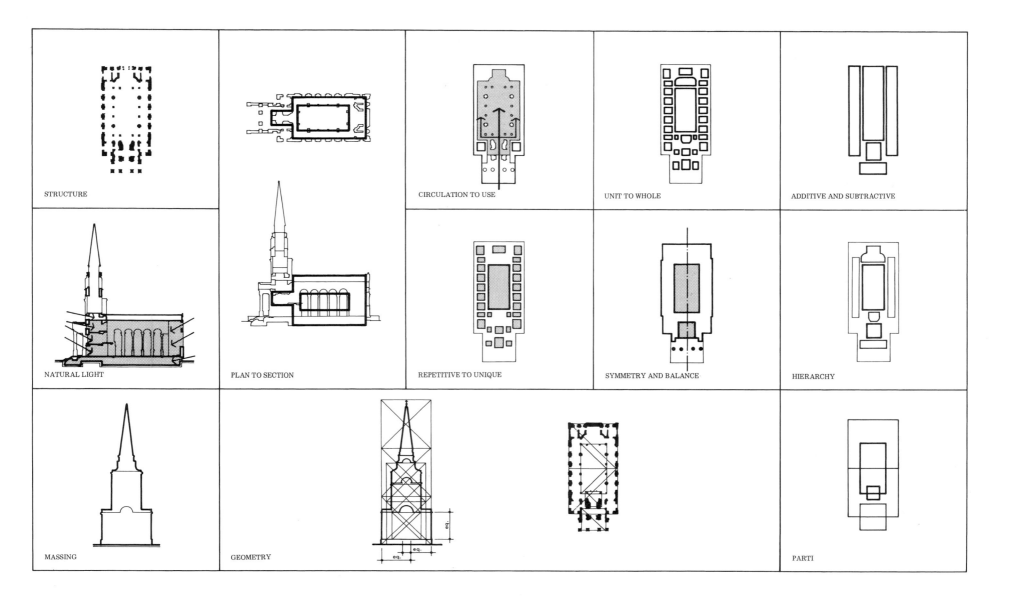

STRUCTURE

CIRCULATION TO USE

UNIT TO WHOLE

ADDITIVE AND SUBTRACTIVE

NATURAL LIGHT

PLAN TO SECTION

REPETITIVE TO UNIQUE

SYMMETRY AND BALANCE

HIERARCHY

MASSING

GEOMETRY

PARTI

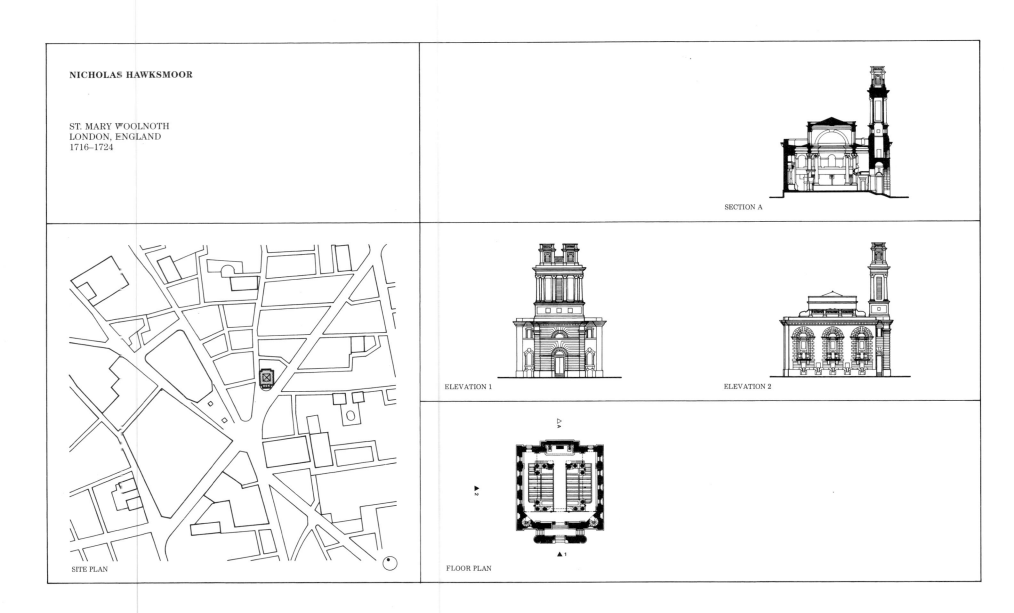

NICHOLAS HAWKSMOOR

ST. MARY WOOLNOTH
LONDON, ENGLAND
1716–1724

SECTION A

ELEVATION 1

ELEVATION 2

SITE PLAN

FLOOR PLAN

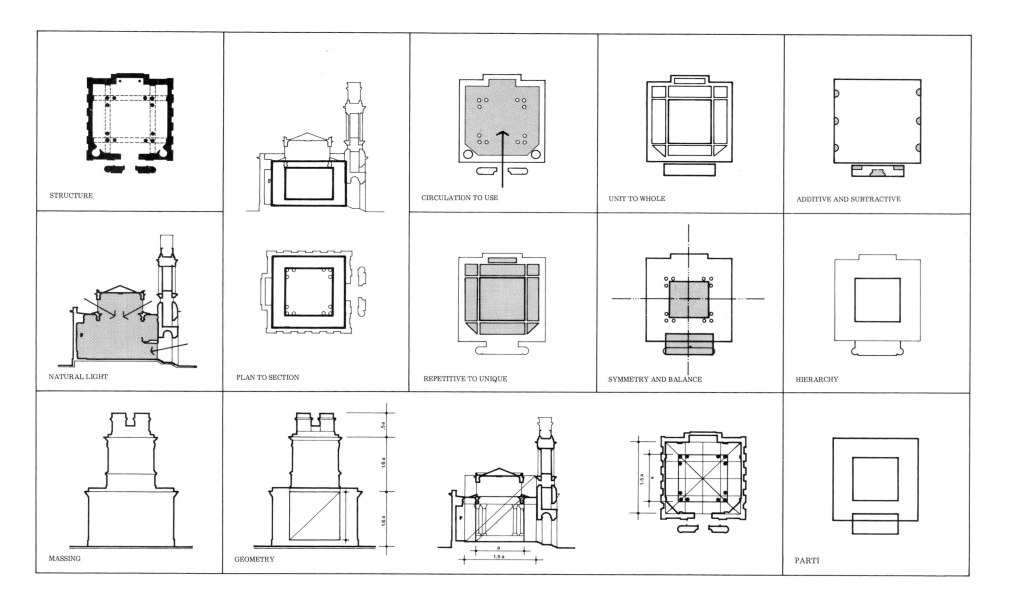

STRUCTURE

NATURAL LIGHT

MASSING

CIRCULATION TO USE

PLAN TO SECTION

GEOMETRY

UNIT TO WHOLE

REPETITIVE TO UNIQUE

SYMMETRY AND BALANCE

ADDITIVE AND SUBTRACTIVE

HIERARCHY

PARTI

HERZOG & DE MEURON

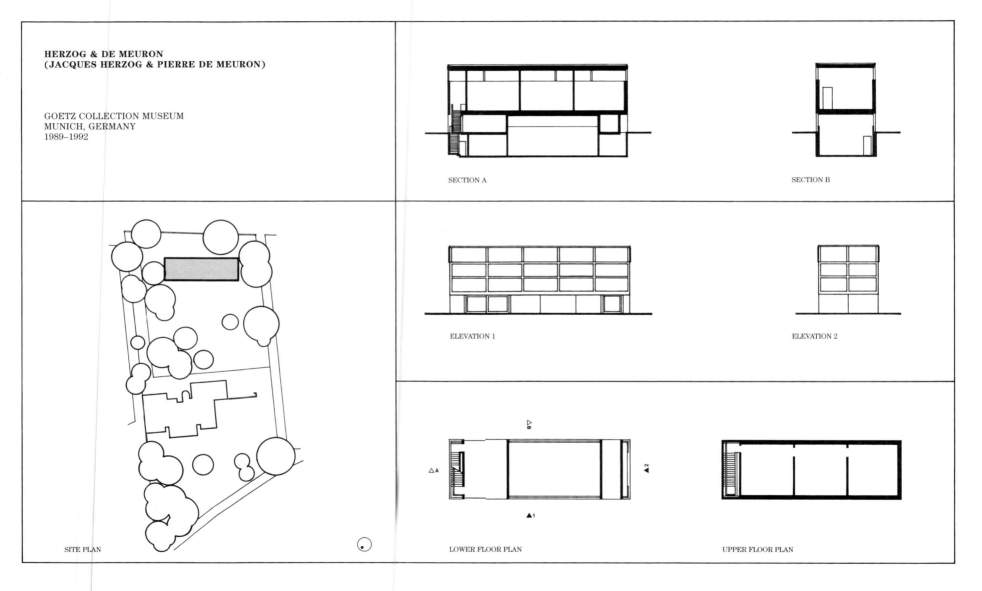

HERZOG & DE MEURON
(JACQUES HERZOG & PIERRE DE MEURON)

GOETZ COLLECTION MUSEUM
MUNICH, GERMANY
1989–1992

SECTION A

SECTION B

ELEVATION 1

ELEVATION 2

SITE PLAN

LOWER FLOOR PLAN

UPPER FLOOR PLAN

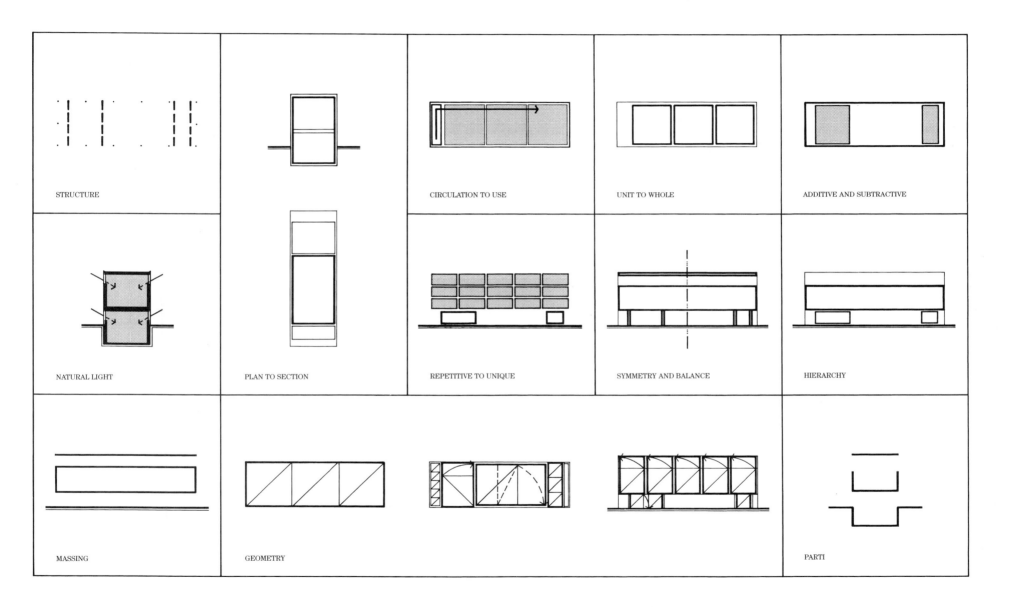

STRUCTURE

CIRCULATION TO USE

UNIT TO WHOLE

ADDITIVE AND SUBTRACTIVE

NATURAL LIGHT

PLAN TO SECTION

REPETITIVE TO UNIQUE

SYMMETRY AND BALANCE

HIERARCHY

MASSING

GEOMETRY

PARTI

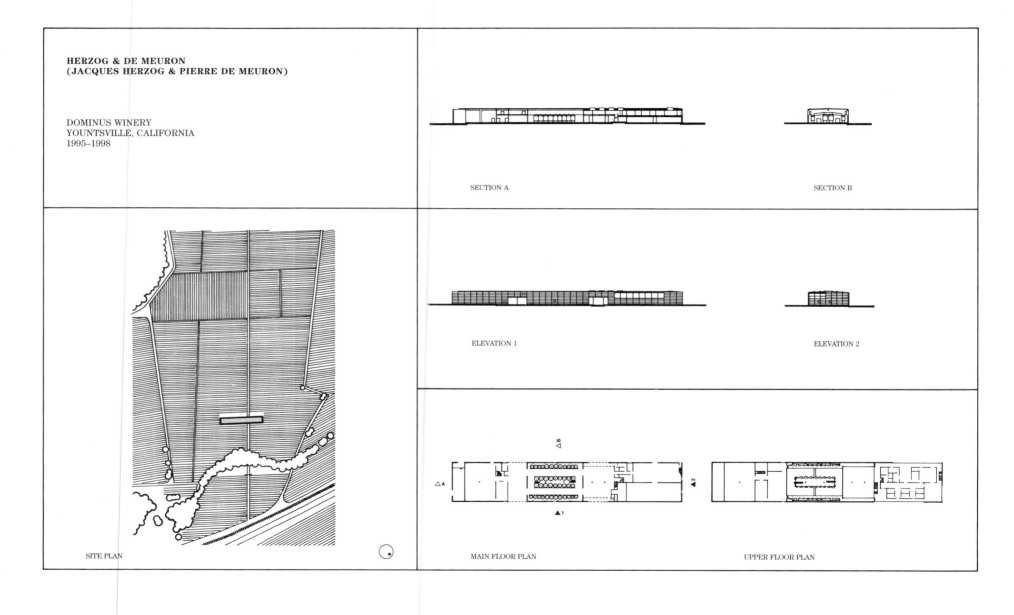

HERZOG & DE MEURON
(JACQUES HERZOG & PIERRE DE MEURON)

DOMINUS WINERY
YOUNTSVILLE, CALIFORNIA
1995–1998

SECTION A

SECTION B

ELEVATION 1

ELEVATION 2

SITE PLAN

MAIN FLOOR PLAN

UPPER FLOOR PLAN

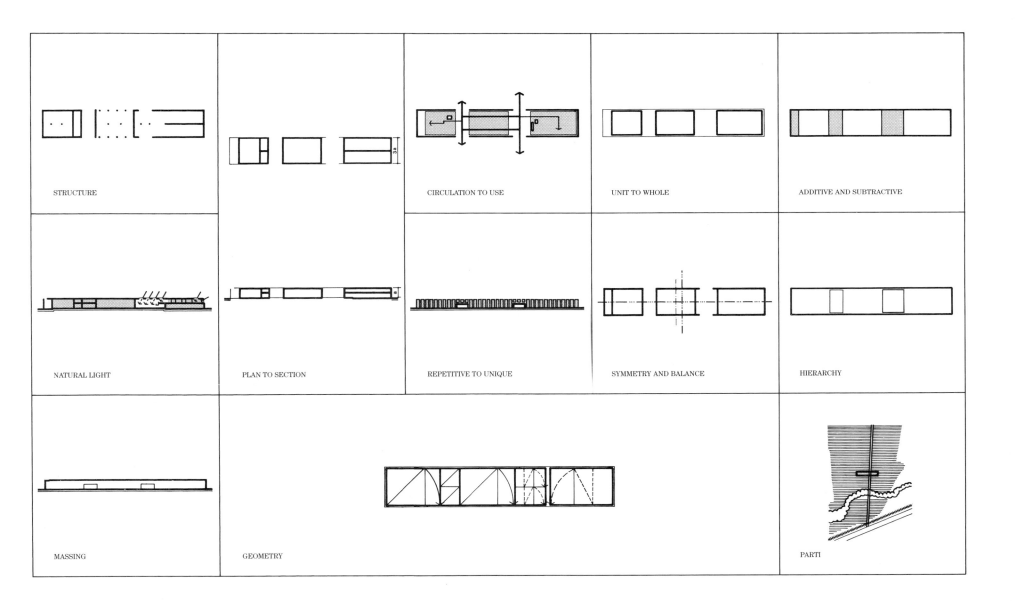

STRUCTURE

CIRCULATION TO USE

UNIT TO WHOLE

ADDITIVE AND SUBTRACTIVE

NATURAL LIGHT

PLAN TO SECTION

REPETITIVE TO UNIQUE

SYMMETRY AND BALANCE

HIERARCHY

MASSING

GEOMETRY

PARTI

STEVEN HOLL

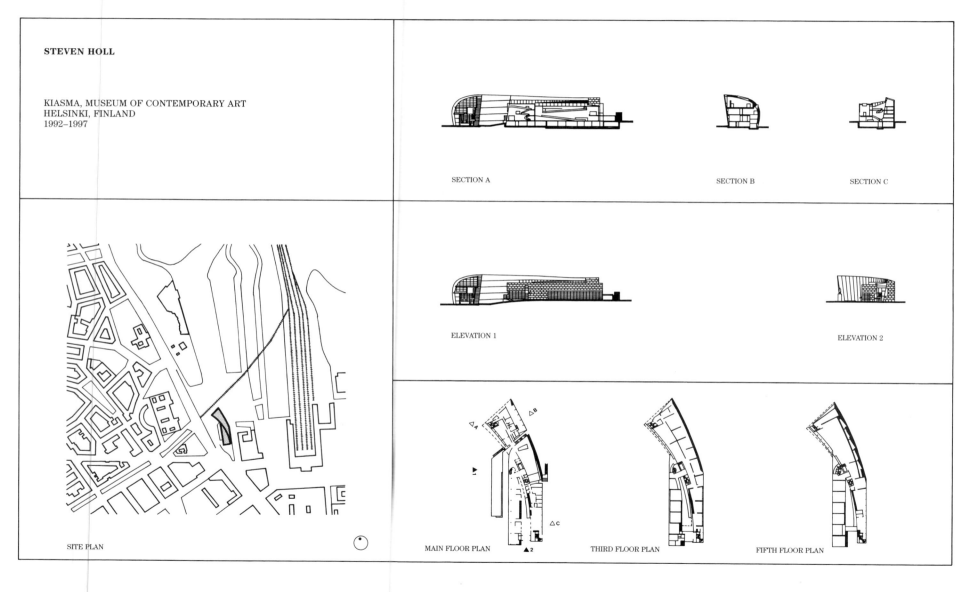

STEVEN HOLL

KIASMA, MUSEUM OF CONTEMPORARY ART
HELSINKI, FINLAND
1992–1997

SECTION A

SECTION B

SECTION C

ELEVATION 1

ELEVATION 2

SITE PLAN

MAIN FLOOR PLAN

THIRD FLOOR PLAN

FIFTH FLOOR PLAN

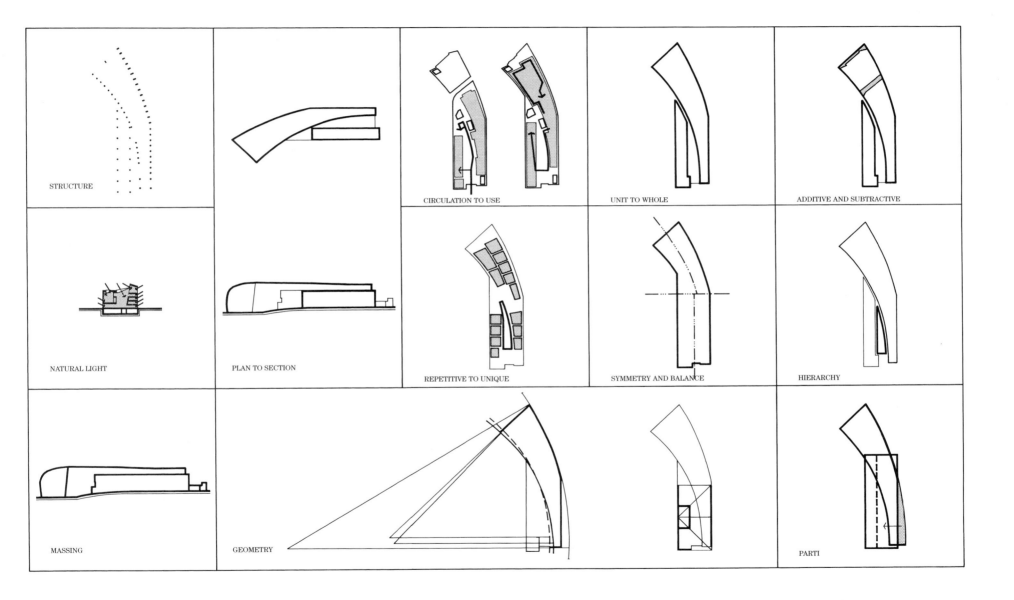

STRUCTURE

NATURAL LIGHT

MASSING

PLAN TO SECTION

GEOMETRY

CIRCULATION TO USE

REPETITIVE TO UNIQUE

UNIT TO WHOLE

SYMMETRY AND BALANCE

ADDITIVE AND SUBTRACTIVE

HIERARCHY

PARTI

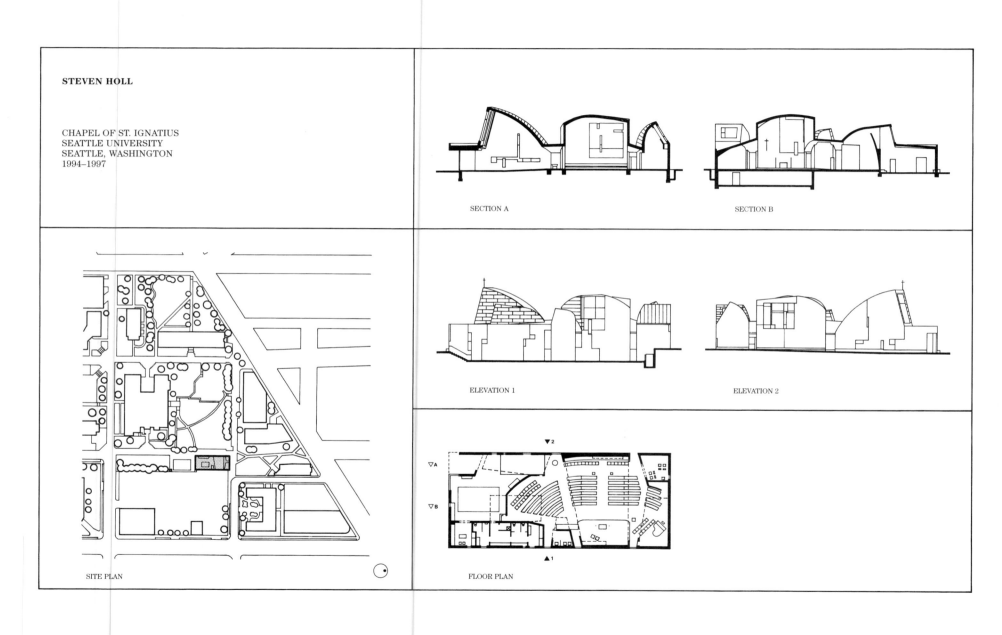

STEVEN HOLL

CHAPEL OF ST. IGNATIUS
SEATTLE UNIVERSITY
SEATTLE, WASHINGTON
1994–1997

SECTION A

SECTION B

ELEVATION 1

ELEVATION 2

SITE PLAN

FLOOR PLAN

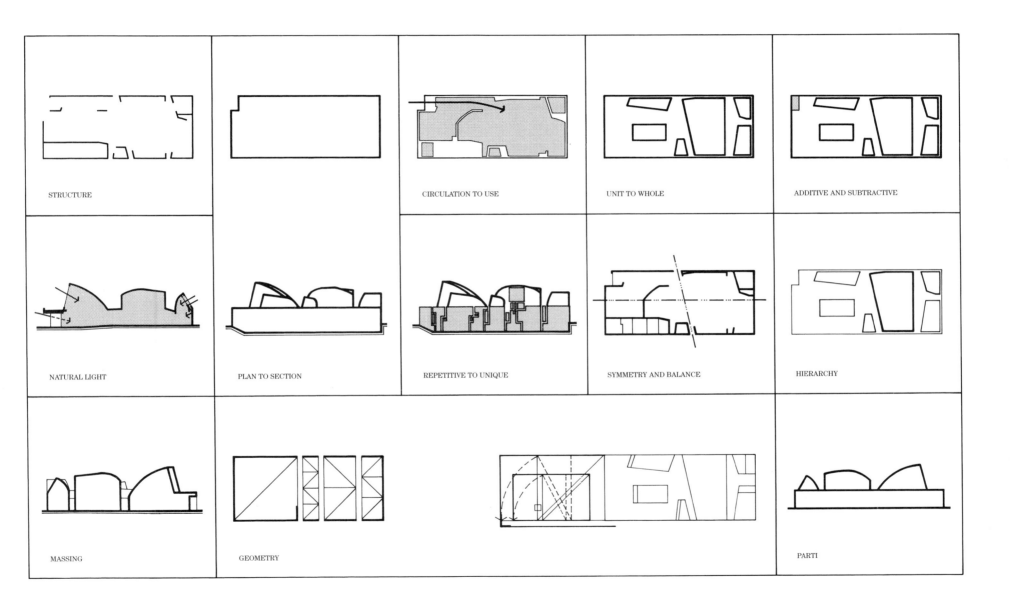

STRUCTURE

CIRCULATION TO USE

UNIT TO WHOLE

ADDITIVE AND SUBTRACTIVE

NATURAL LIGHT

PLAN TO SECTION

REPETITIVE TO UNIQUE

SYMMETRY AND BALANCE

HIERARCHY

MASSING

GEOMETRY

PARTI

LOUIS I. KAHN

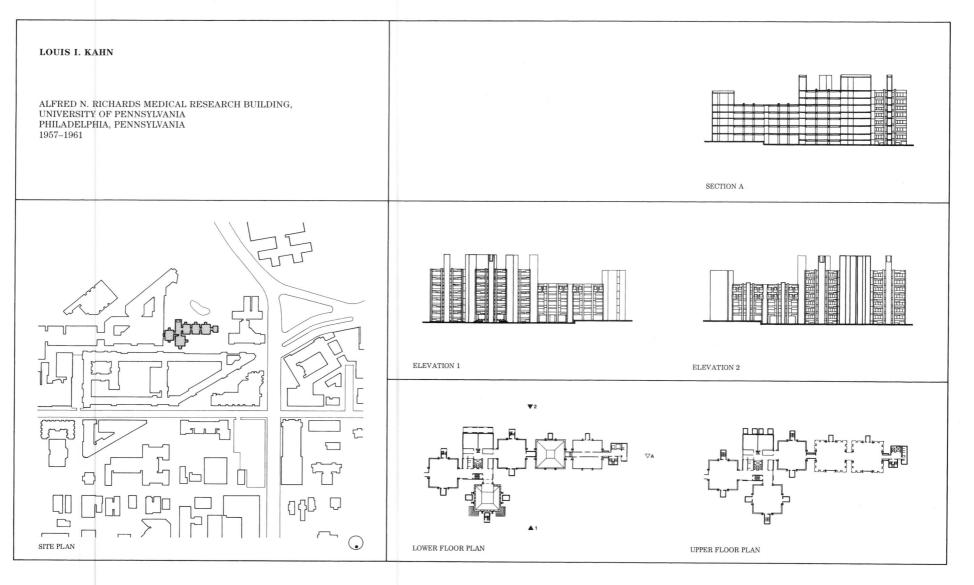

LOUIS I. KAHN

ALFRED N. RICHARDS MEDICAL RESEARCH BUILDING,
UNIVERSITY OF PENNSYLVANIA
PHILADELPHIA, PENNSYLVANIA
1957–1961

SECTION A

ELEVATION 1

ELEVATION 2

SITE PLAN

LOWER FLOOR PLAN

UPPER FLOOR PLAN

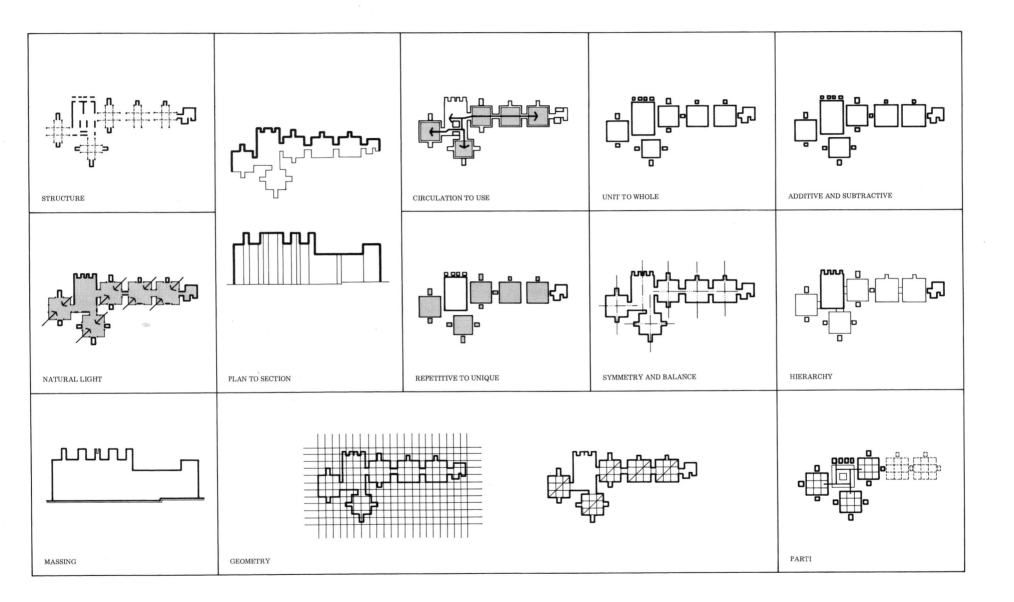

STRUCTURE

CIRCULATION TO USE

UNIT TO WHOLE

ADDITIVE AND SUBTRACTIVE

NATURAL LIGHT

PLAN TO SECTION

REPETITIVE TO UNIQUE

SYMMETRY AND BALANCE

HIERARCHY

MASSING

GEOMETRY

PARTI

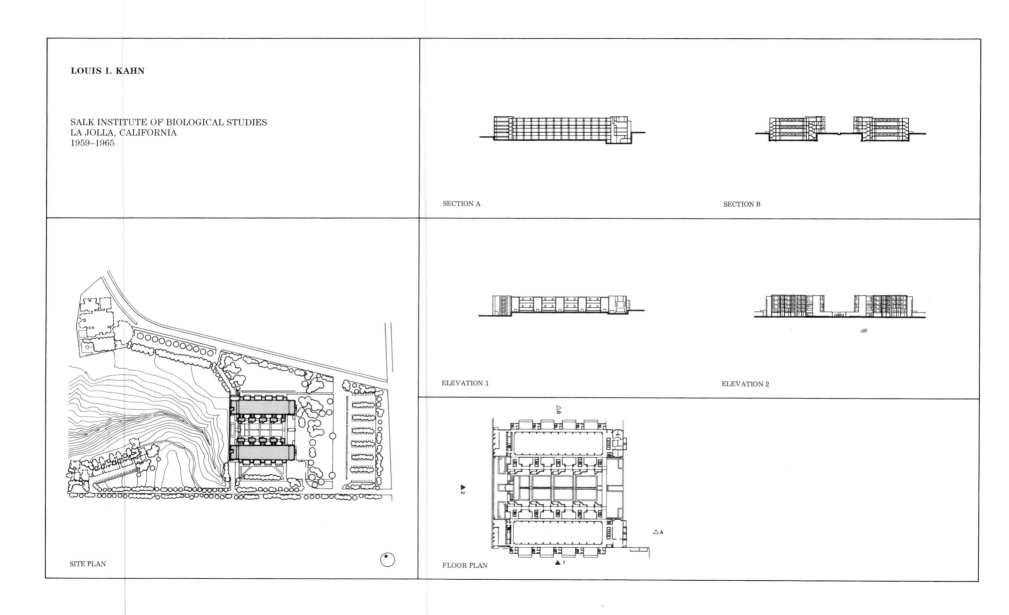

LOUIS I. KAHN

SALK INSTITUTE OF BIOLOGICAL STUDIES
LA JOLLA, CALIFORNIA
1959–1965

SECTION A

SECTION B

ELEVATION 1

ELEVATION 2

SITE PLAN

FLOOR PLAN

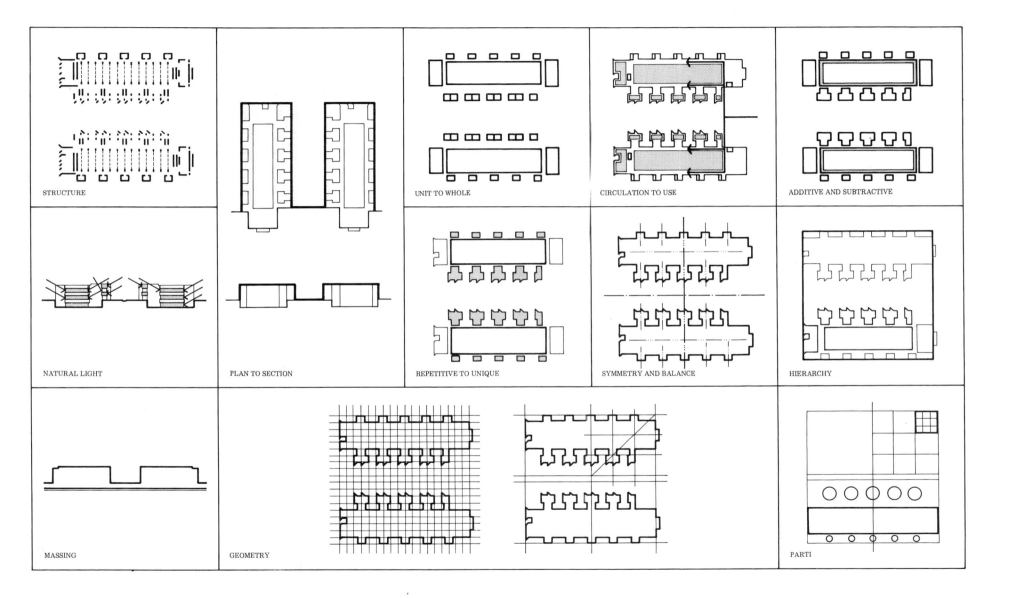

STRUCTURE

UNIT TO WHOLE

CIRCULATION TO USE

ADDITIVE AND SUBTRACTIVE

NATURAL LIGHT

PLAN TO SECTION

REPETITIVE TO UNIQUE

SYMMETRY AND BALANCE

HIERARCHY

MASSING

GEOMETRY

PARTI

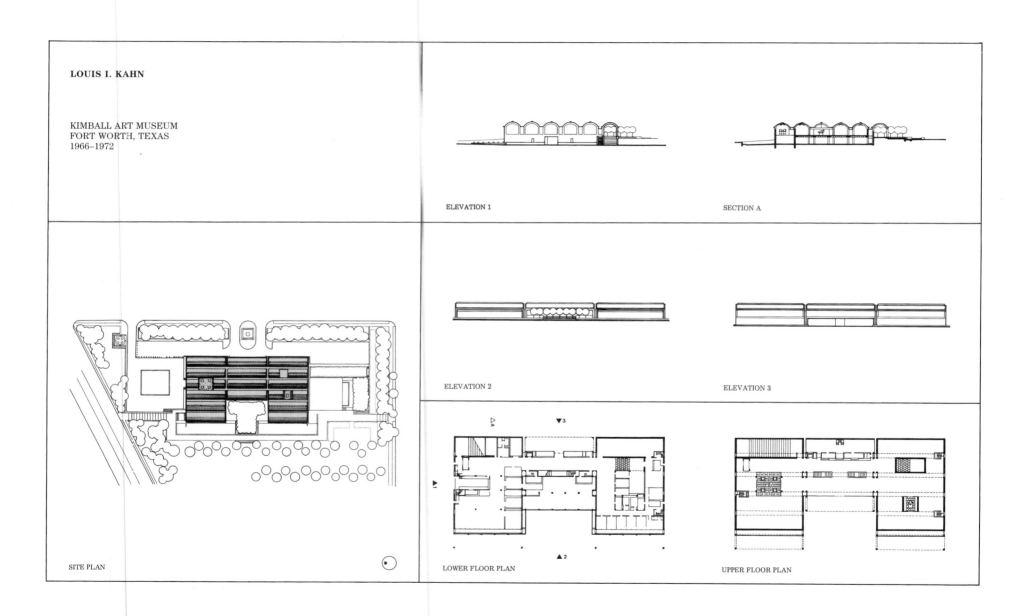

LOUIS I. KAHN

KIMBALL ART MUSEUM
FORT WORTH, TEXAS
1966–1972

ELEVATION 1

SECTION A

ELEVATION 2

ELEVATION 3

SITE PLAN

LOWER FLOOR PLAN

UPPER FLOOR PLAN

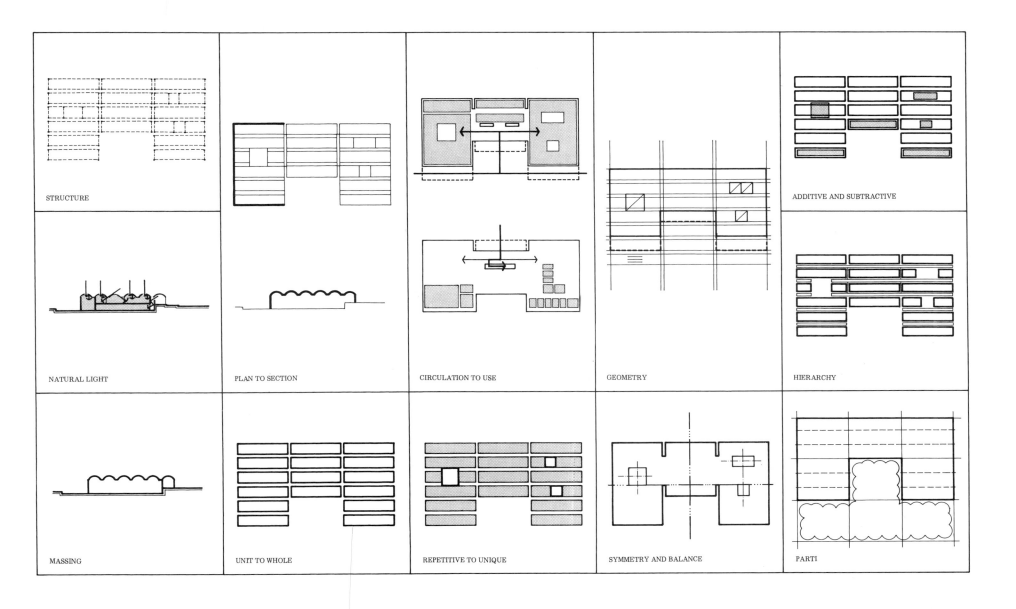

STRUCTURE

NATURAL LIGHT

MASSING

PLAN TO SECTION

UNIT TO WHOLE

CIRCULATION TO USE

REPETITIVE TO UNIQUE

GEOMETRY

SYMMETRY AND BALANCE

ADDITIVE AND SUBTRACTIVE

HIERARCHY

PARTI

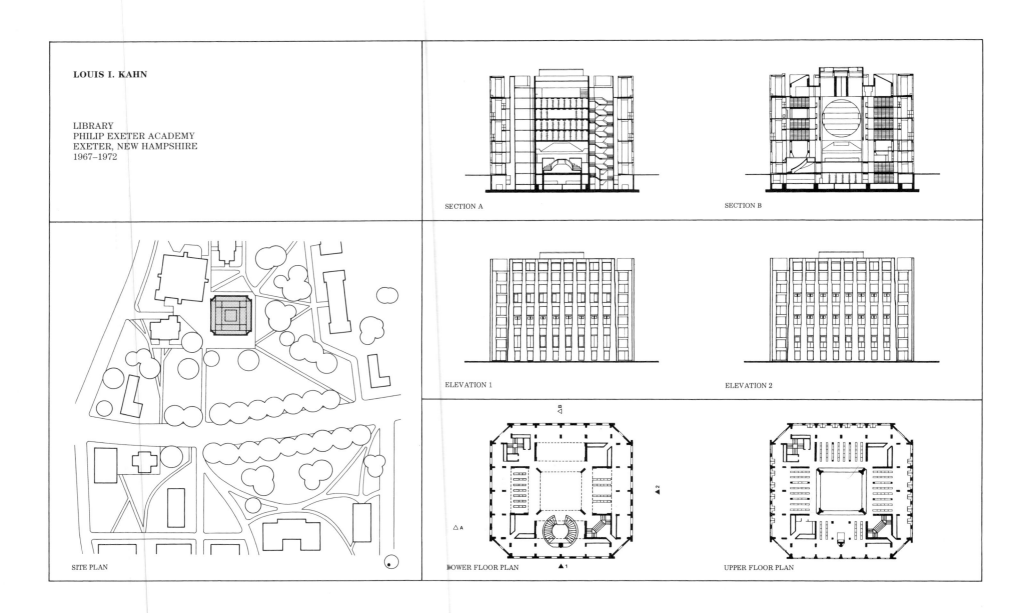

LOUIS I. KAHN

LIBRARY
PHILIP EXETER ACADEMY
EXETER, NEW HAMPSHIRE
1967–1972

SECTION A

SECTION B

ELEVATION 1

ELEVATION 2

SITE PLAN

LOWER FLOOR PLAN

UPPER FLOOR PLAN

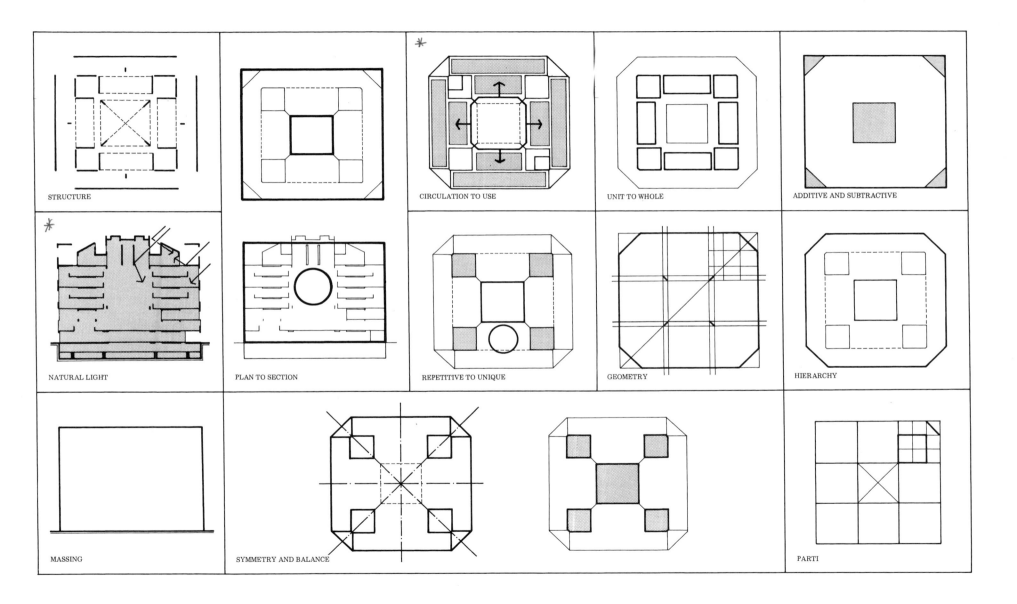

STRUCTURE

CIRCULATION TO USE

UNIT TO WHOLE

ADDITIVE AND SUBTRACTIVE

NATURAL LIGHT

PLAN TO SECTION

REPETITIVE TO UNIQUE

GEOMETRY

HIERARCHY

MASSING

SYMMETRY AND BALANCE

PARTI

87

LE CORBUSIER

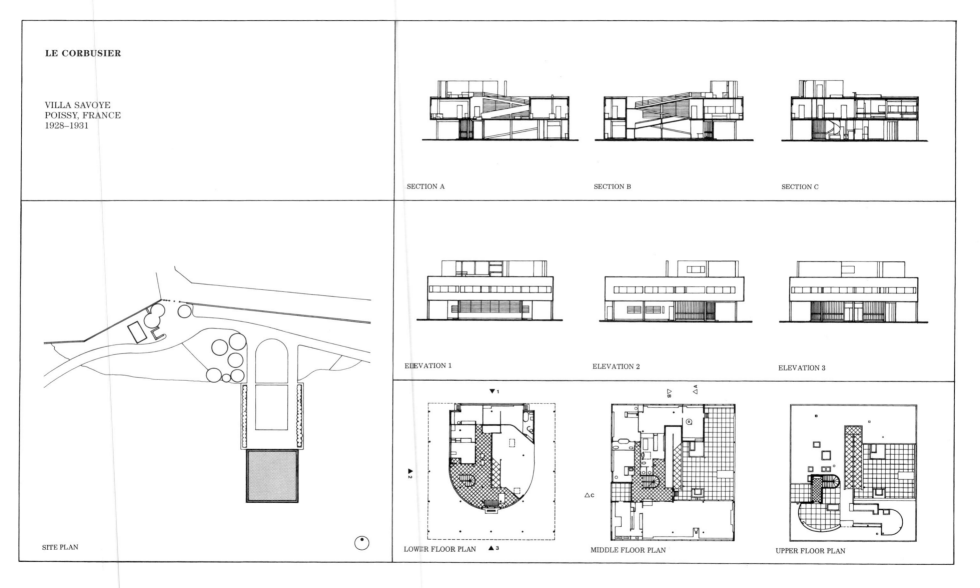

LE CORBUSIER

VILLA SAVOYE
POISSY, FRANCE
1928–1931

SECTION A

SECTION B

SECTION C

ELEVATION 1

ELEVATION 2

ELEVATION 3

SITE PLAN

LOWER FLOOR PLAN

MIDDLE FLOOR PLAN

UPPER FLOOR PLAN

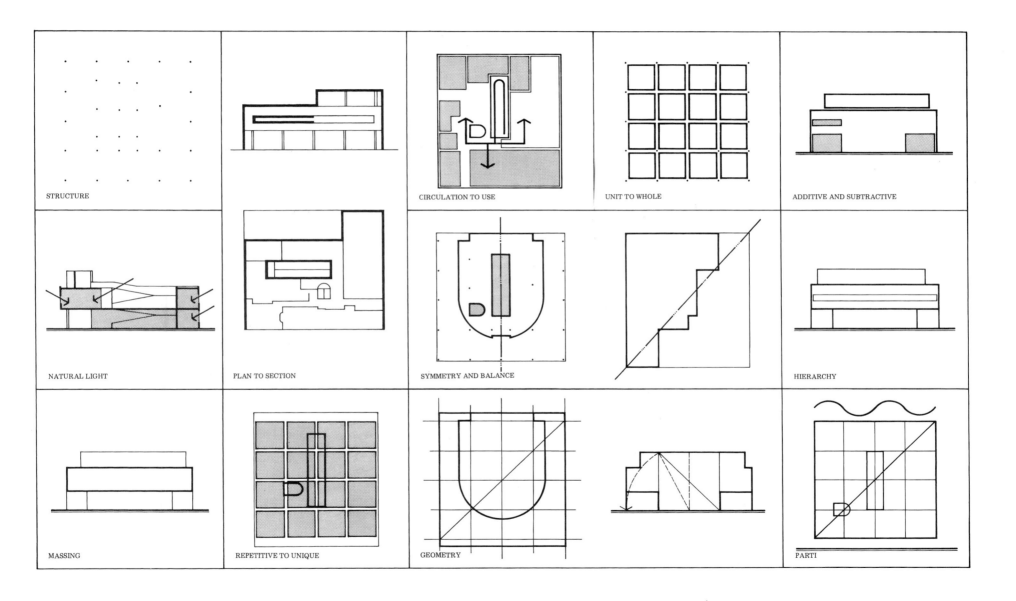

STRUCTURE

CIRCULATION TO USE

UNIT TO WHOLE

ADDITIVE AND SUBTRACTIVE

NATURAL LIGHT

PLAN TO SECTION

SYMMETRY AND BALANCE

HIERARCHY

MASSING

REPETITIVE TO UNIQUE

GEOMETRY

PARTI

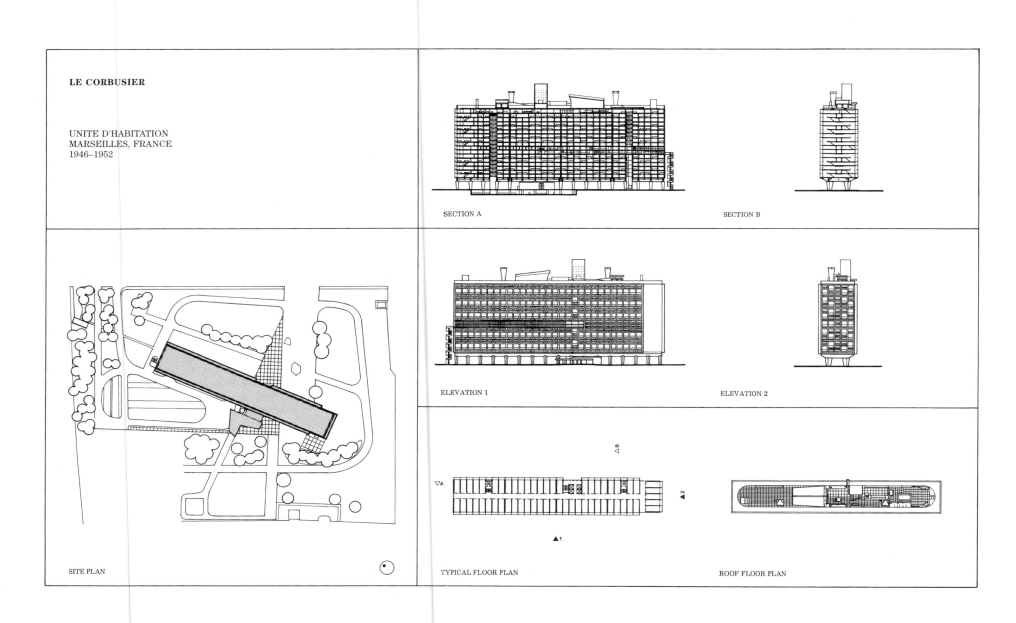

LE CORBUSIER

UNITE D'HABITATION
MARSEILLES, FRANCE
1946–1952

SECTION A

SECTION B

ELEVATION 1

ELEVATION 2

SITE PLAN

TYPICAL FLOOR PLAN

ROOF FLOOR PLAN

90

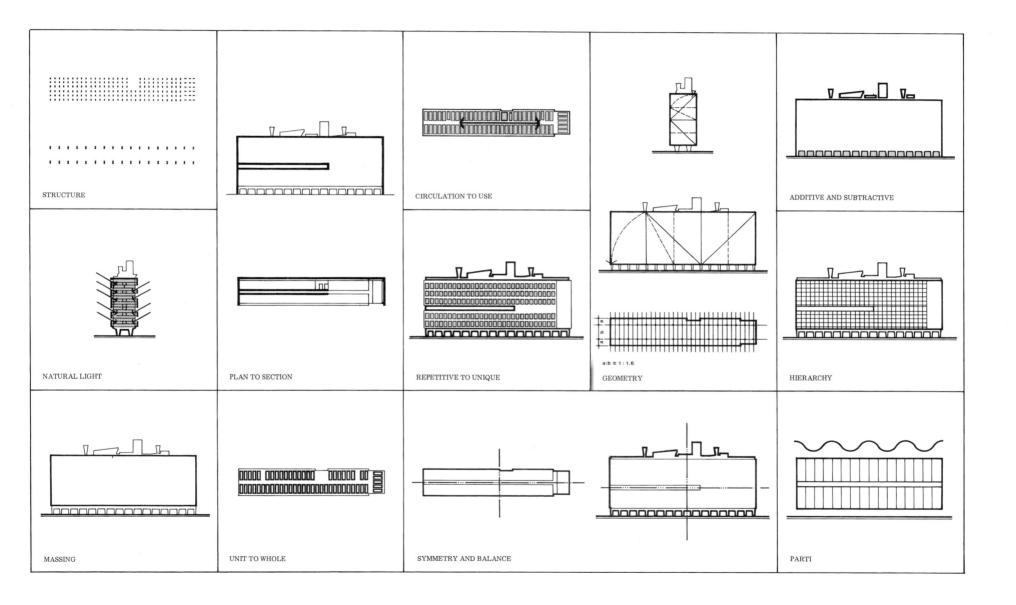

STRUCTURE

CIRCULATION TO USE

ADDITIVE AND SUBTRACTIVE

NATURAL LIGHT

PLAN TO SECTION

REPETITIVE TO UNIQUE

GEOMETRY

a:b = 1 : 1.6

HIERARCHY

MASSING

UNIT TO WHOLE

SYMMETRY AND BALANCE

PARTI

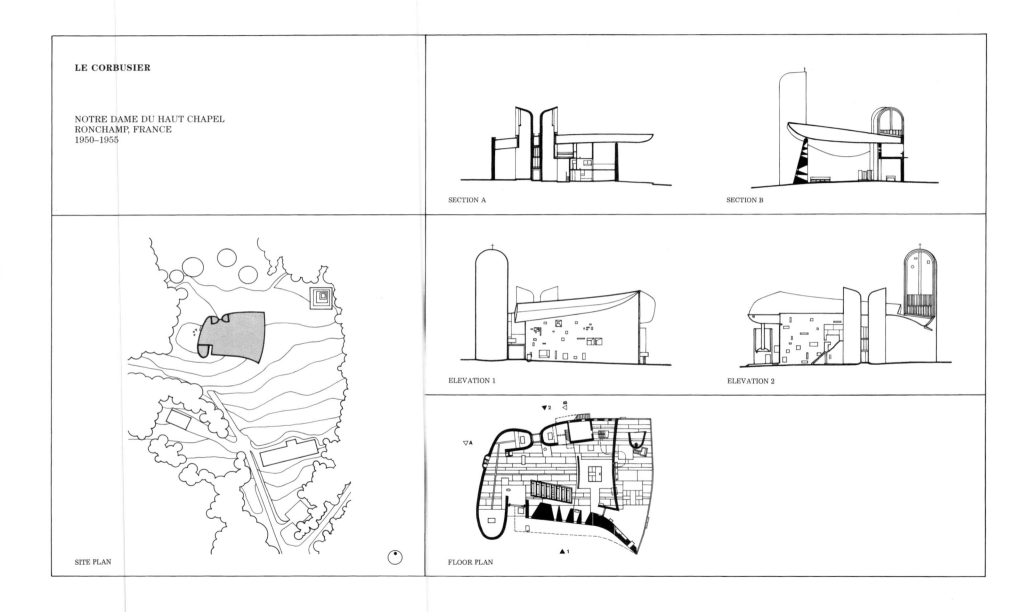

LE CORBUSIER

NOTRE DAME DU HAUT CHAPEL
RONCHAMP, FRANCE
1950–1955

SECTION A

SECTION B

ELEVATION 1

ELEVATION 2

SITE PLAN

FLOOR PLAN

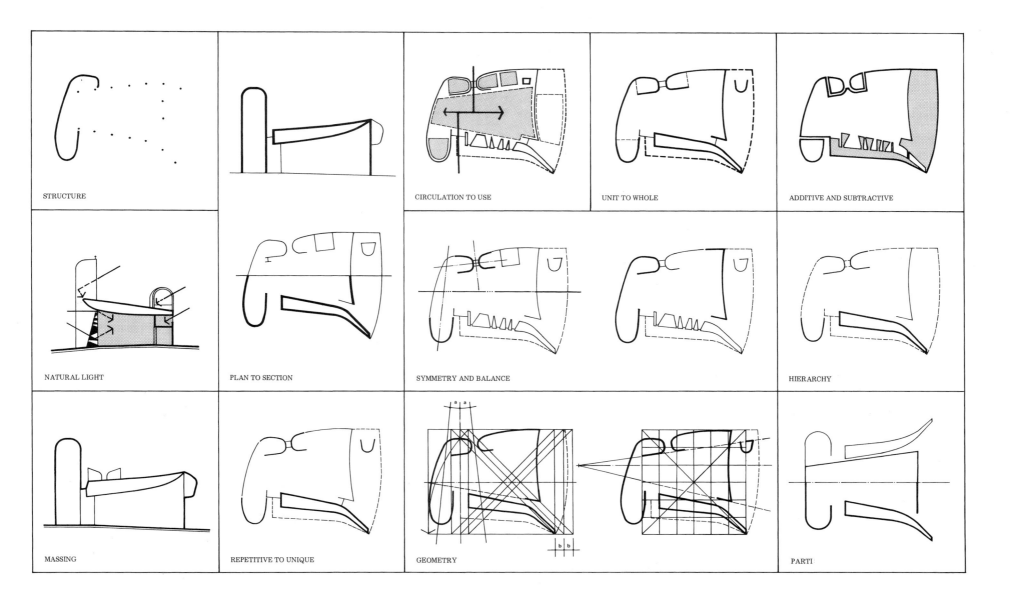

STRUCTURE

CIRCULATION TO USE

UNIT TO WHOLE

ADDITIVE AND SUBTRACTIVE

NATURAL LIGHT

PLAN TO SECTION

SYMMETRY AND BALANCE

HIERARCHY

MASSING

REPETITIVE TO UNIQUE

GEOMETRY

PARTI

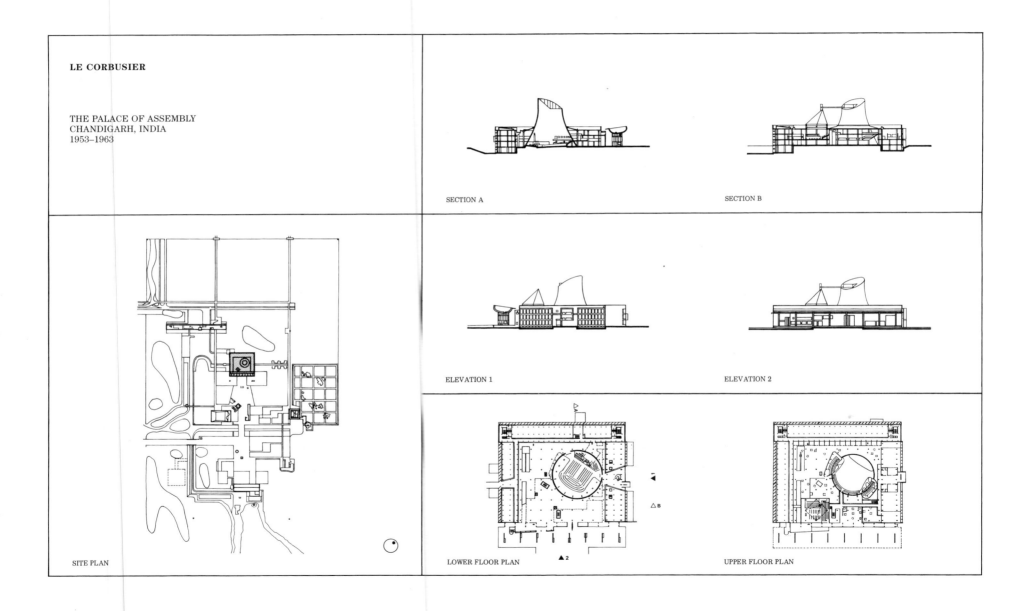

LE CORBUSIER

THE PALACE OF ASSEMBLY
CHANDIGARH, INDIA
1953–1963

SECTION A

SECTION B

ELEVATION 1

ELEVATION 2

SITE PLAN

LOWER FLOOR PLAN

UPPER FLOOR PLAN

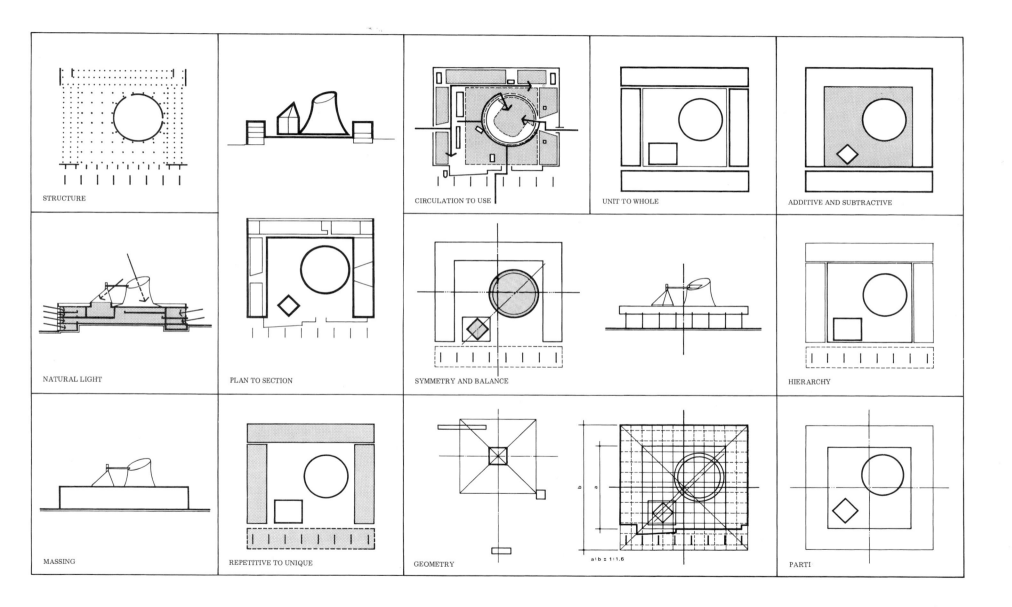

STRUCTURE

CIRCULATION TO USE

UNIT TO WHOLE

ADDITIVE AND SUBTRACTIVE

NATURAL LIGHT

PLAN TO SECTION

SYMMETRY AND BALANCE

HIERARCHY

MASSING

REPETITIVE TO UNIQUE

GEOMETRY

a:b = 1:1.6

PARTI

95

CLAUDE NICHOLAS LEDOUX

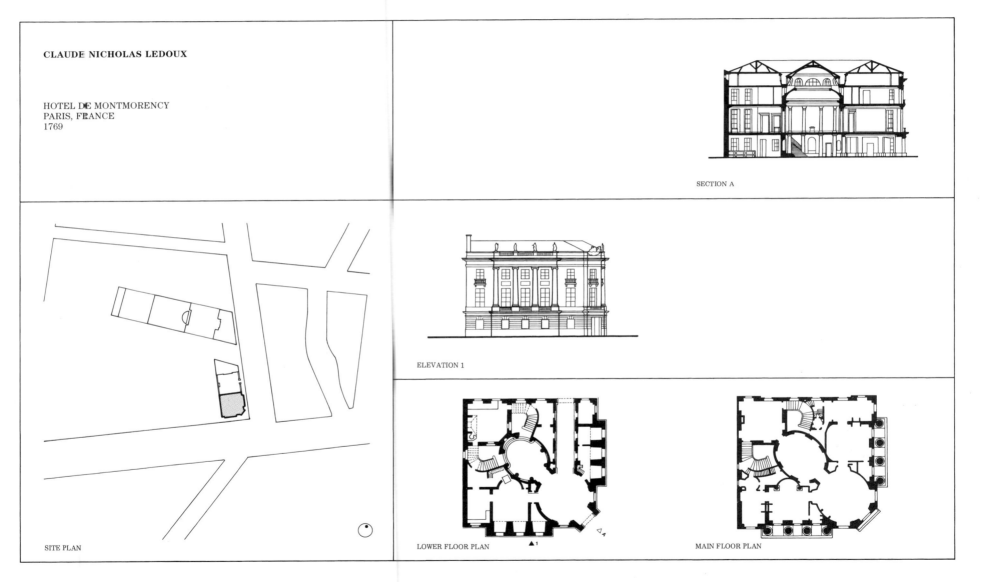

CLAUDE NICHOLAS LEDOUX

HOTEL DE MONTMORENCY
PARIS, FRANCE
1769

SECTION A

ELEVATION 1

SITE PLAN

LOWER FLOOR PLAN

MAIN FLOOR PLAN

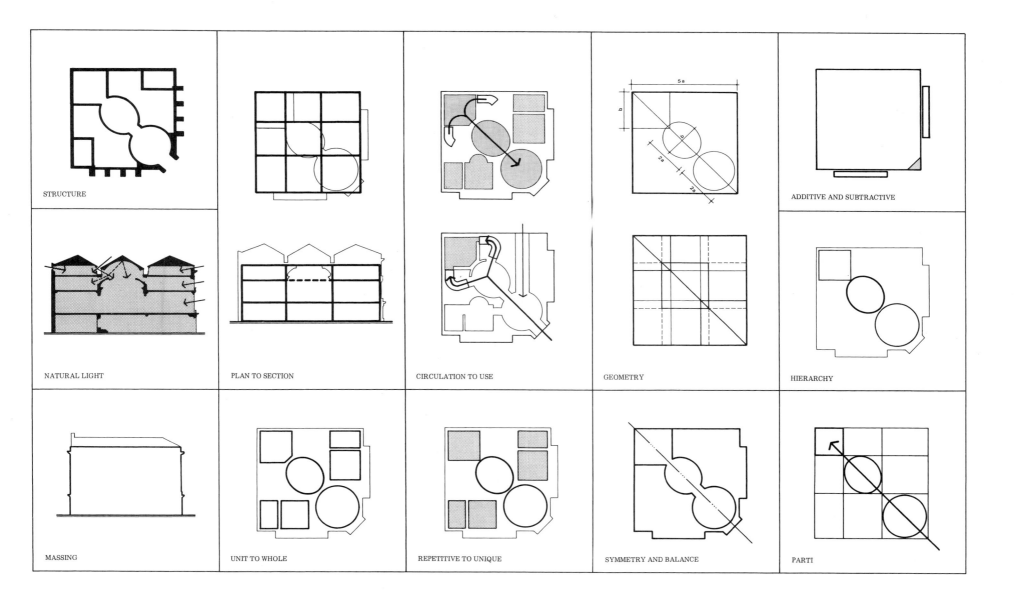

STRUCTURE

NATURAL LIGHT

MASSING

PLAN TO SECTION

UNIT TO WHOLE

CIRCULATION TO USE

REPETITIVE TO UNIQUE

GEOMETRY

SYMMETRY AND BALANCE

ADDITIVE AND SUBTRACTIVE

HIERARCHY

PARTI

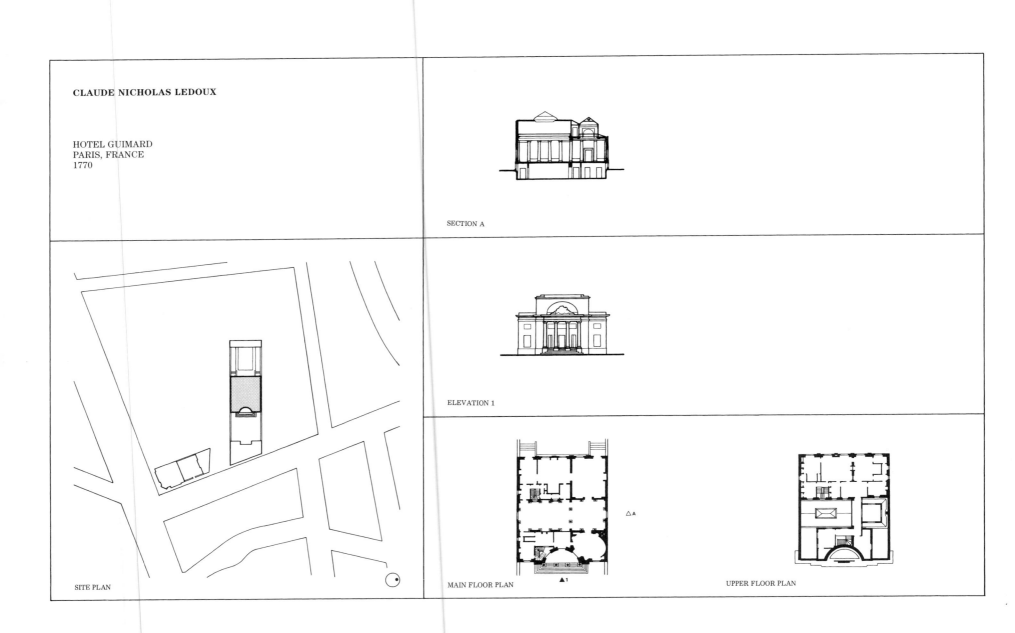

CLAUDE NICHOLAS LEDOUX

HOTEL GUIMARD
PARIS, FRANCE
1770

SECTION A

ELEVATION 1

SITE PLAN

MAIN FLOOR PLAN

UPPER FLOOR PLAN

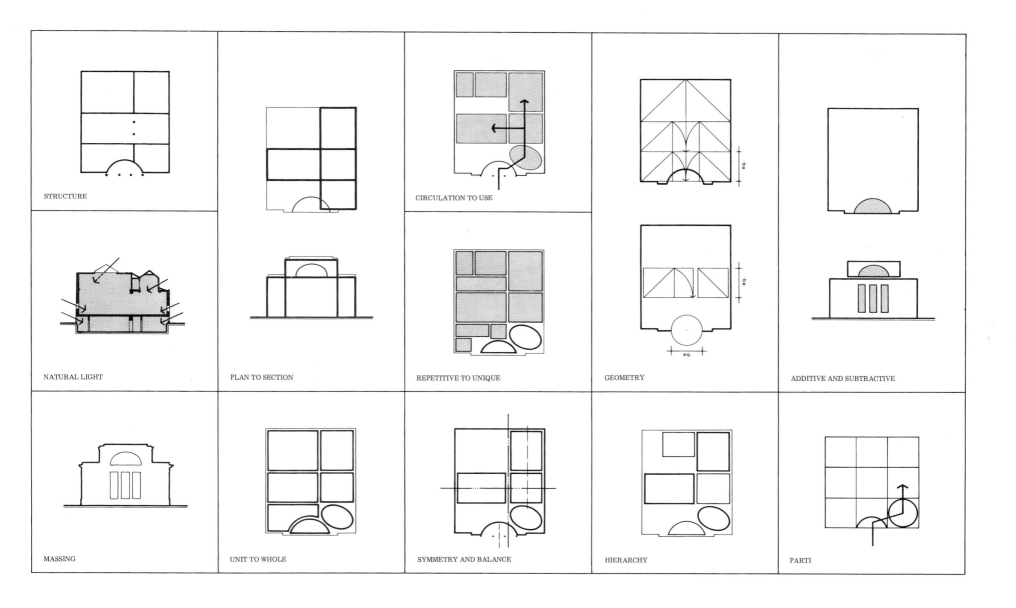

STRUCTURE

NATURAL LIGHT

MASSING

CIRCULATION TO USE

PLAN TO SECTION

UNIT TO WHOLE

REPETITIVE TO UNIQUE

SYMMETRY AND BALANCE

GEOMETRY

HIERARCHY

ADDITIVE AND SUBTRACTIVE

PARTI

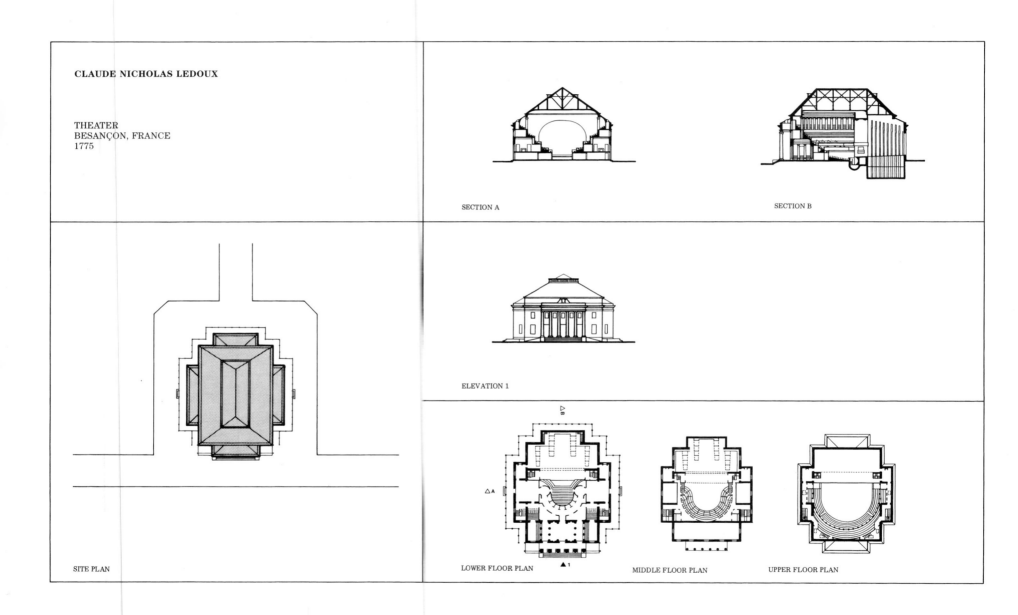

CLAUDE NICHOLAS LEDOUX

THEATER
BESANÇON, FRANCE
1775

SECTION A

SECTION B

ELEVATION 1

SITE PLAN

LOWER FLOOR PLAN

MIDDLE FLOOR PLAN

UPPER FLOOR PLAN

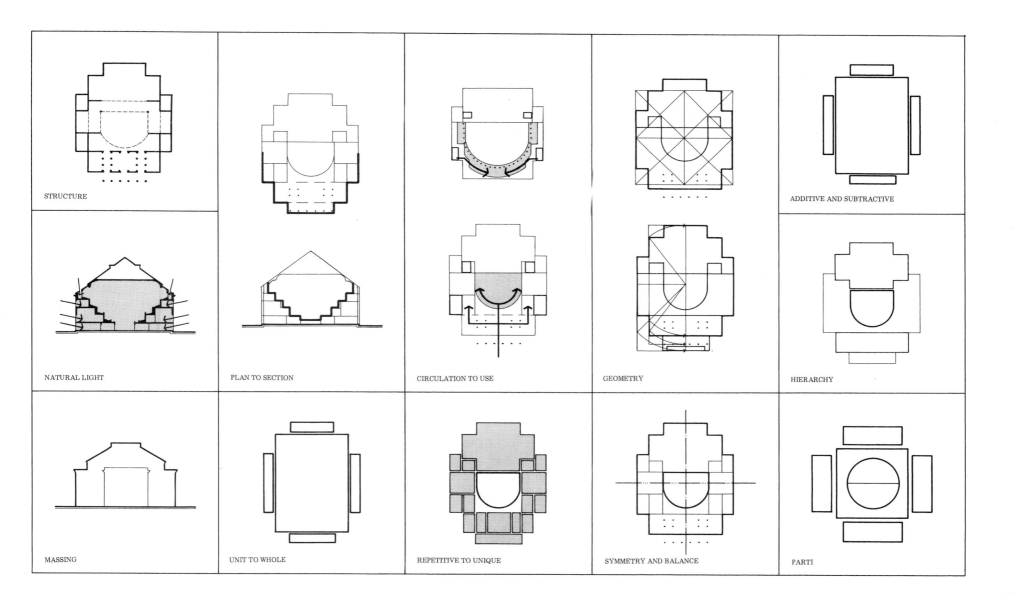

STRUCTURE

NATURAL LIGHT

MASSING

PLAN TO SECTION

UNIT TO WHOLE

CIRCULATION TO USE

REPETITIVE TO UNIQUE

GEOMETRY

SYMMETRY AND BALANCE

ADDITIVE AND SUBTRACTIVE

HIERARCHY

PARTI

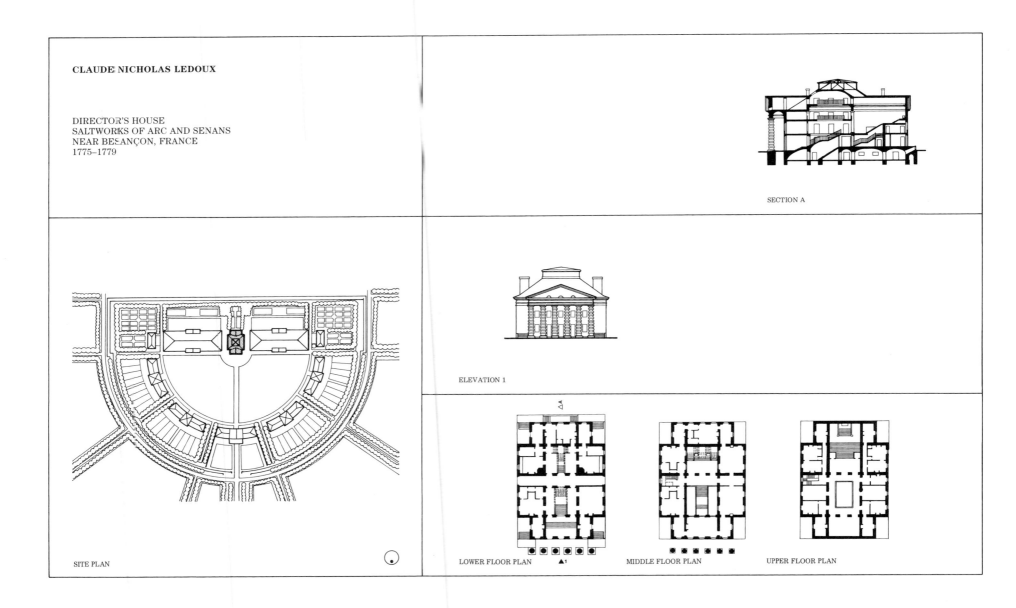

CLAUDE NICHOLAS LEDOUX

DIRECTOR'S HOUSE
SALTWORKS OF ARC AND SENANS
NEAR BESANÇON, FRANCE
1775–1779

SECTION A

ELEVATION 1

SITE PLAN

LOWER FLOOR PLAN   MIDDLE FLOOR PLAN   UPPER FLOOR PLAN

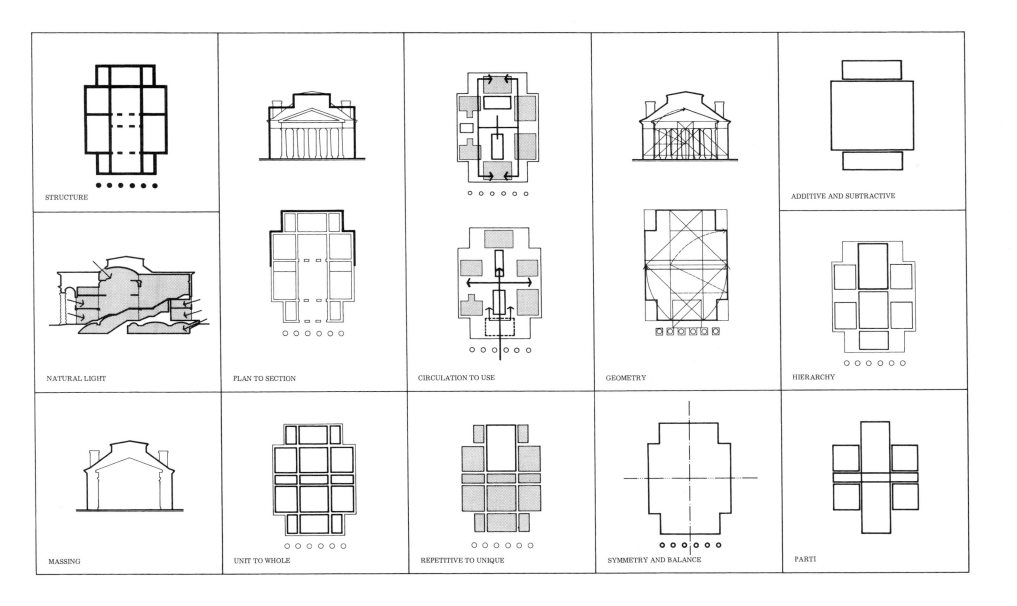

STRUCTURE

NATURAL LIGHT

MASSING

PLAN TO SECTION

UNIT TO WHOLE

CIRCULATION TO USE

REPETITIVE TO UNIQUE

GEOMETRY

SYMMETRY AND BALANCE

ADDITIVE AND SUBTRACTIVE

HIERARCHY

PARTI

SIGURD LEWERENTZ

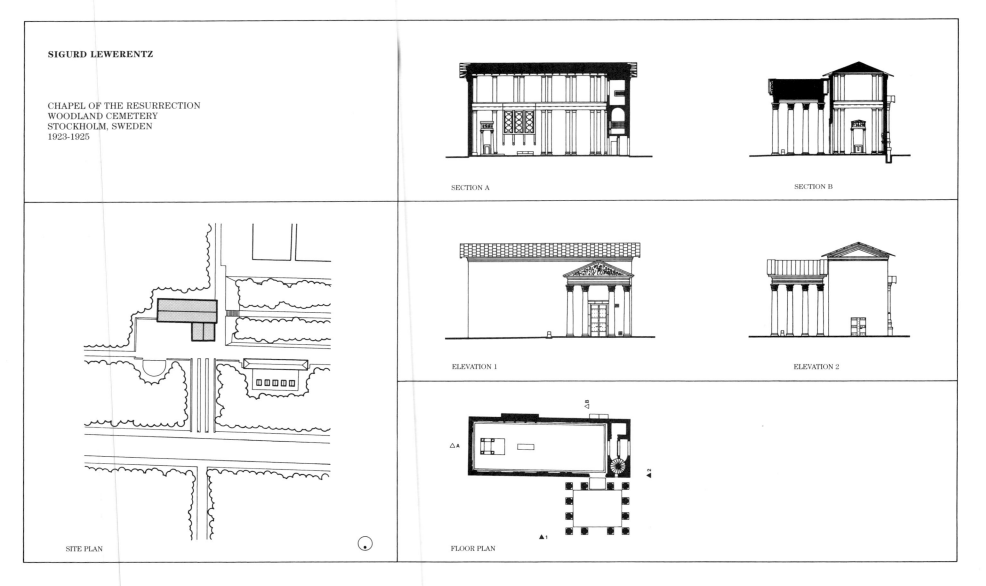

SIGURD LEWERENTZ

CHAPEL OF THE RESURRECTION
WOODLAND CEMETERY
STOCKHOLM, SWEDEN
1923-1925

SECTION A

SECTION B

ELEVATION 1

ELEVATION 2

SITE PLAN

FLOOR PLAN

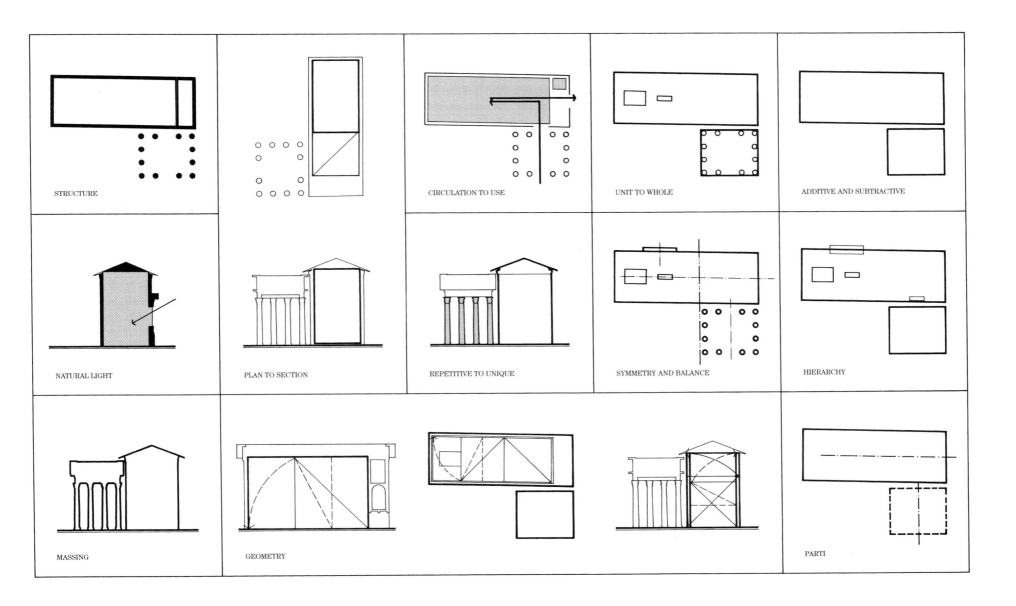

STRUCTURE

CIRCULATION TO USE

UNIT TO WHOLE

ADDITIVE AND SUBTRACTIVE

NATURAL LIGHT

PLAN TO SECTION

REPETITIVE TO UNIQUE

SYMMETRY AND BALANCE

HIERARCHY

MASSING

GEOMETRY

PARTI

105

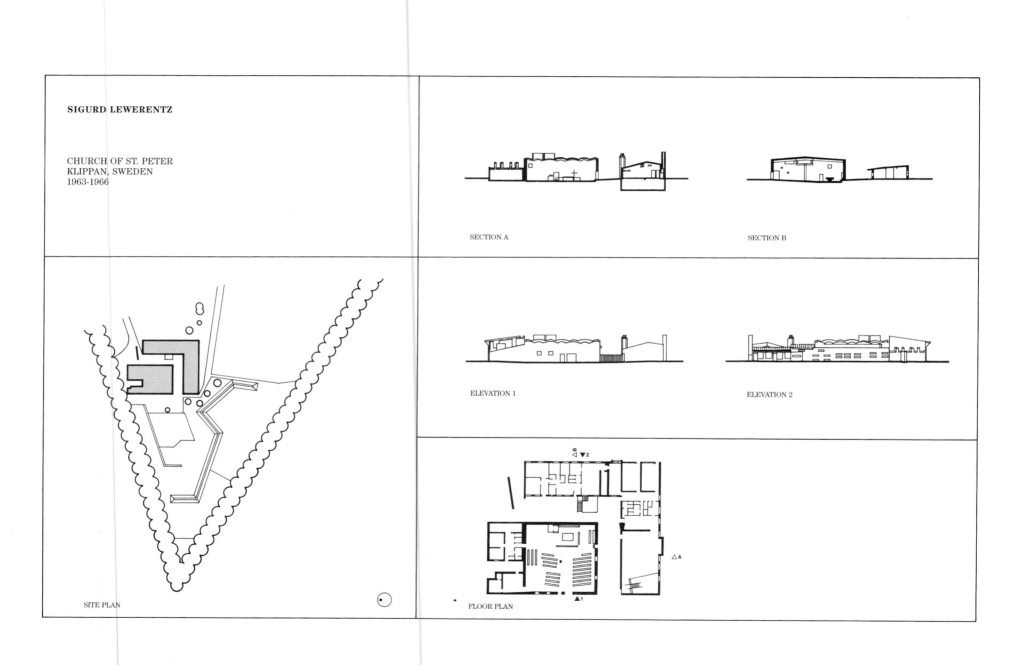

SIGURD LEWERENTZ

CHURCH OF ST. PETER
KLIPPAN, SWEDEN
1963-1966

SECTION A

SECTION B

ELEVATION 1

ELEVATION 2

SITE PLAN

FLOOR PLAN

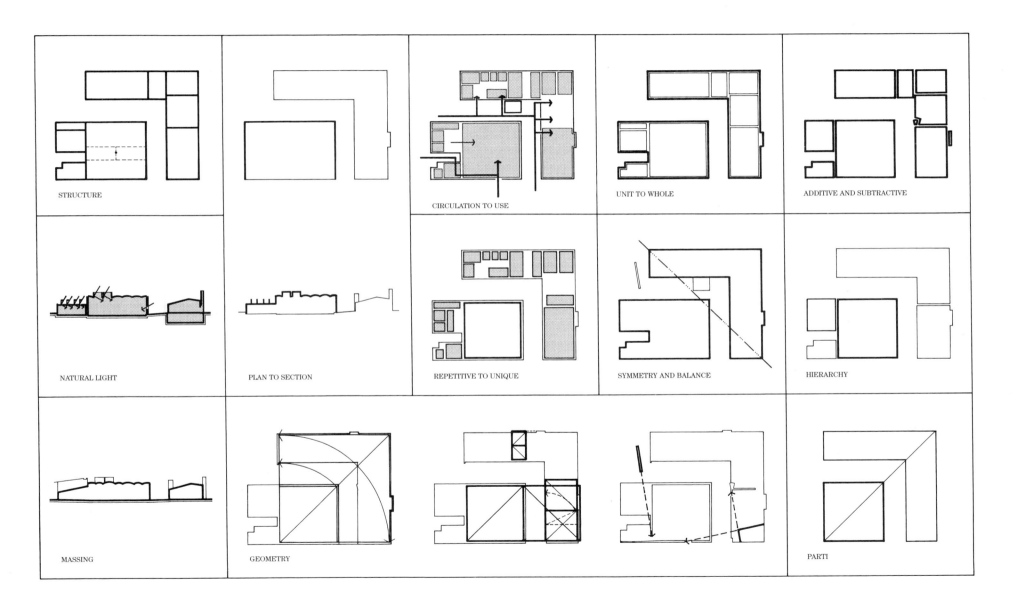

STRUCTURE

CIRCULATION TO USE

UNIT TO WHOLE

ADDITIVE AND SUBTRACTIVE

NATURAL LIGHT

PLAN TO SECTION

REPETITIVE TO UNIQUE

SYMMETRY AND BALANCE

HIERARCHY

MASSING

GEOMETRY

PARTI

EDWIN LUTYENS

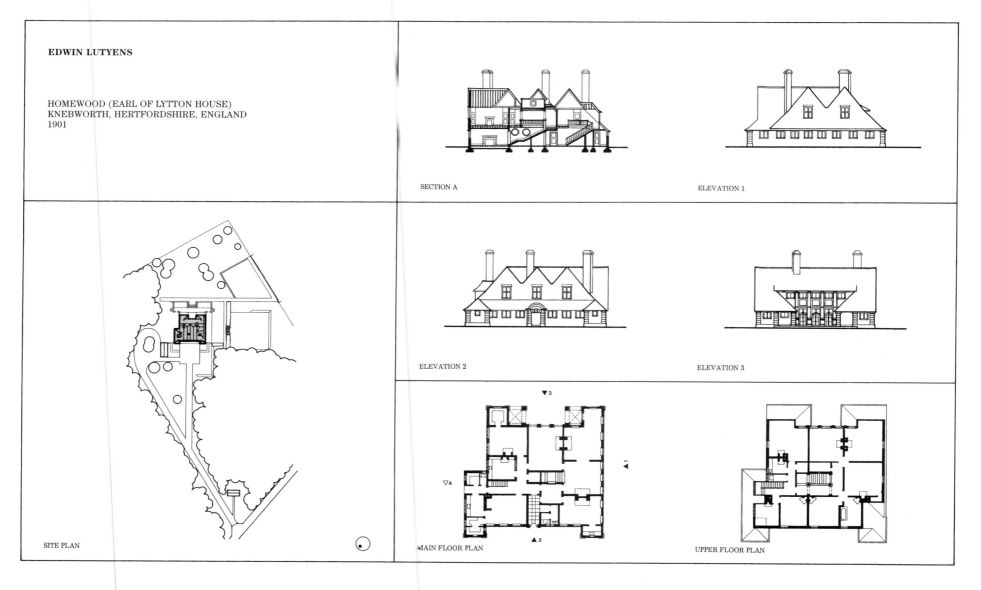

EDWIN LUTYENS

HOMEWOOD (EARL OF LYTTON HOUSE)
KNEBWORTH, HERTFORDSHIRE, ENGLAND
1901

SECTION A

ELEVATION 1

ELEVATION 2

ELEVATION 3

SITE PLAN

MAIN FLOOR PLAN

UPPER FLOOR PLAN

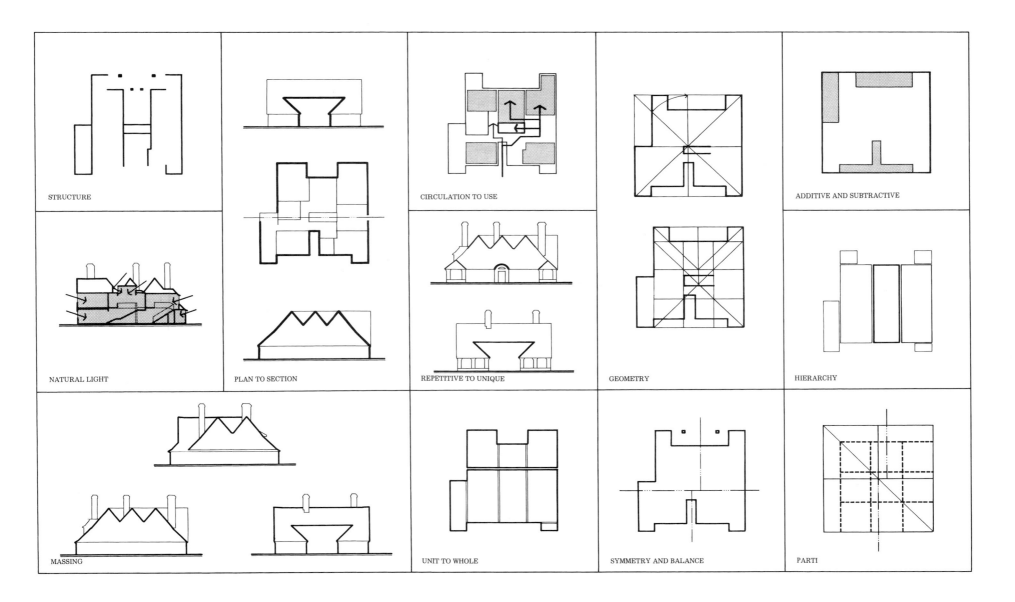

STRUCTURE

NATURAL LIGHT

MASSING

PLAN TO SECTION

UNIT TO WHOLE

CIRCULATION TO USE

REPETITIVE TO UNIQUE

SYMMETRY AND BALANCE

GEOMETRY

ADDITIVE AND SUBTRACTIVE

HIERARCHY

PARTI

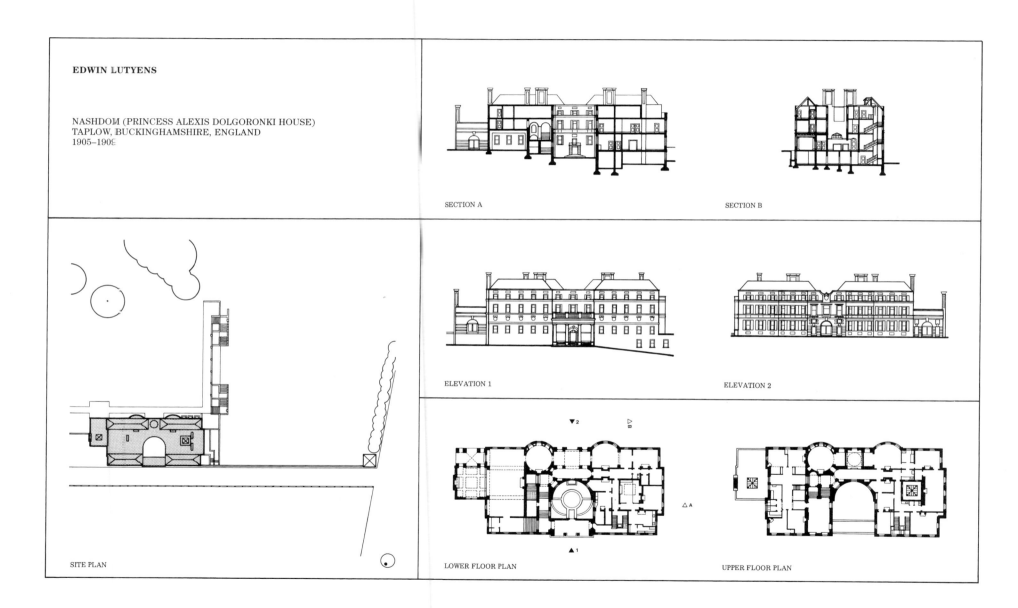

EDWIN LUTYENS

NASHDOM (PRINCESS ALEXIS DOLGORONKI HOUSE)
TAPLOW, BUCKINGHAMSHIRE, ENGLAND
1905–1909

SECTION A

SECTION B

ELEVATION 1

ELEVATION 2

SITE PLAN

LOWER FLOOR PLAN

UPPER FLOOR PLAN

110

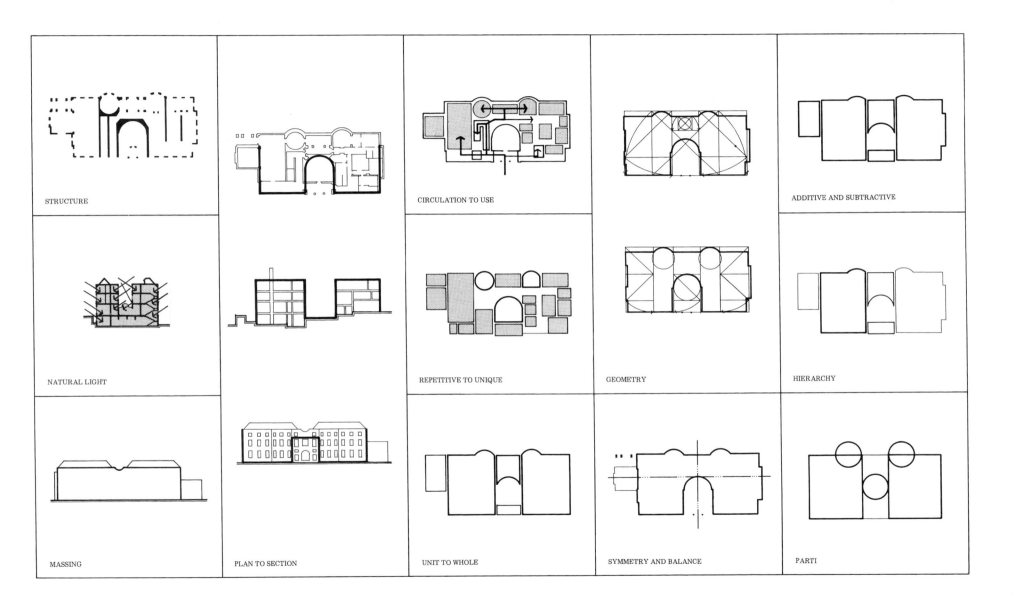

STRUCTURE

CIRCULATION TO USE

ADDITIVE AND SUBTRACTIVE

NATURAL LIGHT

REPETITIVE TO UNIQUE

GEOMETRY

HIERARCHY

MASSING

PLAN TO SECTION

UNIT TO WHOLE

SYMMETRY AND BALANCE

PARTI

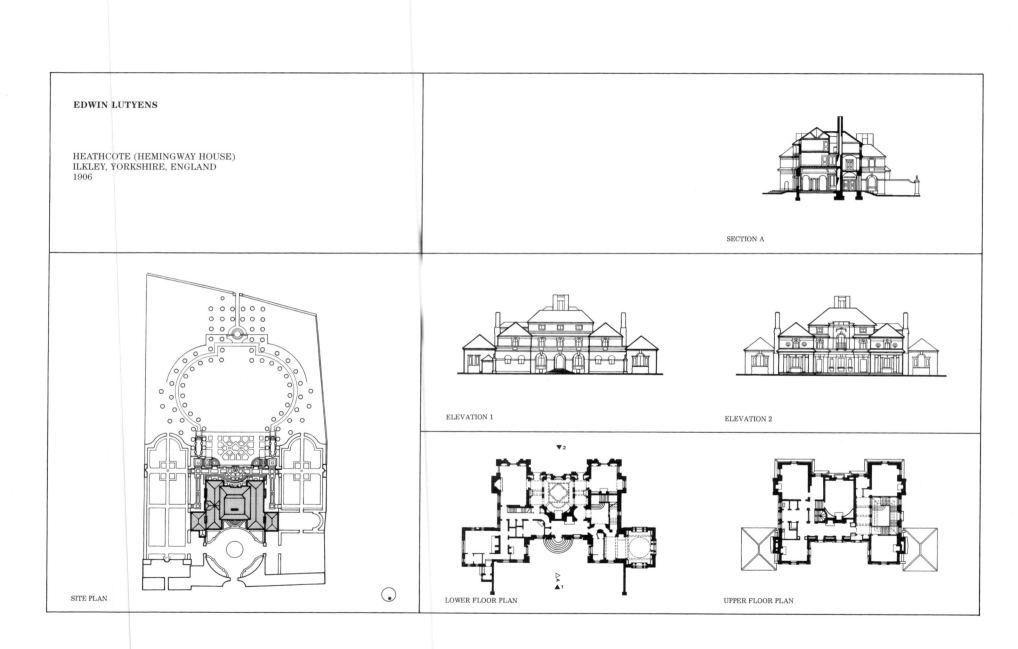

EDWIN LUTYENS

HEATHCOTE (HEMINGWAY HOUSE)
ILKLEY, YORKSHIRE, ENGLAND
1906

SECTION A

ELEVATION 1

ELEVATION 2

SITE PLAN

LOWER FLOOR PLAN

UPPER FLOOR PLAN

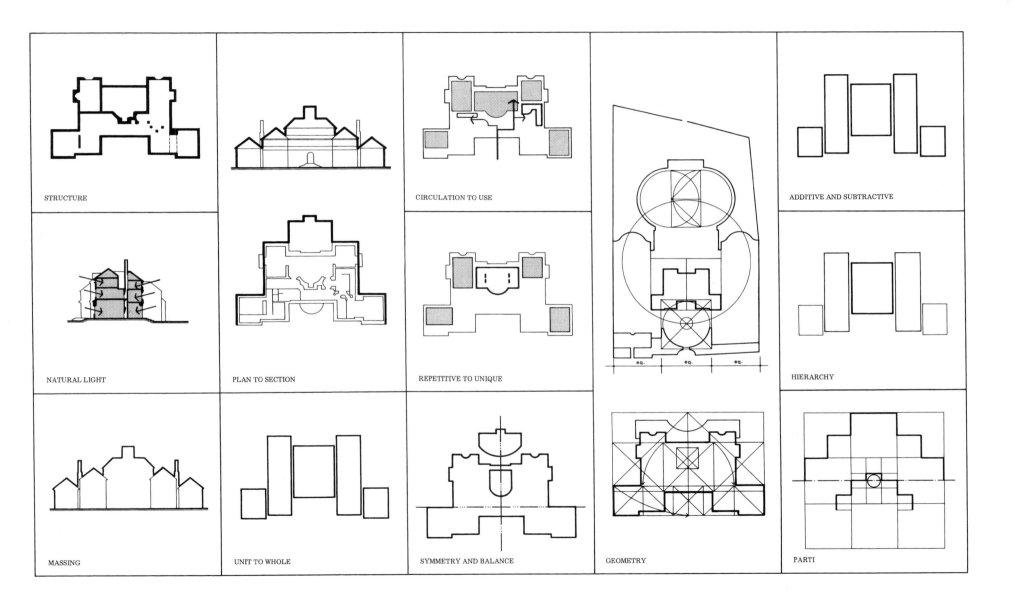

STRUCTURE

CIRCULATION TO USE

ADDITIVE AND SUBTRACTIVE

NATURAL LIGHT

PLAN TO SECTION

REPETITIVE TO UNIQUE

HIERARCHY

MASSING

UNIT TO WHOLE

SYMMETRY AND BALANCE

GEOMETRY

PARTI

113

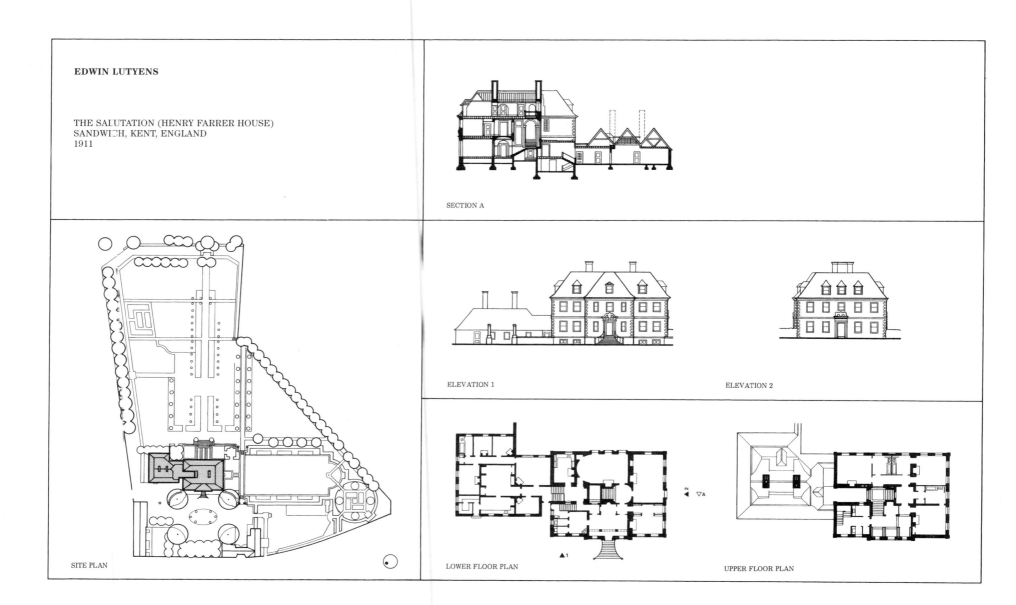

EDWIN LUTYENS

THE SALUTATION (HENRY FARRER HOUSE)
SANDWICH, KENT, ENGLAND
1911

SECTION A

ELEVATION 1

ELEVATION 2

SITE PLAN

LOWER FLOOR PLAN

UPPER FLOOR PLAN

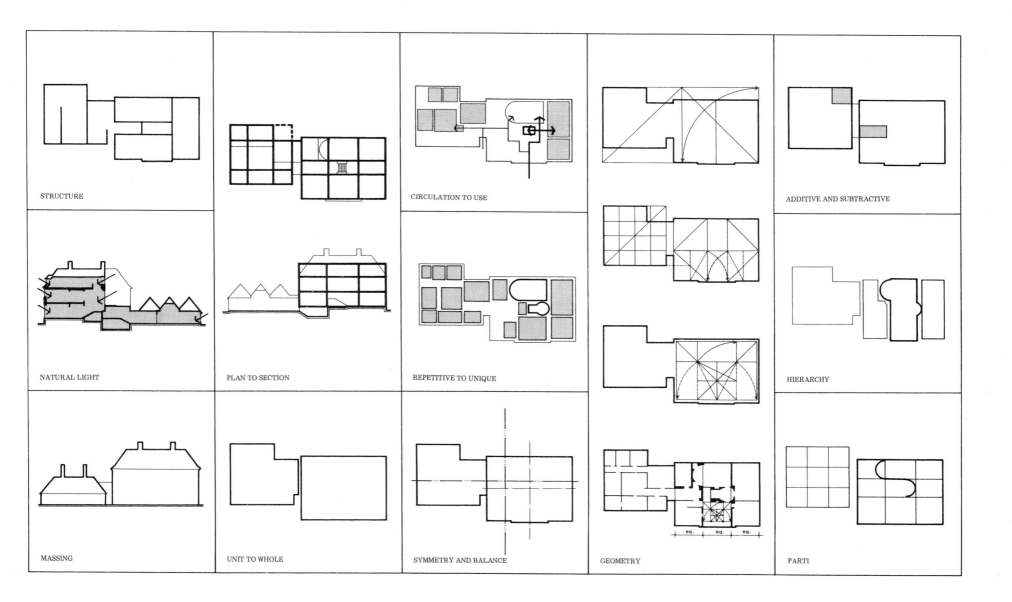

STRUCTURE

CIRCULATION TO USE

ADDITIVE AND SUBTRACTIVE

NATURAL LIGHT

PLAN TO SECTION

REPETITIVE TO UNIQUE

HIERARCHY

MASSING

UNIT TO WHOLE

SYMMETRY AND BALANCE

GEOMETRY

PARTI

115

RICHARD MEIER

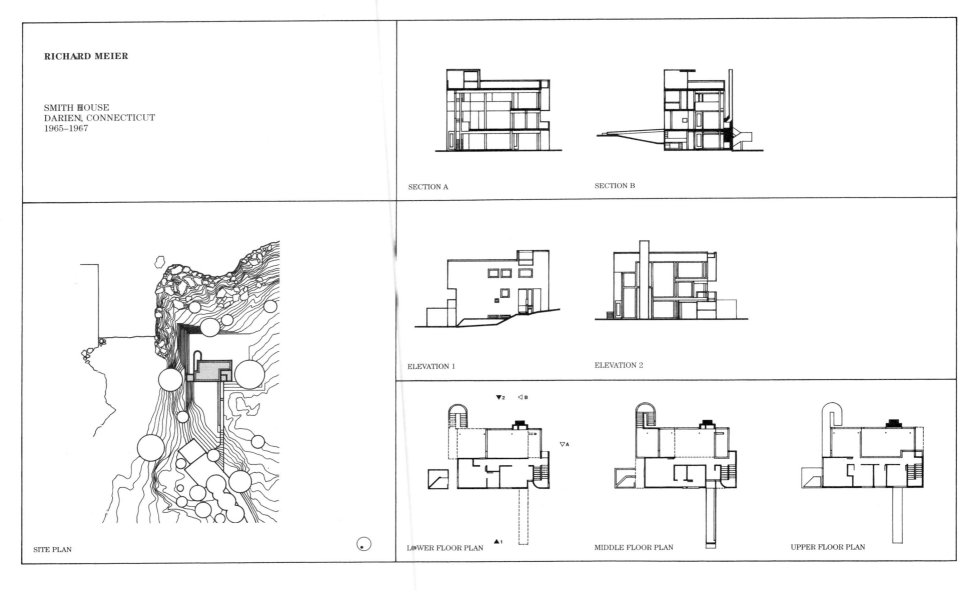

RICHARD MEIER

SMITH HOUSE
DARIEN, CONNECTICUT
1965–1967

SECTION A

SECTION B

ELEVATION 1

ELEVATION 2

SITE PLAN

LOWER FLOOR PLAN

MIDDLE FLOOR PLAN

UPPER FLOOR PLAN

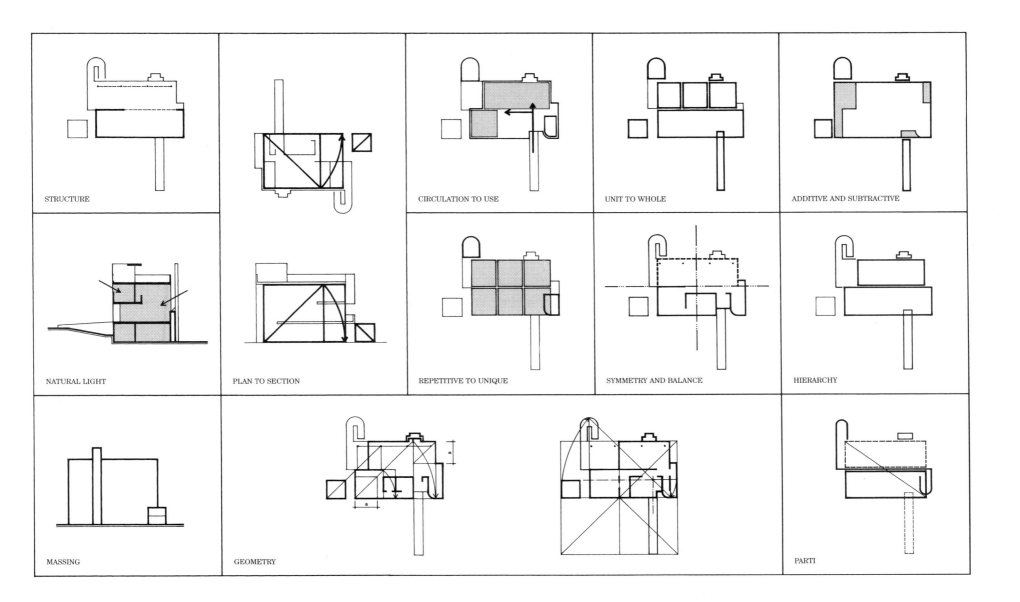

STRUCTURE

CIRCULATION TO USE

UNIT TO WHOLE

ADDITIVE AND SUBTRACTIVE

NATURAL LIGHT

PLAN TO SECTION

REPETITIVE TO UNIQUE

SYMMETRY AND BALANCE

HIERARCHY

MASSING

GEOMETRY

PARTI

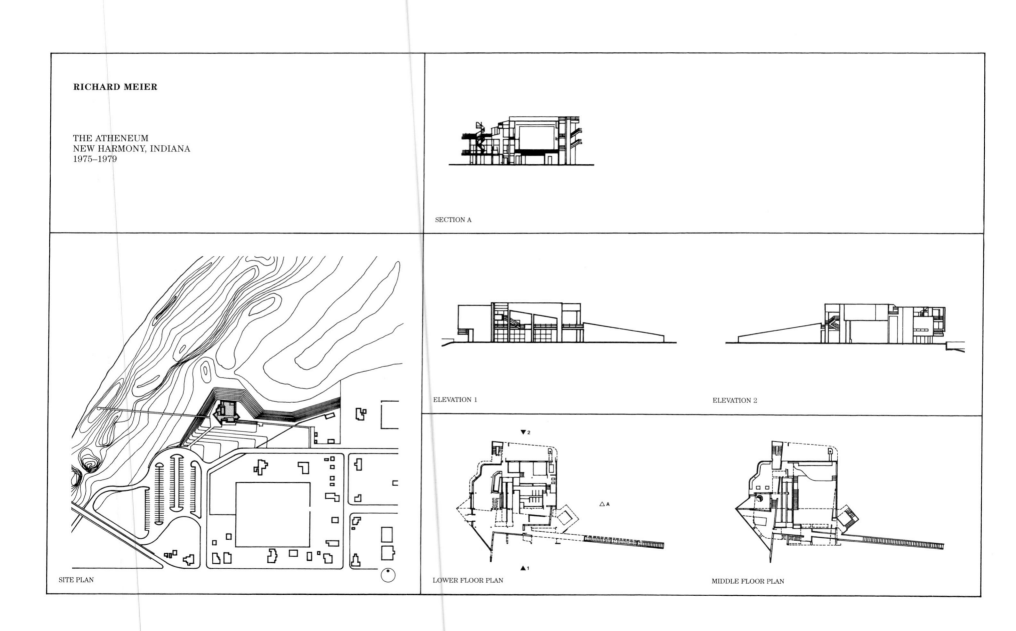

RICHARD MEIER

THE ATHENEUM
NEW HARMONY, INDIANA
1975–1979

SECTION A

ELEVATION 1

ELEVATION 2

SITE PLAN

LOWER FLOOR PLAN

MIDDLE FLOOR PLAN

118

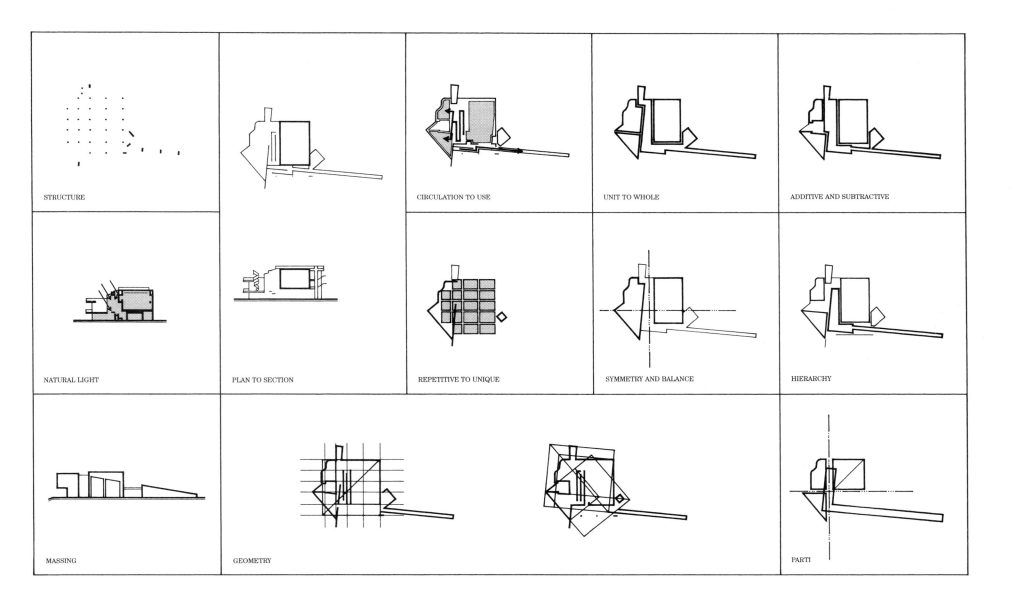

STRUCTURE

CIRCULATION TO USE

UNIT TO WHOLE

ADDITIVE AND SUBTRACTIVE

NATURAL LIGHT

PLAN TO SECTION

REPETITIVE TO UNIQUE

SYMMETRY AND BALANCE

HIERARCHY

MASSING

GEOMETRY

PARTI

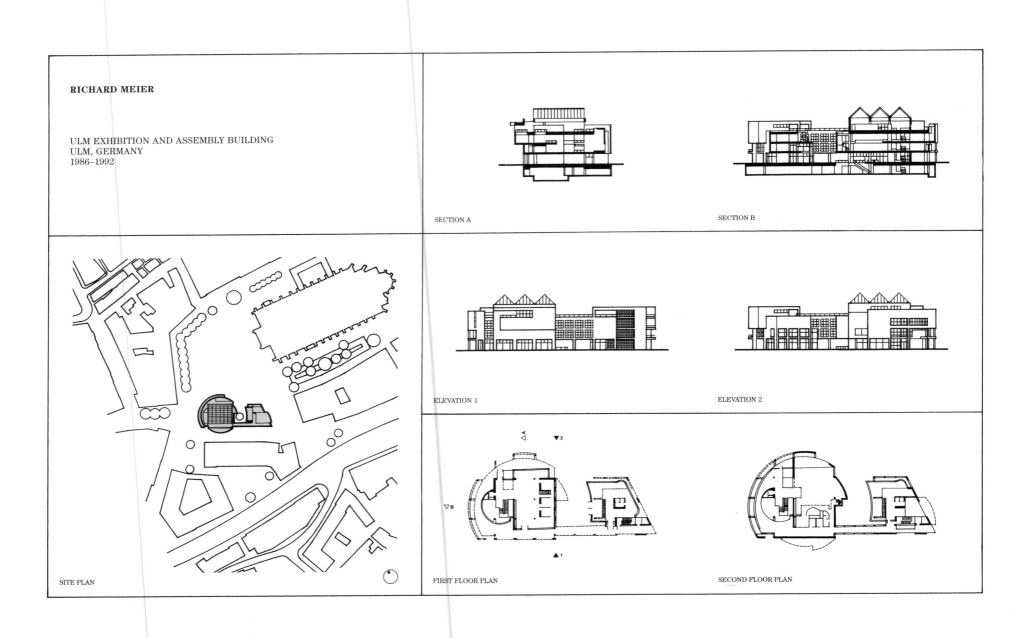

RICHARD MEIER

ULM EXHIBITION AND ASSEMBLY BUILDING
ULM, GERMANY
1986–1992

SECTION A

SECTION B

ELEVATION 1

ELEVATION 2

SITE PLAN

FIRST FLOOR PLAN

SECOND FLOOR PLAN

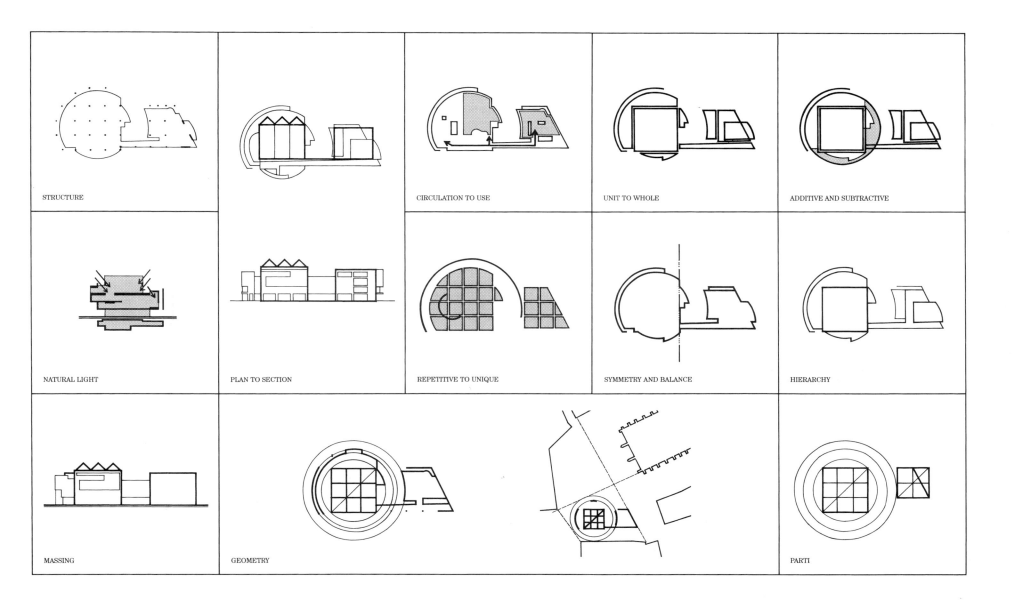

STRUCTURE

CIRCULATION TO USE

UNIT TO WHOLE

ADDITIVE AND SUBTRACTIVE

NATURAL LIGHT

PLAN TO SECTION

REPETITIVE TO UNIQUE

SYMMETRY AND BALANCE

HIERARCHY

MASSING

GEOMETRY

PARTI

121

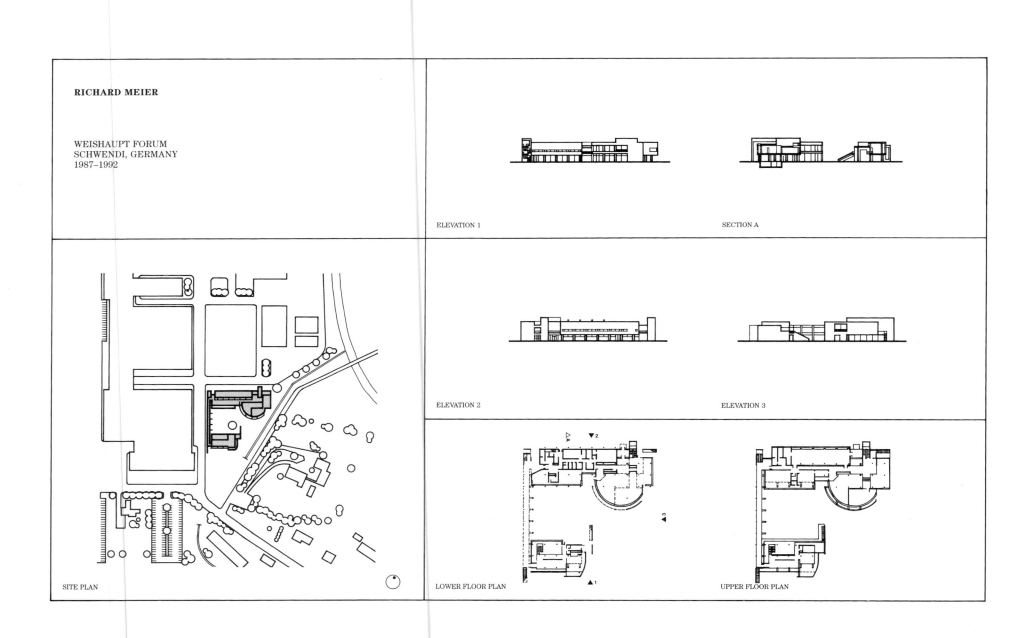

RICHARD MEIER

WEISHAUPT FORUM
SCHWENDI, GERMANY
1987–1992

ELEVATION 1

SECTION A

ELEVATION 2

ELEVATION 3

SITE PLAN

LOWER FLOOR PLAN

UPPER FLOOR PLAN

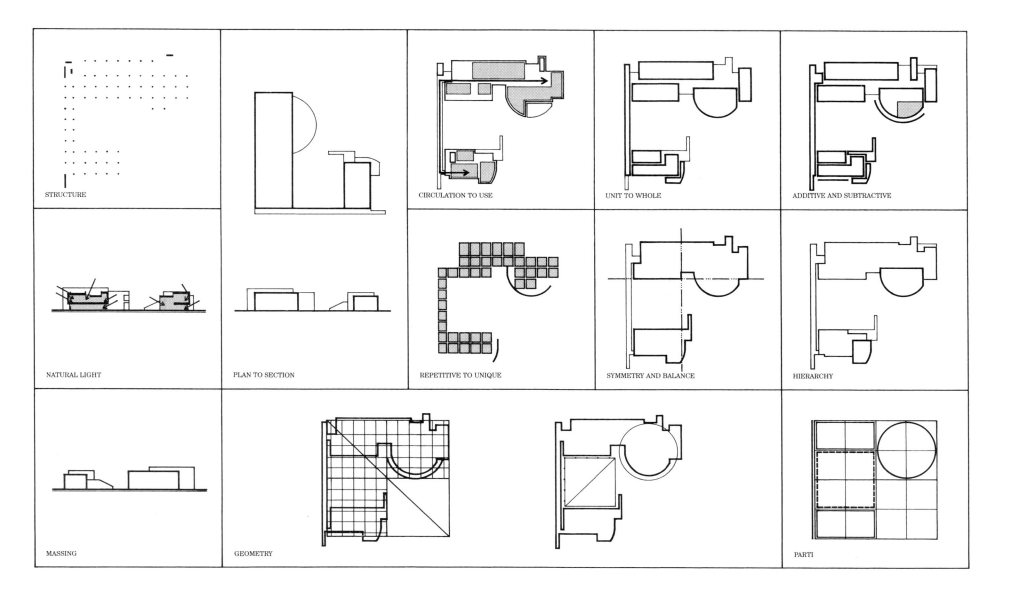

STRUCTURE

CIRCULATION TO USE

UNIT TO WHOLE

ADDITIVE AND SUBTRACTIVE

NATURAL LIGHT

PLAN TO SECTION

REPETITIVE TO UNIQUE

SYMMETRY AND BALANCE

HIERARCHY

MASSING

GEOMETRY

PARTI

RAFAEL MONEO

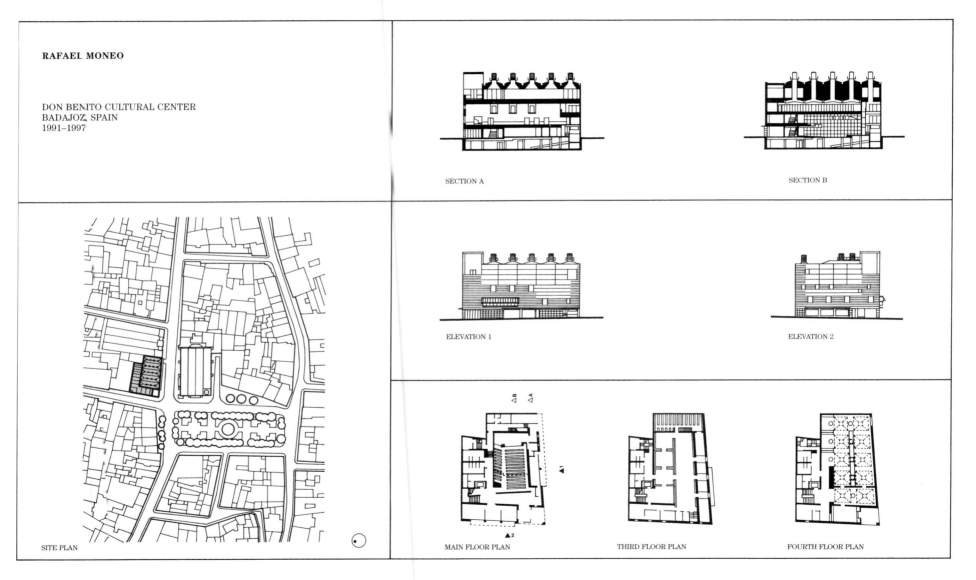

RAFAEL MONEO

DON BENITO CULTURAL CENTER
BADAJOZ, SPAIN
1991–1997

SECTION A

SECTION B

ELEVATION 1

ELEVATION 2

SITE PLAN

MAIN FLOOR PLAN

THIRD FLOOR PLAN

FOURTH FLOOR PLAN

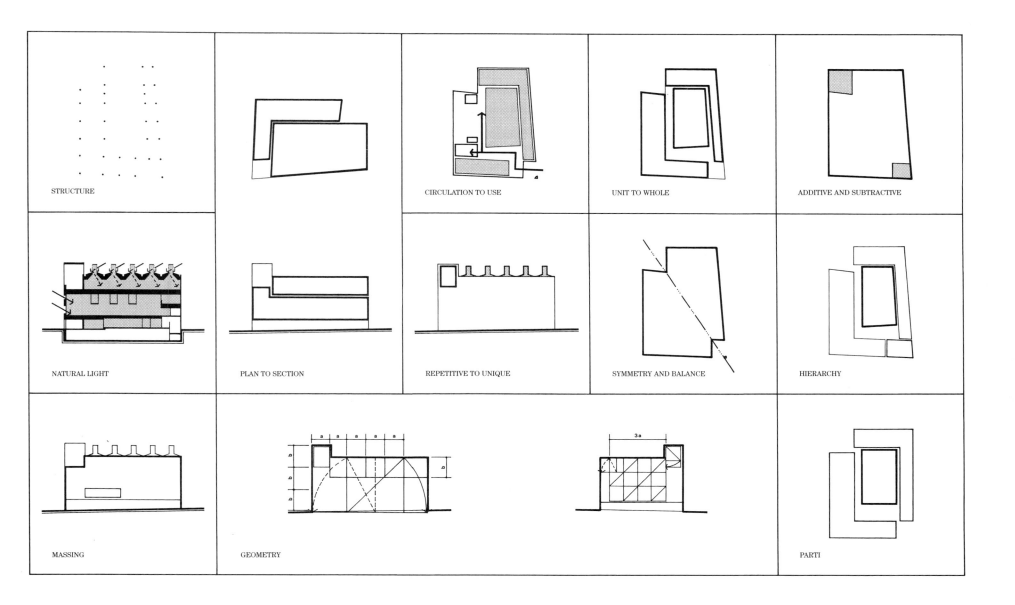

STRUCTURE

CIRCULATION TO USE

UNIT TO WHOLE

ADDITIVE AND SUBTRACTIVE

NATURAL LIGHT

PLAN TO SECTION

REPETITIVE TO UNIQUE

SYMMETRY AND BALANCE

HIERARCHY

MASSING

GEOMETRY

PARTI

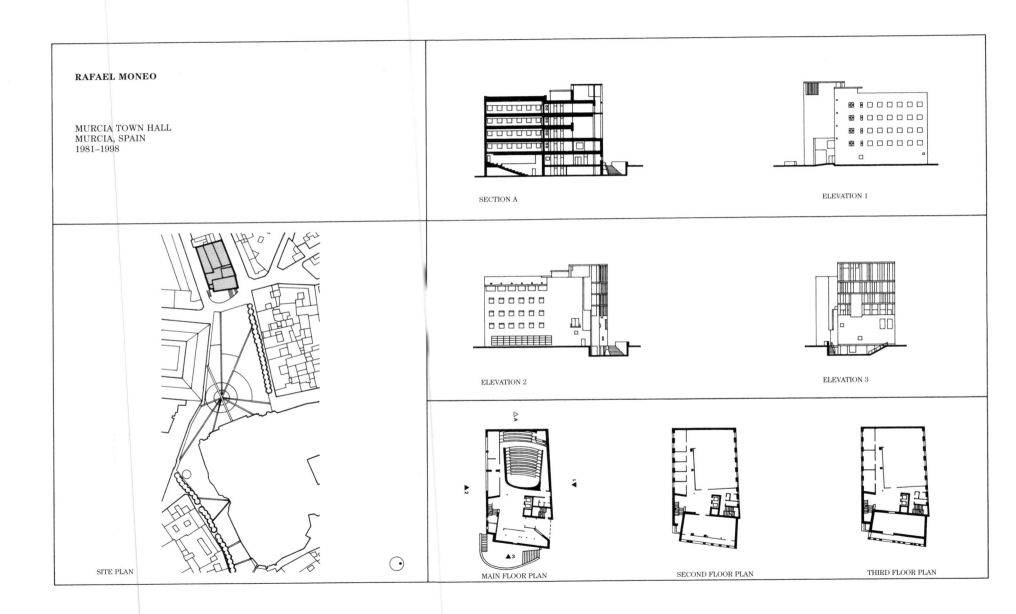

RAFAEL MONEO

MURCIA TOWN HALL
MURCIA, SPAIN
1981–1998

SECTION A

ELEVATION 1

ELEVATION 2

ELEVATION 3

SITE PLAN

MAIN FLOOR PLAN

SECOND FLOOR PLAN

THIRD FLOOR PLAN

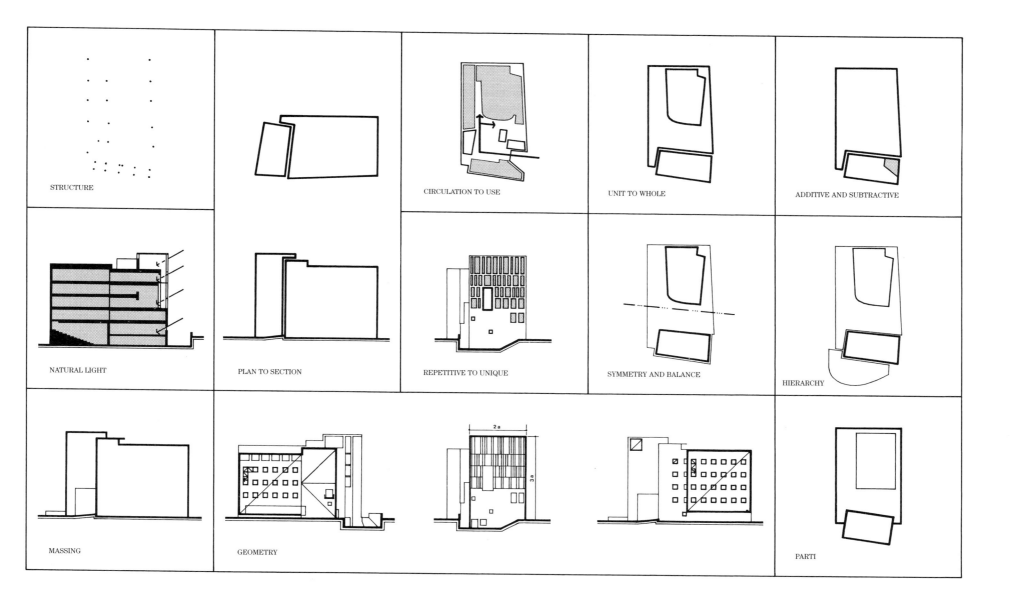

STRUCTURE

CIRCULATION TO USE

UNIT TO WHOLE

ADDITIVE AND SUBTRACTIVE

NATURAL LIGHT

PLAN TO SECTION

REPETITIVE TO UNIQUE

SYMMETRY AND BALANCE

HIERARCHY

MASSING

GEOMETRY

PARTI

CHARLES MOORE

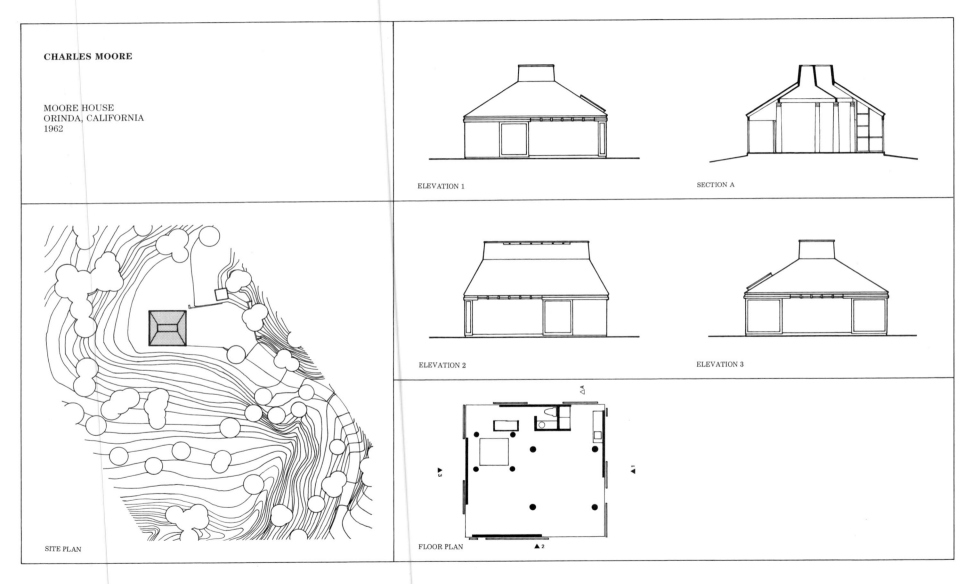

CHARLES MOORE

MOORE HOUSE
ORINDA, CALIFORNIA
1962

ELEVATION 1

SECTION A

ELEVATION 2

ELEVATION 3

SITE PLAN

FLOOR PLAN

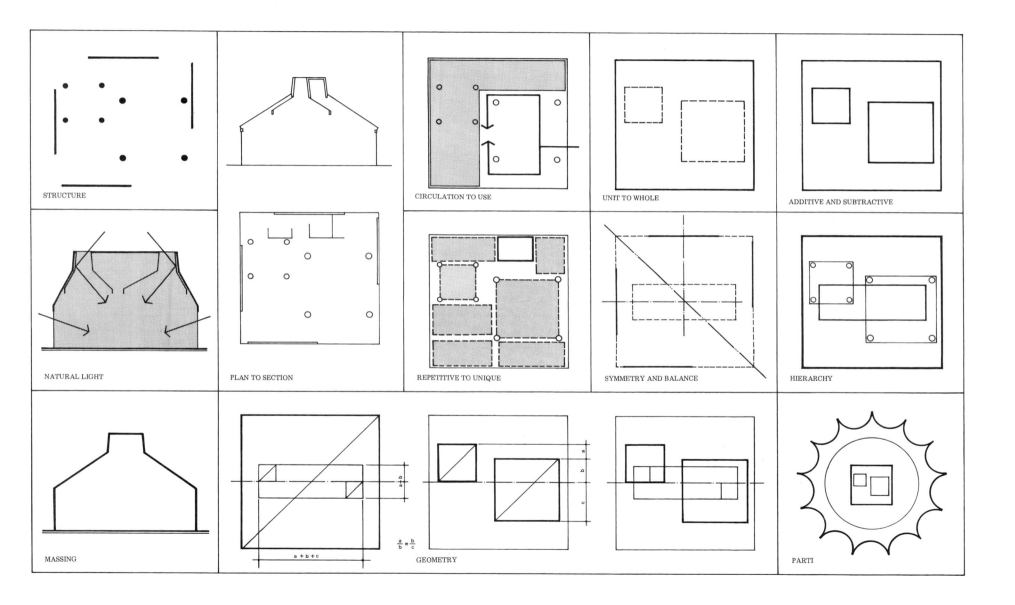

STRUCTURE

CIRCULATION TO USE

UNIT TO WHOLE

ADDITIVE AND SUBTRACTIVE

NATURAL LIGHT

PLAN TO SECTION

REPETITIVE TO UNIQUE

SYMMETRY AND BALANCE

HIERARCHY

MASSING

GEOMETRY

PARTI

129

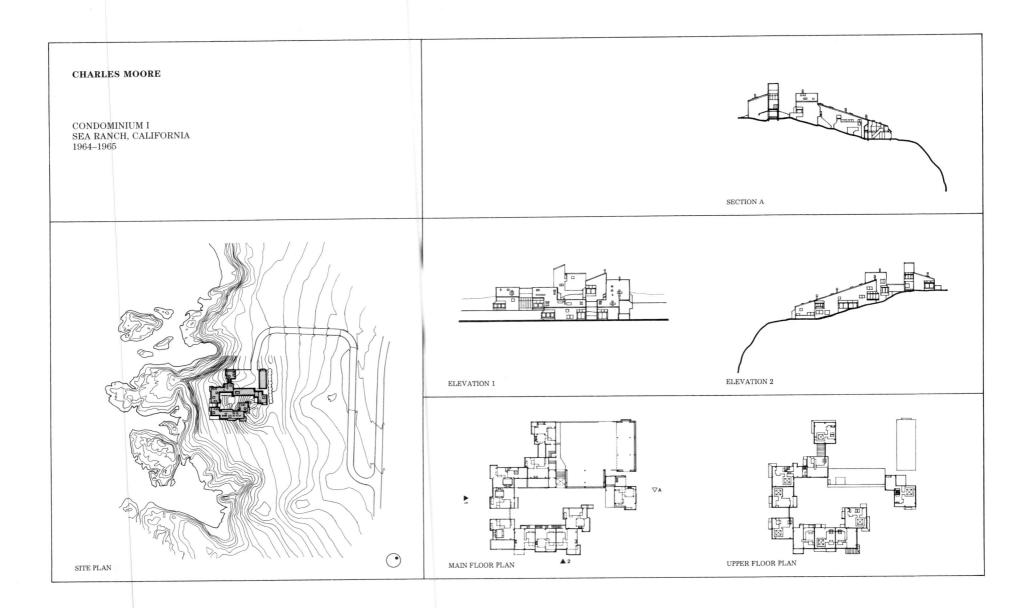

CHARLES MOORE

CONDOMINIUM I
SEA RANCH, CALIFORNIA
1964–1965

SECTION A

ELEVATION 1

ELEVATION 2

SITE PLAN

MAIN FLOOR PLAN

UPPER FLOOR PLAN

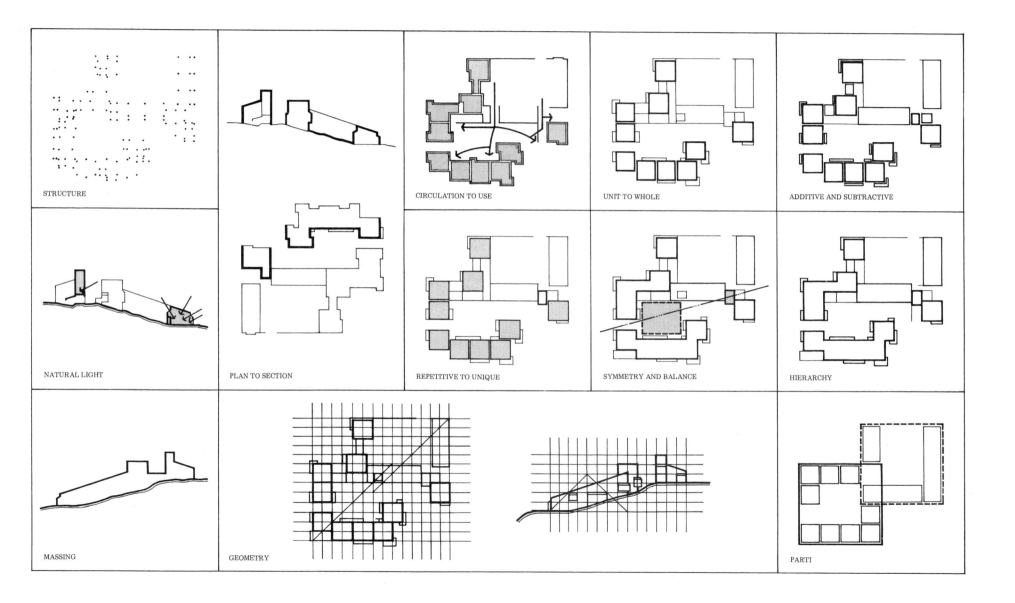

STRUCTURE

NATURAL LIGHT

MASSING

CIRCULATION TO USE

PLAN TO SECTION

GEOMETRY

UNIT TO WHOLE

REPETITIVE TO UNIQUE

ADDITIVE AND SUBTRACTIVE

SYMMETRY AND BALANCE

HIERARCHY

PARTI

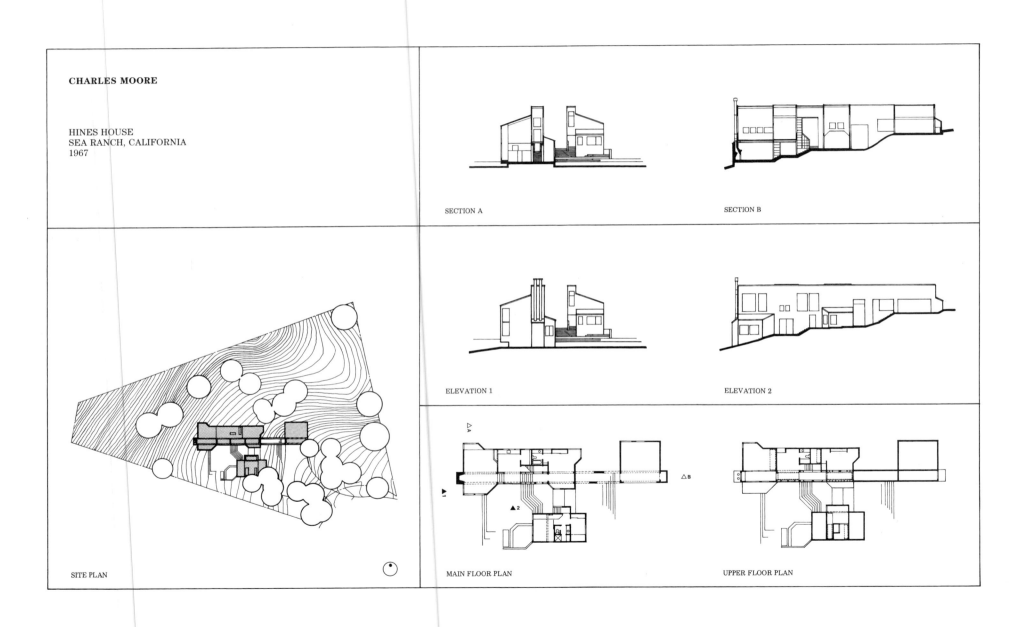

CHARLES MOORE

HINES HOUSE
SEA RANCH, CALIFORNIA
1967

SECTION A

SECTION B

ELEVATION 1

ELEVATION 2

SITE PLAN

MAIN FLOOR PLAN

UPPER FLOOR PLAN

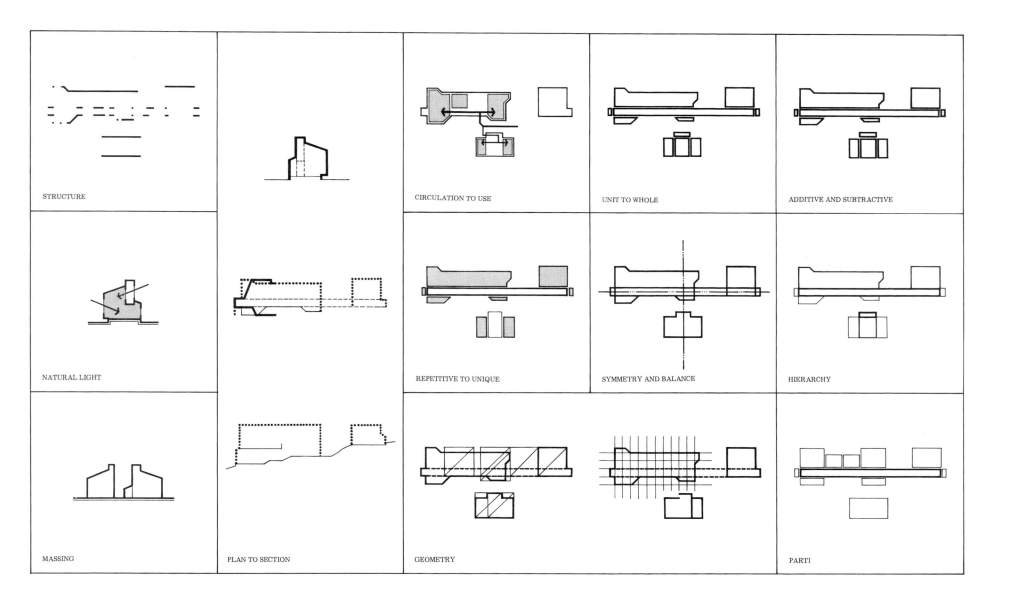

STRUCTURE

CIRCULATION TO USE

UNIT TO WHOLE

ADDITIVE AND SUBTRACTIVE

NATURAL LIGHT

REPETITIVE TO UNIQUE

SYMMETRY AND BALANCE

HIERARCHY

MASSING

PLAN TO SECTION

GEOMETRY

PARTI

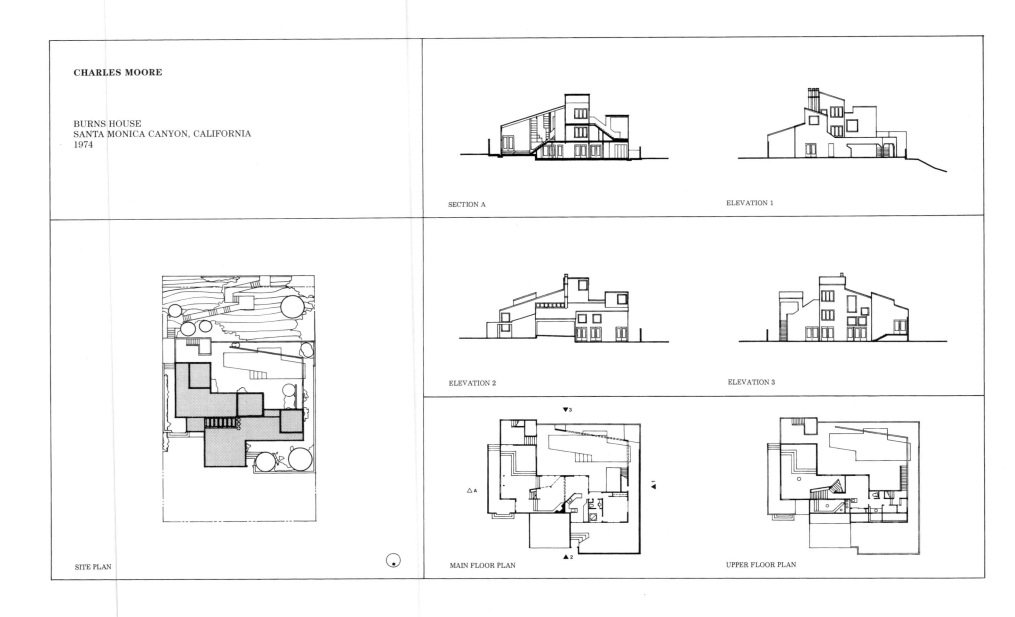

CHARLES MOORE

BURNS HOUSE
SANTA MONICA CANYON, CALIFORNIA
1974

SECTION A

ELEVATION 1

ELEVATION 2

ELEVATION 3

SITE PLAN

MAIN FLOOR PLAN

UPPER FLOOR PLAN

134

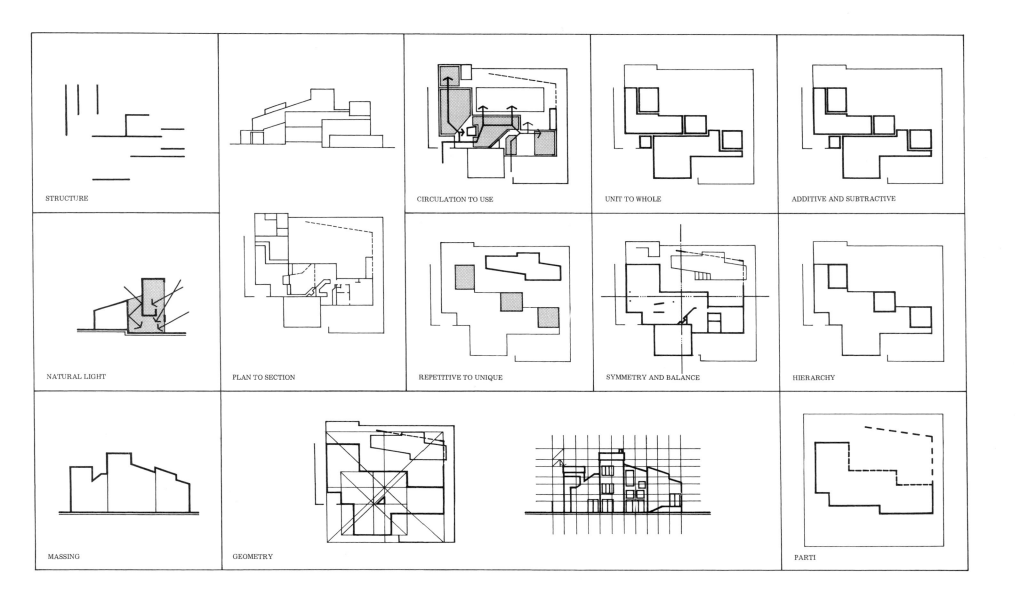

STRUCTURE

CIRCULATION TO USE

UNIT TO WHOLE

ADDITIVE AND SUBTRACTIVE

NATURAL LIGHT

PLAN TO SECTION

REPETITIVE TO UNIQUE

SYMMETRY AND BALANCE

HIERARCHY

MASSING

GEOMETRY

PARTI

GLENN MURCUTT

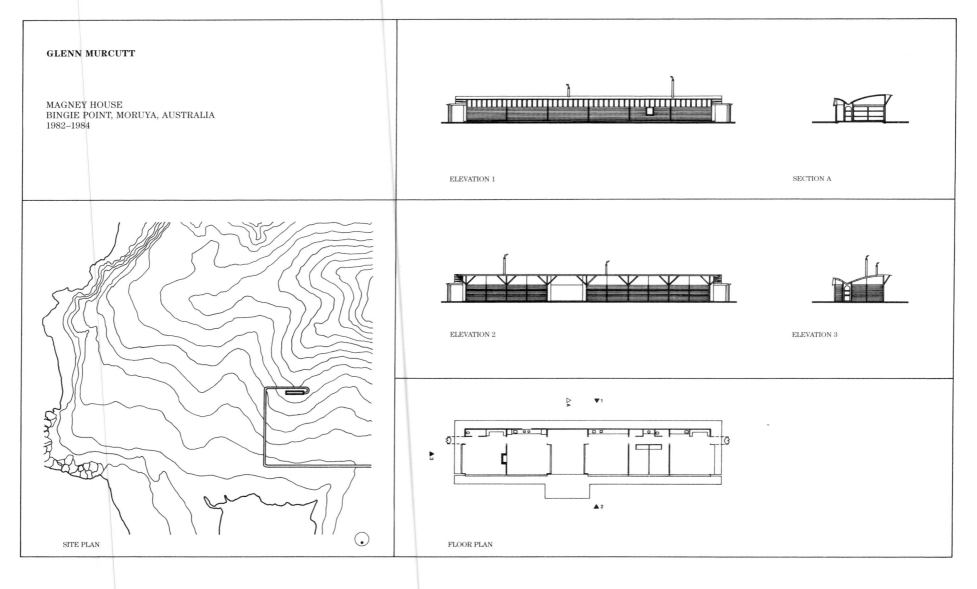

GLENN MURCUTT

MAGNEY HOUSE
BINGIE POINT, MORUYA, AUSTRALIA
1982–1984

ELEVATION 1

SECTION A

ELEVATION 2

ELEVATION 3

SITE PLAN

FLOOR PLAN

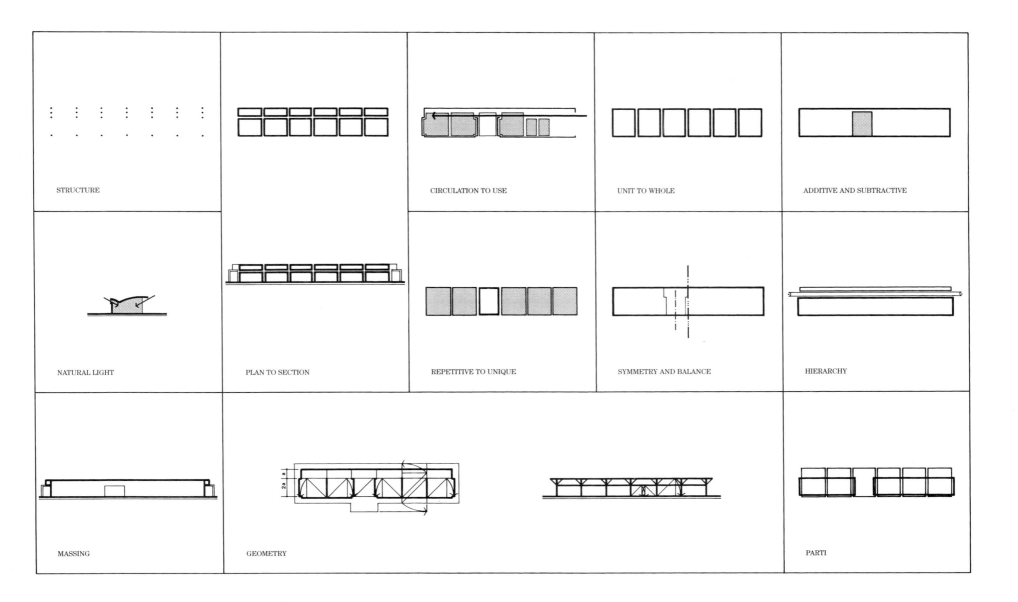

STRUCTURE

CIRCULATION TO USE

UNIT TO WHOLE

ADDITIVE AND SUBTRACTIVE

NATURAL LIGHT

PLAN TO SECTION

REPETITIVE TO UNIQUE

SYMMETRY AND BALANCE

HIERARCHY

MASSING

GEOMETRY

PARTI

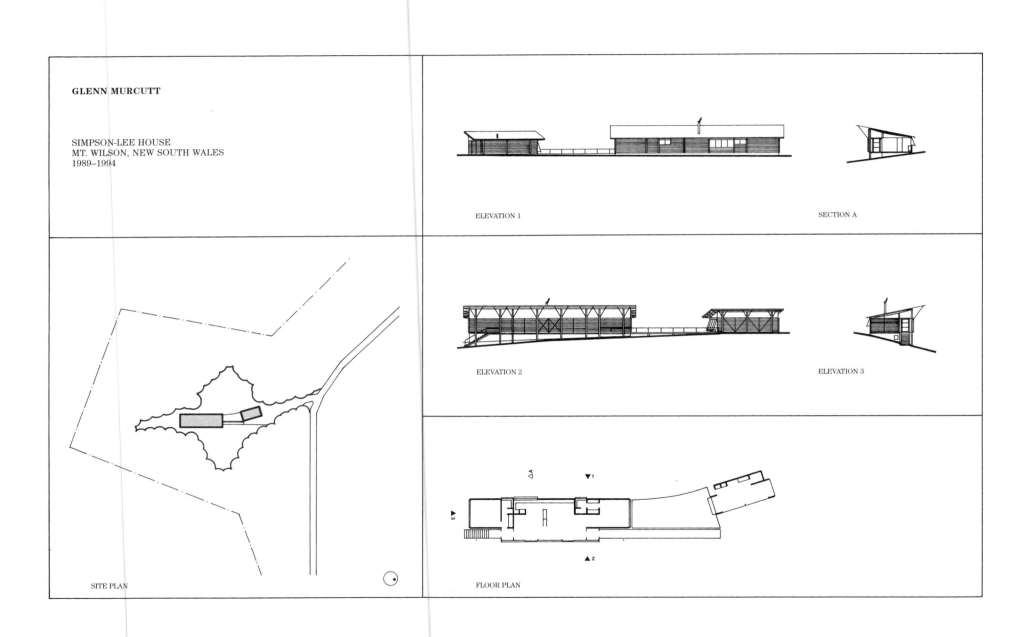

GLENN MURCUTT

SIMPSON-LEE HOUSE
MT. WILSON, NEW SOUTH WALES
1989–1994

ELEVATION 1

SECTION A

ELEVATION 2

ELEVATION 3

SITE PLAN

FLOOR PLAN

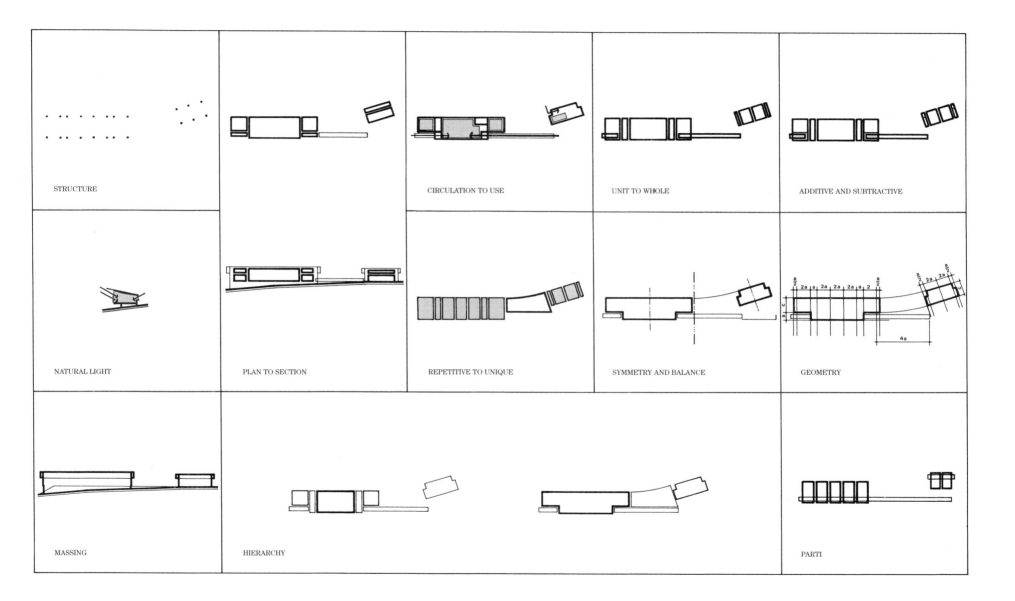

STRUCTURE

CIRCULATION TO USE

UNIT TO WHOLE

ADDITIVE AND SUBTRACTIVE

NATURAL LIGHT

PLAN TO SECTION

REPETITIVE TO UNIQUE

SYMMETRY AND BALANCE

GEOMETRY

MASSING

HIERARCHY

PARTI

JEAN NOUVEL

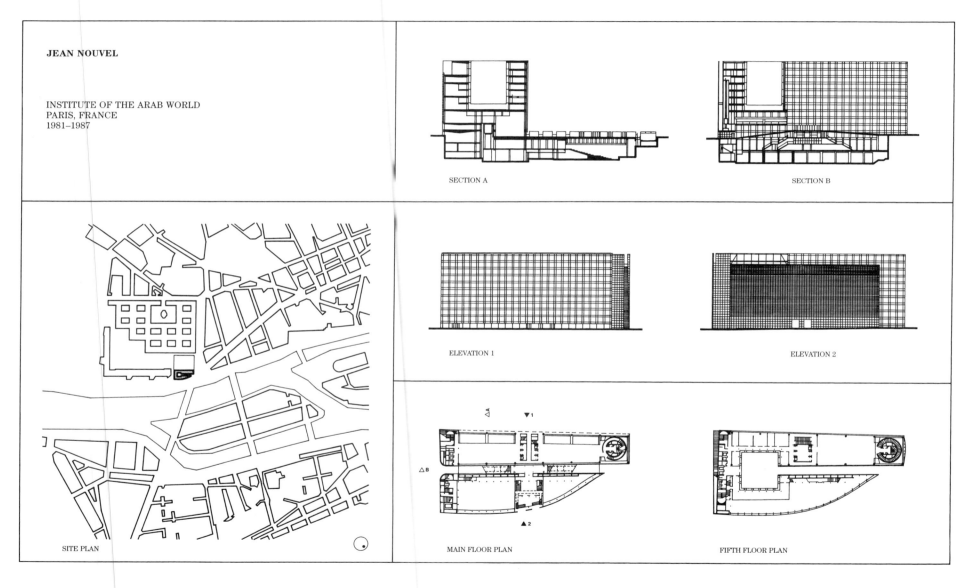

JEAN NOUVEL

INSTITUTE OF THE ARAB WORLD
PARIS, FRANCE
1981–1987

SECTION A

SECTION B

ELEVATION 1

ELEVATION 2

SITE PLAN

MAIN FLOOR PLAN

FIFTH FLOOR PLAN

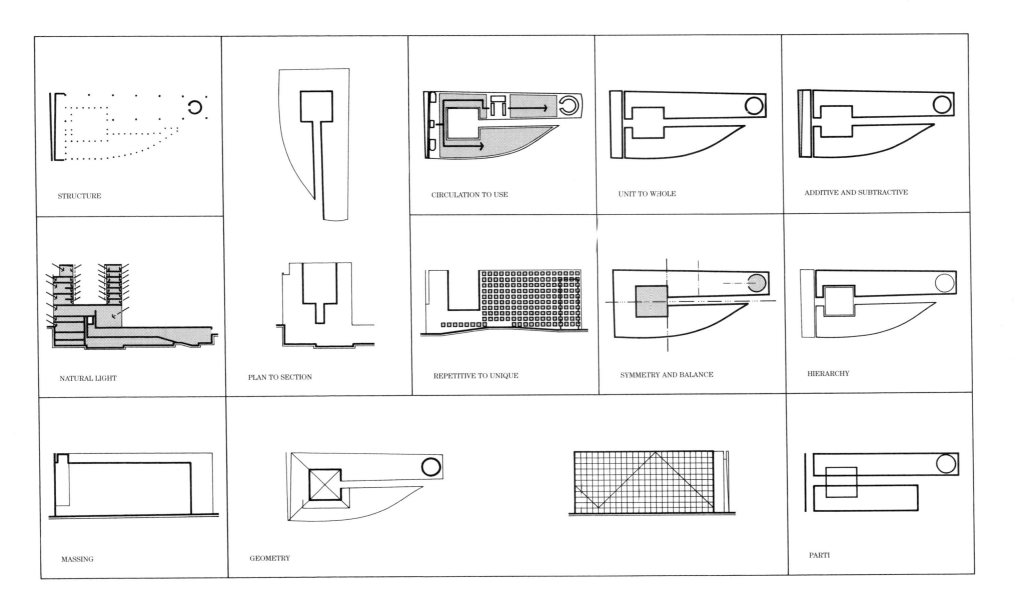

STRUCTURE

CIRCULATION TO USE

UNIT TO WHOLE

ADDITIVE AND SUBTRACTIVE

NATURAL LIGHT

PLAN TO SECTION

REPETITIVE TO UNIQUE

SYMMETRY AND BALANCE

HIERARCHY

MASSING

GEOMETRY

PARTI

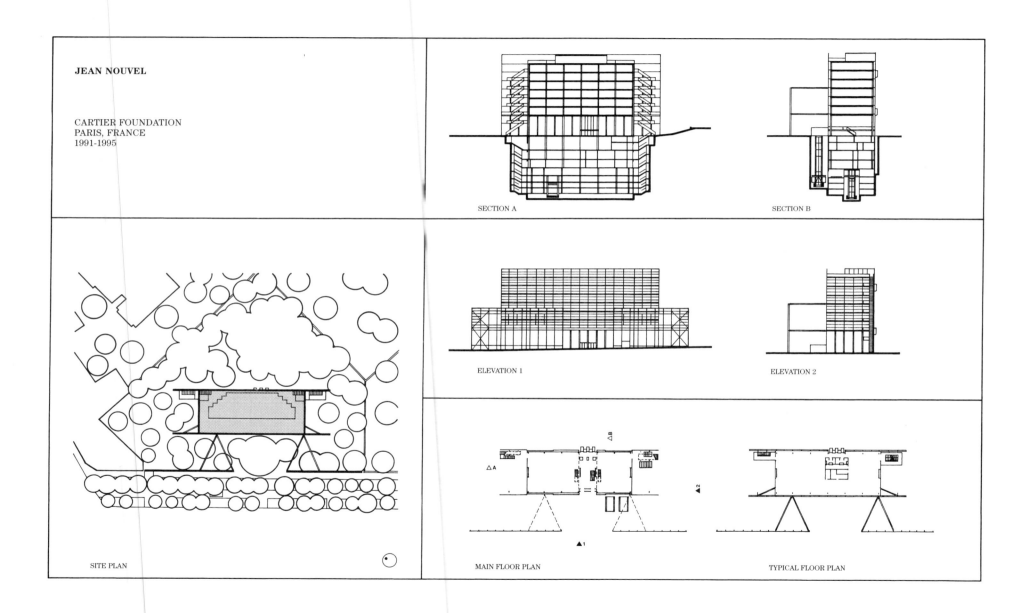

JEAN NOUVEL

CARTIER FOUNDATION
PARIS, FRANCE
1991-1995

SECTION A

SECTION B

ELEVATION 1

ELEVATION 2

SITE PLAN

MAIN FLOOR PLAN

TYPICAL FLOOR PLAN

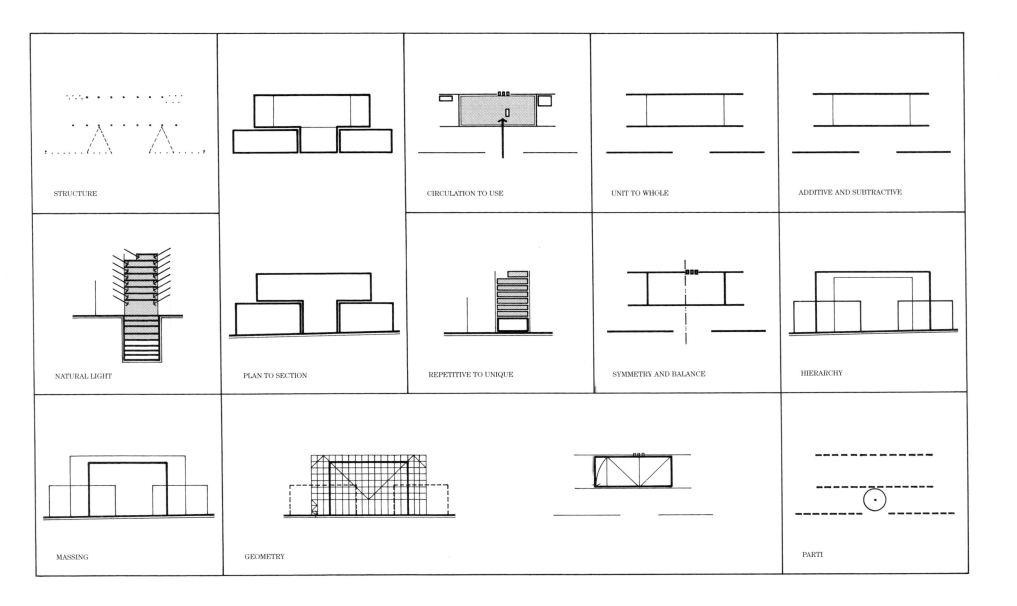

STRUCTURE

CIRCULATION TO USE

UNIT TO WHOLE

ADDITIVE AND SUBTRACTIVE

NATURAL LIGHT

PLAN TO SECTION

REPETITIVE TO UNIQUE

SYMMETRY AND BALANCE

HIERARCHY

MASSING

GEOMETRY

PARTI

ANDREA PALLADIO

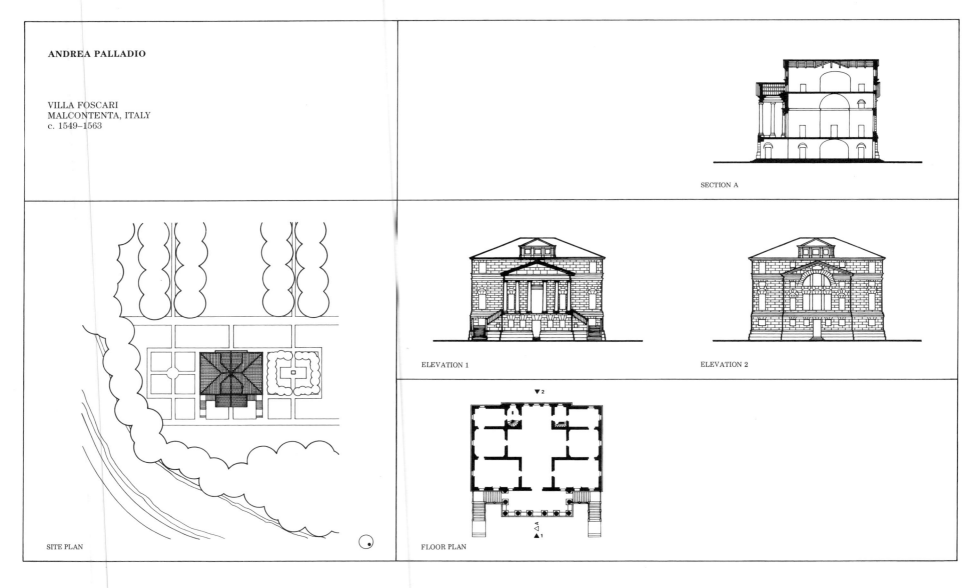

ANDREA PALLADIO

VILLA FOSCARI
MALCONTENTA, ITALY
c. 1549–1563

SECTION A

ELEVATION 1

ELEVATION 2

SITE PLAN

FLOOR PLAN

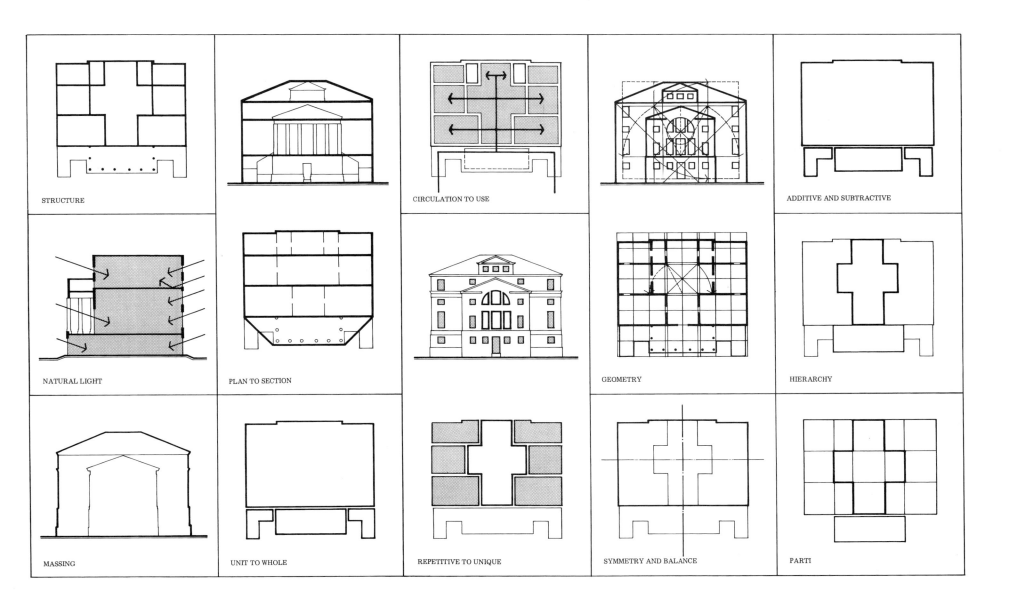

STRUCTURE

CIRCULATION TO USE

ADDITIVE AND SUBTRACTIVE

NATURAL LIGHT

PLAN TO SECTION

GEOMETRY

HIERARCHY

MASSING

UNIT TO WHOLE

REPETITIVE TO UNIQUE

SYMMETRY AND BALANCE

PARTI

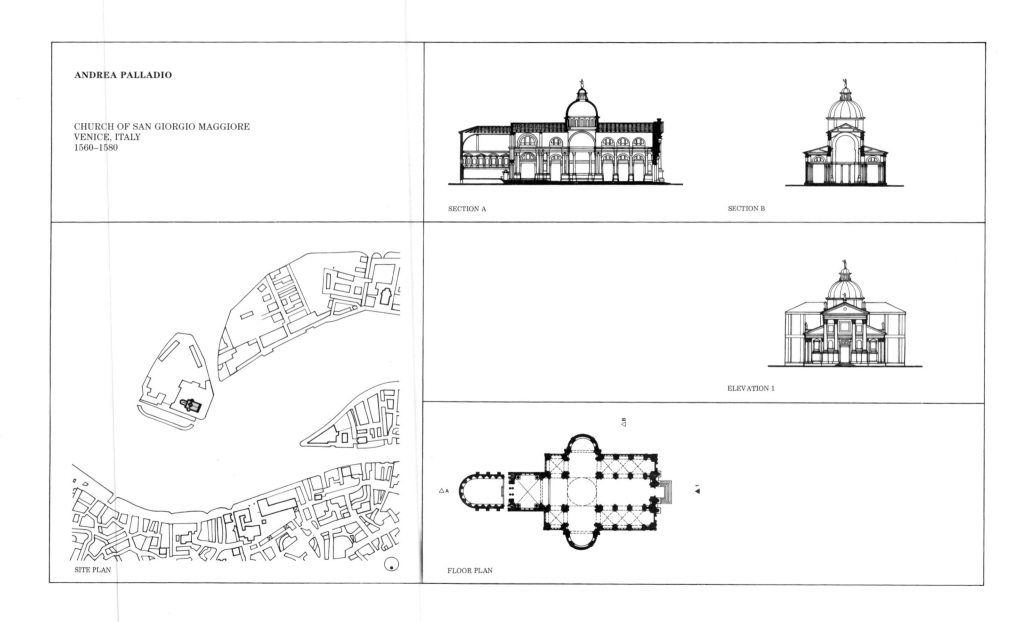

ANDREA PALLADIO

CHURCH OF SAN GIORGIO MAGGIORE
VENICE, ITALY
1560–1580

SECTION A

SECTION B

ELEVATION 1

SITE PLAN

FLOOR PLAN

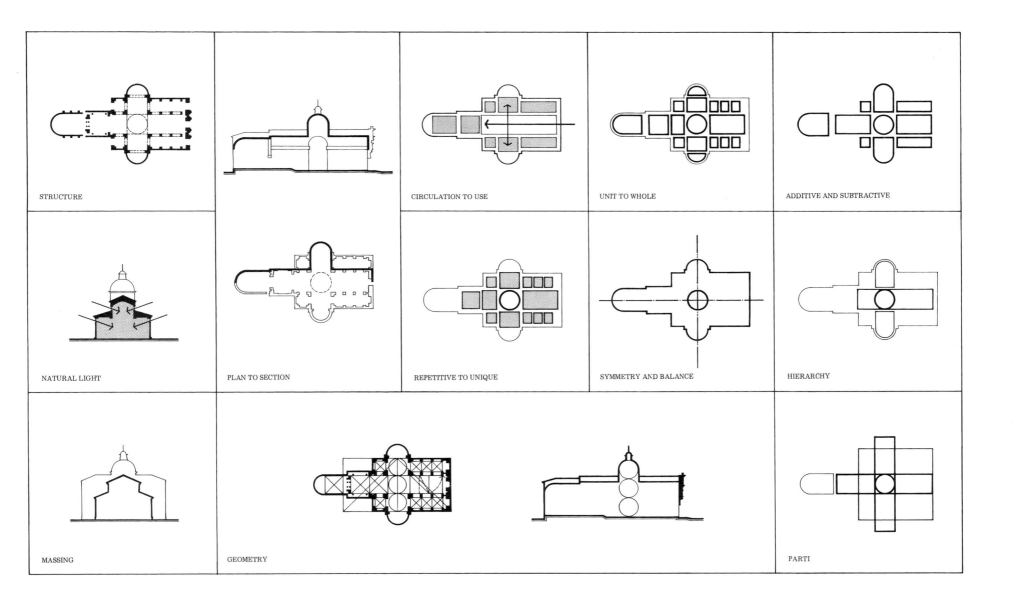

STRUCTURE

CIRCULATION TO USE

UNIT TO WHOLE

ADDITIVE AND SUBTRACTIVE

NATURAL LIGHT

PLAN TO SECTION

REPETITIVE TO UNIQUE

SYMMETRY AND BALANCE

HIERARCHY

MASSING

GEOMETRY

PARTI

147

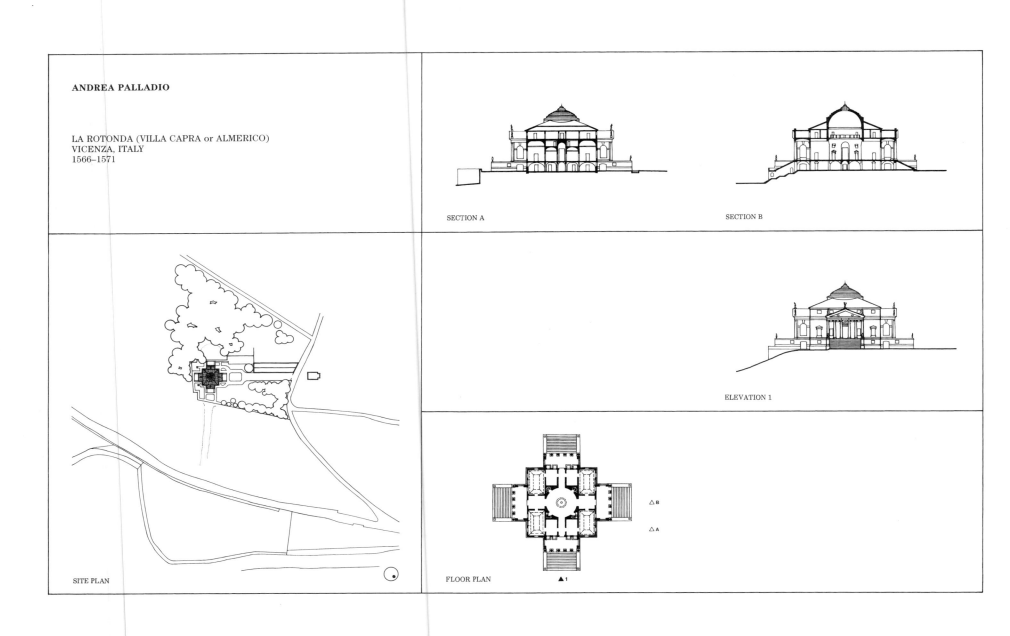

ANDREA PALLADIO

LA ROTONDA (VILLA CAPRA or ALMERICO)
VICENZA, ITALY
1566–1571

SECTION A

SECTION B

ELEVATION 1

SITE PLAN

FLOOR PLAN

△ B

△ A

▲ 1

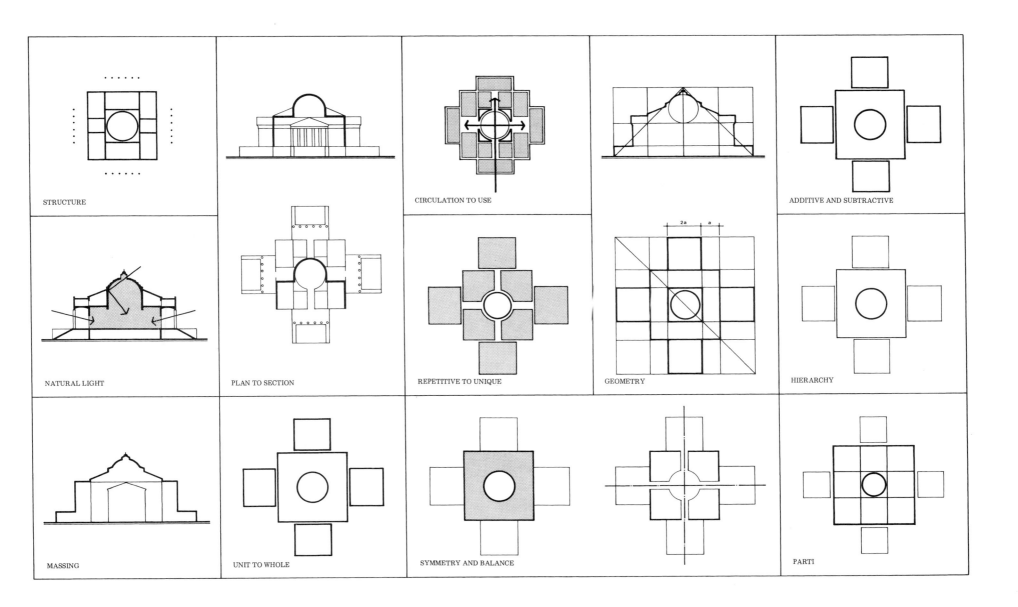

STRUCTURE

CIRCULATION TO USE

ADDITIVE AND SUBTRACTIVE

NATURAL LIGHT

PLAN TO SECTION

REPETITIVE TO UNIQUE

GEOMETRY

HIERARCHY

MASSING

UNIT TO WHOLE

SYMMETRY AND BALANCE

PARTI

149

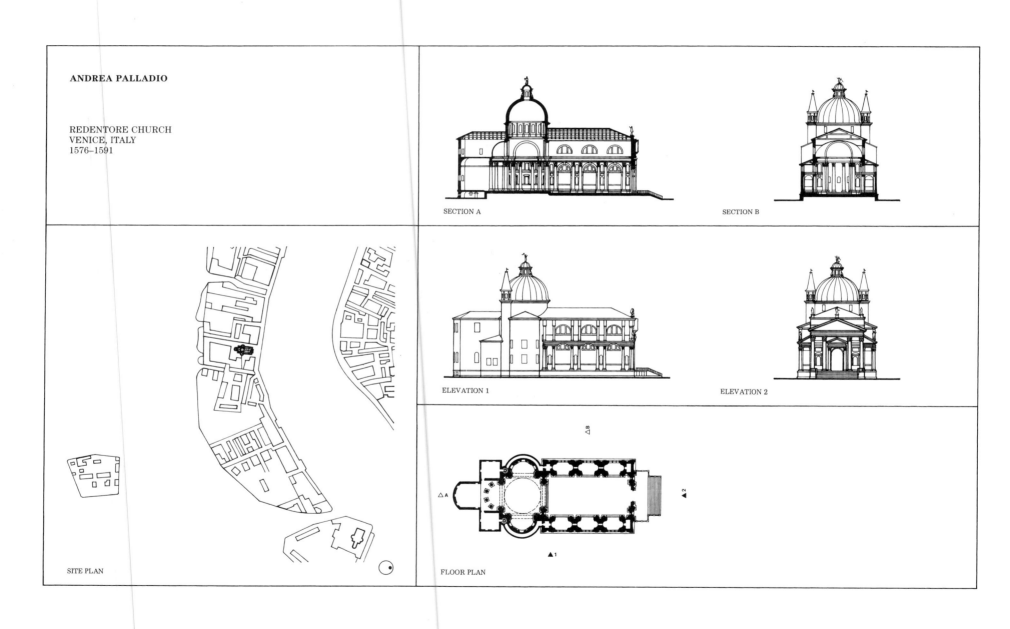

ANDREA PALLADIO

REDENTORE CHURCH
VENICE, ITALY
1576–1591

SECTION A

SECTION B

ELEVATION 1

ELEVATION 2

SITE PLAN

FLOOR PLAN

150

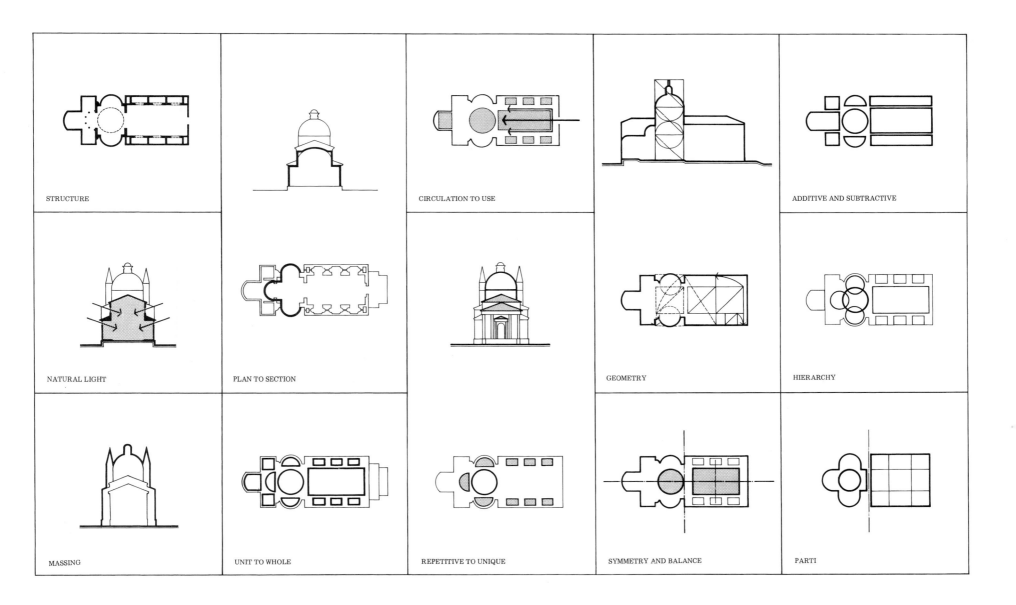

STRUCTURE

CIRCULATION TO USE

ADDITIVE AND SUBTRACTIVE

NATURAL LIGHT

PLAN TO SECTION

GEOMETRY

HIERARCHY

MASSING

UNIT TO WHOLE

REPETITIVE TO UNIQUE

SYMMETRY AND BALANCE

PARTI

151

HENRY HOBSON RICHARDSON

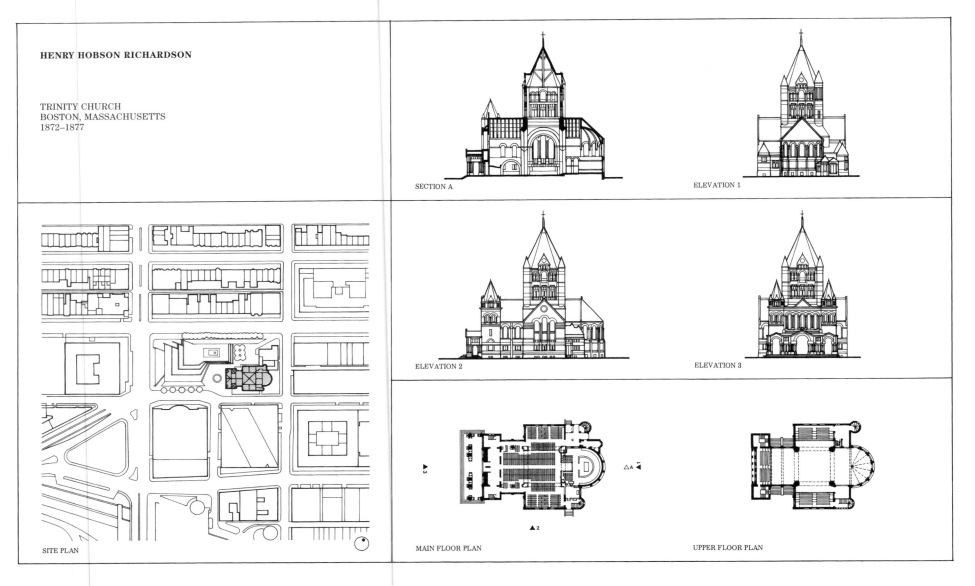

HENRY HOBSON RICHARDSON

TRINITY CHURCH
BOSTON, MASSACHUSETTS
1872–1877

SECTION A

ELEVATION 1

ELEVATION 2

ELEVATION 3

SITE PLAN

MAIN FLOOR PLAN

UPPER FLOOR PLAN

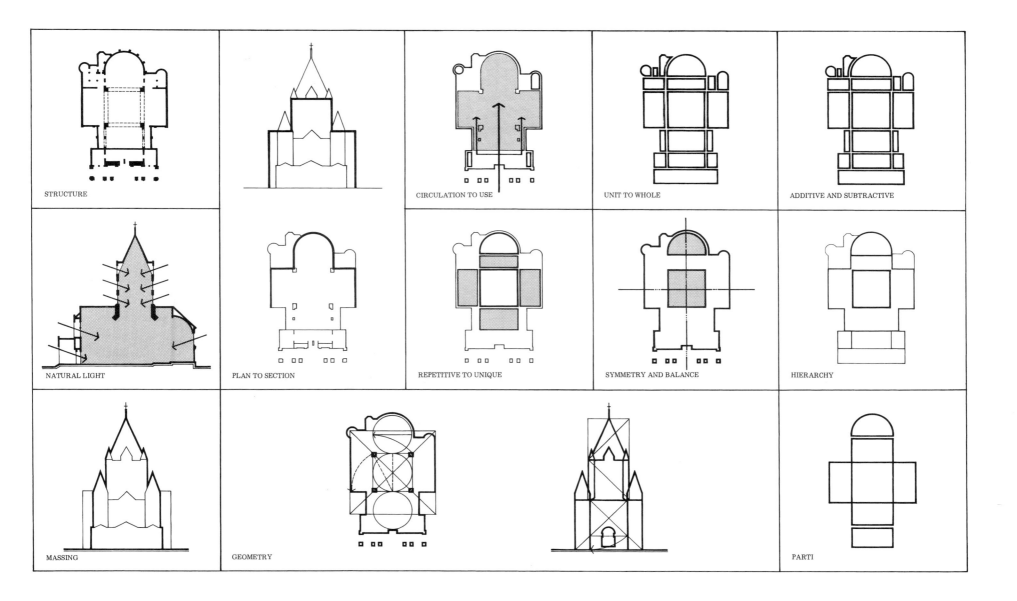

STRUCTURE

CIRCULATION TO USE

UNIT TO WHOLE

ADDITIVE AND SUBTRACTIVE

NATURAL LIGHT

PLAN TO SECTION

REPETITIVE TO UNIQUE

SYMMETRY AND BALANCE

HIERARCHY

MASSING

GEOMETRY

PARTI

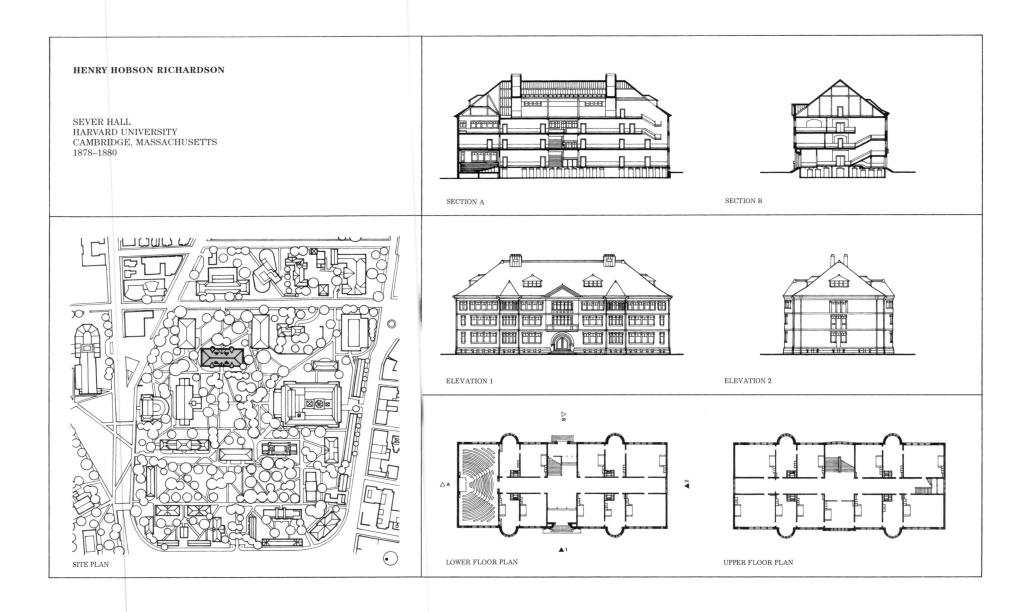

HENRY HOBSON RICHARDSON

SEVER HALL
HARVARD UNIVERSITY
CAMBRIDGE, MASSACHUSETTS
1878–1880

SECTION A

SECTION B

ELEVATION 1

ELEVATION 2

SITE PLAN

LOWER FLOOR PLAN

UPPER FLOOR PLAN

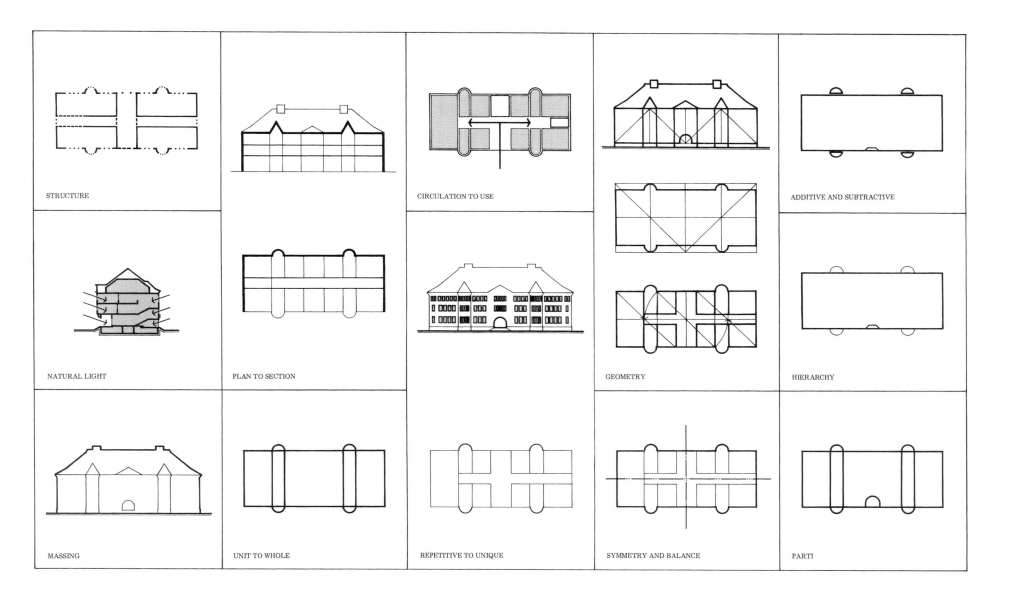

STRUCTURE

CIRCULATION TO USE

ADDITIVE AND SUBTRACTIVE

NATURAL LIGHT

PLAN TO SECTION

GEOMETRY

HIERARCHY

MASSING

UNIT TO WHOLE

REPETITIVE TO UNIQUE

SYMMETRY AND BALANCE

PARTI

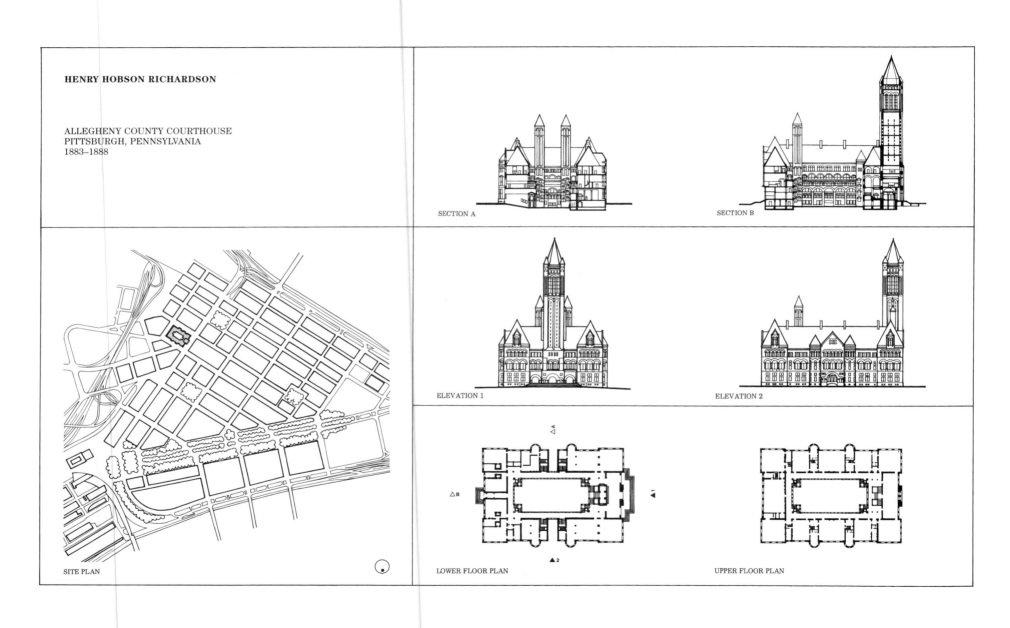

HENRY HOBSON RICHARDSON

ALLEGHENY COUNTY COURTHOUSE
PITTSBURGH, PENNSYLVANIA
1883–1888

SECTION A

SECTION B

ELEVATION 1

ELEVATION 2

SITE PLAN

LOWER FLOOR PLAN

UPPER FLOOR PLAN

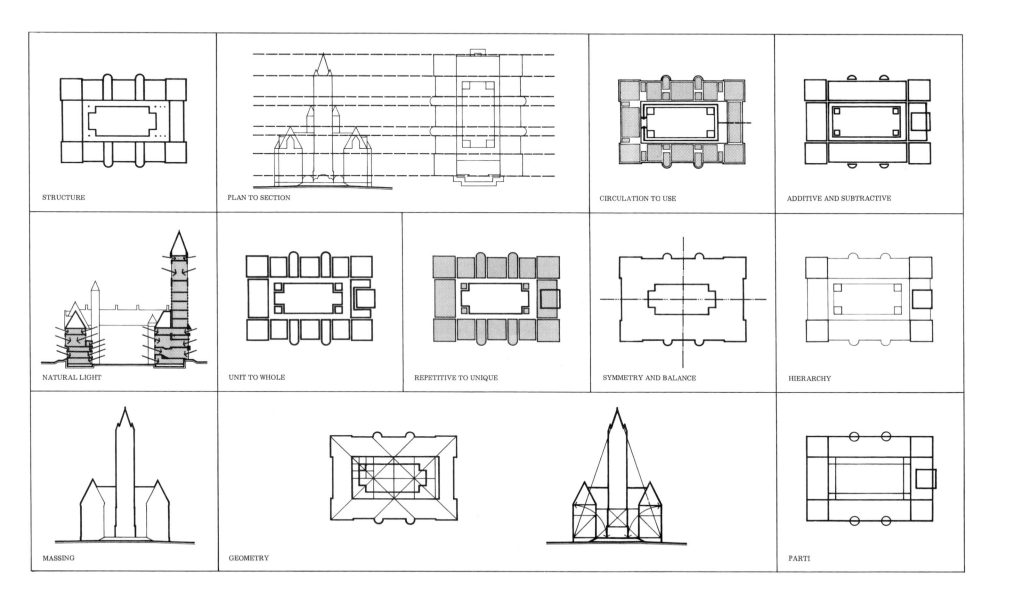

STRUCTURE

PLAN TO SECTION

CIRCULATION TO USE

ADDITIVE AND SUBTRACTIVE

NATURAL LIGHT

UNIT TO WHOLE

REPETITIVE TO UNIQUE

SYMMETRY AND BALANCE

HIERARCHY

MASSING

GEOMETRY

PARTI

157

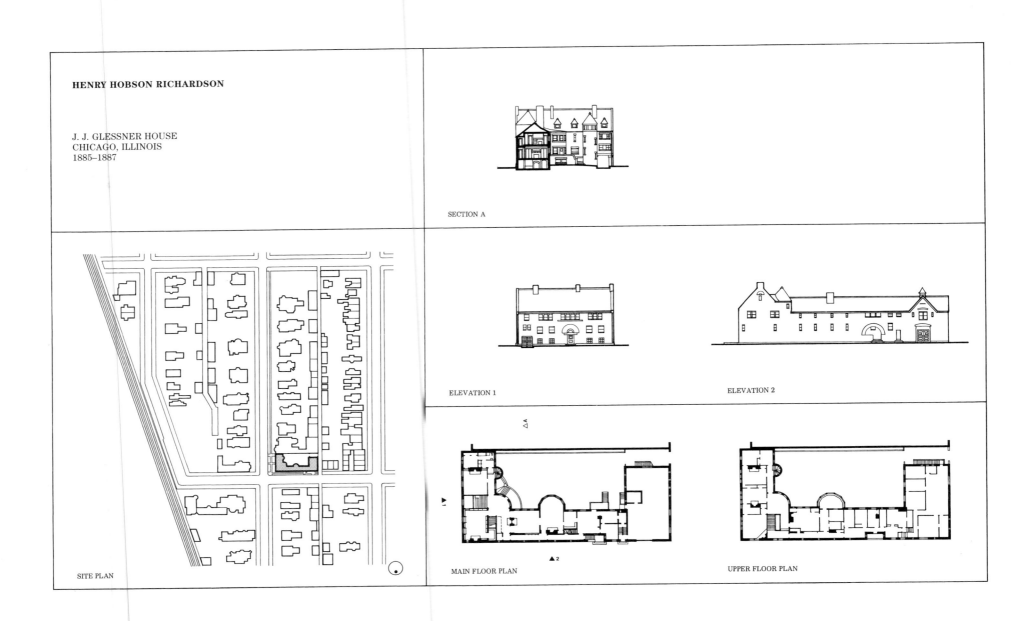

HENRY HOBSON RICHARDSON

J. J. GLESSNER HOUSE
CHICAGO, ILLINOIS
1885–1887

SECTION A

ELEVATION 1

ELEVATION 2

SITE PLAN

MAIN FLOOR PLAN

UPPER FLOOR PLAN

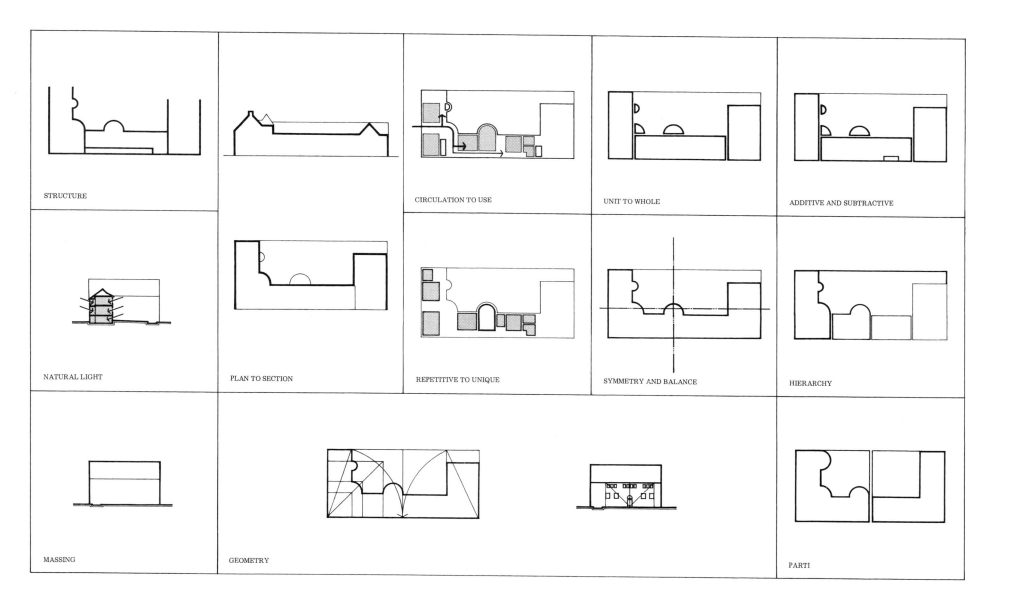

STRUCTURE

CIRCULATION TO USE

UNIT TO WHOLE

ADDITIVE AND SUBTRACTIVE

NATURAL LIGHT

PLAN TO SECTION

REPETITIVE TO UNIQUE

SYMMETRY AND BALANCE

HIERARCHY

MASSING

GEOMETRY

PARTI

159

JAMES STIRLING

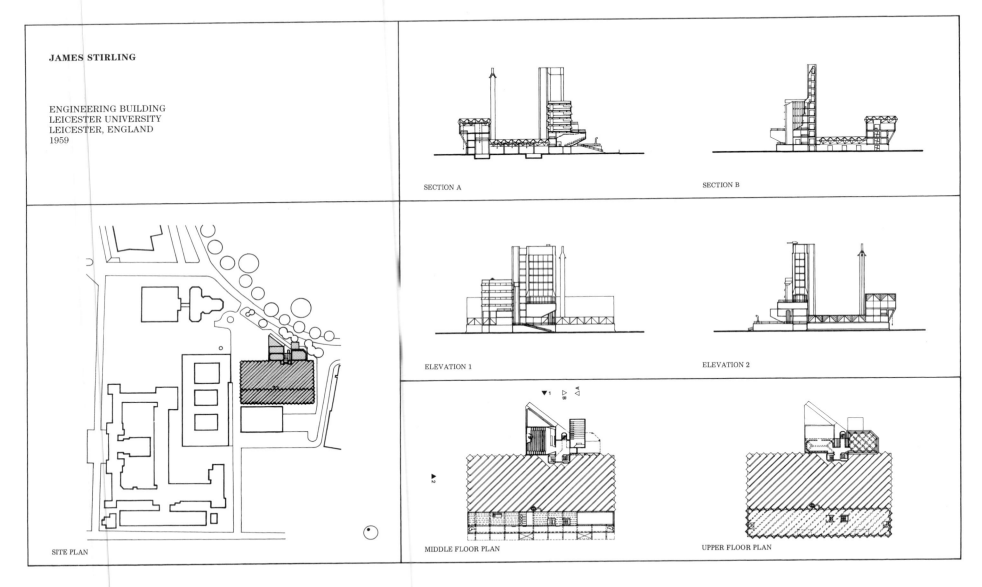

JAMES STIRLING

ENGINEERING BUILDING
LEICESTER UNIVERSITY
LEICESTER, ENGLAND
1959

SECTION A

SECTION B

ELEVATION 1

ELEVATION 2

SITE PLAN

MIDDLE FLOOR PLAN

UPPER FLOOR PLAN

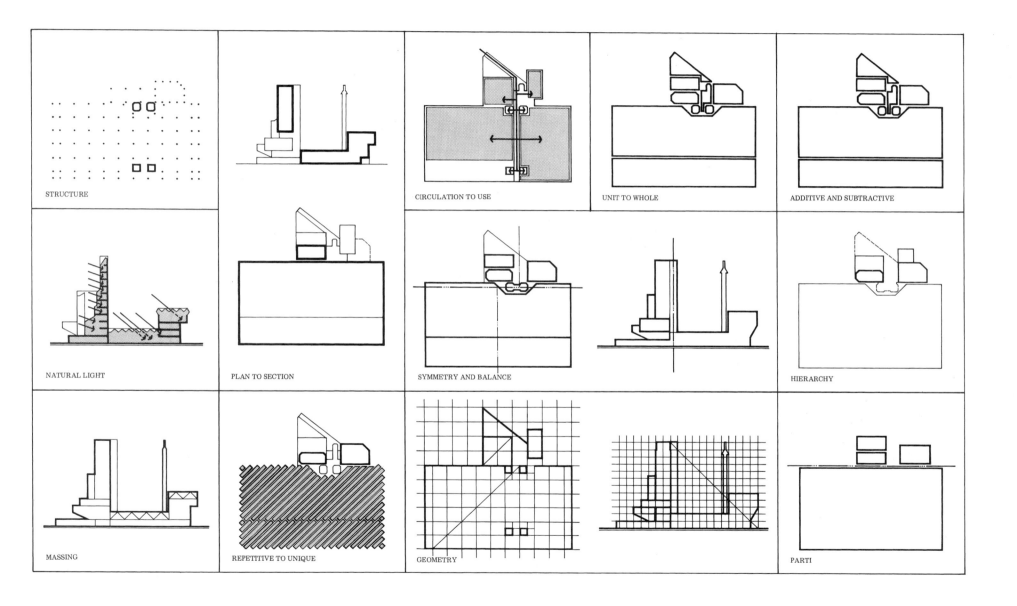

STRUCTURE

CIRCULATION TO USE

UNIT TO WHOLE

ADDITIVE AND SUBTRACTIVE

NATURAL LIGHT

PLAN TO SECTION

SYMMETRY AND BALANCE

HIERARCHY

MASSING

REPETITIVE TO UNIQUE

GEOMETRY

PARTI

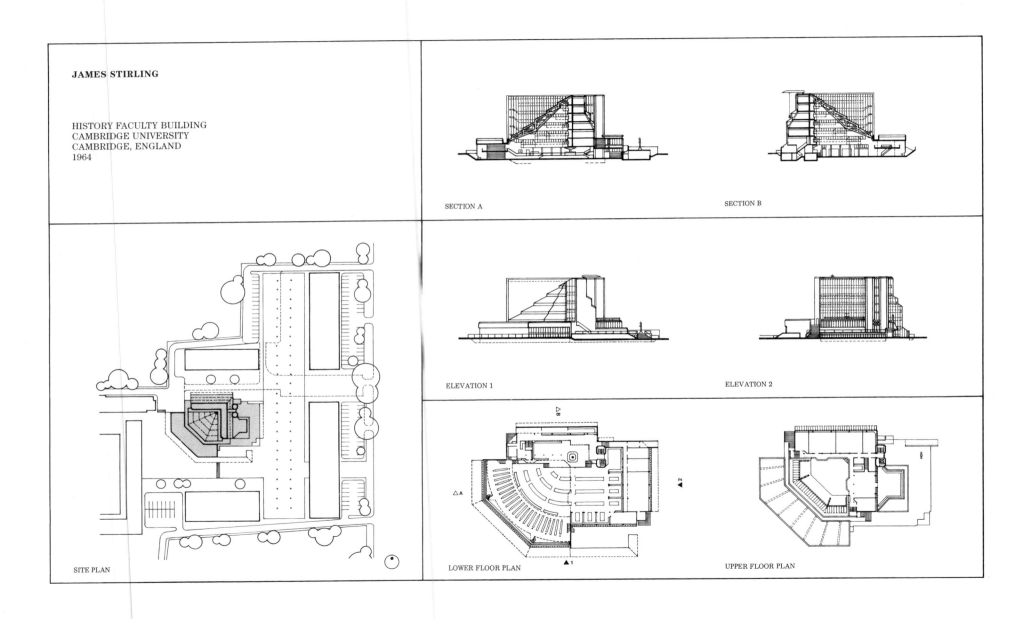

JAMES STIRLING

HISTORY FACULTY BUILDING
CAMBRIDGE UNIVERSITY
CAMBRIDGE, ENGLAND
1964

SECTION A

SECTION B

ELEVATION 1

ELEVATION 2

SITE PLAN

LOWER FLOOR PLAN

UPPER FLOOR PLAN

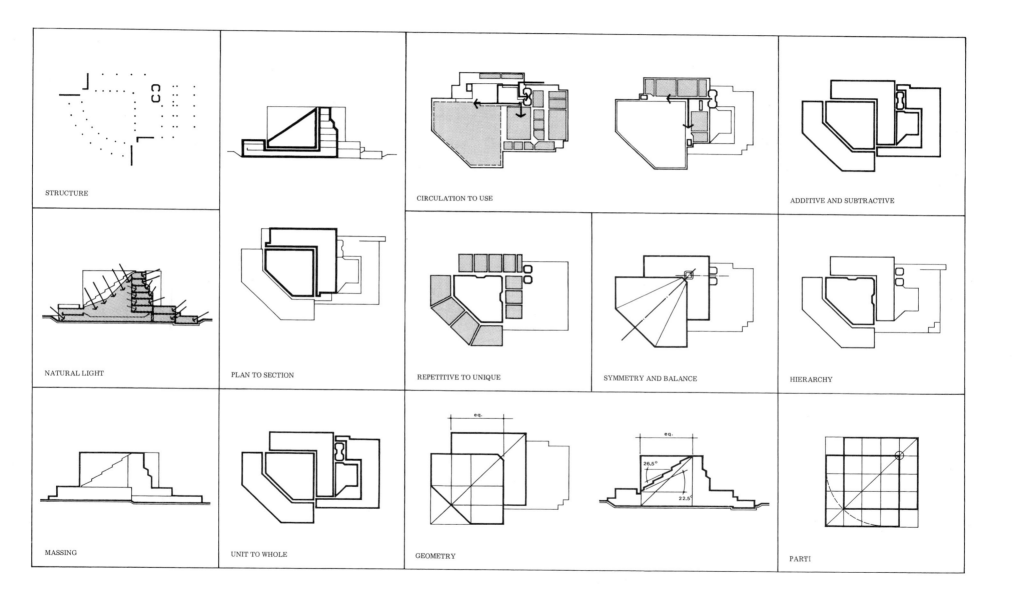

STRUCTURE

CIRCULATION TO USE

ADDITIVE AND SUBTRACTIVE

NATURAL LIGHT

PLAN TO SECTION

REPETITIVE TO UNIQUE

SYMMETRY AND BALANCE

HIERARCHY

MASSING

UNIT TO WHOLE

GEOMETRY

PARTI

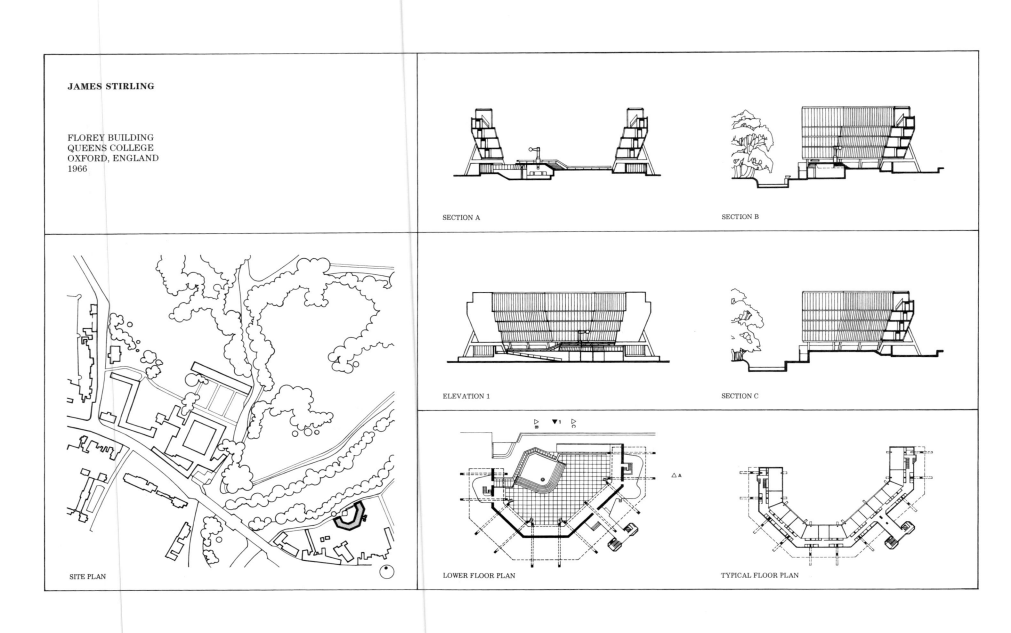

JAMES STIRLING

FLOREY BUILDING
QUEENS COLLEGE
OXFORD, ENGLAND
1966

SECTION A

SECTION B

ELEVATION 1

SECTION C

SITE PLAN

LOWER FLOOR PLAN

TYPICAL FLOOR PLAN

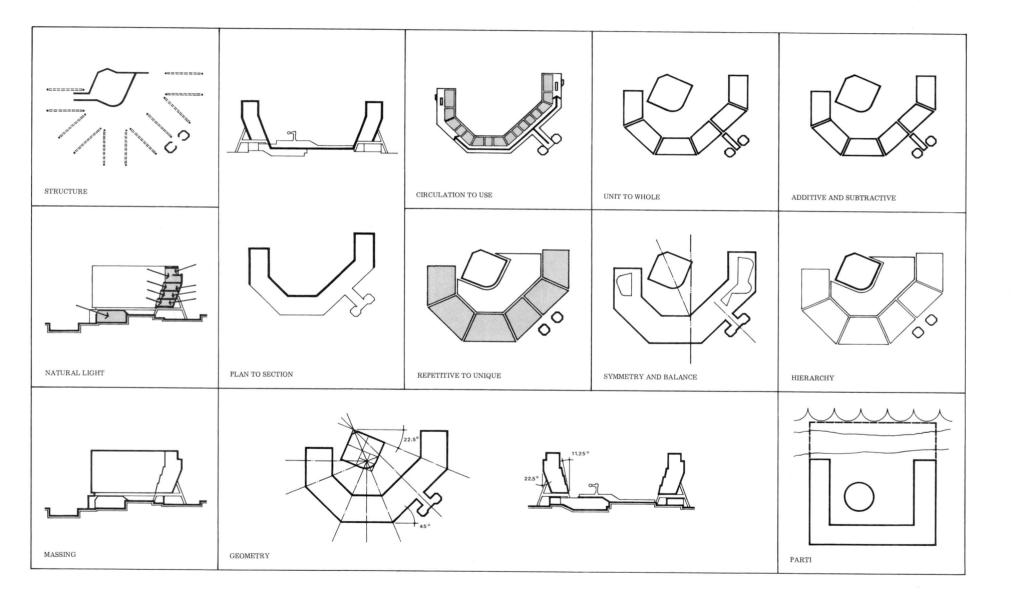

STRUCTURE

CIRCULATION TO USE

UNIT TO WHOLE

ADDITIVE AND SUBTRACTIVE

NATURAL LIGHT

PLAN TO SECTION

REPETITIVE TO UNIQUE

SYMMETRY AND BALANCE

HIERARCHY

MASSING

GEOMETRY

PARTI

165

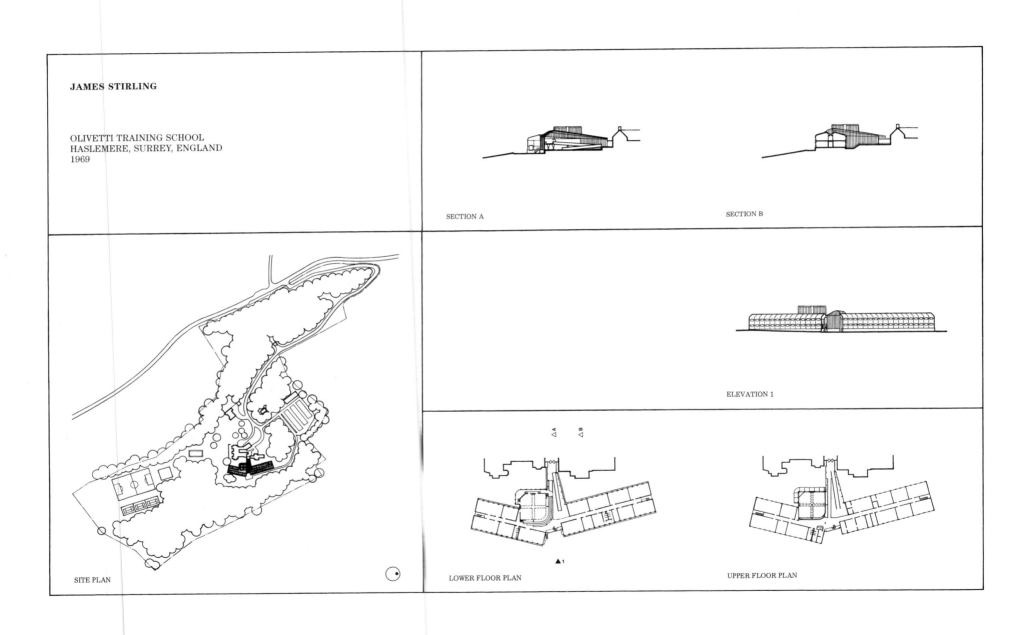

JAMES STIRLING

OLIVETTI TRAINING SCHOOL
HASLEMERE, SURREY, ENGLAND
1969

SECTION A

SECTION B

ELEVATION 1

SITE PLAN

LOWER FLOOR PLAN

UPPER FLOOR PLAN

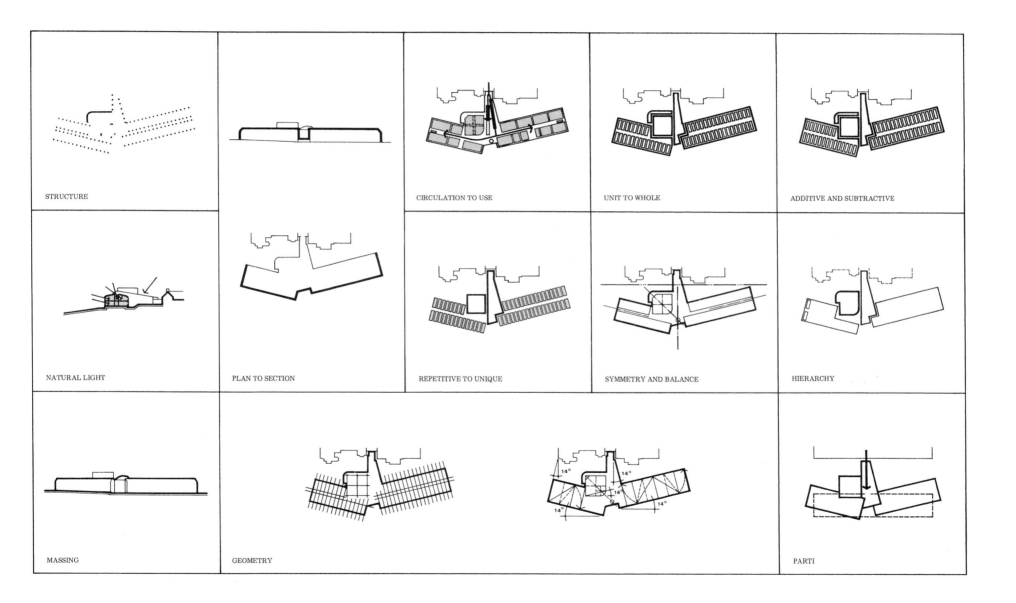

STRUCTURE

CIRCULATION TO USE

UNIT TO WHOLE

ADDITIVE AND SUBTRACTIVE

NATURAL LIGHT

PLAN TO SECTION

REPETITIVE TO UNIQUE

SYMMETRY AND BALANCE

HIERARCHY

MASSING

GEOMETRY

PARTI

LOUIS SULLIVAN

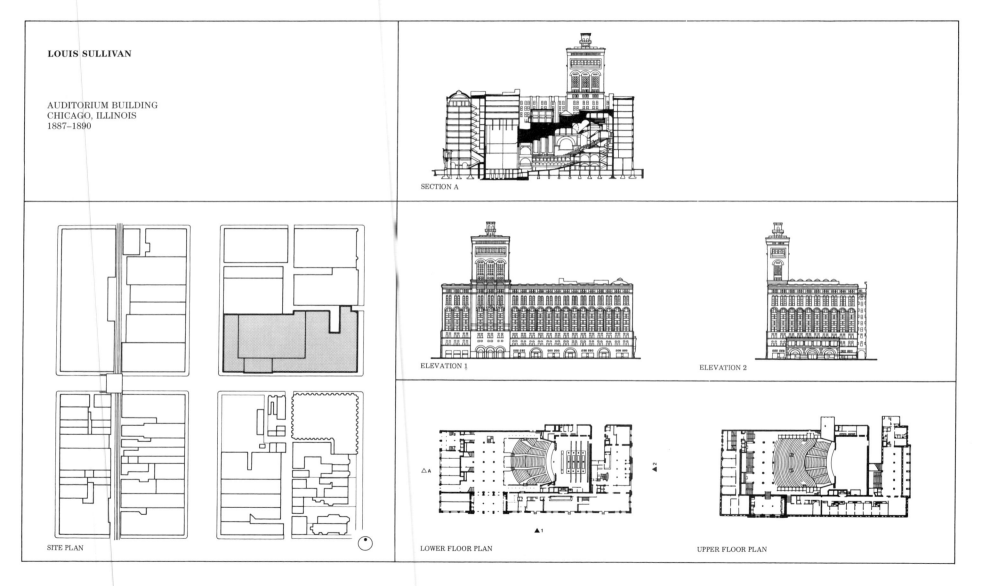

LOUIS SULLIVAN

AUDITORIUM BUILDING
CHICAGO, ILLINOIS
1887–1890

SECTION A

ELEVATION 1

ELEVATION 2

SITE PLAN

LOWER FLOOR PLAN

UPPER FLOOR PLAN

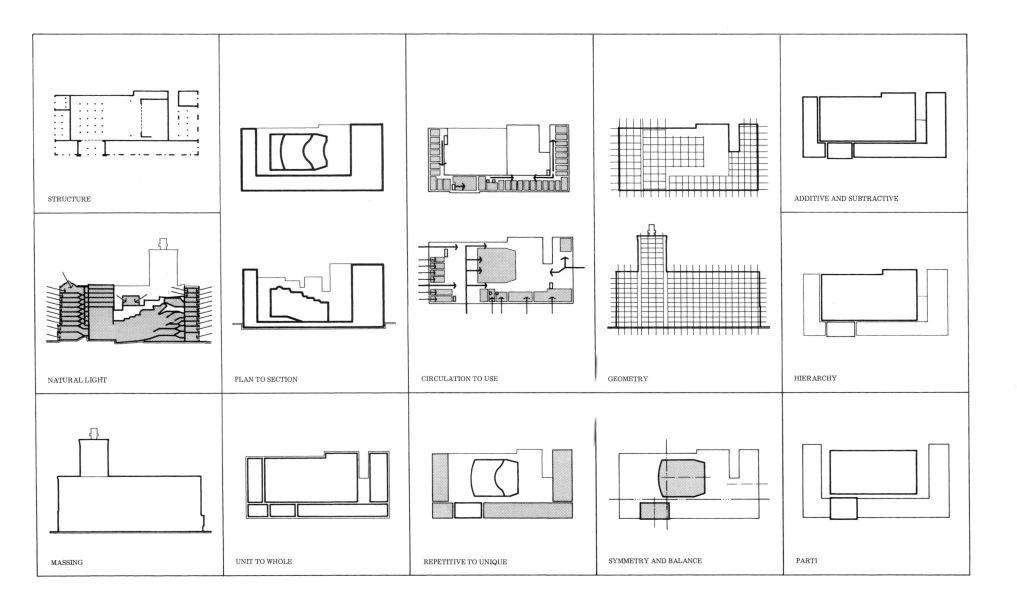

STRUCTURE

ADDITIVE AND SUBTRACTIVE

NATURAL LIGHT

PLAN TO SECTION

CIRCULATION TO USE

GEOMETRY

HIERARCHY

MASSING

UNIT TO WHOLE

REPETITIVE TO UNIQUE

SYMMETRY AND BALANCE

PARTI

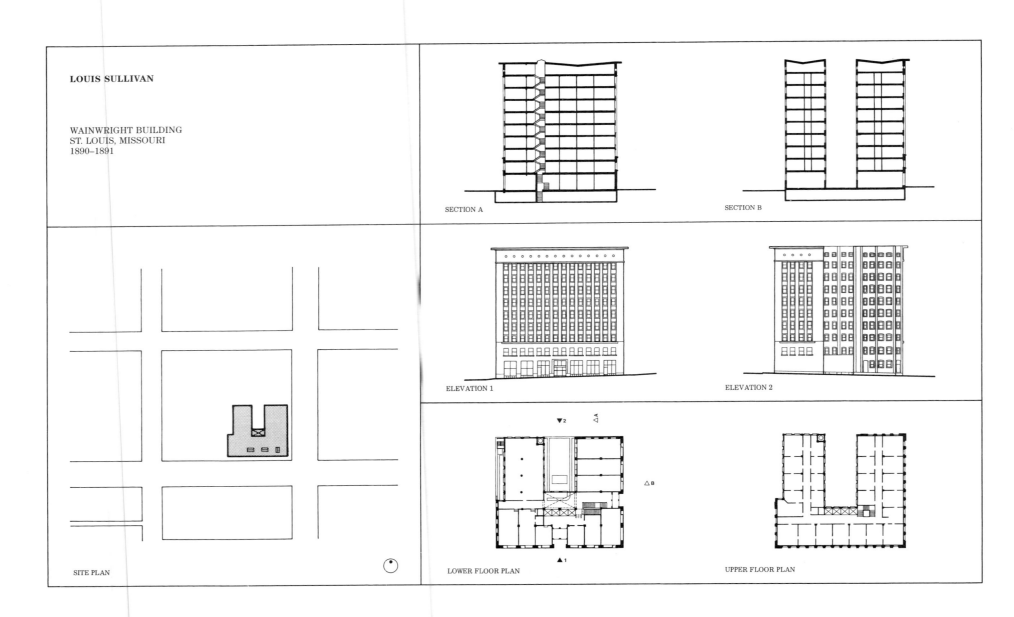

LOUIS SULLIVAN

WAINWRIGHT BUILDING
ST. LOUIS, MISSOURI
1890–1891

SECTION A

SECTION B

ELEVATION 1

ELEVATION 2

SITE PLAN

LOWER FLOOR PLAN

UPPER FLOOR PLAN

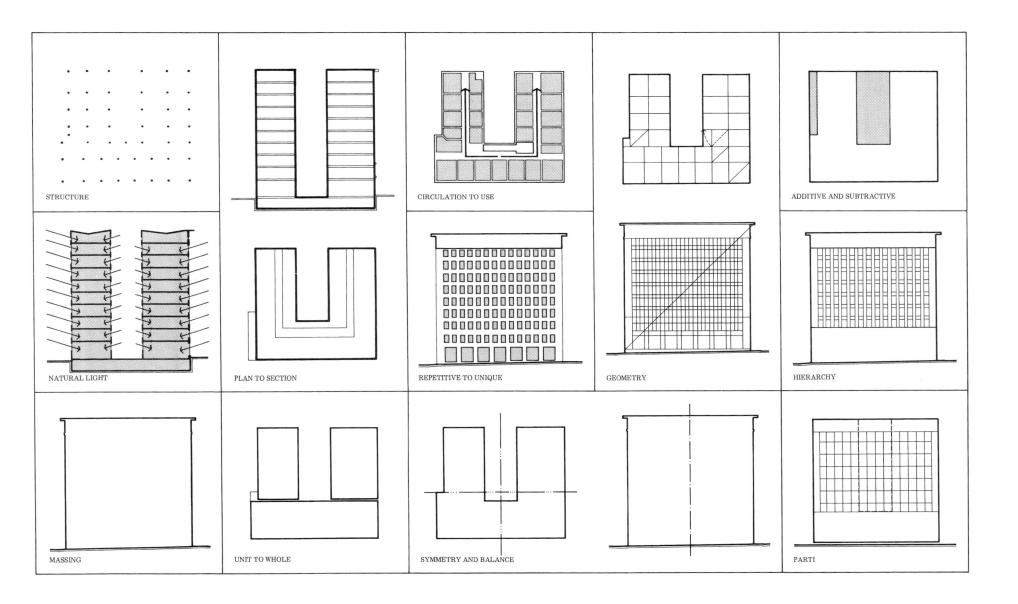

STRUCTURE

CIRCULATION TO USE

ADDITIVE AND SUBTRACTIVE

NATURAL LIGHT

PLAN TO SECTION

REPETITIVE TO UNIQUE

GEOMETRY

HIERARCHY

MASSING

UNIT TO WHOLE

SYMMETRY AND BALANCE

PARTI

171

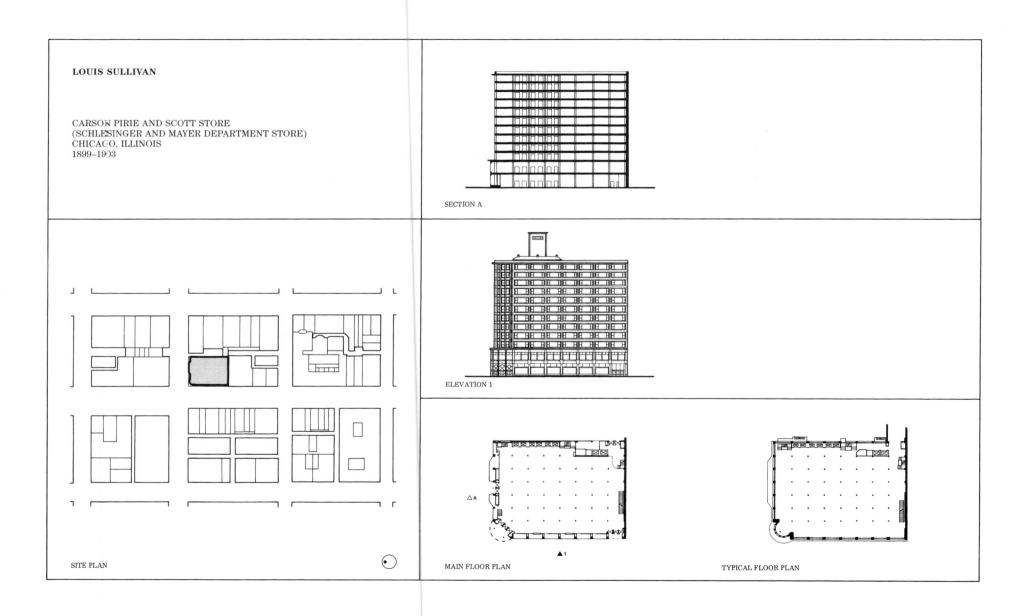

LOUIS SULLIVAN

CARSON PIRIE AND SCOTT STORE
(SCHLESINGER AND MAYER DEPARTMENT STORE)
CHICAGO, ILLINOIS
1899–1903

SECTION A

ELEVATION 1

SITE PLAN

MAIN FLOOR PLAN

TYPICAL FLOOR PLAN

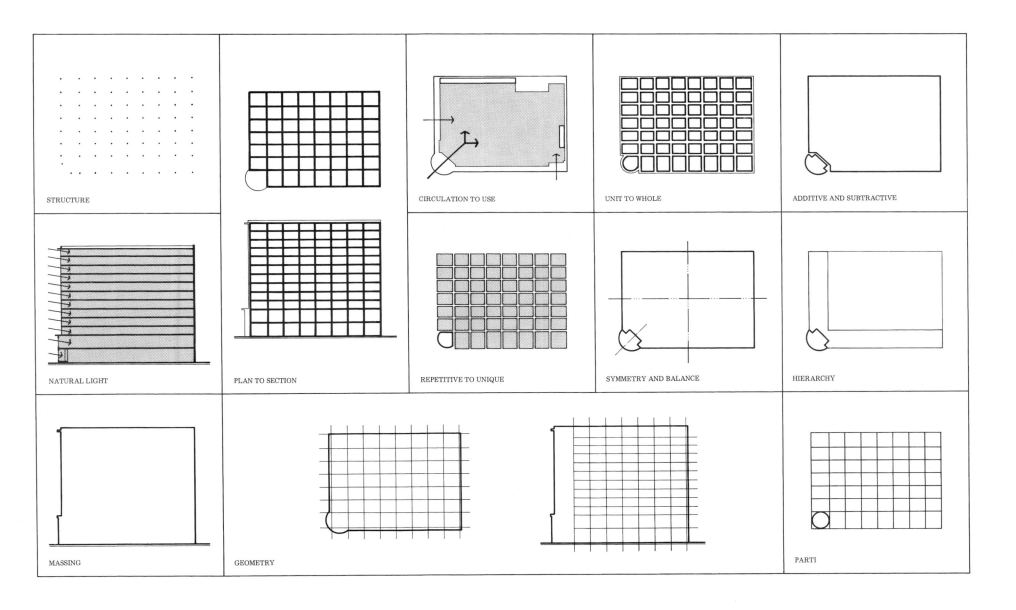

STRUCTURE

CIRCULATION TO USE

UNIT TO WHOLE

ADDITIVE AND SUBTRACTIVE

NATURAL LIGHT

PLAN TO SECTION

REPETITIVE TO UNIQUE

SYMMETRY AND BALANCE

HIERARCHY

MASSING

GEOMETRY

PARTI

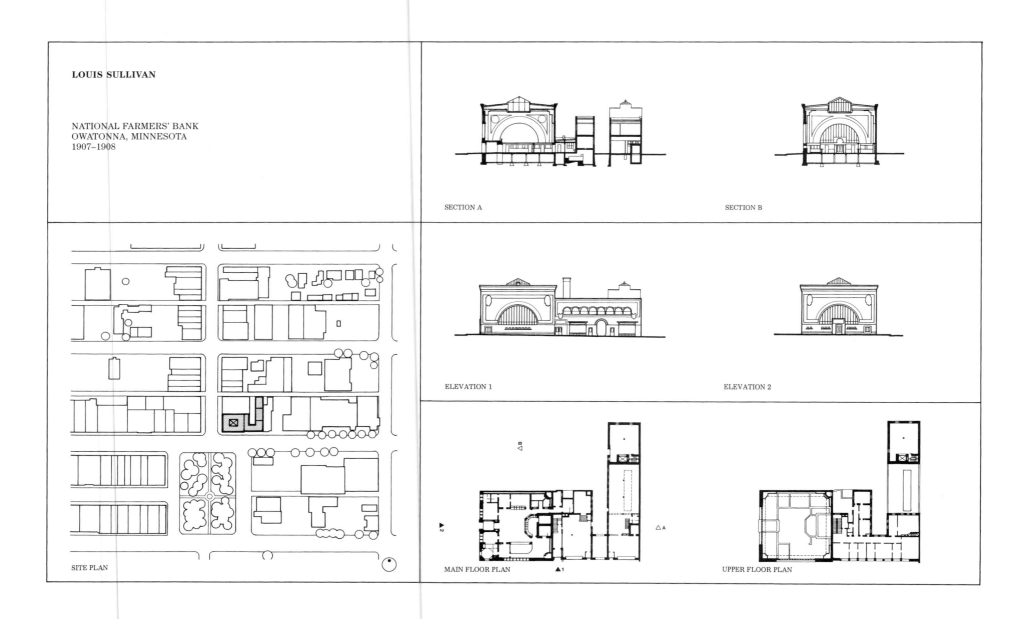

LOUIS SULLIVAN

NATIONAL FARMERS' BANK
OWATONNA, MINNESOTA
1907–1908

SECTION A

SECTION B

ELEVATION 1

ELEVATION 2

SITE PLAN

MAIN FLOOR PLAN

UPPER FLOOR PLAN

174

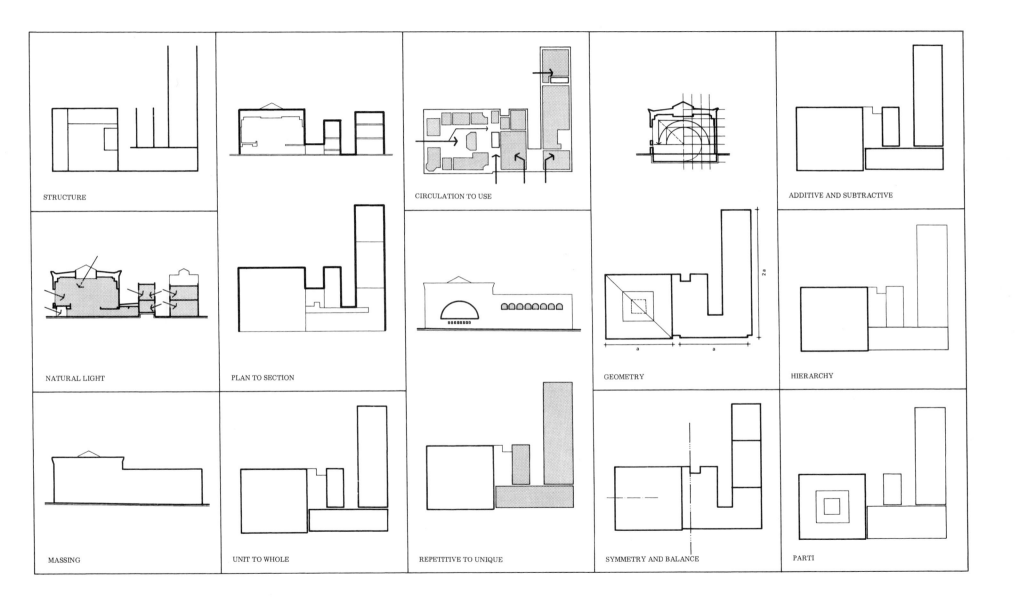

STRUCTURE

CIRCULATION TO USE

ADDITIVE AND SUBTRACTIVE

NATURAL LIGHT

PLAN TO SECTION

GEOMETRY

HIERARCHY

MASSING

UNIT TO WHOLE

REPETITIVE TO UNIQUE

SYMMETRY AND BALANCE

PARTI

175

YOSHIO TANIGUCHI

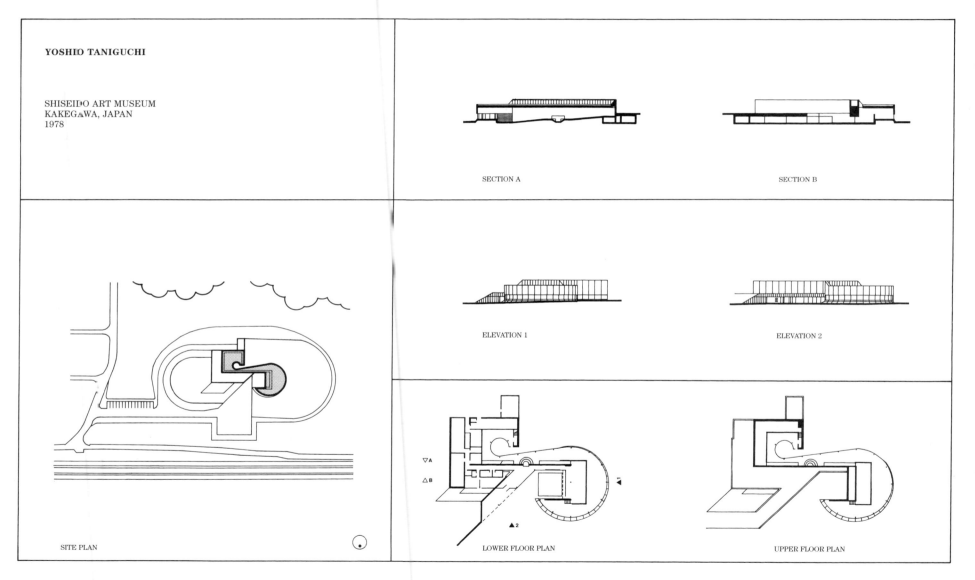

YOSHIO TANIGUCHI

SHISEIDO ART MUSEUM
KAKEGAWA, JAPAN
1978

SECTION A

SECTION B

ELEVATION 1

ELEVATION 2

SITE PLAN

LOWER FLOOR PLAN

UPPER FLOOR PLAN

176

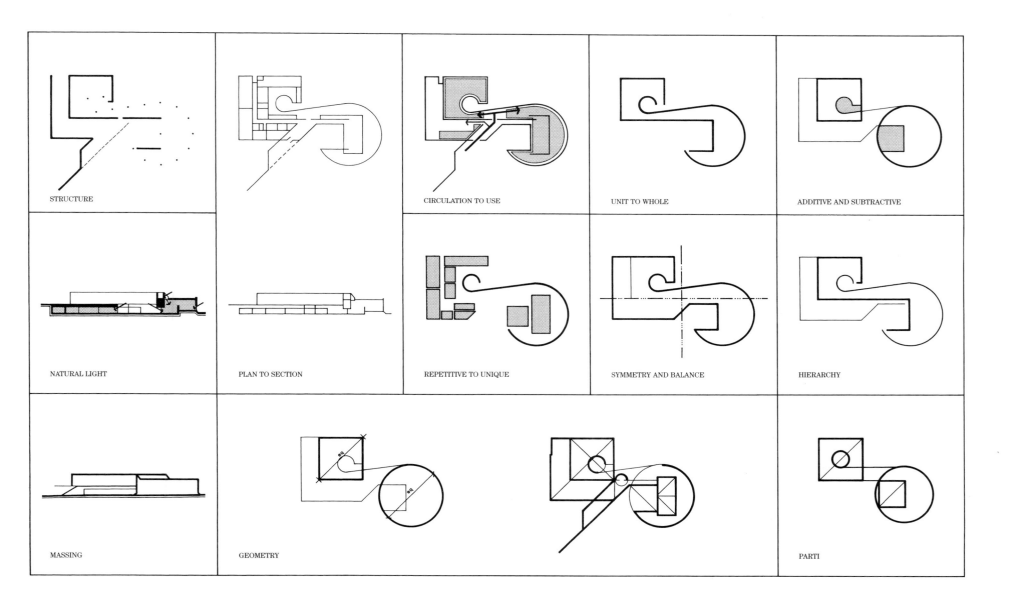

STRUCTURE

CIRCULATION TO USE

UNIT TO WHOLE

ADDITIVE AND SUBTRACTIVE

NATURAL LIGHT

PLAN TO SECTION

REPETITIVE TO UNIQUE

SYMMETRY AND BALANCE

HIERARCHY

MASSING

GEOMETRY

PARTI

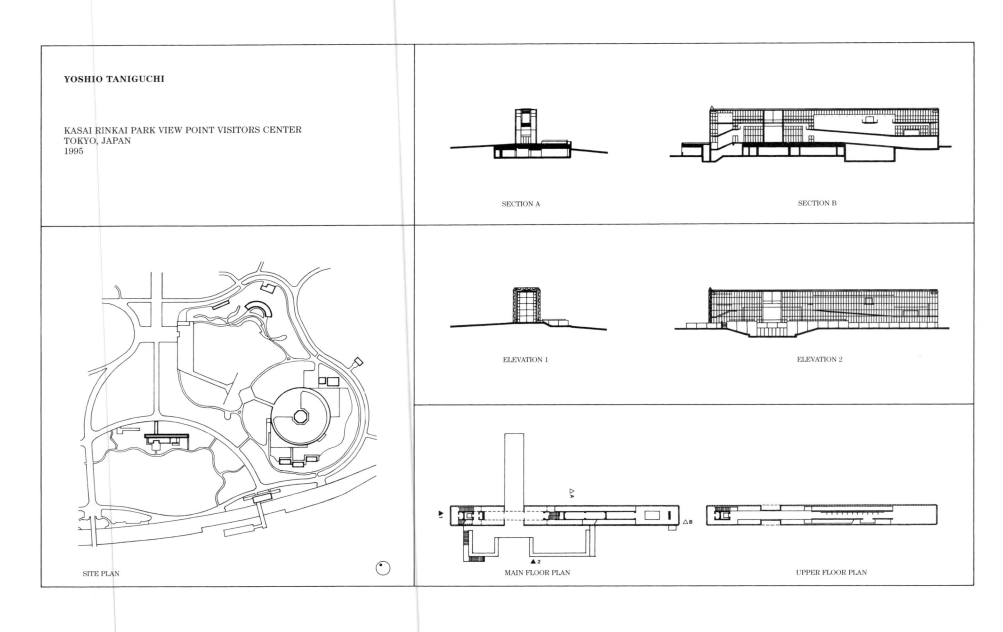

YOSHIO TANIGUCHI

KASAI RINKAI PARK VIEW POINT VISITORS CENTER
TOKYO, JAPAN
1995

SECTION A

SECTION B

ELEVATION 1

ELEVATION 2

SITE PLAN

MAIN FLOOR PLAN

UPPER FLOOR PLAN

178

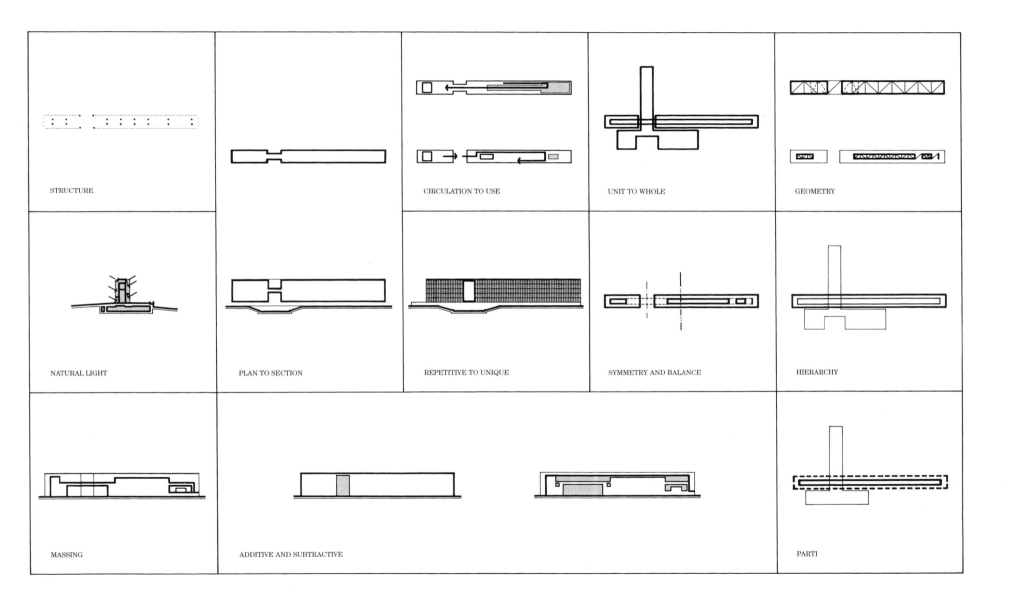

STRUCTURE

CIRCULATION TO USE

UNIT TO WHOLE

GEOMETRY

NATURAL LIGHT

PLAN TO SECTION

REPETITIVE TO UNIQUE

SYMMETRY AND BALANCE

HIERARCHY

MASSING

ADDITIVE AND SUBTRACTIVE

PARTI

GIUSEPPE TERRAGNI

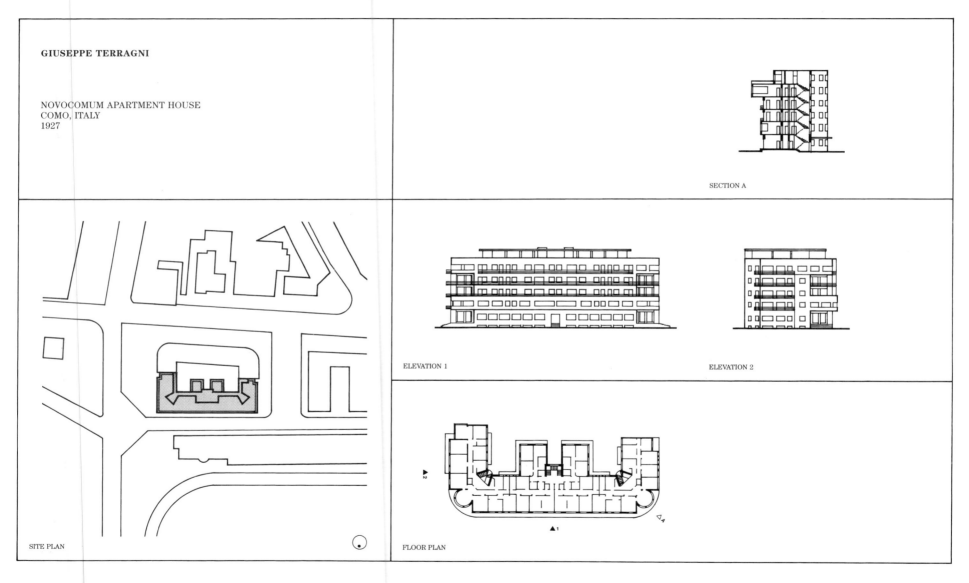

GIUSEPPE TERRAGNI

NOVOCOMUM APARTMENT HOUSE
COMO, ITALY
1927

SECTION A

ELEVATION 1

ELEVATION 2

SITE PLAN

FLOOR PLAN

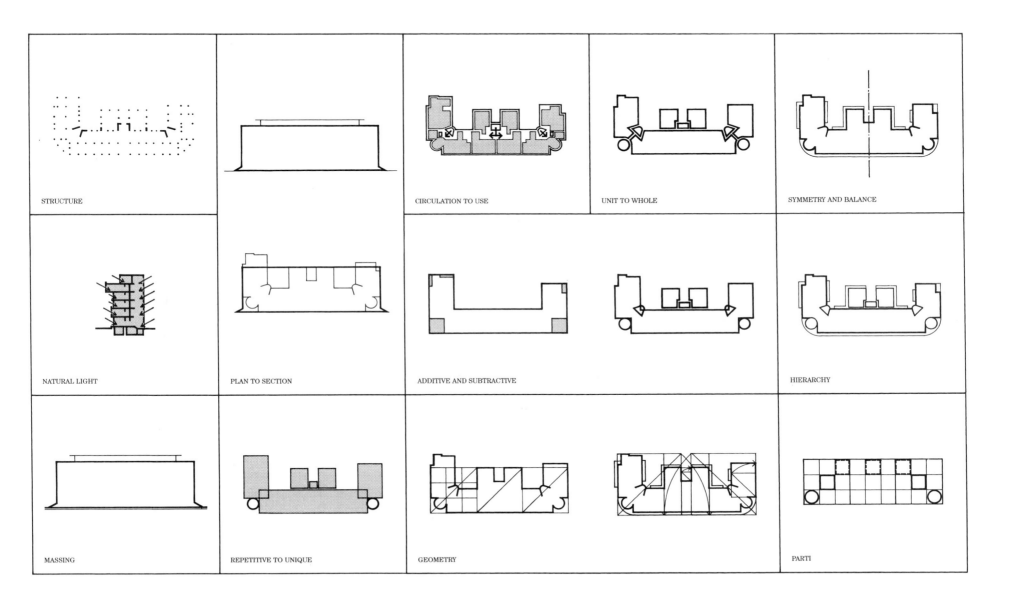

STRUCTURE

CIRCULATION TO USE

UNIT TO WHOLE

SYMMETRY AND BALANCE

NATURAL LIGHT

PLAN TO SECTION

ADDITIVE AND SUBTRACTIVE

HIERARCHY

MASSING

REPETITIVE TO UNIQUE

GEOMETRY

PARTI

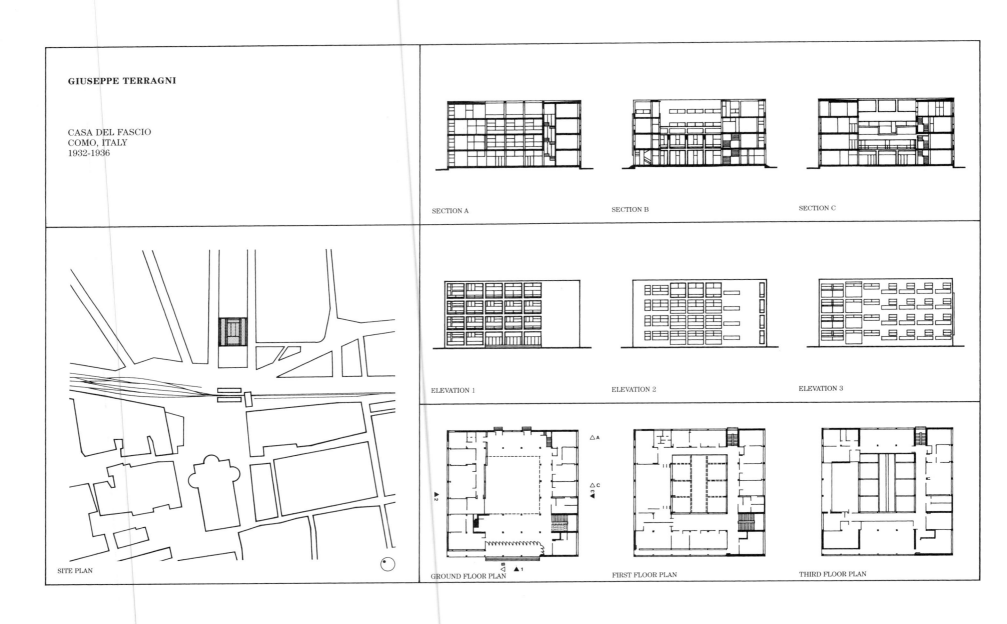

GIUSEPPE TERRAGNI

CASA DEL FASCIO
COMO, ITALY
1932-1936

SECTION A

SECTION B

SECTION C

ELEVATION 1

ELEVATION 2

ELEVATION 3

SITE PLAN

GROUND FLOOR PLAN

FIRST FLOOR PLAN

THIRD FLOOR PLAN

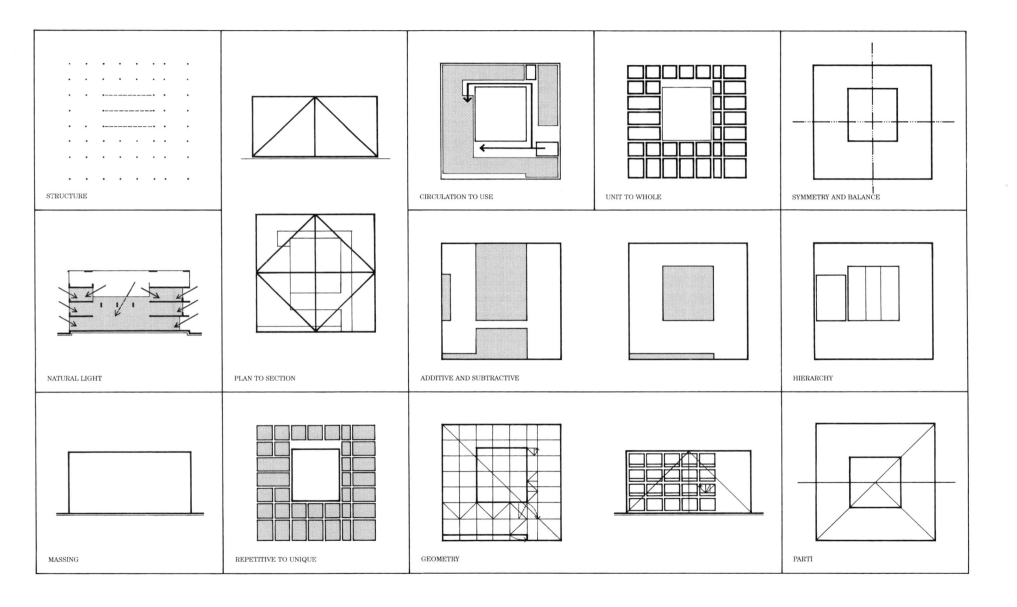

STRUCTURE

CIRCULATION TO USE

UNIT TO WHOLE

SYMMETRY AND BALANCE

NATURAL LIGHT

PLAN TO SECTION

ADDITIVE AND SUBTRACTIVE

HIERARCHY

MASSING

REPETITIVE TO UNIQUE

GEOMETRY

PARTI

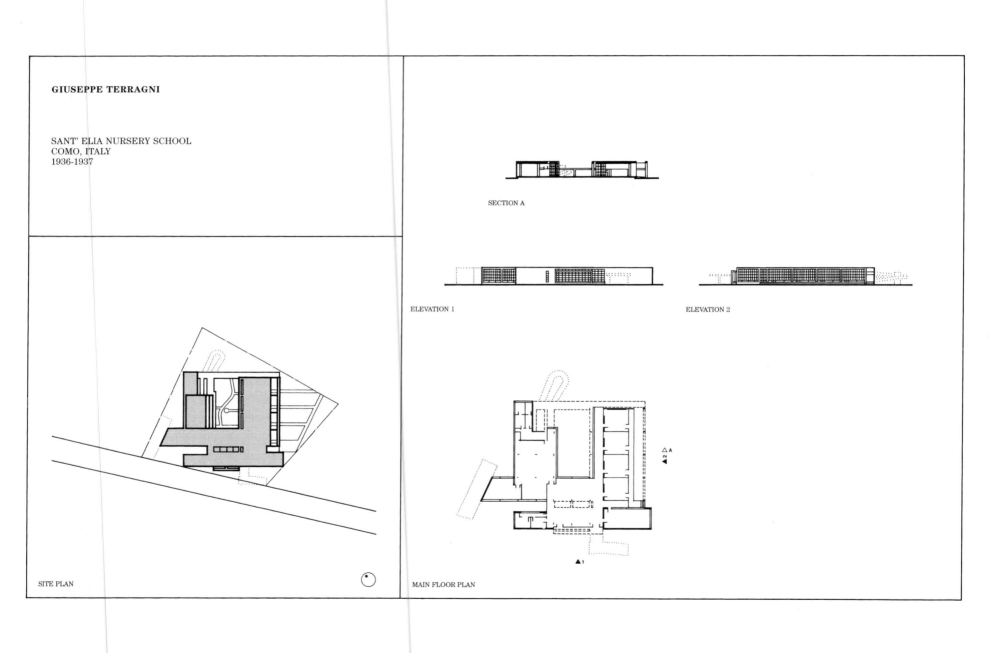

GIUSEPPE TERRAGNI

SANT' ELIA NURSERY SCHOOL
COMO, ITALY
1936-1937

SECTION A

ELEVATION 1

ELEVATION 2

SITE PLAN

MAIN FLOOR PLAN

184

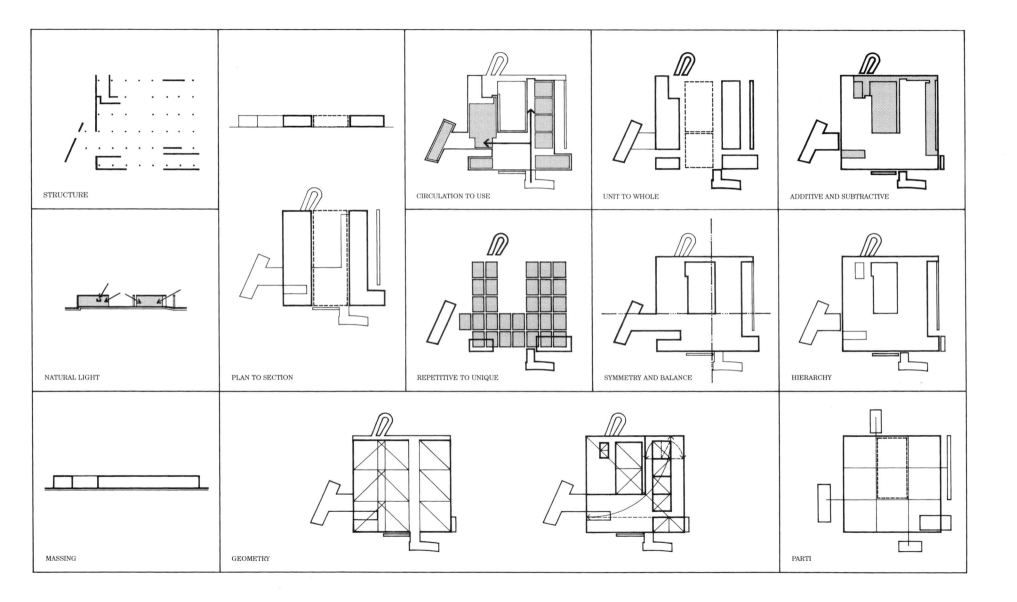

STRUCTURE

CIRCULATION TO USE

UNIT TO WHOLE

ADDITIVE AND SUBTRACTIVE

NATURAL LIGHT

PLAN TO SECTION

REPETITIVE TO UNIQUE

SYMMETRY AND BALANCE

HIERARCHY

MASSING

GEOMETRY

PARTI

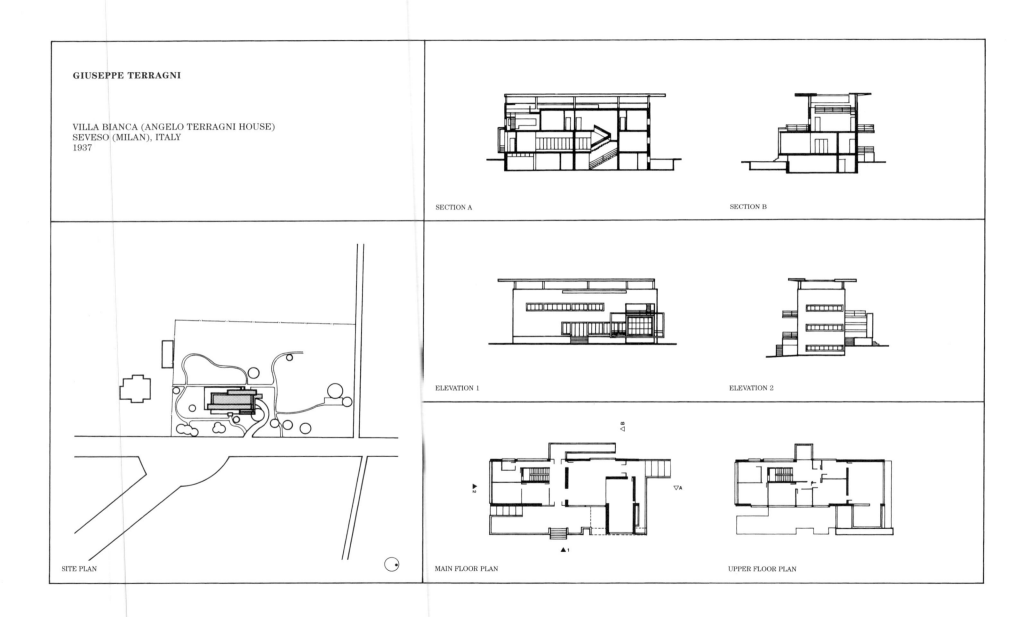

GIUSEPPE TERRAGNI

VILLA BIANCA (ANGELO TERRAGNI HOUSE)
SEVESO (MILAN), ITALY
1937

SECTION A

SECTION B

ELEVATION 1

ELEVATION 2

SITE PLAN

MAIN FLOOR PLAN

UPPER FLOOR PLAN

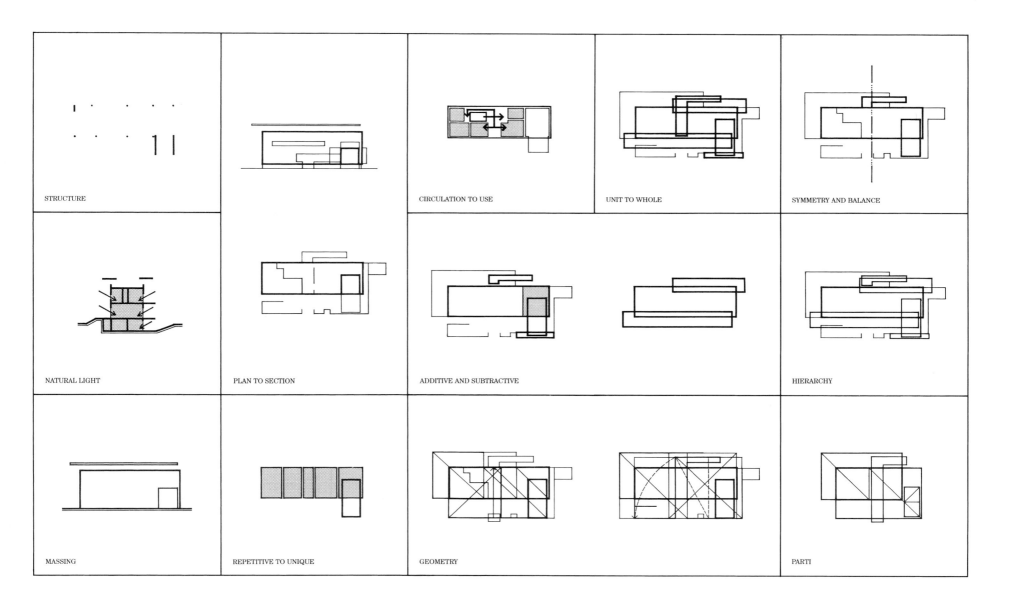

STRUCTURE

CIRCULATION TO USE

UNIT TO WHOLE

SYMMETRY AND BALANCE

NATURAL LIGHT

PLAN TO SECTION

ADDITIVE AND SUBTRACTIVE

HIERARCHY

MASSING

REPETITIVE TO UNIQUE

GEOMETRY

PARTI

LUDWIG MIES VAN DER ROHE

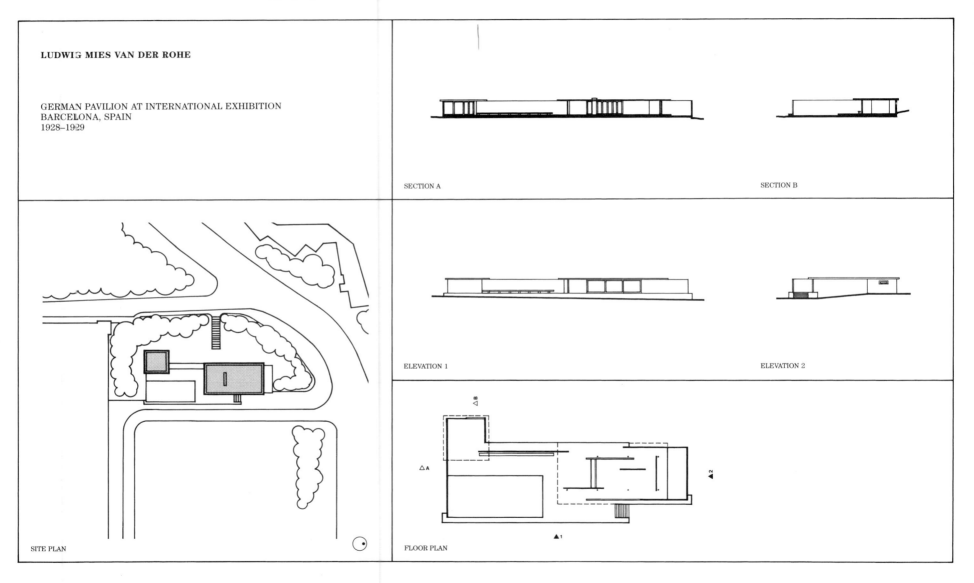

LUDWIG MIES VAN DER ROHE

GERMAN PAVILION AT INTERNATIONAL EXHIBITION
BARCELONA, SPAIN
1928–1929

SECTION A

SECTION B

ELEVATION 1

ELEVATION 2

SITE PLAN

FLOOR PLAN

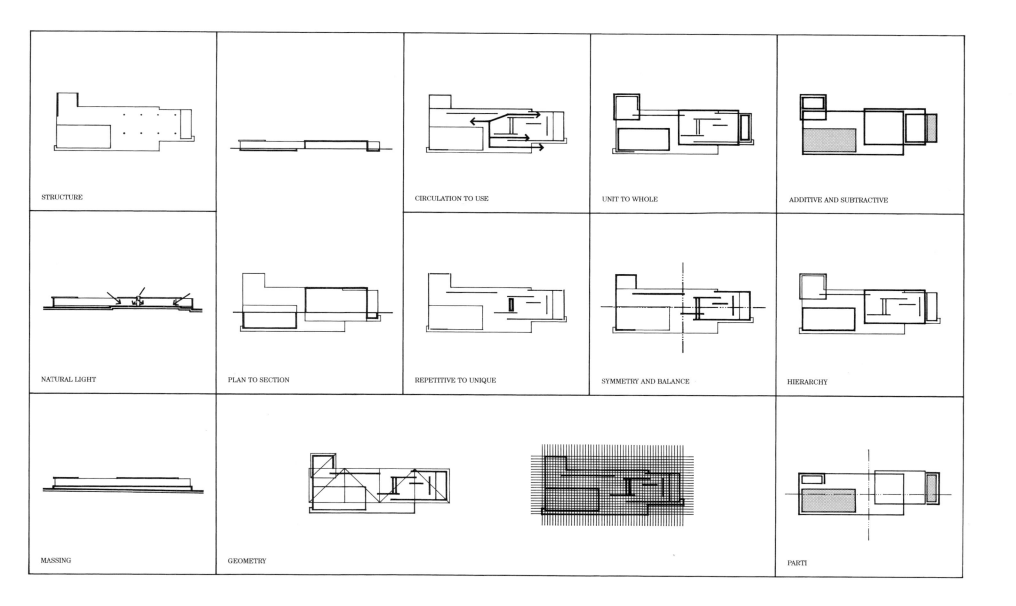

STRUCTURE

CIRCULATION TO USE

UNIT TO WHOLE

ADDITIVE AND SUBTRACTIVE

NATURAL LIGHT

PLAN TO SECTION

REPETITIVE TO UNIQUE

SYMMETRY AND BALANCE

HIERARCHY

MASSING

GEOMETRY

PARTI

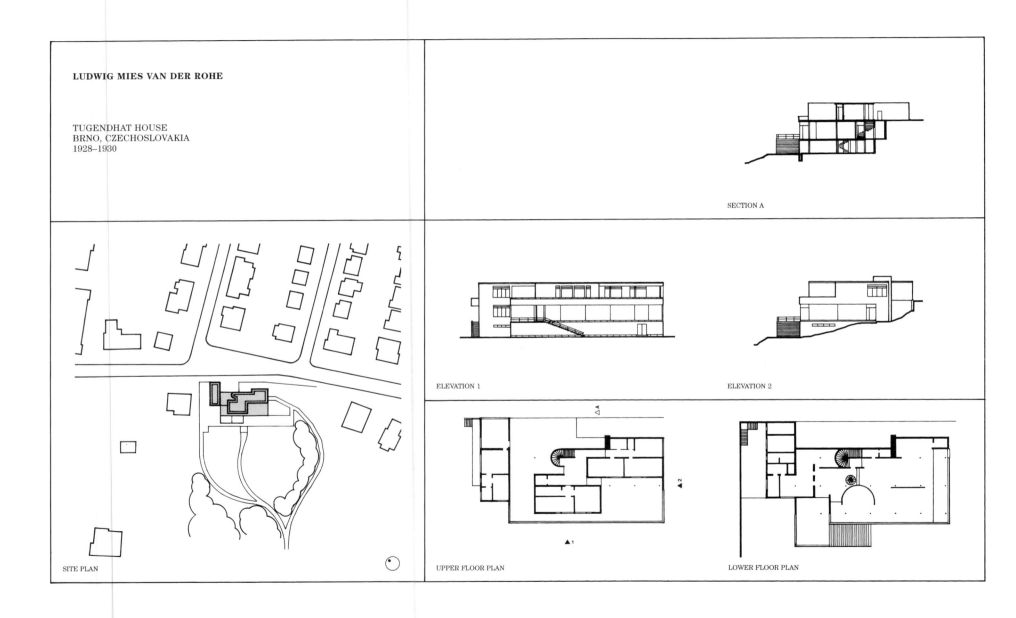

LUDWIG MIES VAN DER ROHE

TUGENDHAT HOUSE
BRNO, CZECHOSLOVAKIA
1928–1930

SECTION A

ELEVATION 1

ELEVATION 2

SITE PLAN

UPPER FLOOR PLAN

LOWER FLOOR PLAN

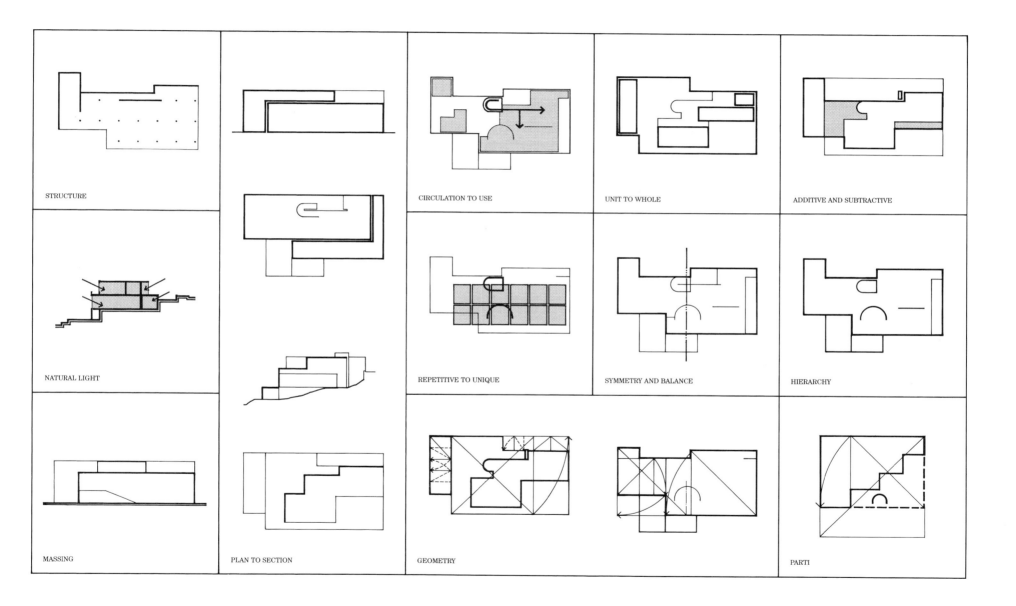

STRUCTURE

NATURAL LIGHT

MASSING

CIRCULATION TO USE

REPETITIVE TO UNIQUE

PLAN TO SECTION

UNIT TO WHOLE

SYMMETRY AND BALANCE

GEOMETRY

ADDITIVE AND SUBTRACTIVE

HIERARCHY

PARTI

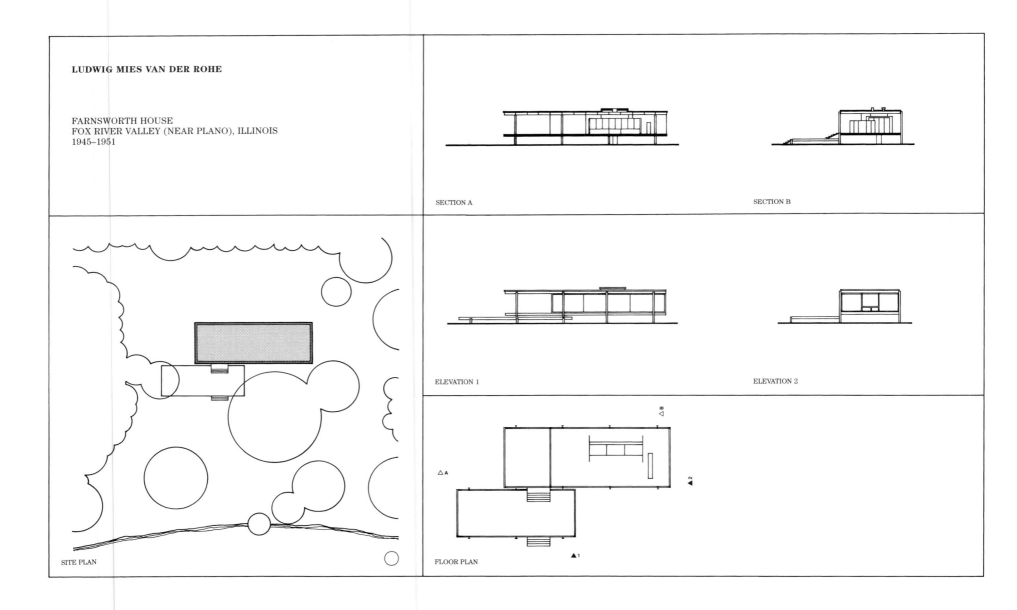

LUDWIG MIES VAN DER ROHE

FARNSWORTH HOUSE
FOX RIVER VALLEY (NEAR PLANO), ILLINOIS
1945–1951

SECTION A

SECTION B

ELEVATION 1

ELEVATION 2

SITE PLAN

FLOOR PLAN

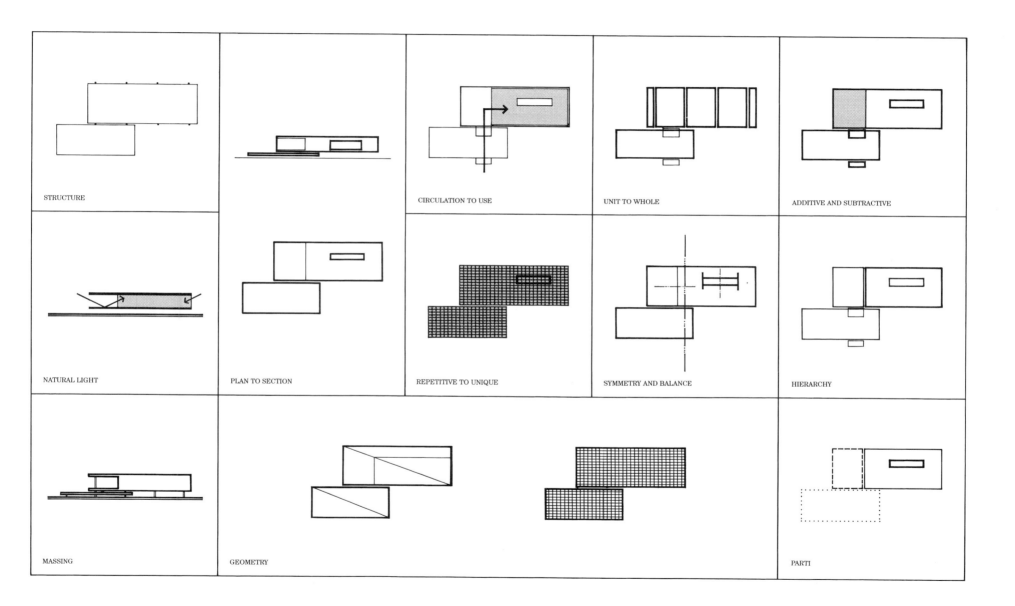

STRUCTURE

CIRCULATION TO USE

UNIT TO WHOLE

ADDITIVE AND SUBTRACTIVE

NATURAL LIGHT

PLAN TO SECTION

REPETITIVE TO UNIQUE

SYMMETRY AND BALANCE

HIERARCHY

MASSING

GEOMETRY

PARTI

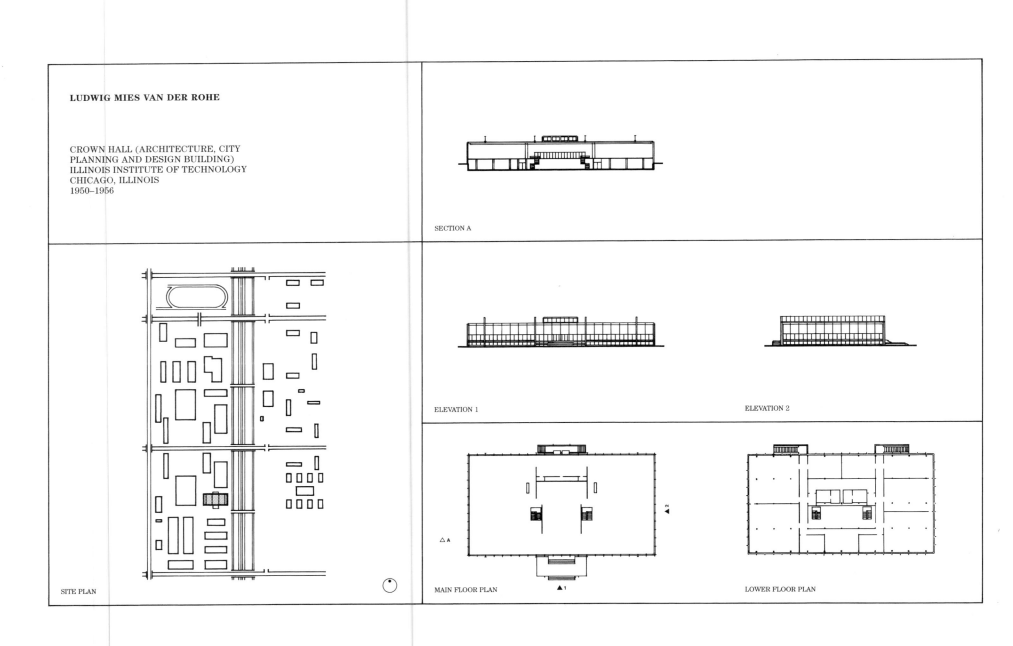

LUDWIG MIES VAN DER ROHE

CROWN HALL (ARCHITECTURE, CITY
PLANNING AND DESIGN BUILDING)
ILLINOIS INSTITUTE OF TECHNOLOGY
CHICAGO, ILLINOIS
1950–1956

SECTION A

ELEVATION 1

ELEVATION 2

SITE PLAN

MAIN FLOOR PLAN

LOWER FLOOR PLAN

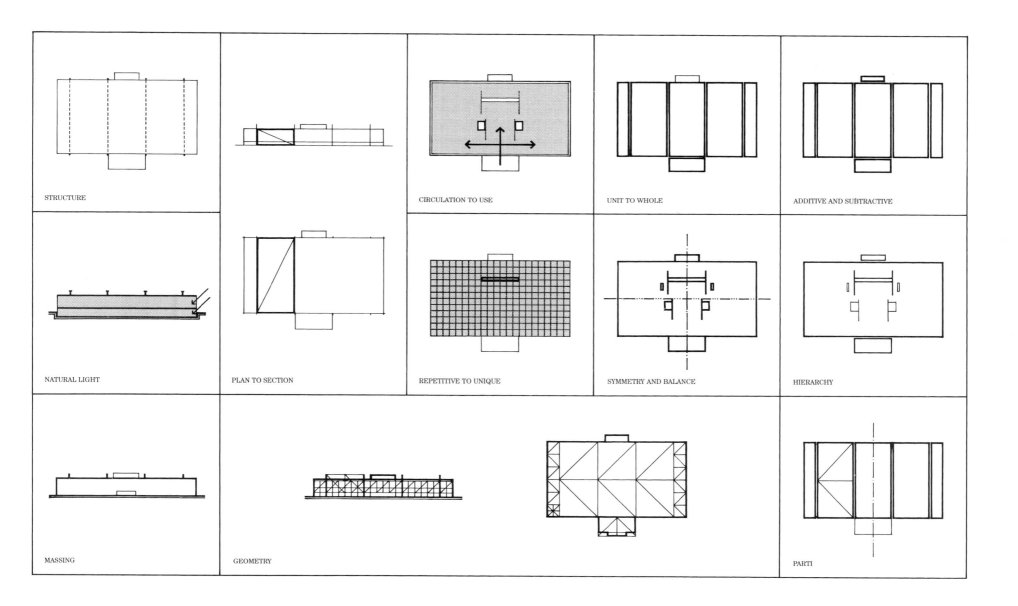

STRUCTURE

CIRCULATION TO USE

UNIT TO WHOLE

ADDITIVE AND SUBTRACTIVE

NATURAL LIGHT

PLAN TO SECTION

REPETITIVE TO UNIQUE

SYMMETRY AND BALANCE

HIERARCHY

MASSING

GEOMETRY

PARTI

ROBERT VENTURI

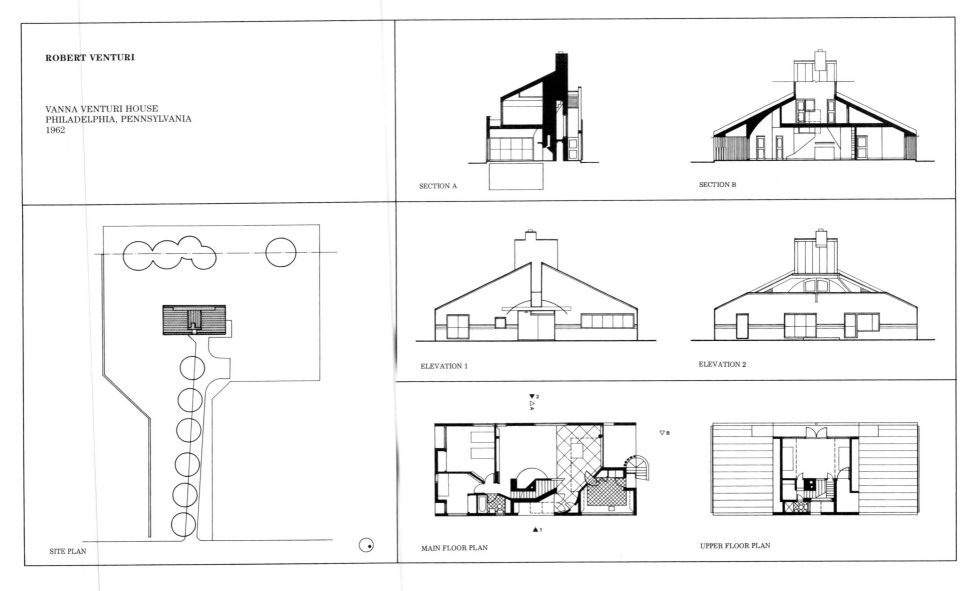

ROBERT VENTURI

VANNA VENTURI HOUSE
PHILADELPHIA, PENNSYLVANIA
1962

SECTION A

SECTION B

ELEVATION 1

ELEVATION 2

SITE PLAN

MAIN FLOOR PLAN

UPPER FLOOR PLAN

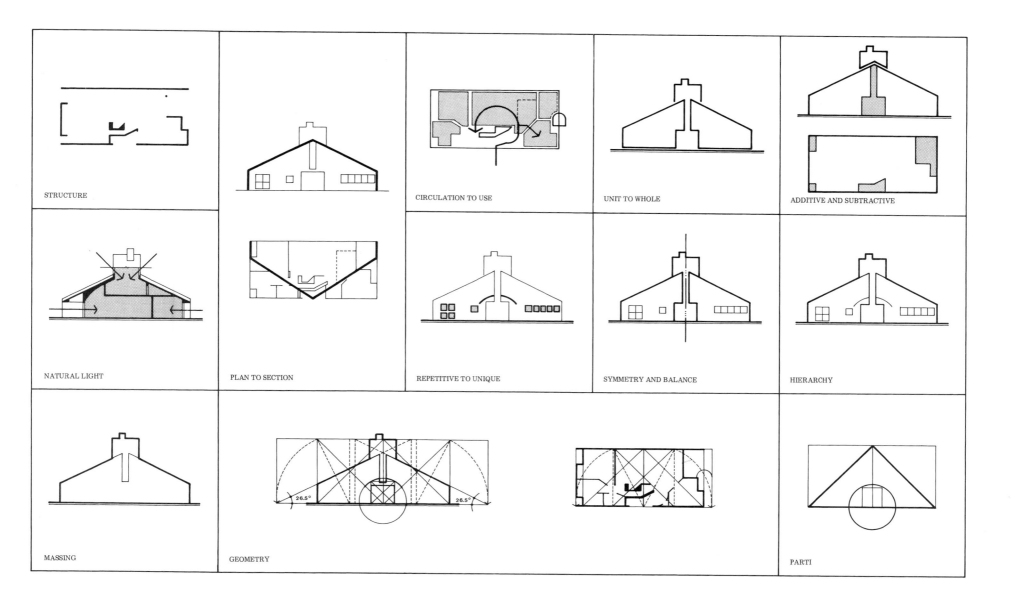

STRUCTURE

CIRCULATION TO USE

UNIT TO WHOLE

ADDITIVE AND SUBTRACTIVE

NATURAL LIGHT

PLAN TO SECTION

REPETITIVE TO UNIQUE

SYMMETRY AND BALANCE

HIERARCHY

MASSING

GEOMETRY

26.5°   26.5°

PARTI

197

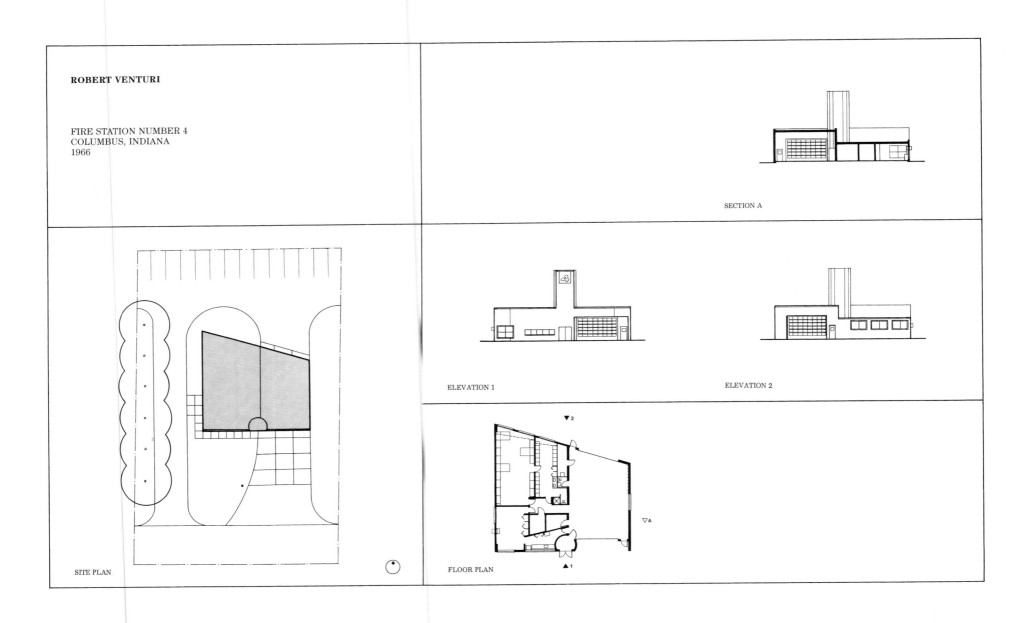

ROBERT VENTURI

FIRE STATION NUMBER 4
COLUMBUS, INDIANA
1966

SECTION A

ELEVATION 1

ELEVATION 2

SITE PLAN

FLOOR PLAN

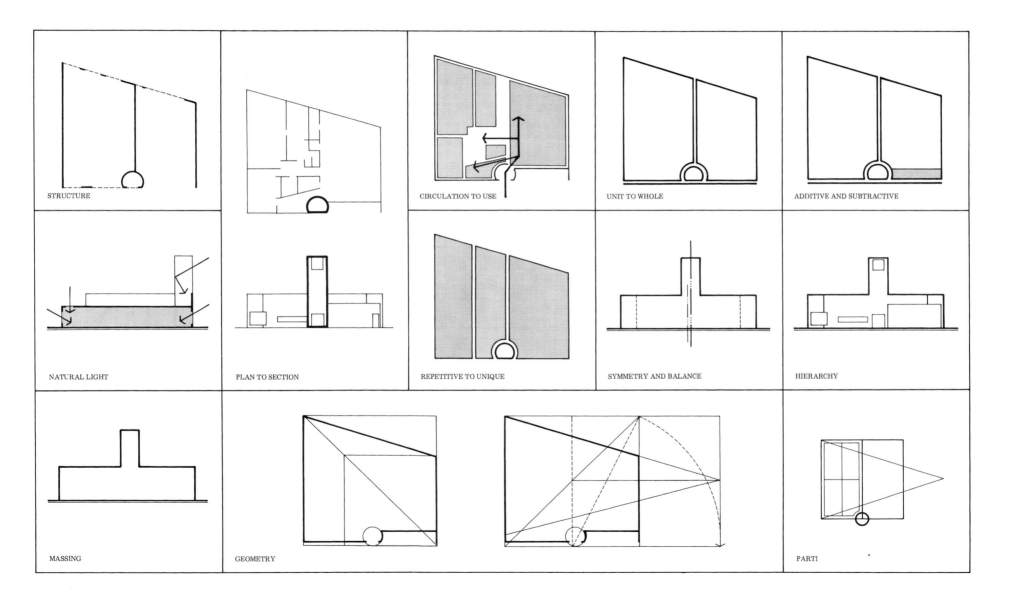

STRUCTURE

CIRCULATION TO USE

UNIT TO WHOLE

ADDITIVE AND SUBTRACTIVE

NATURAL LIGHT

PLAN TO SECTION

REPETITIVE TO UNIQUE

SYMMETRY AND BALANCE

HIERARCHY

MASSING

GEOMETRY

PARTI

199

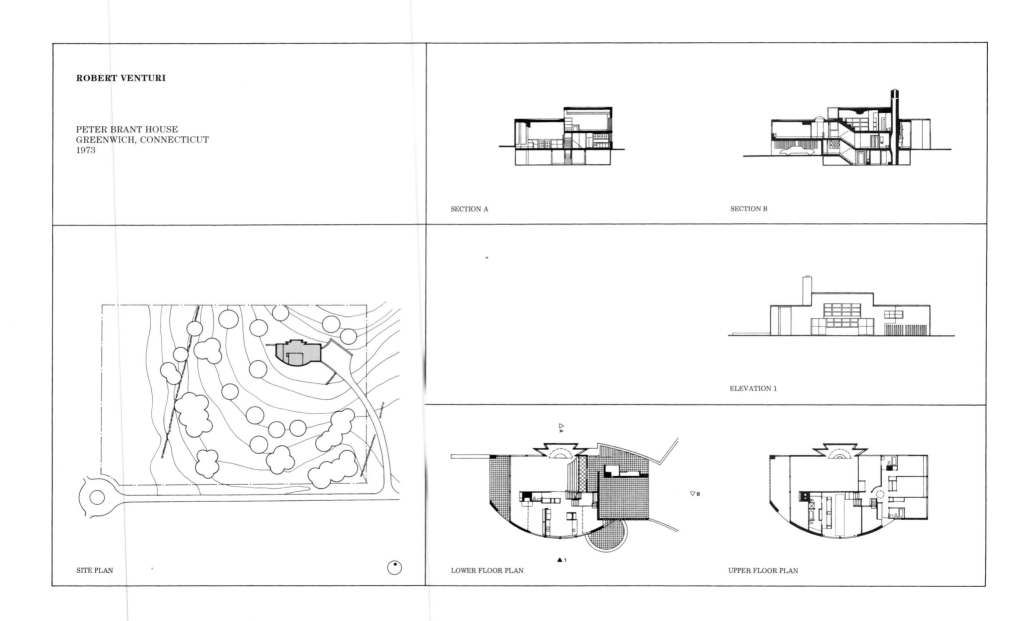

ROBERT VENTURI

PETER BRANT HOUSE
GREENWICH, CONNECTICUT
1973

SECTION A

SECTION B

ELEVATION 1

SITE PLAN

LOWER FLOOR PLAN

UPPER FLOOR PLAN

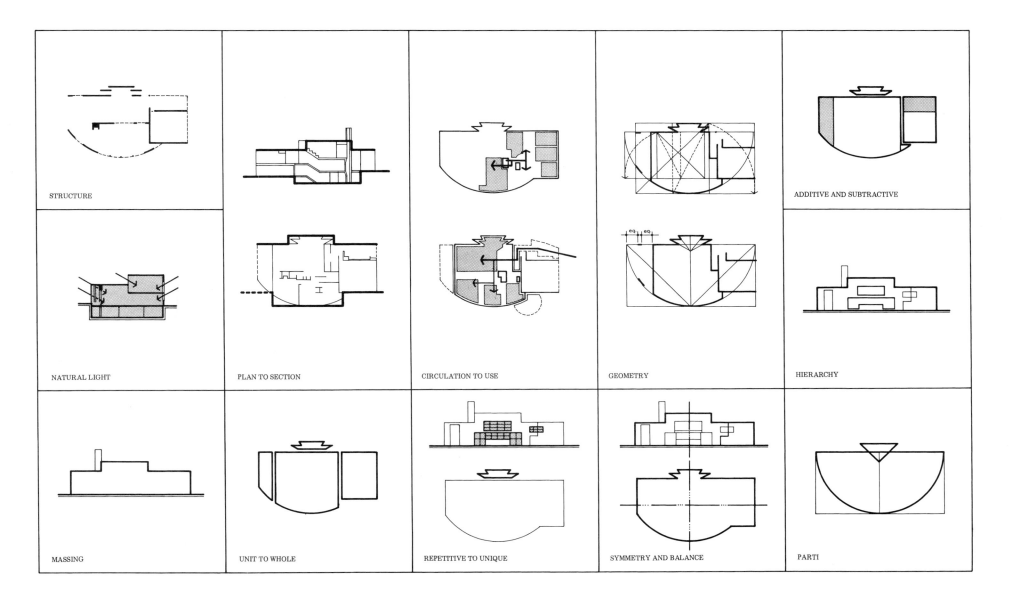

STRUCTURE

NATURAL LIGHT

PLAN TO SECTION

CIRCULATION TO USE

GEOMETRY

ADDITIVE AND SUBTRACTIVE

HIERARCHY

MASSING

UNIT TO WHOLE

REPETITIVE TO UNIQUE

SYMMETRY AND BALANCE

PARTI

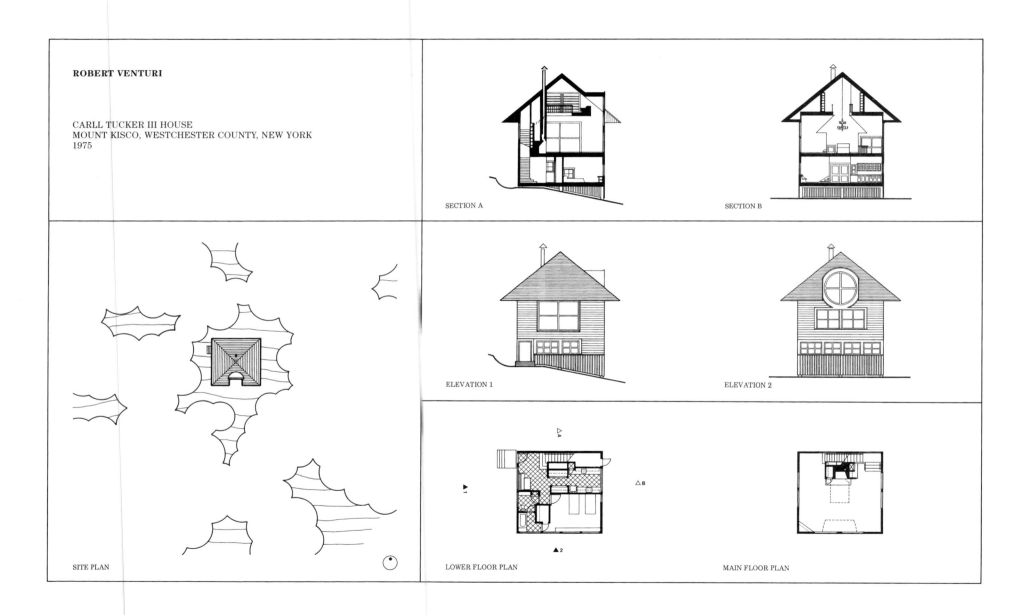

ROBERT VENTURI

CARLL TUCKER III HOUSE
MOUNT KISCO, WESTCHESTER COUNTY, NEW YORK
1975

SECTION A

SECTION B

ELEVATION 1

ELEVATION 2

SITE PLAN

LOWER FLOOR PLAN

MAIN FLOOR PLAN

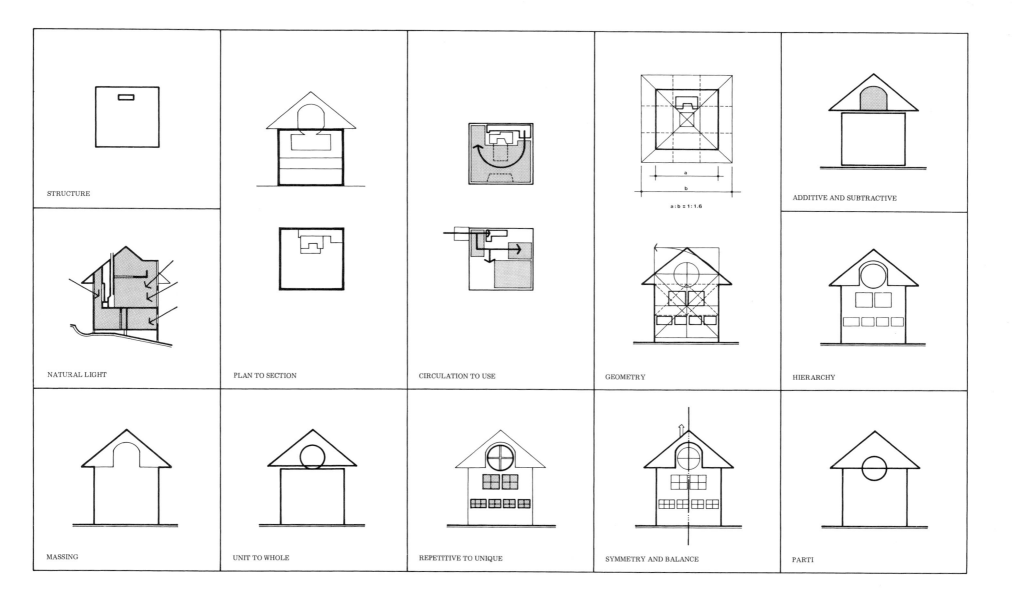

STRUCTURE

NATURAL LIGHT

PLAN TO SECTION

CIRCULATION TO USE

GEOMETRY

a : b = 1 : 1.6

ADDITIVE AND SUBTRACTIVE

HIERARCHY

MASSING

UNIT TO WHOLE

REPETITIVE TO UNIQUE

SYMMETRY AND BALANCE

PARTI

FRANK LLOYD WRIGHT

UNITY TEMPLE
OAK PARK, ILLINOIS
1906

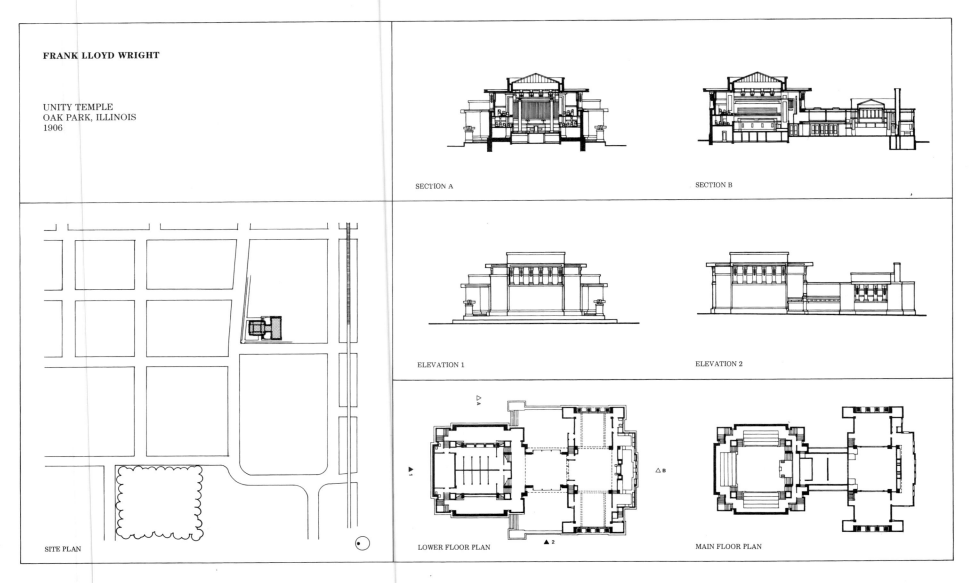

SECTION A

SECTION B

ELEVATION 1

ELEVATION 2

SITE PLAN

LOWER FLOOR PLAN

MAIN FLOOR PLAN

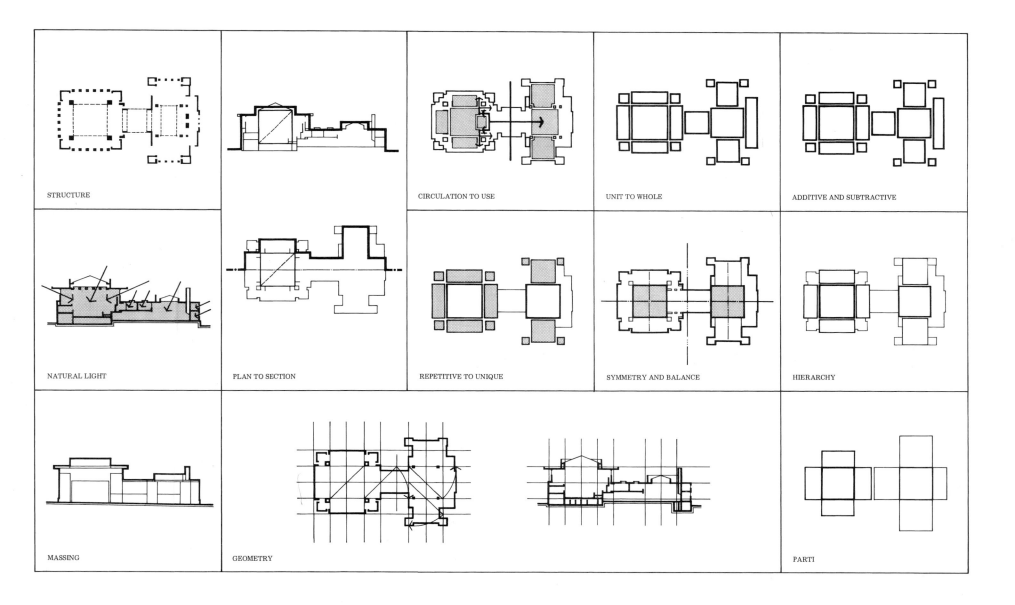

STRUCTURE

CIRCULATION TO USE

UNIT TO WHOLE

ADDITIVE AND SUBTRACTIVE

NATURAL LIGHT

PLAN TO SECTION

REPETITIVE TO UNIQUE

SYMMETRY AND BALANCE

HIERARCHY

MASSING

GEOMETRY

PARTI

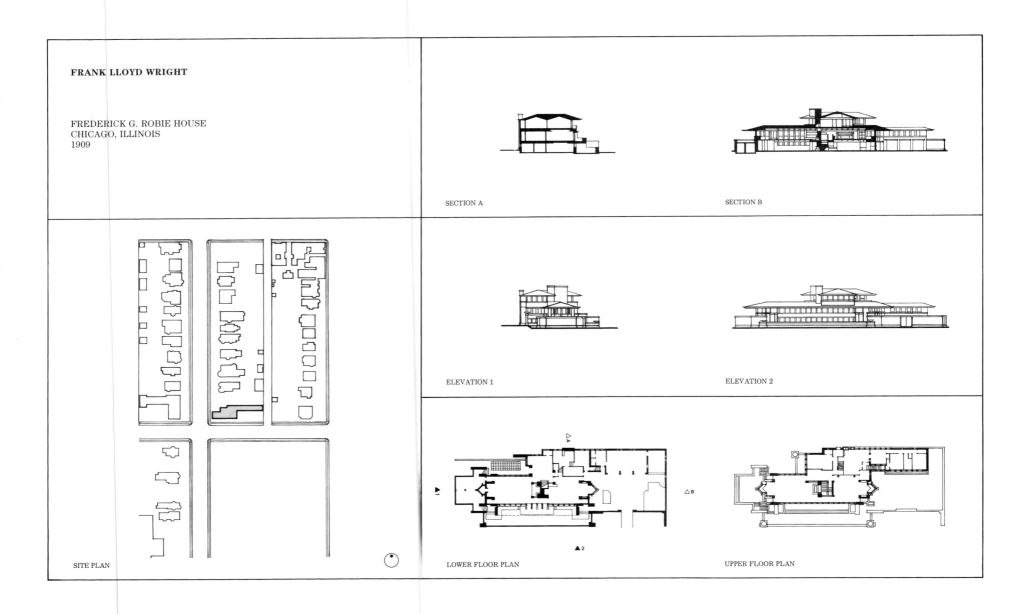

FRANK LLOYD WRIGHT

FREDERICK G. ROBIE HOUSE
CHICAGO, ILLINOIS
1909

SECTION A

SECTION B

ELEVATION 1

ELEVATION 2

SITE PLAN

LOWER FLOOR PLAN

UPPER FLOOR PLAN

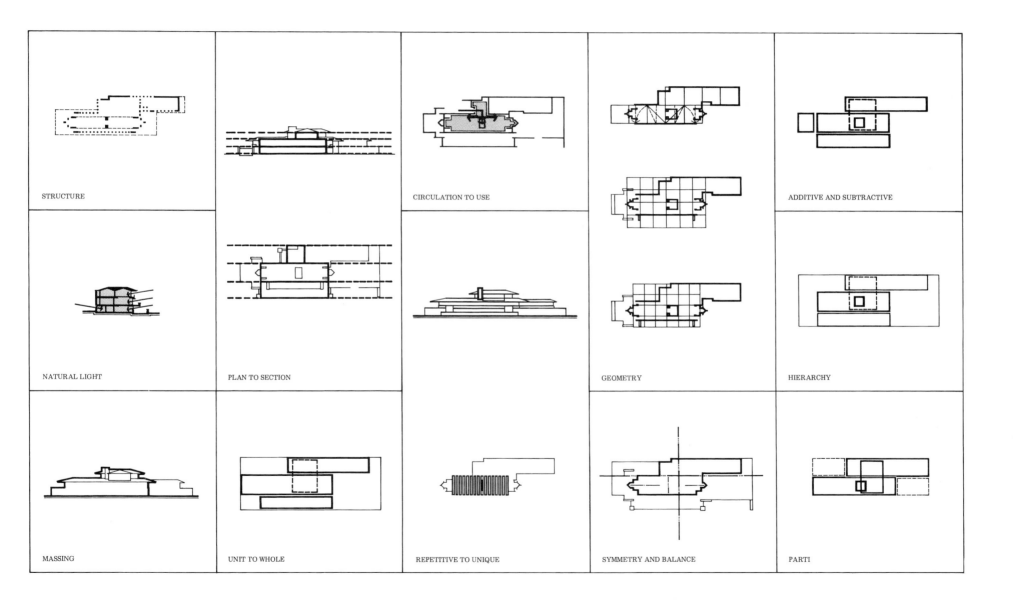

STRUCTURE

CIRCULATION TO USE

ADDITIVE AND SUBTRACTIVE

NATURAL LIGHT

PLAN TO SECTION

GEOMETRY

HIERARCHY

MASSING

UNIT TO WHOLE

REPETITIVE TO UNIQUE

SYMMETRY AND BALANCE

PARTI

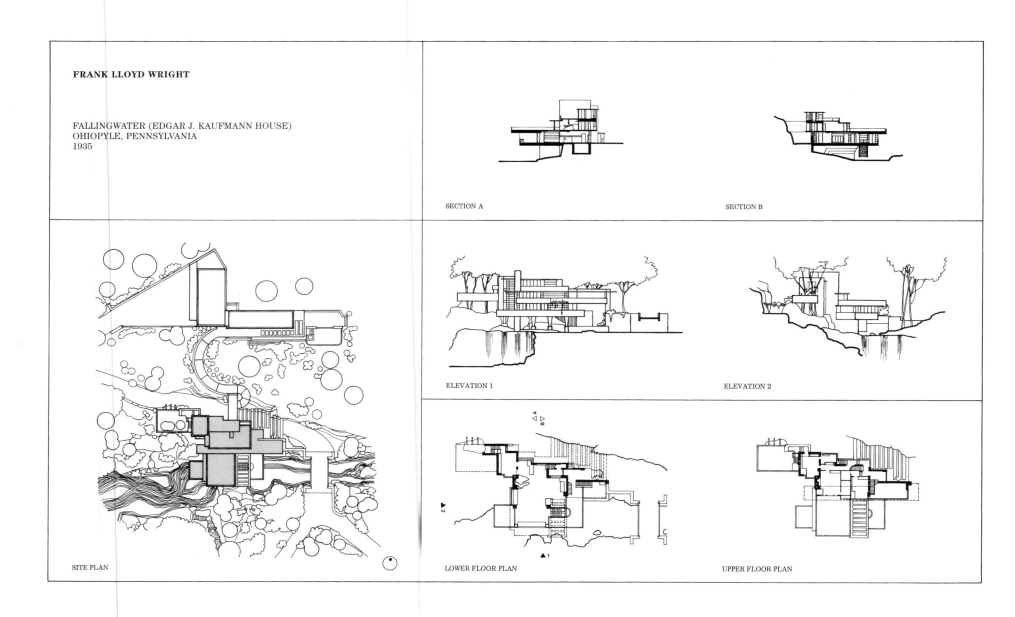

FRANK LLOYD WRIGHT

FALLINGWATER (EDGAR J. KAUFMANN HOUSE)
OHIOPYLE, PENNSYLVANIA
1935

SECTION A

SECTION B

ELEVATION 1

ELEVATION 2

SITE PLAN

LOWER FLOOR PLAN

UPPER FLOOR PLAN

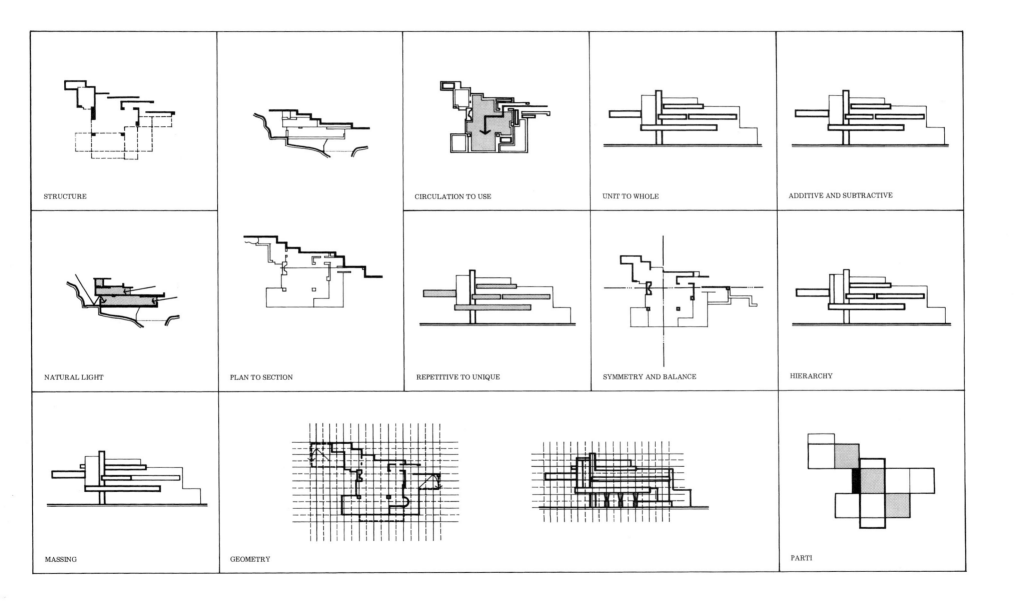

STRUCTURE

CIRCULATION TO USE

UNIT TO WHOLE

ADDITIVE AND SUBTRACTIVE

NATURAL LIGHT

PLAN TO SECTION

REPETITIVE TO UNIQUE

SYMMETRY AND BALANCE

HIERARCHY

MASSING

GEOMETRY

PARTI

209

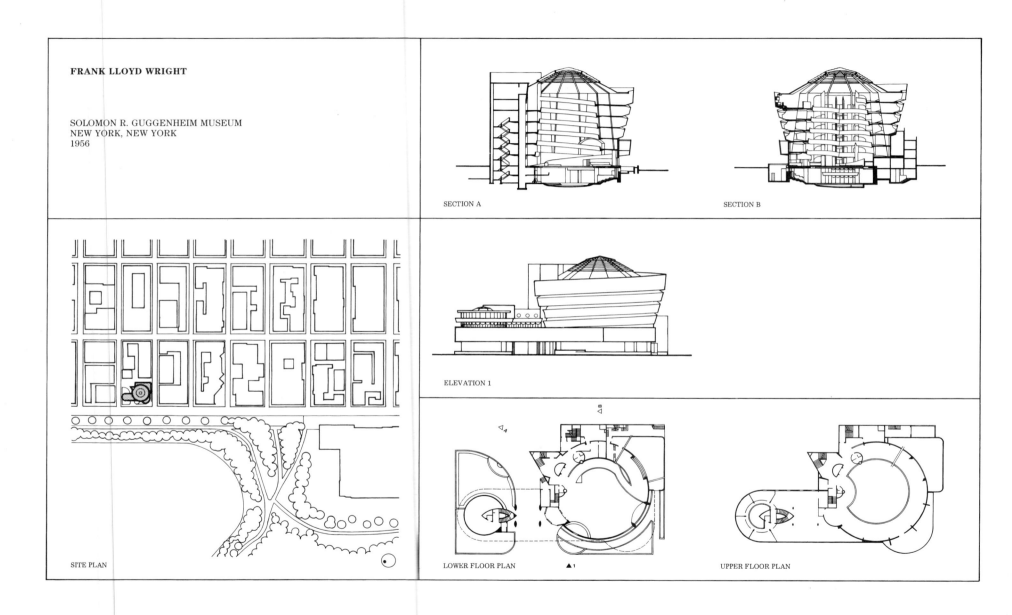

FRANK LLOYD WRIGHT

SOLOMON R. GUGGENHEIM MUSEUM
NEW YORK, NEW YORK
1956

SECTION A

SECTION B

ELEVATION 1

SITE PLAN

LOWER FLOOR PLAN

UPPER FLOOR PLAN

210

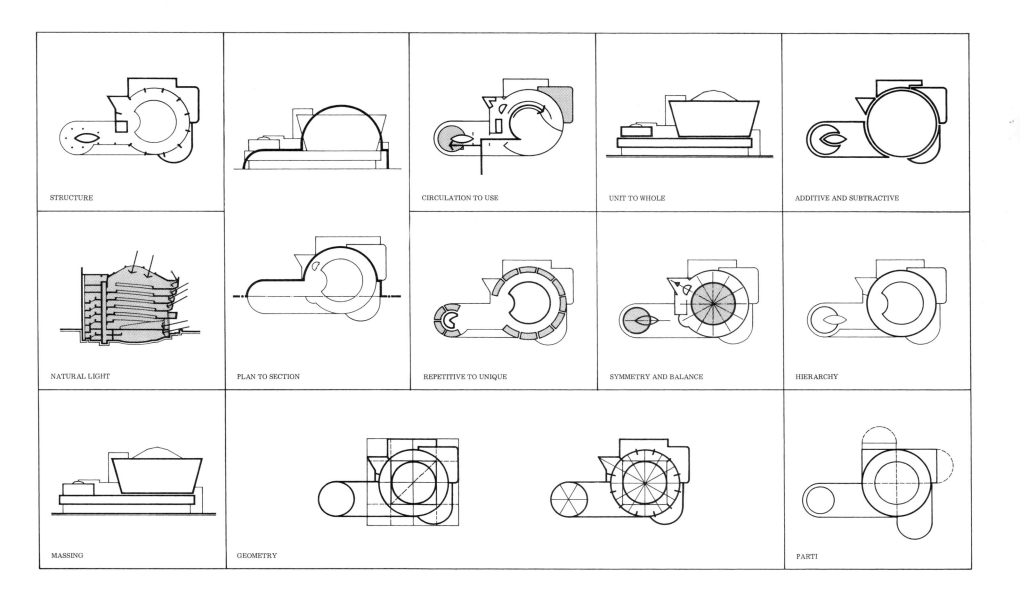

STRUCTURE

CIRCULATION TO USE

UNIT TO WHOLE

ADDITIVE AND SUBTRACTIVE

NATURAL LIGHT

PLAN TO SECTION

REPETITIVE TO UNIQUE

SYMMETRY AND BALANCE

HIERARCHY

MASSING

GEOMETRY

PARTI

PETER ZUMTHOR

PETER ZUMTHOR

CHAPEL OF ST. BENEDICT
SUMVITG, SWITZERLAND
1987–1988

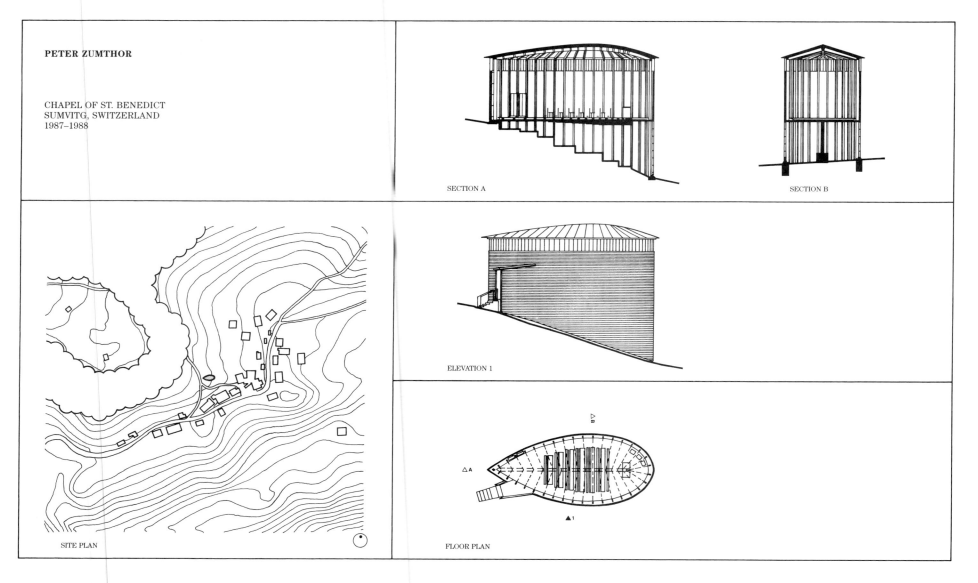

SECTION A

SECTION B

ELEVATION 1

SITE PLAN

FLOOR PLAN

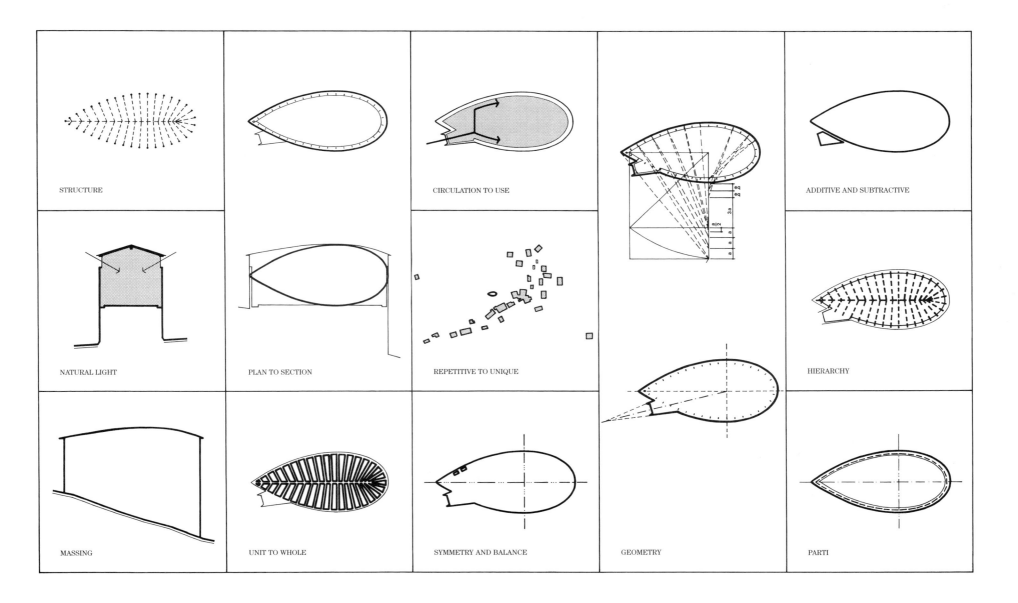

STRUCTURE

CIRCULATION TO USE

ADDITIVE AND SUBTRACTIVE

NATURAL LIGHT

PLAN TO SECTION

REPETITIVE TO UNIQUE

HIERARCHY

MASSING

UNIT TO WHOLE

SYMMETRY AND BALANCE

GEOMETRY

PARTI

213

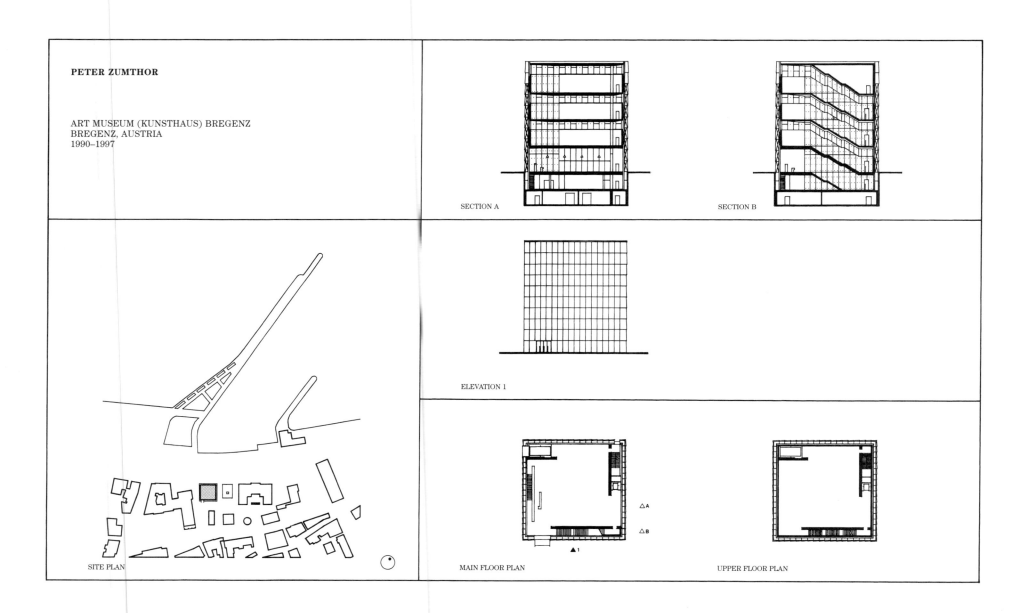

PETER ZUMTHOR

ART MUSEUM (KUNSTHAUS) BREGENZ
BREGENZ, AUSTRIA
1990–1997

SITE PLAN

SECTION A

SECTION B

ELEVATION 1

MAIN FLOOR PLAN

UPPER FLOOR PLAN

214

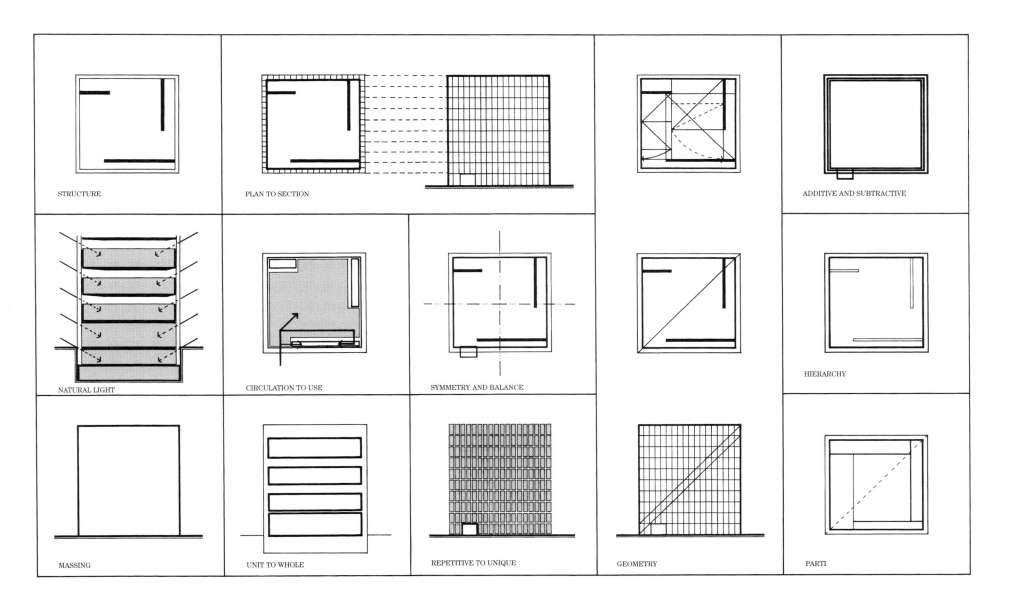

STRUCTURE

PLAN TO SECTION

ADDITIVE AND SUBTRACTIVE

NATURAL LIGHT

CIRCULATION TO USE

SYMMETRY AND BALANCE

HIERARCHY

MASSING

UNIT TO WHOLE

REPETITIVE TO UNIQUE

GEOMETRY

PARTI

215

FORMATIVE IDEAS

FORMATIVE IDEAS

From the analysis of the 104 buildings in the first section, patterns in the design consideration of various architects were identified. Similarities in design approaches appeared among many of the architects' works, independent of time, style, location, function, or type of building. The similarities can be grouped into dominant themes or formative ideas which were conceivably used in the generation of the building designs.

A formative idea is understood to be a concept which a designer can use to influence or give form to a design. The ideas offer ways to organize decisions, to provide order, and to consciously generate form. By engaging one formative idea instead of another, a designer begins to determine the formal result and the manner in which it will differ from other configurations. The use of different ordering ideas may generate different results.

Presented in this section of the book is a series of connections among architects' designs organized by formative idea. Each concept is defined and explored through the presentation of generic manifestations of the idea. The written description is followed by a set of diagrams which exemplify some, but not all, of the generic alternatives. The inventory is not exhaustive: every idea is not explored, nor is every example included. Generally, diagrams developed in the analysis section are supplemented with other examples to illuminate a formative idea. Diagrams were selected which best illustrate the idea, show a variety of manifestations, and represent the widest range of building types from the broadest time frame.

PLAN TO SECTION OR ELEVATION

As a formative idea, the relationship of a plan to a section or an elevation entails design by using an identifiable correlation between the horizontal and vertical configurations of the building. Embodied in this is the linking of the two realms so that decisions in one arena determine or influence the form of the other.

The most direct connection between the plan and section occurs when they are the same—when the delineation of the two is equal. This can be described as a one to one relationship. A sphere, for example, is a figure in which the plan and section are represented by one circle. It is also possible to relate part of one configuration to the whole of the other. For example, a one to one-half relationship exists in a building that has a section or elevation equal in figure and dimension to one-half of the plan. In this case, a circle in plan becomes a half-circle in section, creating a hemisphere. The reciprocal condition is also possible, where the whole plan form of a building is the same as one-half of the section or elevation. In either case, the figures that appear in both plan and section are equal in dimension. In those circumstances in which the section is one-half the plan, a laterally symmetrical plan configuration can be achieved by utilizing the section form twice to create the whole plan. A special condition occurs when the same part of each figure overlaps, such as in the definition of the main space at La Rotonda.

A relationship of proportion by ratio can be used to link the plan with section or elevation. Distinct from the part to whole connection just described, the relationship of proportion establishes the plan and the section as the totality of the other, though different in scale. This relationship is predicated on more information in plan and section being paired than just the outline of each. Examples of ratios which are often used because of their compatibility with primary geometry are $1:2$, $2:3$, and $1:5$. In each case, the plan and section have configurations that differ by dimension in one direction only.

In the case of a 1 : 2 relationship, the plan and the section have the same shape, but one is twice the other in one dimension. For example, a circle in plan would be an oval in section, with the height one-half the width. It is not necessary, though, for each of the parts in the plan to be reduced or increased at the same rate when they are utilized in the section or elevation. In Christ Church, by Nicholas Hawksmoor, for instance, while one element is reduced when it appears in the other realm, the other element is increased.

Plan and section or elevation can have a relationship identified specifically as analogous when the information from one is seen to resemble generally the shape of the other. This type of relationship between the plan and section is the most common, and often involves part of the plan and section rather than the entire plan or section form. Differences between the two may be due to a form language change, size or location shift, or irregular increments of change. In a form language change an orthogonal element in plan or section may be paired with a comparable curve form in the other realm. When size and location shifts occur, an element in the horizontal arena is larger or smaller, or in a slightly different location than in the vertical dimension. In increment change the plan or section information changes at one rate while the correlative information in the other changes in a similar way, but at a different rate.

An inverse relationship exists between the plan and section when the configuration of one is paralleled with some opposite condition in the other. For example, when the plan form has components which are large, or simple or positive, or random, and that correspond to section elements that are small, or complex, or negative, or ordered, respectively, then an inverse relationship exists between the two.

Whereas the relationships of equal, part to whole, proportional, analogous, and inverse establish a link between plan and section in which decisions about one determine the configuration of the other, it is also possible to have a connection that is less deterministic and more influential in nature. In this type of relationship, decisions about the plan or section establish a range of possible configurations for the other.

A part to whole relationship can be created between the plan and the section. In this context, one configuration serves as the whole shape, which, by reduction, becomes a part in the other configuration. The whole is evident in this relationship in its entirety as a part in the other domain, but in reduced dimensions. An example of this form of relationship exists in the Yano House by Arata Isozaki. In this house, which is diagrammed on page 291, the whole configuration of the plan is repeated as part of the section.

Plan and section can also have a coincident relationship when significant points and limits in the plan form coincide with important points in the section. Essential is the alignment of the locations where major changes occur in both plan and section even though the actual configurations are quite varied. The Allegheny Courthouse by H. H. Richardson, which is analyzed in the first part of this book, exemplifies this relationship.

A final alternative to the plan and section relationship is that of common derivation or common origin. In this case, the plan and the section configurations are determined by separate derivation from a common origin. For example, in San Maria degli Angeli by Filippo Brunelleschi, which is also in the analysis section, the plan and section forms are both developed from two overlapped squares that are rotated 45 degrees to each other. In the plan, the two squares have a common center, while in the section, the corner of one square intersects the middle of a side of the other. Both plan and section derive from the same size squares, but the resulting configurations are quite different.

UNIT TO WHOLE

The unit to whole relationship is a formative idea which involves the concept of unit and the understanding that units can be related to other units in specific ways to create built form. A unit is a major recognizable component of a building that generally has a scale that approaches, or is one level removed from, the scale of a whole building. Units can exist within a building at several scales. However, while a brick can be seen as a unit at the scale of a wall, it is less productive to view the brick as a unit at the scale of a building; otherwise, all brick buildings will have the same unit to whole relationship. Units, then, are normally spatial volumes, use-spaces, structural elements, massing blocks, or composites of these elements.

The most direct relationship between a unit and the whole occurs when the two are the same entity—when the unit is equal to the whole. This usually occurs in buildings which are designed as minimal monolithic forms. For example, Cheop's pyramid comprised enormous quantities of stone blocks and cladding pieces. Yet, the dominant perception of this building is that of an identifiable entity. At a greatly reduced level of importance this perception may be qualified to include the surface texture or pattern developed by the fine scale cladding units. Similarly, the glass, tight-skinned cladding on some modern buildings is secondary to the overall monolithic form.

The most prevalent form of unit to whole relationship is the aggregation of units to create the whole. To aggregate units is to put the units in proximity with each other such that some relationship is perceived to exist. The units may or may not be in physical contact with each other for a relationship to be identified. The alternative forms of creating a whole through the aggregation of units are characterized as adjoining, separate, and overlapped.

Adjoining is the most common form of aggregation. In this relationship the units are visible, perceived as entities, and relate to other units through face to face, face to edge, or edge to edge contact. Interlocking is one variation of face to face adjoining.

Units may be separate and at the same time related to other units to form a whole. Separation can occur through physical isolation or through the articulation of the connec-

tion between the units such that the units are perceived to be separate. Essential to this type of relationship is the perceived segregation of units and the proximity of the units so as to establish a compositional relationship.

Units may also aggregate to form a whole through overlap. Since architecture is a three-dimensional phenomenon, the overlap of units in the volumetric realm is by interpenetration. For this to happen the units are identified as entities that partially share form or space with other units. The portion of the overlap is seen as part of each unit and at the same time common to both.

Units can also be contained within a built whole. To distinguish this relationship from units adjoined to form a whole, the building as a whole is the dominant expression with the units contained and not expressed. Embodied in this relationship is the concept of a building as a wrapper or container for units which are usually spatial or structural volumes.

It is possible for a building whole to have more built form than that generated by the assemblage of the identified units. This relationship can be described as one in which the whole is greater than the sum of the parts. In this case, some of the built form serves as a matrix which holds, connects, or at times, just has contact with the units. The units may be formal or spatial, and visible or not. Important to this relationship is the concept of poche, which is the defined difference between interior volume and exterior configuration.

REPETITIVE TO UNIQUE

The formative idea of relating repetitive and unique elements entails the design of built form through the establishment of relationships between components which have multiple and singular manifestations. Fundamental to this idea is the understanding of unique to be a difference within a class or a kind. This distinction allows for the common reference frame of class or kind to couple the domain of the repetitive with the unique. The definition of the unique, in terms of the repetitive, permits the identification of the differences in attributes of common elements. For example, massing units are compared with massing units to determine the differentiating features which make one unit unique. If massing units were compared to windows or structure, the nature of the difference might never be discerned because of the disparity of characteristics to be compared. Repetitive and unique elements can occur at a number of varied scales and levels within a building. As with the unit to whole relationship, the concern is with the dominant manifestation of the idea.

In the realm of architecture, the repetitive and unique elements are usually three-dimensional, and, as such, can be communicated through the conventions of plan and section. In most cases, the repetitive and unique will appear in the same vertical or horizontal arena. However, it is possible for the repetitive elements to occur in plan and the unique element to occur in section, or conversely for the unique to appear in plan and the repetitive in section. San Maria degli Angeli by Brunelleschi is an example of this separation.

A unique element can be developed through the transformation of repetitive units through changes in size, color, location, and orientation. Shape, geometry, and articulation changes can also render an element unique. The distinction between a change in shape and one in geometry is determined by the degree of difference between the two figures. If the unique element is in part the same configuration as the repetitive, then a transformation by shape exists. For example, a square can be transformed into a figure that has three straight, equal length lines at right angles to each other and is closed by an arc of a circle. If the unique component is different in form language from the repetitive, then a transformation by geometry occurs. In this situation, a circle is unique to repeated squares. A change in articulation happens when the same form or configuration is made manifest in two ways. For example, a transparent cube is unique by articulation to a series of opaque cubes.

The unique component can be surrounded by the repetitive. In this case, the unique is central and has its own configuration. The repetitive elements are located around it. It is possible, but not necessary, for the repetitive elements to be coincident with the boundary of the unique. However, a change in the arrangement of the repetitive elements will not change the unique that is surrounded. The counterpart relationship where the unique surrounds the repetitive is also possible.

An alternative to the unique surrounded configuration occurs when the unique is defined by the arrangement of the repetitive. The distinction between this alternative and the unique surrounded model is determined by the manner in which the unique is established. In this case, the unique is dependent upon the configuration of the repetitive elements for its shape or form. The unique does not exist without the repetitive, or, at least, its form will change if the repetitive elements or their arrangement changes.

Unique and repetitive elements can be added together to create built form. The determination of whether repetitive is added to unique or unique is added to repetitive is made perceptually by consideration of relative scales, configuration, location, or some combination. Generally, that which is added to will appear to be dominant.

Unique elements can be formed as a result of overlapping repetitive units where the shared configuration is unique. In some cases, the unique component in a building is the remainder of the built form after the repetitive units have been defined. In this instance, the unique is the difference between the overall building configuration and the sum of the repetitive parts.

If units are in proximity to each other so that a relationship exists, then the unique element can be separate from the repetitive. The nature of the separation can be physical or perceptual, as it is in the unit to whole relationship. Unique elements may also be located within a field in which the repetitive elements have a scale, configuration, and uniformity of relationship that renders them a larger unit that can be identified as a field or network. In this relationship, the difference between the repetitive and the unique is heightened by the disruption of the field by the unique.

Location can establish an element as unique. Singular occurrence in a linear arrangement can be the basis of uniqueness. Therefore, a unit at the center, one which is a terminus to a path, or one that is shifted out of alignment, can be rendered unique. It is also possible in a linear configuration to view the ends as unique units connected by repetitive elements.

ADDITIVE AND SUBTRACTIVE

Additive and subtractive are formative ideas which entail the design of buildings through the aggregation or removal of built form. Basic to these related ideas is the understanding that an additive design has perceptually dominant parts and a subtractive scheme has a perceptually dominant whole. The image a person has of an additive design is that the building is an assemblage of identifiable units. A person engaging a subtractive design understands the building to be a recognizable totality from which parts are removed. Buildings may embody both images, but it is the dominant perception of parts added or parts subtracted from a whole which renders them additive or subtractive, respectively. Generally, these ideas have the greatest bearing on formal considerations of a building, with massing a particular concern. However, as with any formal issue, spatial consequences can result from decisions made in this realm. Although additive and subtractive, as formative ideas, operate at the scale of the building, it is possible to use these concepts to make design decisions at other scales, like parts of buildings and rooms.

Additive and subtractive differ from the other concepts presented in that they are the generic examples of the idea. Alternatives are possible when the ideas are used in conjunction with each other to determine a building design. As noted previously, the potential for design richness is enhanced by the use of the two concepts in consort. This normally occurs when the use of the alternative is sequenced in some manner. For example, the creation of a form by subtracting pieces from a recognized whole, and then after adding parts to form a new whole, subtracting again. The amount of imagery developed by any one step, the dominance of the perception, and the sequence of the processes allow a broad range of alternatives within this formative idea.

SYMMETRY AND BALANCE

Symmetry and balance are formative ideas which entail the design of buildings through the establishment of perceived and conceived equilibrium between components. Intrinsic to an understanding of balance and symmetry in architecture are the notions that elements can be identified as equivalent, and that the nature of the equivalency can be discerned. The generic alternatives for balance and symmetry exist in the nature of these equivalencies. Balance and symmetry both create a stable state relationship between components on either side of an implied line or point. Generally, balance is perceptually based and focuses on the composition of elements. It becomes a conceptual phenomenon when components are given added value and meaning.

Symmetry, as a specialized form of balance, is perceptual in nature. Symmetry differs from balance in that the same unit occurs on both sides of the line of symmetry. The most familiar form of symmetry is referred to as axial, reflected, or mirrored, because the components are oriented such that one unit appears to be reflected in a mirror to create a second unit. In this type of symmetry, the elements are equal in configuration and opposite in handedness. That which occurs on the left side of one element will be on the right side of the other. Biaxial or bilateral symmetry is reflected symmetry that occurs in two directions.

A second form of symmetry is developed through the rotation of components about a common center. Implied in this situation is the central point, which by definition establishes patterns that are different from those developed by symmetry about a line. The central point can be located within, at the edge of, or outside the figure. If the point of rotation is within the figure, a series of overlapping forms will be created. This type of symmetry might also result in pinwheel configurations if the center of rotation is asymmetrically located in both directions. Besides the location of the center of rotation, other important variables are the number of times the figure is rotated and the increments between the rotations.

Symmetry by translation occurs when elements with identical shape and orientation are shifted. This symmetry allows for the development of linear organizations through the aggregation of multiple, equal units, where the symmetrical relationship exists between any two components. Configurations are not limited to straight lines, and can be serial in nature. It is also possible to incorporate more than one sequence of translation into a design. For example, the atrium housing by Jørn Utzon utilizes two sets of symmetrically related units, each with a different orientation.

While symmetry is predicated on equal units occurring on each side of a line or point, balance exists when the units on each side are different in some identifiable way. Differences in attributes which can create a balanced situation between elements include geometry, orientation, location, size, configuration, and a positive-negative reversal. Balance by geometry results from the relationship of equivalent units that vary in form language. For example, one element could be circular and the other rectilinear.

Equal units that have an orientation difference other than those stipulated in reflected and rotational symmetry can be balanced about an implied line. Unit size and relative distance from the line of equilibrium determine balance by location, which closely parallels the concept of balance by weights on a scale.

Units that vary in size can be equidistant from the line of balance when balanced by ratio. In this relationship, the difference in size is balanced by an intensification or concentration of other attributes within the smaller unit, such that the line of balance is created midway between the two. This occurs when a special condition, given importance, like a jewel, balances a much larger, less significant component. For example, two dissimilar size units can be related to a balance line midway between them through the utilization of special materials on the smaller unit.

Balance can also be developed through configuration differences in two and three dimensions. Visual equilibrium on a surface or in a form is achieved by the manipulation of area or mass, respectively. This distinction applies to a building elevation which can be understood in two dimensions, and to architecture which is a three-dimensional phenomenon. In this relationship, the issues of number, shape, and pattern are engaged through consideration of ranges of attributes like open-closed, few-many, and simple-complex.

Finally, balance can occur when two equivalent components exist in positive and negative form. It is this type of balance that can utilize the very essence of architecture, for it embodies equilibrium between mass and space. In this context, the positive tower form balances the void of the courtyard.

GEOMETRY AND GRID

As a formative idea geometry entails the use of the tenets of both plane and solid geometry to determine built form. Geometry in one form or another exists in all buildings, but as a formative idea it must be knowingly central to decisions regarding form at several levels.

The most fundamental use of this idea incorporates the basic figures of geometry as form or space to determine the overall configuration of a building. Thus, a building might be a circle, a square, a triangle, a hexagon, an octagon, or any other singular describable and recognizable geometric form. While the geometric figure may not totally incorporate every piece of the building, it is necessary that the basic figure be dominant and perceptible.

Although architecture might be developed from one geometric figure, these forms can also be combined to generate a building; that is, a circle and square can be added together to create a building. Similarly, any two or more other basic forms might be combined, providing each is perceptible as a whole figure. The forms do not have to physically exist, but each must at least be implied. Within the realm of combinations, it is possible to locate one geometry that is within, contiguous to, or overlaps the other. When one geometry is located inside the other, the inner geometry might be an object, a room, a courtyard, a defined precinct, or an implied space.

A specialized form of geometric overlap prevalent in architecture is the combination of a rectangle and a smaller circle. A circle or a series of circular forms can overlap the rectangle at a side or corner. The overlap can result in a number of specific configurations, including the circle engaged on the centerline of the major side of the rectangle. A circle at the corner of the rectangle can overlap both sides, can have its center at the corner, or can be tangent to one of the sides.

As differing geometries are assembled, so too can similar geometries be combined. For example, buildings may consist of two circles, three triangles, or two hexagons of the same or different size. When square figures of the same size are combined in specific ways, some interesting and very particular phenomena occur.

Two identical squares combined with one congruent face create a rectangle with a 2:1 proportion. However, these same squares can be overlapped to make other rectangles smaller than 2:1, or separated to imply rectangles larger than this proportion. Normally, the space formed by the overlap or the space implied by the separation is used for special purposes, like entrances, or the main hall of building. Two squares can also be overlapped and rotated about a central point such that an eight-cornered figure is developed. It is also possible to unite two squares by attaching the corner of one to the face of the other.

Particular combinations of squares have the characteristic of being either multiples or equal subdivisions of a square. The distinguishing characteristic of these combinations is that they actually form another larger square. When four squares are assembled into a two-square by two-square configuration, the result is a figure that can be viewed as a four-part subdivision of the larger square or as a multiple of the smaller square. Similarly, nine squares can be assembled into a three-square by three-square configuration. By extension, squares can be assembled into 16-square and 25-square constructs.

In a nine-square configuration there are three types of squares, each with its own characteristics. Four of the squares are located on the corners and are bounded by two other squares. Four others are located on the sides and are bounded on three sides by other squares. The final square is located in the center and is completely surrounded. This bounded center square makes the nine-square format an identifiable and unique configuration. Whereas this arrangement emphasizes a central square or space, the four-square format articulates a central point.

Identifiable variations within the nine-square configuration are possible by removing certain squares, while maintaining others in their normal location. Thus, by using only the eight squares on the perimeter, a square ring is created. An "X" form is possible by using only the corner and center squares. By utilizing the middle square on each side and the square in the center, a "plus" configuration is made. Leaving out two side squares opposite each other results in an "H" shape. Finally, a stepped configuration is possible by removing one corner and the two contiguous side squares.

Forms can also be derived by using parts of the basic geometric shapes. In the simplest terms, this might be one-half or some other fraction of a circle, square, or triangle. However, more complex configurations are possible through combinations of forms derived from several geometric shapes. Though clearly derived from geometry, these configurations are not describable in simple geometric terms. Another geometric derivation is the implying of a larger geometric shape by points located within the architectural configuration. For example, at the Guild House by Robert Venturi, the corners of the building align to project a large triangle.

Certain derivations from a square result in three different rectangles with sides of particular proportions. The proportions are all less than the 2:1 proportion that results from combining two squares. The first, the square-root-of-two rectangle, is derived from the 45 degree rotation of the diagonal of a square, to form the long side. A 1.5:1 rectangle can be formed by adding one-half of a square to a square. The third, the golden-section rectangle, is derived from the rotation of the diagonal of one-half the square to form the major side of the figure. The center of rotation in this case is the midpoint of one of the sides of the square. Each of these rectangles, used either alone or in combinations, is frequently utilized to form buildings or parts of buildings.

Another series of configurations can be developed through the manipulation of geometries by rotation, shift, and overlap. These manipulations, all described by a process of implied movement, can be used in combinations to create more complex forms: for instance, rotation used in conjunction with overlapping.

Rotation is the conceptual process of moving a part or parts about a center. This center of rotation may be, but is not necessarily, the same for all the parts. Rotational movement naturally changes the orientation of the part involved. A particular configuration that results from rotation is the hinge in which two linear and connected elements are normally oriented in different directions. In some examples, the pin of the hinge or connector actually appears as a figure in the building; in other cases, it is implied.

When the manipulation by shifting occurs, the parts move, but unlike rotation, the orientation of the parts remains the same. While the shifting is often orthogonal in nature, a diagonal shift can create added richness by resulting in change in two directions through movement in one. Shifting might also be understood as sliding of two parts against one another. When this occurs, a third space or form is usually introduced between the shifting parts to neutralize the fissuring.

Overlap has the unique characteristic of creating a third figure from the combining of two other figures. The overlap of relatively simple shapes can result in a common space, as well as a total configuration, that is quite complex. Depending upon the nature of the overlap, the figure of the common area might be quite different from either of the overlapping figures.

The geometric configurations of radial, pinwheel, and spiral share the common attribute of originating from a center. Buildings that can be considered radial have dominant multiple elements that extend from a center. These raylike elements may be intersected with other elements that are in a concentric arrangement. Both spiral and pinwheel configurations are more dynamic than radial. Spirals move away from a center at a constant rate of change and in a rotational direction. Pinwheels consist of offset linear elements that are connected to a common core or abut to form an implied core. The parts of this configuration are positioned so that the centerlines of the elements do not intersect at a common center. These elements do, however, occur radially at regular intervals, and have similar relationships to the core and to each other. Spinning is the implied dynamic of a pinwheel configuration.

Grids are developed from the repetition of the basic geometries. Multiplication, combination, subdivision, and manipulation are the processes used to create the repetitions. Conceptually, grids are infinite fields in which all units relate equally to all other units. A grid can be described as a series of parallel lines that intersects at least one other series of parallel lines.

The intervals between lines can repeat or vary. In the series' simplest form, all intervals would be equal. The complexity of the series can be altered by increasing the number of intervals that occur within it. The frequency with which a particular interval occurs, and its relationship to another interval and its frequency, will determine whether a discernible patterns exists, and the nature of that pattern. Thus, if "a," "b," and "c" represent intervals on a grid, and if "a" is to occur at the frequency of every fourth interval, then the pattern might be "a, b, c, a, b, c, a, b, . . ."; but it might also be "a, b, b, a, c, c, a, b, . . ." or "a, b, c, a, c, b, a, b, . . ."

Another aspect of grid is the relationship between one series and another. Two series might or might not be orthogonal to each other. If the relationship is orthogonal, with all intervals in both series equal, a square grid results. A regular rectangular grid occurs when two series, each with a different interval, are orthogonal, and the intervals within each series are equal. Two orthogonal series, each with more than one equal interval, create a rectangular, plaid grid. Two nonorthogonal series of lines constitute a parallelogram grid. A triangular grid is formed by three intersecting series of lines which have common points of intersection. The number of series of lines which might exist coincidentally is conceptually infinite, but practically, the number is significantly lower.

Within the grid, a critical construct is the intersection created by any two lines in the series. However, intersections alone do not provide enough information to describe a grid accurately. For instance, a series of intersections arranged in what is apparently a square grid configuration, also can describe a parallelogram or triangular grid if the intersections are connected differently.

Important to the total understanding of a grid is the method of articulating both the line and the intersection. As discussed, both must exist conceptually and be defined, but either may be implied by the existence of the other; that is, at least two points or intersections must exist in order to imply a line. If enough of the field exists so that an expected pattern can be perceived, then it is also possible for an intersection or part of a line in the grid to be removed. Expectations, then, complete or fill in the implied piece. Articulation of the lines and intersections can establish importance or give major and minor emphasis to the grid. Like the basic geometric figures, grids can be combined or manipulated through the processes of rotation, shift, and overlap.

CONFIGURATION PATTERNS

As a formative idea, patterns of configuration describe the relative disposition of parts. The patterns are essentially themes that have the potential for making space and organizing groups of spaces and forms. The terms that describe these basic patterns are: central, linear, cluster, concentric, nested, double-centered, and binuclear.

Central configuration patterns can be classified as those that are central-dominant and those in which the central space is used to organize other spaces. How the center is engaged is the primary difference in each of these cases. In the first, one goes to or around the center while in the second, one goes through the center. A third model of central configuration, but one that is not included in this study, is that of a central solid, such as a fireplace.

In the central-dominant model, the center is the focus with the most important use-space located in that position. If this space is covered, it is very often done so by forms that are higher in the center than at the edges—a hemisphere or dome, a cone, or a pyramid. Thus, the idea of center is reinforced by the roof or ceiling configuration. A primary characteristic of central-dominant space is that the center appears to generate the entirety of volume and form. This space can be functionally or symbolically dominant. In some cases it is considered sacred; in others it is less sacred, but no less important. The configuration of this pattern may suggest a singular volume or a spatial composition that extends from the center. These volumetric extensions, which might create complex patterns, emanate from the center. Each successive volume reinforces the center, but lessens its own importance. Excessive extensions will at some point diminish the importance of the center itself. A fundamental difficulty in this configuration is maintaining the center focus or dominance while introducing entrance. Ideally, though it is not usually feasible, the entrance should be introduced at the center or through a continuous series of openings equally spaced around the perimeter.

Circulation within the central-dominant configuration is either to or around the center space. Therefore, the central space can be an outdoor space that one walks around, but generally not through. A cloister, in which the outdoor space is a sanctuary, or a multistoried atrium that one walks around, might be examples of voids that are central-dominant. Within this idea, the central space does not necessarily have to have external visual impact.

The other model of central configuration employs the center as an organizer of spaces. In this case, the center space can be considered a servant space that is used for circulation and as a clearinghouse that resolves circulation problems. The classic rotunda is an example of such a space. It may have great significance externally, and formally may unify the building, but functionally it is not important as a use-space. This configuration, like the central-dominant organization, does not necessarily have to be expressed externally. It can be a void, such as a courtyard or atrium, that is used for circulation.

Whereas the previous configurations developed from the concept of center, linear configuration patterns focus on line and movement. They entail the critical issues of path and direction. As with central configuration, linear patterns are classified into two types. The primary distinction is identified by the relationship of use-space and how one engages it through circulation. In the first model, the circulation is separate from the use-space, and can be referred to as a spine. In the second type, circulation is through the use-space and the

spaces are linked, much as the chain of a necklace links beads by passing through them.

The spine is a servant space that provides access to a series of independent parts or rooms. Often, the common circulation route allows parts that have no direct relationship to each other to be grouped. The spine may be dominant in the form of the building, or it may be hidden within. In the latter case, the spine is reduced to a single- or double-loaded corridor. Symmetrical or asymmetrical arrangements of parts is possible along the spine. By nature, a spine is not hierarchical, nor is it of a given length, but what it serves may begin to determine its limits. Other architectural issues, like entrance, also influence the actual spine configuration and the way it is experienced. Normally, spines are assumed to be straight, but they can be bent to create enclosed space, to focus view, to reduce its apparent length, or to respond to some exterior situation. Within a building there also may be more than one spine. In these instances, spines that cross and the nature in which they cross might suggest hierarchy or special areas.

A use-space that is traversed longitudinally, or a series of spaces that are linked to suggest movement from one to another, describes that second type of linear configuration. Thus, a path is either through the space or from space to space. In the space to space circumstance, the pattern of the location of openings between spaces will determine the configuration and the legibility of that path. Volumetric extensions may enrich the path if the extensions are rendered secondary to the primary space and are located in a manner that reinforces the linear quality of the space.

In this type of linear configuration exists the opportunity to exploit the potentials of serial progressions. While progressions themselves are discussed later, it is important to realize that space to space linear configurations are normally engaged sequentially. Therefore, it is possible to place importance on any space in the sequence. Accent can be at the beginning of, along, at the center of, or at the end of the path.

Cluster organizations refer to groupings of spaces or

forms in which there is no discernible pattern. The units, whether forms or spaces, need to be in proximity to one another, yet the relationship between these units is irregular. While not a prerequisite for clustering, the random character of the relationships may permit the units to be irregular. Spaces can cluster within an overall form and in a way that influences or determines three-dimensional forms. Forms that cluster may have spatial subdivisions that are not important or dominant within them.

The concentric configuration pattern is analogous to the pattern created by dropping a pebble into water. The pattern is concentric when a series of units of differing sizes have the same center. This configuration can also be viewed as layering in which one element is viewed in the context of another. A characteristic of concentric organizations is that several rings are necessary to begin to see the pattern. However, it is important to note that the rings, though they share a common center, may not be of the same form language.

Nested configuration patterns share certain characteristics with concentric patterns. While both patterns have units inside one another, in nested patterns the center of each unit is different. Nested units can have other parts, such as one or more sides or a centerline, in common. Both nested and concentric patterns can be created at the formal or spatial level, and both imply layering.

A configuration pattern with two equally important foci is called double-centered. Prominent to the understanding of double-center is the idea of a precinct or field that has definite boundaries. The precinct can be either solid or void. If a void, the field can be a room, a large interior volume, or an outside space, like a court or a discernible area.

If the building is considered a mass, then the precinct is a solid. In either case of precinct as void or as solid, the double-centers are rendered opposites within the field. Thus, if the precinct is void, the double-centers refer to objects within a defined space. If the precinct is considered solid, the double-centers are spaces that are hollowed from the mass, and the remainder is considered poche.

Binuclear configuration patterns have the primary attribute of two equally dominant parts, which, as forms, comprise the general building configuration. The two forms establish a line of symmetry or balance. While the nuclear parts may be the same, they also may be different through changes of geometry, orientation, configuration, or state. A third form may create a link between the nuclear forms, but it is not essential. Normally, this connector is a secondary or neutral space which is exclusive of both dominant parts. On occasion, though, it can be a major use-space or a solid in the form of a wall. The dominant parts are often engaged by entering between them, or by entering into one and then proceeding to the other in a linear fashion.

PROGRESSIONS

The archetypal themes that comprise the formative idea of progressions focus on patterns of incremental change that occur between one condition and another. Progressions embrace ideas of multiplicity, rather than duality. Therefore, to discern a pattern, more than two increments of change are normally necessary. Hierarchy, transition, transformation, and mediation are the generic progression types discussed in this study. An important distinction between these generics and the overall progression category is that the generics are bounded subsets of progressions. Whereas progressions can be infinite, the four generic examples are finite, with definite beginnings and ends. In these bounded sets, the characteristics of the increment are describable in relation to the next increment, rather than as an isolate. Similarly, the increment can be understood in relation to the boundaries. Something large in one instance, for example, is actually small in another.

Hierarchy refers to the rank ordering of parts relative to a common attribute. This ranking differentiates among the parts by assigning importance. Sacred to profane, large to small, figure to poche, center to edge, servant to served, tall to short, few to many, and inclusive to exclusive are some of the hierarchies often found, either alone or in any number of combinations, in architecture. In some instances, it is necessary to determine more about the attribute before knowing the importance. Large, for instance, is not necessarily more important than small. Rank orderings from large to small and from small to large are both evident in buildings.

The dominance of hierarchy within a building is often reinforced through the layering of more than one progression type. The Temple of Horus at Edfu, for example, employs several architectural hierarchies to reinforce the importance of the room for the main god. These architectural hierarchies support the religious and social hierarchical beliefs of the society. The Temple's hierarchies are based upon the importance of the sacred to the profane, and are architecturally rendered as small to large, one to many, dark to light, rooms to areas, and closed to open. The openings between the various precincts of the building change with gates in the profane areas and with the openings of increasingly smaller size that are closed by doors at the more sacred rooms. Changes in floor height through steps and sloping floors even though slight in nature, also signal the movement to the sacred. The most holy space, which is protected and separated from the outside world by a series of walls, then, is the smallest, darkest, most enclosed, and roomlike precinct in the Temple. This sanctuary is for a few worshippers and the main god, as opposed to the many lesser gods found in other areas of the Temple. Immediately behind the large entrance gate is the great court or "hall for the masses." This precinct is large, open to the sky, and the least roomlike area in the Temple.

In other buildings, evidence indicates that the most important increment in a hierarchy is often rendered by architects with the most ornament, the most intense polychromy, the most precious materials, or the highest level of detail and texture. Location, as in the center, or at the end of an axis,

might also reinforce the specialness of a space or form. In general, those qualities which make something special or precious in relation to others suggest the devices which are available to create importance in a piece of architecture.

Transitions are bounded progressions in which change takes place in an attribute without a change in form. A change from open to closed, inside to outside, simple to complex, movement to rest, individual to collective, and one size to another are typical transitions. As with hierarchy, transitions have definite limits, but as opposed to hierarchy, there is no value placed on the end condition of the limits; that is, simple is not seen as being more important than complex, or vice-versa. While the end states are seen as equal, the individual conditions between those ends must also be equal. Aldo van Eyck's discussions of the "inbetween" and "twin phenomena" are of value in understanding transition and its potentials. Within a transition there is necessarily a series of intermediate steps. Each of the increments between the extreme conditions of the transition will suggest what is on either side, and thus will form a link for the conditions on either side.

Transformation is a progression in which changes in form take place within the boundary of the object itself. It is similar to transition, but more specific in that the attribute being changed is the configuration. This configuration change may have impact on either the two or three dimensional form. A reference frame of multiple images is necessary so the change from one form to another is perceptible. Transformation is not, then, a comparison between two forms, but a series of form changes, with each form in the series hierarchically undifferentiated.

Mediation is distinct from the other generic progressions in that the end states are conditions which exist outside the building itself. The building is viewed as a bridge, or a piece of connective tissue, between conditions that exist in the context. Thus, the building cannot be considered autonomous, but must be seen in relation to its context. In order to utilize mediation as a formative idea, a position is taken or a statement is made about the context in which a building is to exist. Generally, this is achieved by a certain amount of abstraction. For example, Richard Meier in the Atheneum at New Harmony abstracts the river on one side as a wavy wall and the grid of the town on the other side as orthogonal geometry. Preferably, such a position entails at least two conditions which might be in either the natural or the built context. Thus, the new building might mediate between two built situations, between two circumstances in the natural environment, or between a built condition and a natural one.

Within this idea, the building is seen as a fragment of a larger piece. Through mediation the building reconciles differences that exist in the context. In the building, a series of gestures might be made which modulate the form to reflect the external conditions. Alternately, one condition can be repeated in some form in part of the building and then altered to be more like the other external condition. Another possibility is that the building is a midpoint or series of intermediates between the two external circumstances.

REDUCTION

Reduction is a formative idea in which a configuration is repeated at a lesser size within the building. This miniaturization can occur in two ways: part of the whole, and large to small. In the first type, the whole, or a large portion of the whole, is reduced in size, and utilized as a part. Normally, in this case, the reduced piece is located within the whole. Alternately, a large unit and at least one reduction of that unit are combined to form a building or part of a building. The reduced unit may be repeated or reduced further. In this type, the reduced piece is usually located next to, rather than within, the larger unit. In either case, but particularly in the part of the whole type, the reduction may involve a positive to negative state change. At one size, for instance, the configuration might be a solid or mass while at the other size the configuration might be a void or space.

A unique quality of the part of the whole type of reduction is that an observer can learn about the whole by encountering a part. With this capacity to inform the observer, this type transcends the perceptual to the conceptual. Thus, by observing the configuration of a room, a court, or a wing of a building, it is possible to infer the configuration of the entire building. The conceptual transference of information may also take place between the plan and the section. In this case, the whole of the plan or section may be repeated in miniature form in the other position. For example, the section of a space or room may correspond to the configuration of the plan of the entire building, as in the Yano House by Isozaki.

On the other hand, in large to small type reduction, comprehending one part may inform about only another part, and not the whole. Therefore, this type remains purely perceptual. In many cases, large to small reductions are incorporated into buildings with major and minor parts so that less important aspects of the building occur in the reduced piece. Typical examples of this are the several buildings in which servant spaces, literal and otherwise, are the small parts. An interesting reversal to this more typical interpretation, though, is that small might mean intense, and thus more important. Alvar Aalto's Town Hall at Saynatsalo is an example where the small piece, which is the town meeting space, is the more important in the large to small reduction.

1. **SNELLMAN HOUSE**
ERIK GUNNAR ASPLUND
1917–1918
2. **SMITH HOUSE**
RICHARD MEIER
1965–1967

3. **PANTHEON**
ARCHITECT UNKNOWN
c. 100
4. **CARLL TUCKER III HOUSE**
ROBERT VENTURI
1975

5. **OLD SACRISTY**
FILIPPO BRUNELLESCHI
1421
6. **VILLA STEIN**
LE CORBUSIER
1927

PLAN TO SECTION
OR ELEVATION

Plan, section, and elevation are conventions common to the horizontal and vertical configuration of all buildings. Decisions made in one of these arenas can determine or influence the form of the other. Illustrated are examples of equal, one to one-half, proportional, inverse, and analogous relationships.

Equal

The most direct relationship between the plan and section or elevation occurs when they are the same. In its simplest form, this equal relationship entails only the overall building configuration. At Asplund's Snellman House (1) the rectangle of the main house becomes the figure of the elevation, excluding the roof. Similarly, the rectangle of the overall plan form at the Old Sacristy (5) is repeated in the major mass of the elevation. Richard Meier, in the Smith House (2), employs a 1.4 rectangle for both the plan and section. The small outbuilding is a cube that is related to the major house form in the same way in both arenas. In the Pantheon (3), the circle that forms the major space in plan determines the interior configuration of that space. The dome of this space is a hemisphere with its crown located at a height equal to the diameter of the circle in plan. This space may be as close to a sphere in form as practically can be achieved. The Tucker House (4) by Robert Venturi is, without the roof form, a cube. Le Corbusier's Villa Stein (6) has plan and elevation configurations which are the same, not only in overall form, but also in their plaid grid subdivisions.

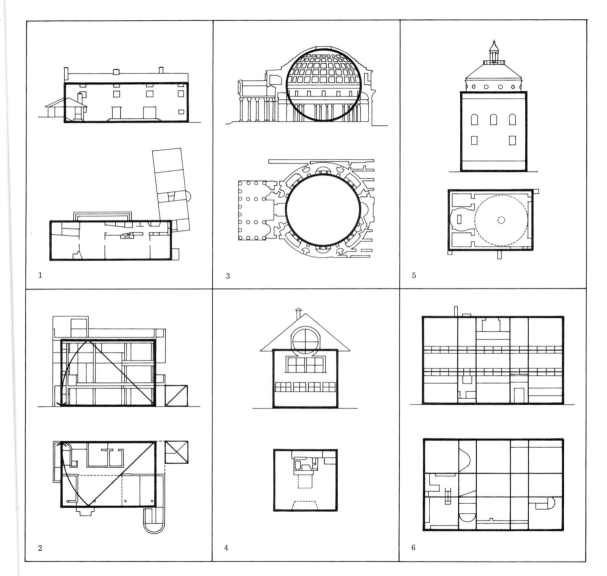

1. **STOCKHOLM EXHIBITION HALL**
   LE CORBUSIER
   1962
2. **NAKAYAMA HOUSE**
   ARATA ISOZAKI
   1964

3. **CHAPEL AT RONCHAMP**
   LE CORBUSIER
   1950–1955
4. **YALE HOCKEY RINK**
   EERO SAARINEN
   1956–1958

5. **RUSAKOV CLUB**
   KONSTANTIN MELNIKOV
   1927
6. **ST. JOHN'S ABBEY**
   MARCEL BREUER
   1953–1961

7. **SAN GIORGIO MAGGIORE**
   ANDREA PALLADIO
   1560–1580
8. **LA ROTONDA**
   ANDREA PALLADIO
   1566–1571

One to One-Half

The configuration of the whole plan or section can be equal to a part of the other, as in the Stockholm Pavillion (1) by Corbusier in which the elevation wall is the same as one-half the plan. The large, dominant squares and smaller square skylights which constitute the major portion of the elevation in Isozaki's Nakayama House (2) are repeated as part of the plan. Generally, one-half the plan at Ronchamp (3) becomes the elevation where the thick wall corresponds to the roof. Saarinen, at the Yale Hockey Rink (4), utilizes the exact curve form that is the center rib of the roof as the outside configuration of each side. On the other hand, one-half the plan at Melnikov's Rusakov Club (5) and Breuer's St. John's Abbey (6) approximates the general configuration of the sections. In Palladio's San Giorgio Maggiore Church (7) the configuration of the main ceiling forms is equal to one-half of the plan form of this space. At Villa Rotonda (8), one-half of the plan is similar to the dominant exterior form.

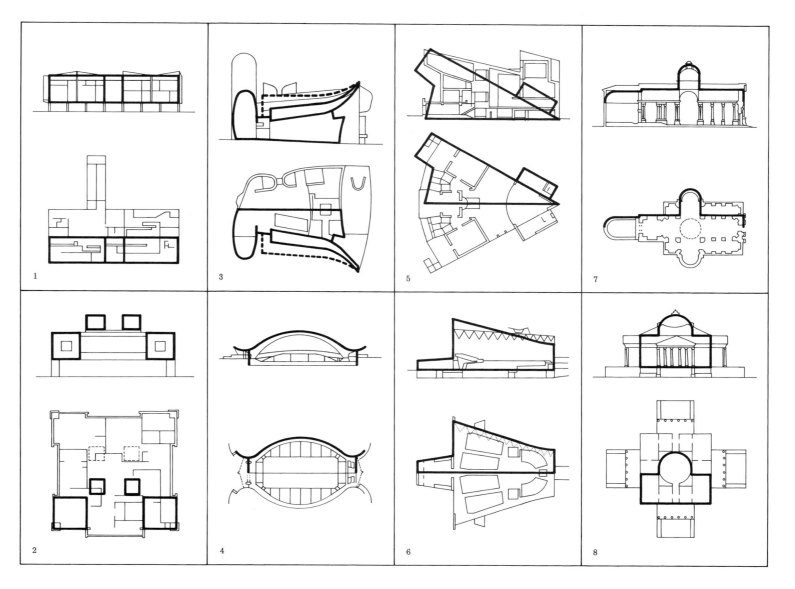

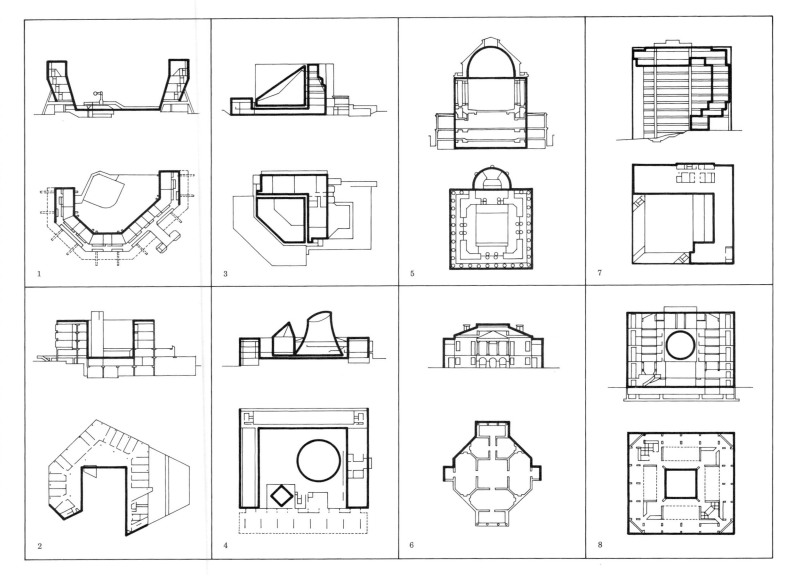

1. **FLOREY BUILDING**
   JAMES STIRLING
   1966
2. **ADULT LEARNING LABORATORY**
   ROMALDO GIURGOLA
   1972
3. **CAMBRIDGE HISTORY FACULTY**
   JAMES STIRLING
   1964
4. **THE PALACE OF ASSEMBLY**
   LE CORBUSIER
   1953–1963
5. **TEMPLE OF THE SCOTTISH RITE**
   JOHN RUSSELL POPE
   1910
6. **POPLAR FOREST**
   THOMAS JEFFERSON
   c. 1806
7. **THE FORD FOUNDATION BUILDING**
   ROCHE-DINKELOO
   1963–1968
8. **EXETER LIBRARY**
   LOUIS I. KAHN
   1967–1972

Analogous

An analogous relationship exists between plan and section when the configuration of one generally resembles the shape of the other. Differences in form language, size, location, or irregular increments of change may account for the resemblance rather than equivalence. The Florey Building (1) and Adult Learning Labs (2) have 'U'-shaped configurations in plan and section. Differences in size occur between plan and section in the Scottish Rite (5), Poplar Forest (6), Salutation (9), and Sullivan's bank (16). In the Hines House (13) size differences occur in two directions. Increment changes account for the variations in plan and section in the Ford Foundation Building (7), Fallingwater (14), Wolfsburg Cultural Center (15), Enso-Gutzeit (17), and the Besançon theater (18). Plan and section differ by form language in Exeter Library (8), Sever Hall (10), and Redentore Church (11). Location shift renders the plan of St. Clement Danes (12) somewhat different from the section. A combination of form language and size changes create the variation in the Palace of Assembly (4). Form language and increment changes make the plan and section of the History Faculty Building (3) analogous, rather than equal.

234

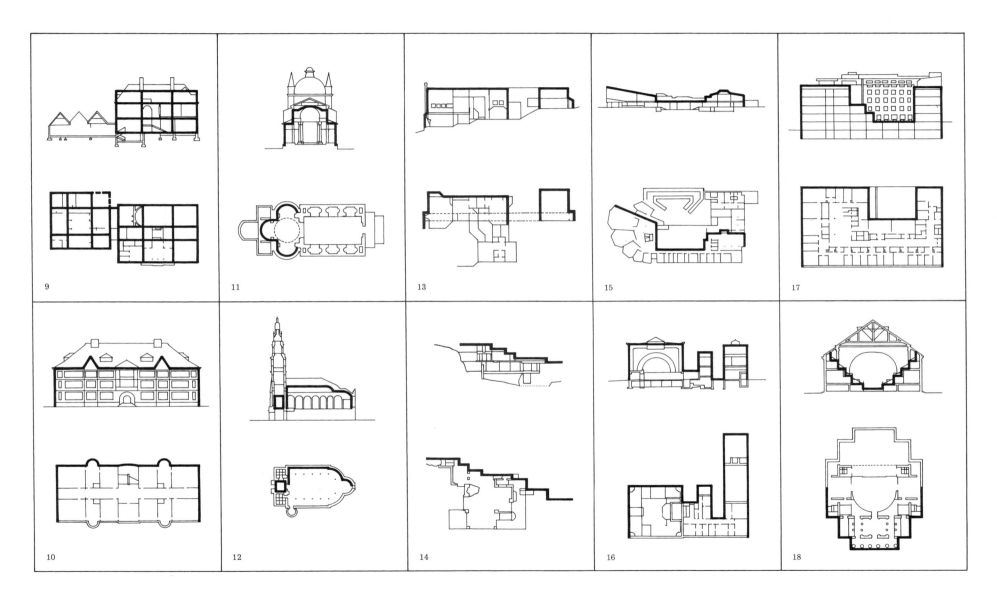

1. **FARNSWORTH HOUSE**
   LUDWIG MIES VAN DER ROHE
   1945–1950
2. **HOTEL DE MONTMORENCY**
   CLAUDE NICHOLAS LEDOUX
   1769

3. **VILLA SAVOYE**
   LE CORBUSIER
   1928–1931
4. **RESIDENCE IN BERLIN**
   KARL FRIEDRICH SCHINKEL
   1823

5. **UNITE D'HABITATION**
   LE CORBUSIER
   1946–1952
6. **CHAROF RESIDENCE**
   GWATHMEY-SIEGEL
   1974–1976

Proportional

In the proportional plan to section relationship, the plan and section or elevation are totalities of each other, but have a dimension change in one direction. Connections between the two realms should involve more than just outlines of the plan and section. Most of the examples have section configurations that are uniformly smaller than the plans, but Unite d'Habitation (5) and the residence in Cadenazzo (10) are exceptions. At Carson Pirie and Scott (11), the increments between parts in plan reduce in section, but the number of increments in section increases. In Christ Church (7) a reversal occurs in the proportional change between plan and section. The in-terior form in section increases in plan while the exterior form decreases. Different parts of the Khuner Villa (13) have different rates of change between plan and section. The Brant House (14) and Lister Courthouse (15) both have modified form languages in plan or section. The Farnsworth House (1), Hotel de Montmorency (2), Villa Savoye (3), Schinkel's Residence (4), and the Charof Residence (6) exemplify proportional plan to section relationships with the sections smaller than the plan, and some but not all of the interior configuration related. Additional examples of this are St. Mary Woolnoth (8), the Lang Music Center (9), and the Salk Institute (12).

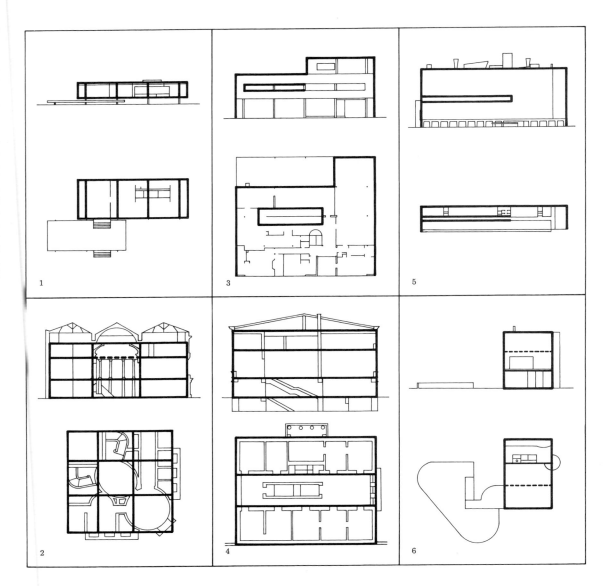

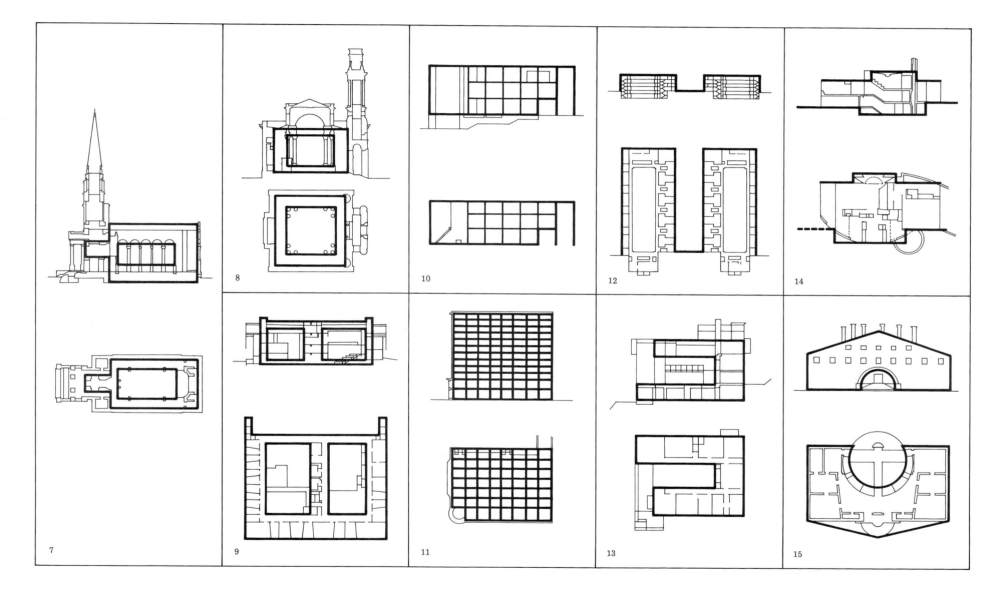

7. CHRIST CHURCH
NICHOLAS HAWKSMOOR
1715–1729

8. ST. MARY WOOLNOTH
NICHOLAS HAWKSMOOR
1715–1724

9. LANG MUSIC BUILDING
ROMALDO GIURGOLA
1973

10. RESIDENCE IN CADENAZZO
MARIO BOTTA
1970–1971

11. CARSON PIRIE AND SCOTT STORE
LOUIS SULLIVAN
1899–1903

12. SALK INSTITUTE
LOUIS I. KAHN
1959–1965

13. KHUNER VILLA
ADOLF LOOS
1930

14. PETER BRANT HOUSE
ROBERT VENTURI
1973

15. LISTER COUNTY COURTHOUSE
ERIK GUNNAR ASPLUND
1917–1921

1. **FIRE STATION NUMBER 4**
   ROBERT VENTURI
   1966
2. **ST. MARY LE BOW**
   CHRISTOPHER WREN
   1670–1683

3. **LEICESTER ENGINEERING BUILDING**
   JAMES STIRLING
   1959
4. **STOCKHOLM PUBLIC LIBRARY**
   ERIK GUNNAR ASPLUND
   1920–1928

5. **VOUKSENNISKA CHURCH, IMATRA**
   ALVAR AALTO
   1956–1958
6. **WEEKEND HOUSE**
   EDWARD LARABEE BARNES
   1963

7. **KIMBALL ART MUSEUM**
   LOUIS I. KAHN
   1966–1972
8. **ANNEX TO OITA MEDICAL HALL**
   ARATA ISOZAKI
   1970–1972

Inverse

An inverse relationship exists between plan and section when the configuration of one is connected to some opposite condition in the other. In the fire station (1) and St. Mary Le Bow (2), a lesser plan form is the dominant element in section or elevation. This reversal of dominance occurs twice in the Leicester Engineering Building (3), where the major plan form is less significant in elevation and the dominant elevation component is small in plan. The inverse configurations in the Stockholm Library (4) have positive and negative manifestations, the central drum in elevation and the recess in plan. The church in Imatra (5) has a sequence of three curved and increasingly larger plan forms related to three decreasing forms in section. In the weekend house (6), the long side of the plan is low in section and the short side is tall. Simple plan forms relate inversely to a complex section and elevation in the Kimball Art Museum (7). At the medical building (8), two forms in elevation, one curvilinear and simple, the other rectilinear and articulated, reverse their characteristics in plan.

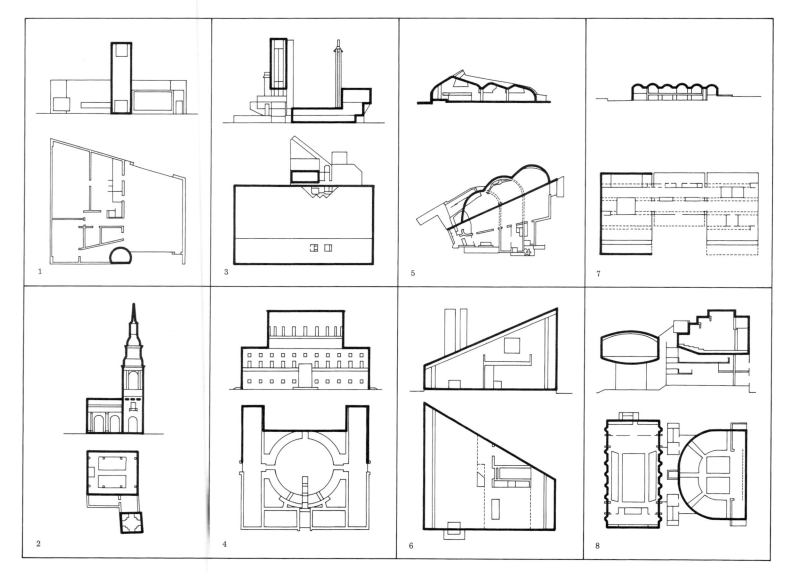

1. **PYRAMID OF CHEOPS**
   ARCHITECT UNKNOWN
   c. 3733 B.C.
2. **RUFER HOUSE**
   ADOLF LOOS
   1922
3. **FROG HOLLOW**
   STANLEY TIGERMAN
   1973–1974

4. **HOUSE AT WEISSENHOF**
   LE CORBUSIER
   1927
5. **UNITED NATIONS PLAZA**
   ROCHE-DINKELOO
   1969–1975
6. **KRESGE AUDITORIUM**
   EERO SAARINEN
   1955

7. **RESIDENCE IN RIVA SAN VITALE**
   MARIO BOTTA
   1972–1973
8. **ELPHINSTONE TOWER**
   ARCHITECT UNKNOWN
   16th CENTURY
9. **SMALL OLYMPIC ARENA**
   KENZO TANGE
   1961–1964

UNIT TO WHOLE

The unit to whole relationship is a formative idea that relates units to other units and to the whole in specific ways to create built form. Illustrated are examples of units equal to, contained within, less than, and aggregated to form the whole.

Unit Equals Whole

The most direct relationship between a unit and the whole occurs when the unit equals the whole. In Cheop's Pyramid (1) and the Rufer House (2) surface material, color, and form render the unit as the whole. At Frog Hollow (3), the application of the color black unifies the roof, walls, and windows into a single entity. The unified grid becomes a wrapper that makes the United Nations Plaza (5) a unit and whole concurrently. As a segment of a sphere, Kresge Auditorium (6) is at once a unit and the whole. Le Corbusier's house at Weissenhof (4) and Mario Botta's house in Switzerland (7) are examples of whole forms that are subtractive. Thick walls that are unified in material and color along with the simple block form of Elphinstone Tower (8) render it a unit equal to the whole. A singular sculptural form makes the unit and whole equal in the Olympic Arena (9).

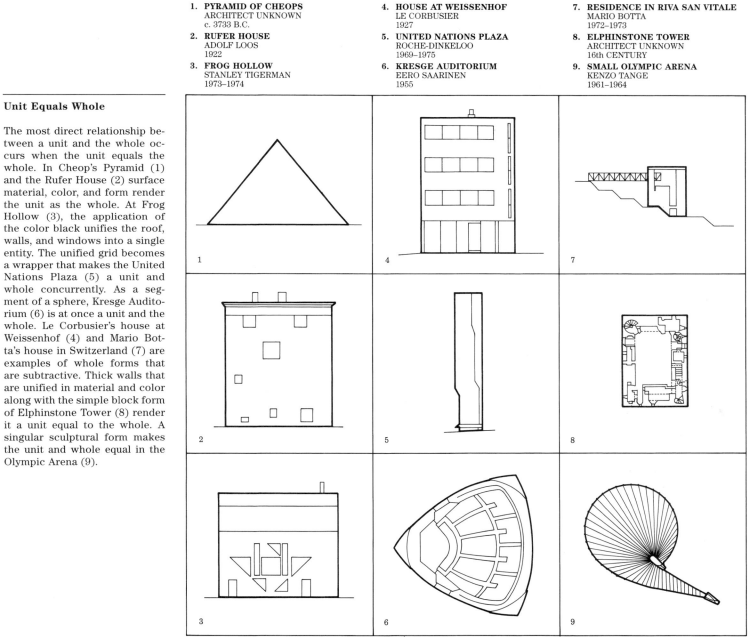

1. **SAN GIORGIO MAGGIORE**
   ANDREA PALLADIO
   1560–1580
2. **STUDENT UNION**
   ROMALDO GIURGOLA
   1974
3. **CHURCH OF SAN SPIRITO**
   FILIPPO BRUNELLESCHI
   1434

4. **REDENTORE CHURCH**
   ANDREA PALLADIO
   1576–1591
5. **CARSON PIRIE AND SCOTT STORE**
   LOUIS SULLIVAN
   1899–1903
6. **CHRIST CHURCH**
   NICHOLAS HAWKSMOOR
   1715–1729

7. **AUDITORIUM BUILDING**
   LOUIS SULLIVAN
   1887–1890
8. **ST. MARY WOOLNOTH**
   NICHOLAS HAWKSMOOR
   1716–1724
9. **OLD SACRISTY**
   FILIPPO BRUNELLESCHI
   1421–1440

10. **DIRECTOR'S HOUSE**
    CLAUDE NICHOLAS LEDOUX
    1775–1779
11. **LANG MUSIC BUILDING**
    ROMALDO GIURGOLA
    1973
12. **HOTEL GUIMARD**
    CLAUDE NICHOLAS LEDOUX
    1770

Units Contained in Whole

In the relationship of units contained in the whole, the units are structural components, use-spaces, or blocks of use-spaces. The whole is the dominant image, with the units not expressed on the exterior. Christ Church (6) and the churches of San Giorgio (1), San Spirito (3), and Redentore (4) are composed of implied spatial units in configurations that emphasize major subdivisions in the forms. The Student Union (2) and Carson Pirie and Scott store (5) are designed with units that are structural modules. In the Auditorium Building (7), the units are blocks of use-spaces which generally are divided into different types of uses. Lesser spatial units are organized around the main central space in St. Mary Woolnoth (8). Spatial volumes form the major units in the Old Sacristy (9), while domed ceiling forms create secondary units. In the Director's House (10) the units generally coincide with use and circulation spaces. Major rooms and groupings of smaller rooms create the units in the Lang Music Building (11) and the Hotel Guimard (12).

1. **EXETER LIBRARY**
LOUIS I. KAHN
1967–1972

2. **TREDYFFRIN PUBLIC LIBRARY**
ROMALDO GIURGOLA
1976

3. **HOTEL DE MONTMORENCY**
CLAUDE NICHOLAS LEDOUX
1769

4. **TENDERING HALL**
JOHN SOANE
1784–1790

5. **J. PIERPONT MORGAN LIBRARY**
McKIM, MEAD, AND WHITE
1906

6. **ANNAGLEE**
RICHARD CASTLE
1740–1770

7. **TEMPLE OF HORUS**
ARCHITECT UNKNOWN
237 B.C.–57 B.C.

8. **THE PALACE OF ASSEMBLY**
LE CORBUSIER
1953–1963

9. **FALLINGWATER**
FRANK LLOYD WRIGHT
1935

10. **MUSGUM VILLAGE**
ARCHITECT UNKNOWN
DATE UNKNOWN

11. **SEA RANCH CONDOMINIUM I**
CHARLES MOORE
1964–1965

12. **FINLANDIA HALL**
ALVAR AALTO
1967–1971

Whole Greater than Sum of the Units

In this relationship, the whole incorporates more built form than that ascribed to the identified units. The central space in the Exeter Library (1) is not a use-space and, therefore, not a unit. Tredyffrin Library (2) is more than the major use-space formed by the structural bays. In Hotel de Montmorency (3), Tendering Hall (4), Morgan Library (5), the Irish house (6), and Finlandia Hall (12), the major figured use-spaces form the units, and the lesser, servant spaces are poche. The units in Edfu Temple (7) are major building blocks set within a whole defined by a wall; the difference between the wall and the units is exterior space. In the Palace of Assembly (8), the units are the two unique central forms and the blocks of use-spaces at the perimeter; the remainder of the interior court is the excess. At Fallingwater (9), the units are expressed in elevation by balcony forms and chimney mass, viewed against the remainder of the building. A wall defines the whole in the Musgum Village (10), which is more than the units combined. At Sea Ranch (11), the units are the living spaces, while the whole also includes the central space and the secondary units added to each dwelling.

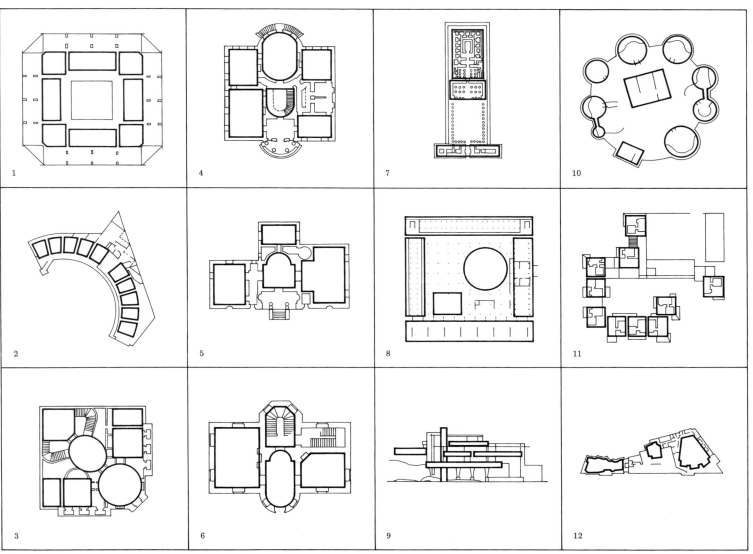

1.	LEICESTER ENGINEERING BUILDING JAMES STIRLING 1959	4.	EASTON NESTON NICHOLAS HAWKSMOOR c. 1695–1710	7.	NASHDOM EDWIN LUTYENS 1905–1909
2.	CAMBRIDGE HISTORY FACULTY JAMES STIRLING 1964	5.	ST. GEORGE-IN-THE-EAST NICHOLAS HAWKSMOOR 1714–1729	8.	TRINITY CHURCH HENRY HOBSON RICHARDSON 1872–1877
3.	FLOREY BUILDING JAMES STIRLING 1966	6.	THEATER IN BESANÇON, FRANCE CLAUDE NICHOLAS LEDOUX 1775	9.	ALLEGHENY COUNTY COURTHOUSE HENRY HOBSON RICHARDSON 1883–1888

Units Aggregate to Form Whole

Units are aggregated to form a whole when they are arranged in proximity to other units to establish a perceived relationship. This is done by adjoining, separating, and overlapping.

Units Adjoin

Units adjoin to form a whole when the units are visible, perceived as entities, and relate to other units through surface contact. Adjoining, indicative of

James Stirling's work at this time, is exemplified in the Engineering Labs (1), History Faculty (2), and the Florey Building (3). At Easton Neston (4) and Nashdom (7), assembled units emphasize the classic central entrance. Built form and spatial units are combined in St. George (5). The Besançon Theater (6) and Trinity Church (8) exemplify units added around a dominant central form. In Richardson's Courthouse (9) and Aalto's Town Hall (13), units as groups of use-spaces adjoin around a central court, and at Aalto's Church (12), Cultural Center (14), and Sanitorium (15) they adjoin to create the building itself. At Unity Temple (10), two sets of added units are combined. Major and minor units connected by a third unit define the Guggenheim Museum (11). In La Rotonda (16), the units are added symmetrically about a central space, while at Karlskirche (19) the use-space units adjoin symmetrically. Major volumes and components comprise the fire station (17) and the Brant House (18), and units occur around a central form or space in Stockholm Library (20) and Santa Maria (21). Structural units adjoin in Villa Savoye (22) and the Kimball Art Center (23). Kahn's Convent (24) is a series of forms partially contained by units which are groups of spaces.

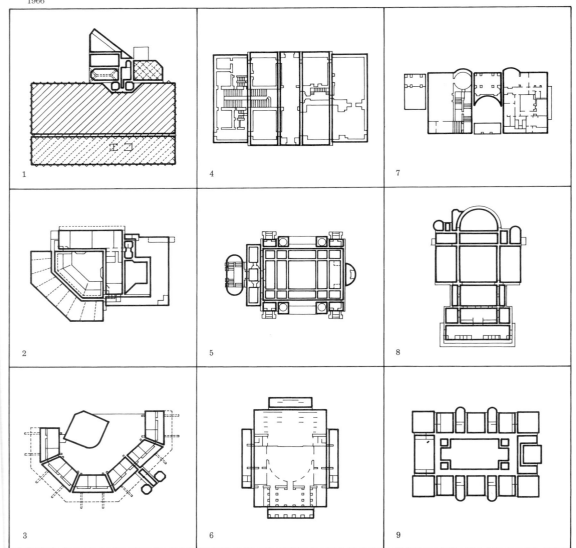

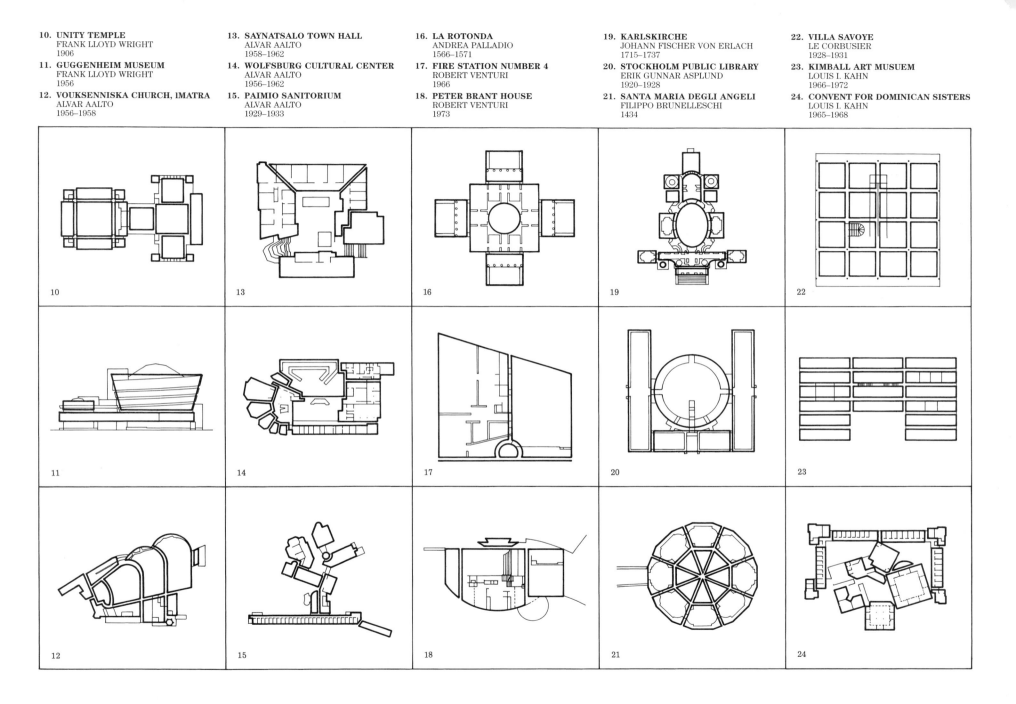

Units Overlap

Units overlap to form a whole through volumetric interpenetration. Two elongated forms defined by four towers overlap the main block of Sever Hall (1), and an upper level wing with perpendicular orientation connects the two masses of the Robie House (2). In the Yale Architecture Building (3), a series of overlapping trays define interior space. The circular main space of Lister Courthouse (4) is partially engaged into the central mass, while the circle unites the triangle of the roof to the square of the building in the Tucker House (5). Overlapping corners allow for continuous circulation in the Bryn Mawr Dormitories (6). Rotated sets of forms overlap in the Occupational Health Building (7), the Pratt Residence (8), and the Salisbury School (9). At the Bridgehampton Residence (10), implied circles overlap a rectangle and each other, and in the Cooper Residence (11), the overlapping forms create spatial subdivisions and imply a partial pinwheel. The Barcelona Pavilion (12) is a complex series of interpenetrating, orthogonal, and implied spatial volumes.

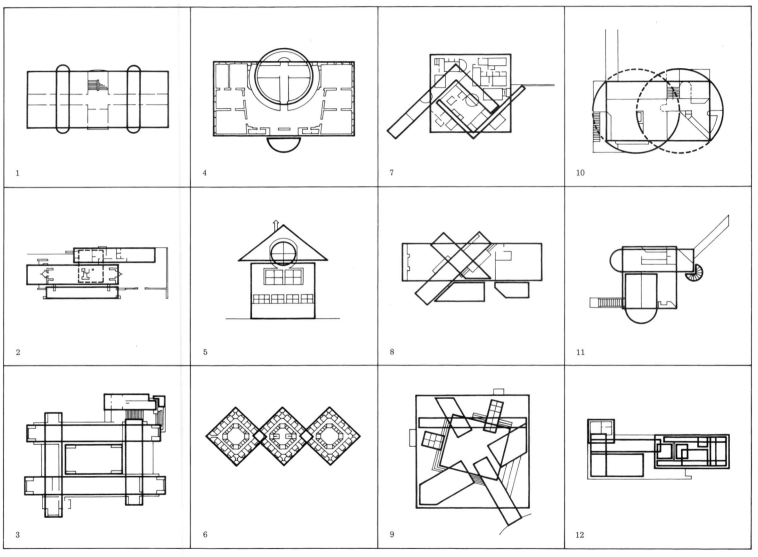

1. DEERE WEST OFFICE BUILDING
ROCHE-DINKELOO
1975–1976

2. OLYMPIC ARENA
KENZO TANGE
1961–1964

3. RESIDENCE IN STABIO
MARIO BOTTA
1981

4. COLLEGE LIFE INSURANCE COMPANY
ROCHE-DINKELOO
1967–1971

5. RESIDENCE ON MT. DESERT ISLAND
EDWARD LARABEE BARNES
1975

6. PAUL MELLON ARTS CENTER
I. M. PEI
1970–1973

7. EVERSON MUSEUM OF ART
I. M. PEI
1968

8. NATIONAL ASSEMBLY
LOUIS I. KAHN
1962–1974

9. CHAPEL AT RONCHAMP
LE CORBUSIER
1950–1955

Units Separate

Units which are related to other units can be separated through isolation or articulation of the connection to create perceived separation. In the Deere Office Building (1), the units are separated by glass, a defined circulation element, and an atrium space. Glass is used to create perceptual separation in the Olympic Arena (2) and the house in Switzerland (3). The College Life Insurance Buildings (4) are isolated forms tenuously connected by a bridge at one level. A deck serves to unify isolated elements in the Mt. Desert house (5), and separated forms share a common roof in the Mellon Arts Center (6). Glass perceptually separates the units of the Everson Museum (7), and is also used to create apparent separation of units in the National Assembly (8) and the Chapel at Ronchamp (9).

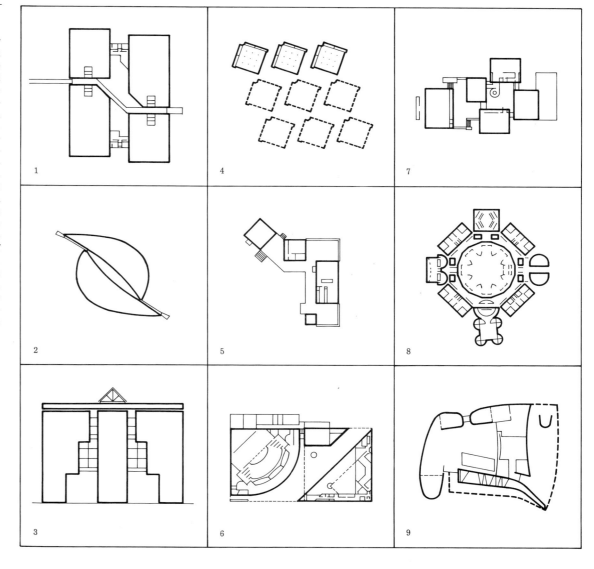

1. **ALTES MUSEUM**
KARL FRIEDRICH SCHINKEL
1824–1830

2. **HUNTING LODGE**
KARL FRIEDRICH SCHINKEL
1822

3. **RHODE ISLAND STATE CAPITOL**
McKIM, MEAD, AND WHITE
1895–1903

4. **UNITY TEMPLE**
FRANK LLOYD WRIGHT
1906

5. **GUGGENHEIM MUSEUM**
FRANK LLOYD WRIGHT
1956

6. **SHENBOKU ARCHIVES**
FUMIHIKO MAKI
1970

7. **ST. GEORGE-IN-THE-EAST**
NICHOLAS HAWKSMOOR
1714–1729

8. **CHRIST CHURCH**
NICHOLAS HAWKSMOOR
1715–1729

9. **KHUNER VILLA**
ADOLF LOOS
1930

REPETITIVE TO UNIQUE

The formative idea of relating repetitive and unique elements is the design of buildings by establishing relationships between components which have singular and multiple manifestations. Illustrated are examples of unique surrounded by repetitive; formed by transformation in a repetitive field; added to repetitive; and defined by repetitive.

Unique Surrounded by Repetitive

Repetitive elements surround a unique unit when the unique is a bounded form and is ringed by multiple equal units. Unique elements are located in larger spaces formed by the repetitive units in Schinkel's museum (1), the Florey Building (10), and the Palace of Assembly (18). In the Hunting Lodge (2) the unique center is surrounded. It is partially surrounded in the Adult Learning Lab (16). Unique elements are surrounded in the Rhode Island Capitol (3), Unity Temple (4), and San Spirito (23), and are partially ringed in the Guggenheim Museum (5), the Convent (13), the Auditorium Building (15), and the Lang Music Center (17). The repetitive elements form a pinwheel in the Archives Building (6), and a 'U' shape in both the Khuner Villa (9) and the Stockholm Library (22). St. George (7), Cambridge History (11), Trinity Church (12), and San Spirito (23) exemplify two kinds of repetitive elements. In Christ Church (8) and Villa Foscari (20), the multiple units relate to the unique element in more than one way. A central unique element is totally surrounded at Exeter Library (14), the theater (19), and La Rotonda (21). Santa Maria (24) has a unique center surrounded by two sets of repetitive elements, one spatial and one structural.

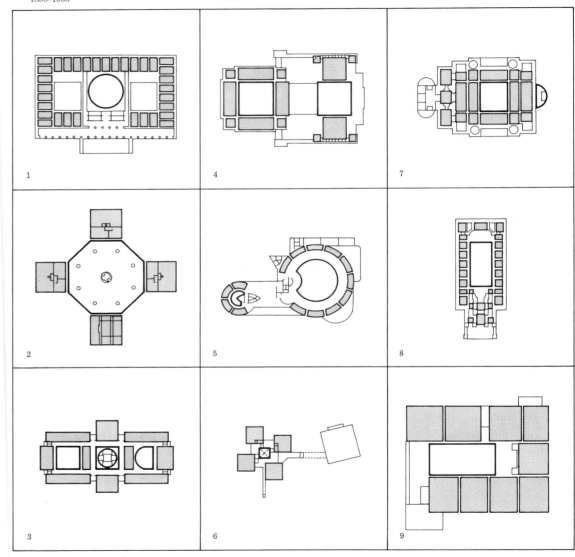

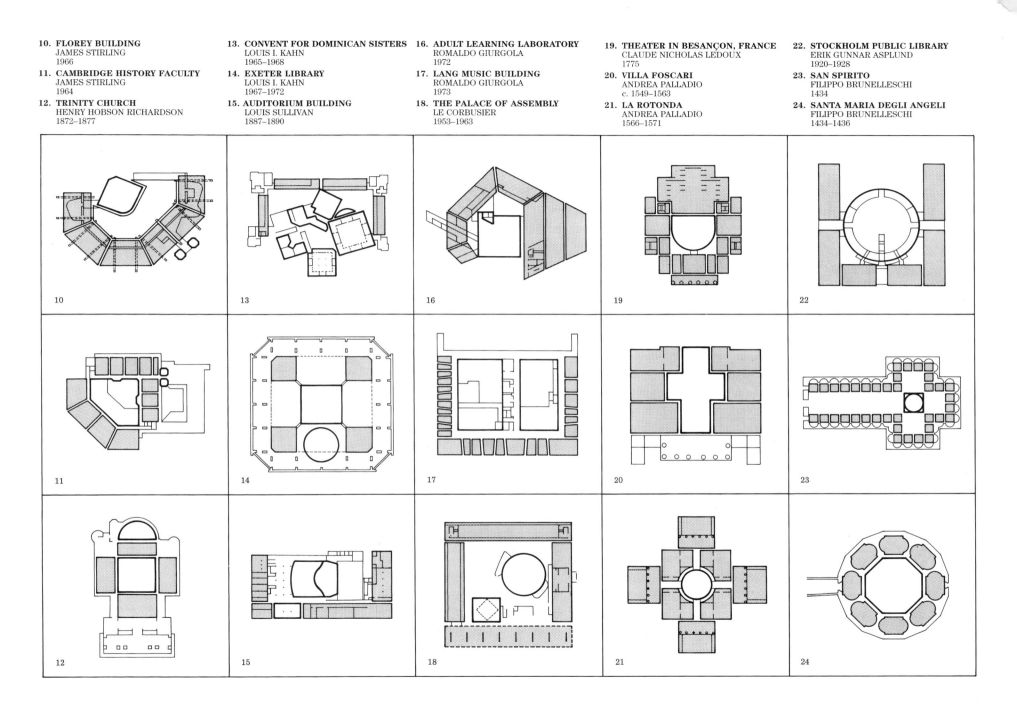

10. FLOREY BUILDING
JAMES STIRLING
1966

11. CAMBRIDGE HISTORY FACULTY
JAMES STIRLING
1964

12. TRINITY CHURCH
HENRY HOBSON RICHARDSON
1872–1877

13. CONVENT FOR DOMINICAN SISTERS
LOUIS I. KAHN
1965–1968

14. EXETER LIBRARY
LOUIS I. KAHN
1967–1972

15. AUDITORIUM BUILDING
LOUIS SULLIVAN
1887–1890

16. ADULT LEARNING LABORATORY
ROMALDO GIURGOLA
1972

17. LANG MUSIC BUILDING
ROMALDO GIURGOLA
1973

18. THE PALACE OF ASSEMBLY
LE CORBUSIER
1953–1963

19. THEATER IN BESANÇON, FRANCE
CLAUDE NICHOLAS LEDOUX
1775

20. VILLA FOSCARI
ANDREA PALLADIO
c. 1549–1563

21. LA ROTONDA
ANDREA PALLADIO
1566–1571

22. STOCKHOLM PUBLIC LIBRARY
ERIK GUNNAR ASPLUND
1920–1928

23. SAN SPIRITO
FILIPPO BRUNELLESCHI
1434

24. SANTA MARIA DEGLI ANGELI
FILIPPO BRUNELLESCHI
1434–1436

1. **CARSON PIRIE AND SCOTT STORE**
   LOUIS SULLIVAN
   1899–1903
2. **STEINER HOUSE**
   ADOLF LOOS
   1910
3. **ALEXANDER HOUSE**
   MICHAEL GRAVES
   1971–1973

4. **SNELLMAN HOUSE**
   ERIK GUNNAR ASPLUND
   1917–1918
5. **HOTEL DE MONTMORENCY**
   CLAUDE NICHOLAS LEDOUX
   1769
6. **TENDERING HALL**
   JOHN SOANE
   1784–1790

7. **CARLL TUCKER III HOUSE**
   ROBERT VENTURI
   1975
8. **HOMEWOOD**
   EDWIN LUTYENS
   1901
9. **EASTON NESTON**
   NICHOLAS HAWKSMOOR
   c. 1695–1710

10. **MOORE HOUSE**
    CHARLES MOORE
    1962
11. **FALLINGWATER**
    FRANK LLOYD WRIGHT
    1935
12. **GUMMA MUSEUM OF FINE ARTS**
    ARATA ISOZAKI
    1971–1974

Unique by Transformation of Repetitive

Unique elements can be developed by the transformation of repetitive units through changes in size, shape, configuration, orientation, geometry, color, and articulation. The changes of shape and geometry are similar and related, but usually shape involves less form change than does geometry. Carson Pirie and Scott store (1), Snellman Residence (4), and Hotel de Montmorency (5) exemplify unique elements developed by geometric transformations. This is also the case at Tendering Hall (6), the Tucker House (7), and Homewood (8). Related changes by shape occur in the Steiner House (2) and the Alexander House (3). Transformation by size creates the unique two-story spaces in Easton Neston (9). Unique by change in the articulation of the repetitive units is exemplified in the Moore House in Orinda (10). The unique components in Wright's Fallingwater (11) and the Gumma Museum (12) are created by change in orientation of the repetitive elements.

1. **TEMPLE OF ARTEMIS**
   PAEONIUS AND DEMETRIUS
   c. 356 B.C.
2. **KIMBALL ART MUSEUM**
   LOUIS I. KAHN
   1966–1972
3. **INSTITUTE FOR ADVANCED STUDIES**
   GBQC
   1968–1972

4. **STUDENT UNION**
   ROMALDO GIURGOLA
   1974
5. **BROOKLYN CHILDREN'S MUSEUM**
   HARDY-HOLZMAN-PFIEFFER
   1977
6. **OCCUPATIONAL HEALTH CENTER**
   HARDY-HOLZMAN-PFIEFFER
   1973

7. **FREDERICK G. ROBIE HOUSE**
   FRANK LLOYD WRIGHT
   1909
8. **ST. STEPHENS WALBROOK**
   CHRISTOPHER WREN
   1672–1687
9. **VILLA SAVOYE**
   LE CORBUSIER
   1928–1931

Unique in Repetitive Field

A field or network made from equal units in uniform relationships may be interrupted by a unique element. In the Artemis Temple (1), walls are located within a columnar field. Open courts that interrupt the structural system form the unique units in the Kimball Art Center (2) and the Student Union (4). At the Institute for Advanced Studies (3), unique geometric forms are placed within an orthogonal structural grid. A circulation element rotated in a structural field forms the unique element in the Brooklyn Museum (5), while at the Occupational Health Building (6), a skylight, rotated in the orthogonal grid, is unique. Structural fields are disrupted by a fireplace mass in the Robie House (7), by a dome in St. Stephens (8), and by two different vertical circulation elements in the Villa Savoye (9).

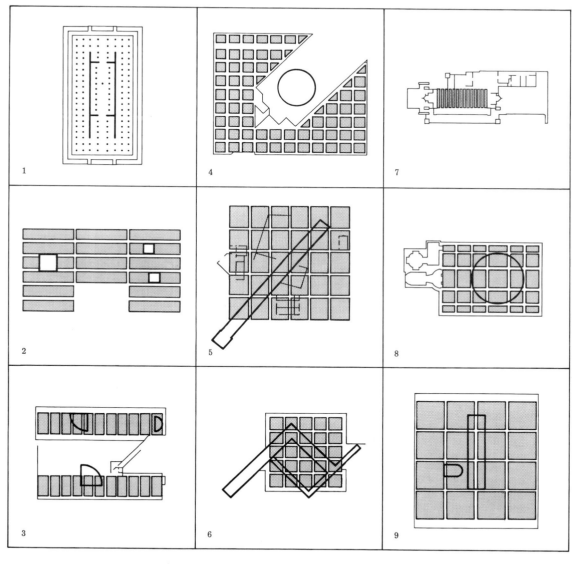

Unique Added to Repetitive

When the scale and mass of the repetitive elements are dominant, the unique is viewed as added to the repetitive. In the Seinajoki Town Hall (1), the unique component, added to the end of the repetitive, becomes a terminus. The Kamioka Town Hall (2) has a unique form added to the midpoint of a series of multiple elements. Three unique units are placed into an implied arena in Boyer Hall (3), and a cloister is formed by the joining of the unique and repetitive at La Tourette (4). In the Unite d'Habitation (5) elevation, the special forms are added to the top and bottom of the main block. A different kind of end is created in the Wainwright Building (6) with the addition of the unique top. The unique form is added to the front of St. Nicholas (7). At the Olivetti Center (8), two unique elements are adjoined to the middle of the multiple units, while the two unique components at Leicester Engineering Building (9) are added adjacent to the main blocks of the building.

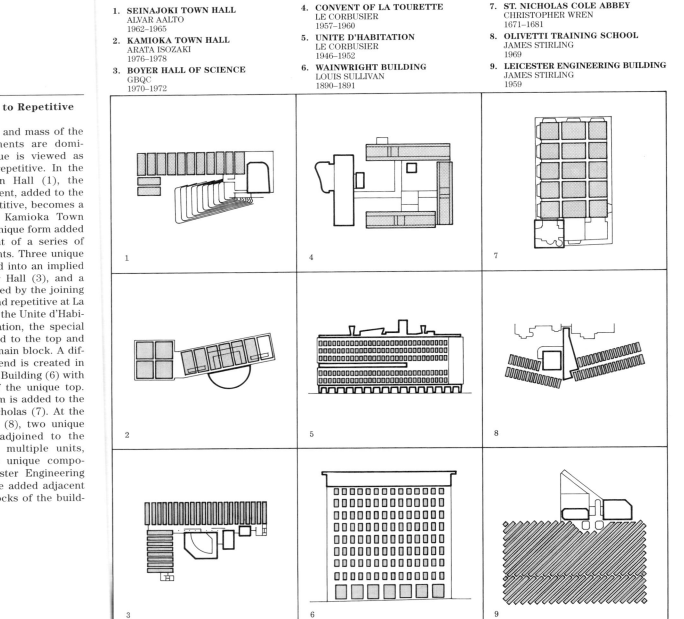

250

1. **COLOSSEUM**
ARCHITECT UNKNOWN
70–82

2. **ST. LEOPOLD AM STEINHOF**
OTTO WAGNER
1905–1907

3. **ST. ANTHOLIN**
CHRISTOPHER WREN
1678–1691

4. **HOUSE OF THE MENANDER**
ARCHITECT UNKNOWN
C. 300 B.C.

5. **BOSTON PUBLIC LIBRARY**
MCKIM, MEAD, AND WHITE
1898

6. **SAYNATSALO TOWN HALL**
ALVAR AALTO
1950–1952

7. **YALE ART AND ARCHITECTURE**
PAUL RUDOLPH
1958

8. **LARKIN BUILDING**
FRANK LLOYD WRIGHT
1903

9. **ALLEGHENY COUNTY COURTHOUSE**
HENRY HOBSON RICHARDSON
1883–1888

Unique Defined by Repetitive

Unique is defined by repetitive when the form of the unique element is established by the configuration of the repetitive elements. All of the examples have unique forms that are either interior or exterior spaces. In the Colosseum (1), Pompeii House (4), and Boston Public Library (5), a major exterior space is formed by the arrangement of the multiple units. This is also the case in Aalto's town hall (6) and the Allegheny Courthouse (9). Major interior spaces that are expressed on the exterior are the singular units in Wagner's Steinhof Church (2) and Wren's St. Antholin (3). Multistoried, unique spaces that serve as the foci for surrounding repetitive spaces are exemplified in the Yale Architecture Building (7) and the Larkin Building (8).

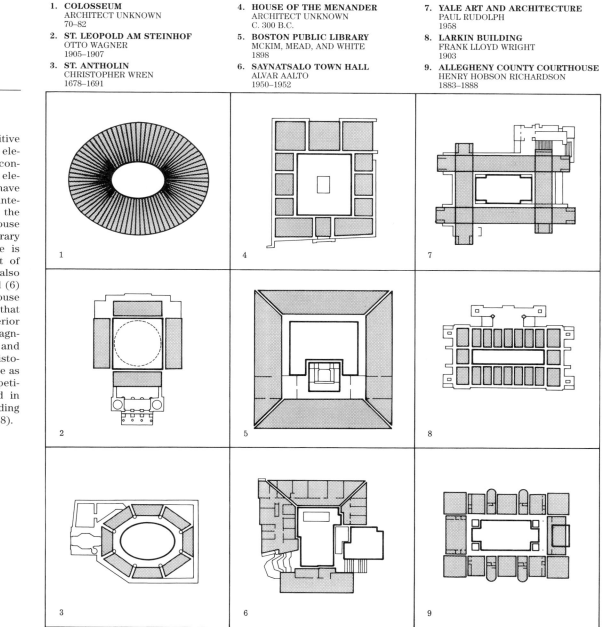

251

1. **HOMEWOOD**
   EDWIN LUTYENS
   1901
2. **WAINWRIGHT BUILDING**
   LOUIS SULLIVAN
   1890–1891
3. **WHITNEY MUSEUM OF AMERICAN ART**
   MARCEL BREUER
   1966

4. **VILLA SAVOYE**
   LE CORBUSIER
   1928–1931
5. **STOCKHOLM PUBLIC LIBRARY**
   ERIK GUNNAR ASPLUND
   1920-1928
6. **VANNA VENTURI HOUSE**
   ROBERT VENTURI
   1962

7. **ENSO-GUTZEIT HEADQUARTERS**
   ALVAR AALTO
   1959–1962
8. **EXETER LIBRARY**
   LOUIS I. KAHN
   1967–1972
9. **STUDENT UNION**
   ROMALDO GIURGOLA
   1974

ADDITIVE AND SUBTRACTIVE

Additive and subtractive are formative ideas which involve the assemblage of parts or the removal of pieces to create built form. In additive, the parts are dominant, while in subtractive, the whole is dominant.

Subtractive

All of the examples present simple orthogonal configurations that are eroded to generate the building design. At Homewood (1), terraces and the entry are developed by the subtractions, while in the Wainwright Building (2), a light well is made. The Whitney Museum (3) shows erosion in section, which allows for light to enter lower floors, the entry to be defined, and the building to establish a unique contact with the street. In Villa Savoye (4), the subtraction occurs within a bounded frame, and in the Stockholm Library (5), a drum is added into the courtyard created by the removal. The Venturi House (6) and Enso-Gutzeit Headquarters (7) are similar in that the subtraction establishes the entry. It also allows for the introduction of light into the interior at Enso. The major interior central space in Exeter Library (8) results from subtraction, while at the Student Union (9) a major exterior space, as well as the entry and smaller exterior spaces, is created by removal.

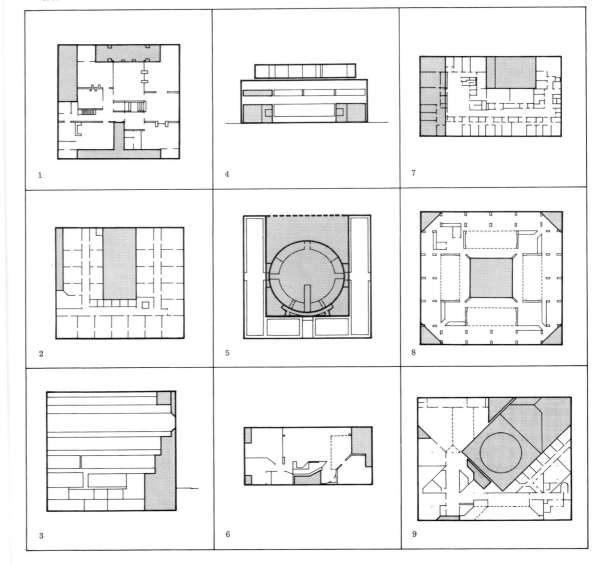

1. **LA ROTONDA**
ANDREA PALLADIO
1566–1571
2. **RICHARDS RESEARCH BUILDING**
LOUIS I. KAHN
1959–1961
3. **THE SALUTATION**
EDWIN LUTYENS
1911

4. **LISTER COUNTY COURTHOUSE**
ERIK GUNNAR ASPLUND
1917–1921
5. **FLOREY BUILDING**
JAMES STIRLING
1966
6. **SEA RANCH CONDOMINIUM I**
CHARLES MOORE
1964–1965

7. **UNITY TEMPLE**
FRANK LLOYD WRIGHT
1906
8. **ALLEGHENY COUNTY COURTHOUSE**
HENRY HOBSON RICHARDSON
1883–1888
9. **ST. GEORGE-IN-THE-EAST**
NICHOLAS HAWKSMOOR
1714–1729

10. **WOLFSBURG CULTURAL CENTER**
ALVAR AALTO
1958–1962
11. **SAN MARIA DEGLI ANGELI**
FILIPPO BRUNELLESCHI
1434–1436
12. **BASILICA OF SAN VITALE**
ARCHITECT UNKNOWN
c. 530–548

Additive

Additive designs are perceptually parts-dominant. In Villa Rotonda (1), the parts are attached to a major central unit. At Richards Medical Labs (2), a series of aggregations occur; service towers added to individual research labs form a composite unit, which is added to other similar parts and to a central service core. In Salutation (3), the servants' quarters are a minor element that is joined to the major form. A major use-space is added into the dominant building form in the Lister Courthouse (4). In the Florey Building (5), a series of segments aggregate to create an exterior space into which the unique common space is added. The units at Sea Ranch (6), each a collection of forms, are assembled under a common roof. Two sets of repetitive, orthogonal units are joined to make the two dominant building parts in Unity Temple (7). In the Allegheny Courthouse (8), the parts form a central open space. Lesser units are assembled around the nave in Saint George-in-the-East (9), and components that are generally consistent with use areas are aggregate to form the Wolfsburg Cultural Center (10). In San Maria (11) and San Vitale (12) a series of lesser spaces ring a major space.

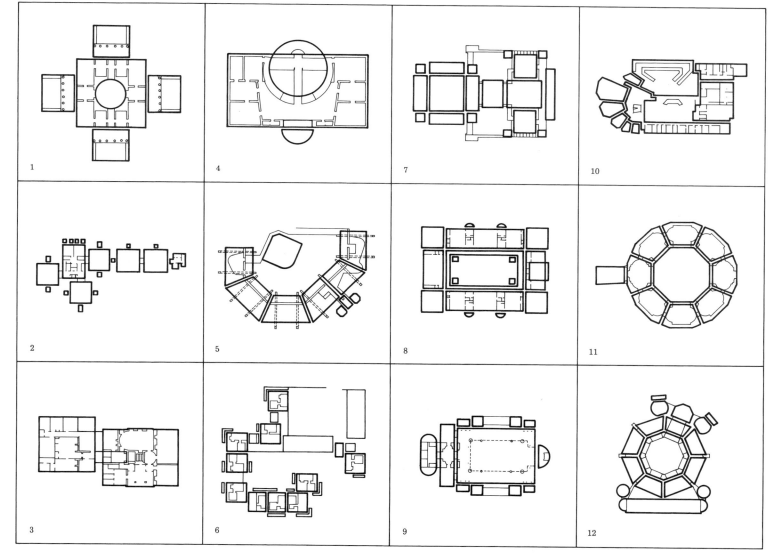

1. **SALK INSTITUTE**
   LOUIS I. KAHN
   1959–1965
2. **DIRECTOR'S HOUSE**
   CLAUDE NICHOLAS LEDOUX
   1775–1779
3. **UNITY TEMPLE**
   FRANK LLOYD WRIGHT
   1906

4. **CHRIST CHURCH**
   NICHOLAS HAWKSMOOR
   1715–1729
5. **REDENTORE CHURCH**
   ANDREA PALLADIO
   1576–1591
6. **CHURCH OF SAN SPIRITO**
   FILIPPO BRUNELLESCHI
   1434

7. **SAN MARIA DEGLI ANGELI**
   FILIPPO BRUNELLESCHI
   1434–1436
8. **LISTER COUNTY COURTHOUSE**
   ERIK GUNNAR ASPLUND
   1917–1921
9. **STOCKHOLM PUBLIC LIBRARY**
   ERIK GUNNAR ASPLUND
   1920–1928

SYMMETRY AND BALANCE

Symmetry and balance are formative ideas in which states of perceived and conceived equilibrium are established between components to create built form. Illustrated are examples of axial, biaxial, rotational, and translational symmetry and balance by configuration, geometry, and positive and negative.

Symmetry

Symmetry, a specialized form of balance, entails the use of equal units on each side of an implied line or about a point. At Salk Institute (1), the line of axial symmetry is established through the major exterior space. In the Director's House (2), Unity Temple (3), Christ Church (4), Redentore Church (5), and San Spirito (6), it is through the major usespaces. In Santa Maria (7), radial symmetry is changed to axial by the location of two opposite entries. Symmetry occurs through the main interior space in the Lister Courthouse (8) and the Stockholm Library (9). Biaxial symmetry in the Temple of Venus and Rome (10) is through and between the major spaces. In Exeter Library (11), it bisects the dominant space, and in La Rotonda (12), it occurs in the main circulation area. Symmetry by rotation in St. Mark's Tower (13) has four units about a point, while Castle del Monte (14) shows eight, and St. John Nepomuk (15) has five. St. Ivo (16), the Pilgrimage Church (17), and the Sepulchral Church (18) each has three units in symmetry by rotation. Units as rooms and groups of rooms are symmetrically translated into linear configurations at St. Andrews (19) and in a school by Botta (20). Two sets of units are translated in different directions in Utzon's atrium housing (21).

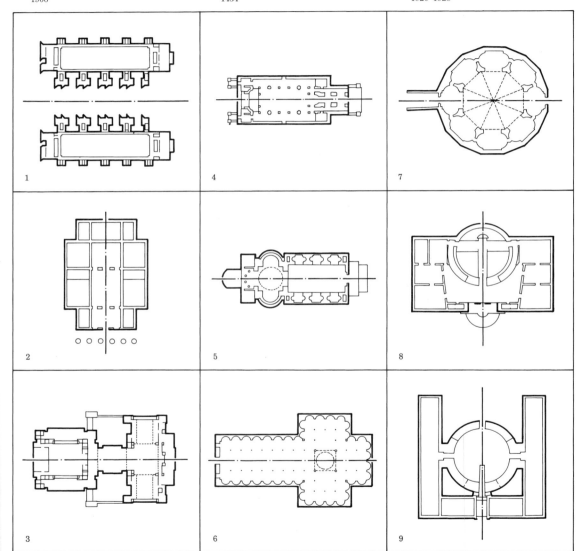

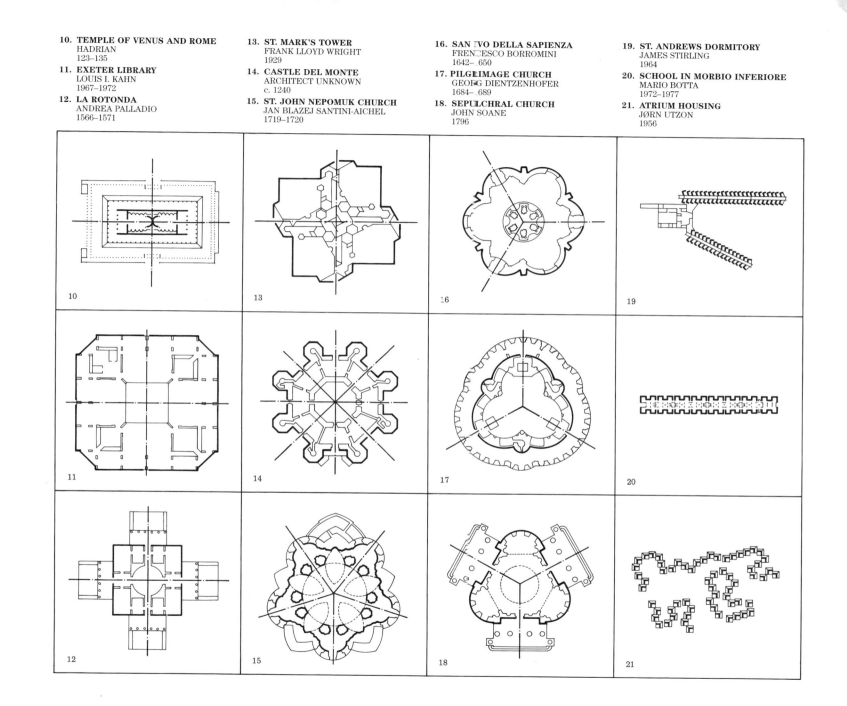

10. TEMPLE OF VENUS AND ROME
HADRIAN
123–135

11. EXETER LIBRARY
LOUIS I. KAHN
1967–1972

12. LA ROTONDA
ANDREA PALLADIO
1566–1571

13. ST. MARK'S TOWER
FRANK LLOYD WRIGHT
1929

14. CASTLE DEL MONTE
ARCHITECT UNKNOWN
c. 1240

15. ST. JOHN NEPOMUK CHURCH
JAN BLAZEJ SANTINI-AICHEL
1719–1720

16. SAN IVO DELLA SAPIENZA
FRENCESCO BORROMINI
1642–1650

17. PILGRIMAGE CHURCH
GEORG DIENTZENHOFER
1684–1689

18. SEPULCHRAL CHURCH
JOHN SOANE
1796

19. ST. ANDREWS DORMITORY
JAMES STIRLING
1964

20. SCHOOL IN MORBIO INFERIORE
MARIO BOTTA
1972–1977

21. ATRIUM HOUSING
JØRN UTZON
1956

1. **OLIVETTI TRAINING SCHOOL**
   JAMES STIRLING
   1969
2. **OSPEDALE DEGLI INNOCENTI**
   FILIPPO BRUNELLESCHI
   1421–1445
3. **SEA RANCH CONDOMINIUM I**
   CHARLES MOORE
   1964–1965

4. **UNITY TEMPLE**
   FRANK LLOYD WRIGHT
   1906
5. **FREDERICK G. ROBIE HOUSE**
   FRANK LLOYD WRIGHT
   1909
6. **J. J. GLESSNER HOUSE**
   HENRY HOBSON RICHARDSON
   1885–1887

7. **ADULT LEARNING LABORATORY**
   ROMALDO GIURGOLA
   1972
8. **SAN GIORGIO MAGGIORE**
   ANDREA PALLADIO
   1560–1580
9. **PETER BRANT HOUSE**
   ROBERT VENTURI
   1973

Balance by Configuration

Balance by configuration occurs when equilibrium between components that are different in form or shape is established. The Olivetti Training Center (1) balances the older existing building. Within it, the long wing equalizes the short wing plus the special space. The Ospedale (2) exemplifies balance of masses—one with a void, the other with an additional unit. In Sea Ranch (3), a diagonal balance line is established with six living units on one side, and four units with two garages on the other. Equal cores are rendered differently by the addition of secondary units in Unity Temple (4). Public and private separation creates one line of balance in the Robie House (5) and the Glessner House (6). In Giurgola's Research Labs (7), the balance is developed through geometry and mass. San Giorgio (8) is symmetrical in one direction and balanced in the other with simple and complex shapes that reflect the sacred and secular areas. The configuration differences in the Brant House (9) occur at changes of floor plane and mass. At Ronchamp (10) in plan and at the Riola Parish Center (14) in section, single, larger units balance multiple smaller units. Fallingwater (11) is balanced between smaller enclosed and larger open spaces. In one direction, Lister Courthouse (23) and Dulwich Gallery (13) are symmetrical; in the other, the differences between public areas for Lister and gallery size for Dulwich define the balance. External symmetry in Hotel Guimard (15) is shifted to balance by location of three major living spaces. Balance in the Florey Building (16) occurs between a form weighted with a pair of towers and another with a special space. A special space, with a detached form, balances the remainder of the town hall (17), and the tower balances the void of the main space in two directions in the Auditorium Building (18). At Easton Neston (19), the two unique two-story spaces create the difference in configuration. Balance at Homewood (20) occurs at the line of shift between front and back arrangement. The configuration change at Snellman House (21) occurs between servant and main use-spaces in two directions. At Unite d'Habitation (22), the shopping street locates the balance line between the subtracted base and the additive top. At Leicester Engineering (12), the difference is between vertical and horizontal, and in the Venturi House (24), symmetry is shifted to balance by the window pattern.

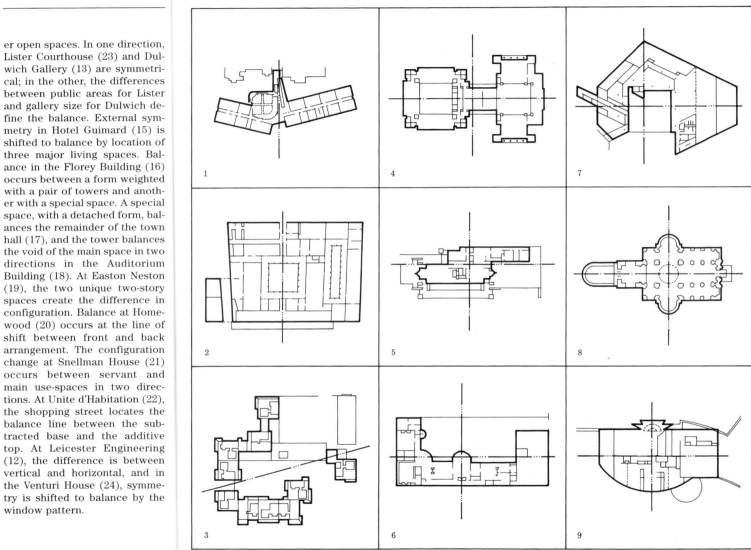

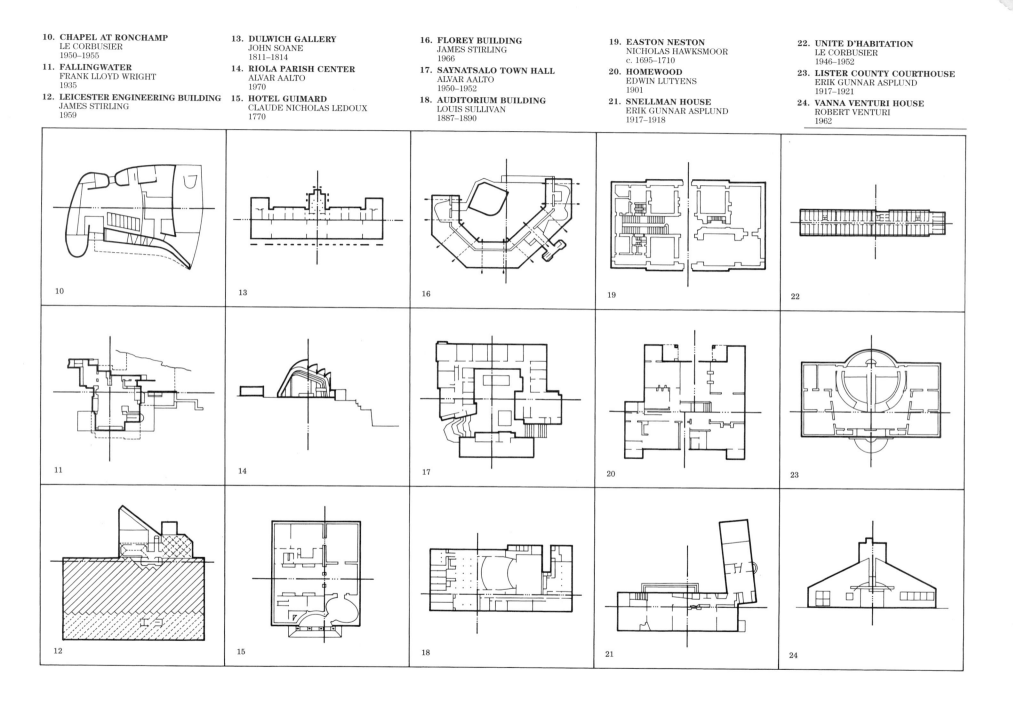

10. CHAPEL AT RONCHAMP
LE CORBUSIER
1950–1955

11. FALLINGWATER
FRANK LLOYD WRIGHT
1935

12. LEICESTER ENGINEERING BUILDING
JAMES STIRLING
1959

13. DULWICH GALLERY
JOHN SOANE
1811–1814

14. RIOLA PARISH CENTER
ALVAR AALTO
1970

15. HOTEL GUIMARD
CLAUDE NICHOLAS LEDOUX
1770

16. FLOREY BUILDING
JAMES STIRLING
1966

17. SAYNATSALO TOWN HALL
ALVAR AALTO
1950–1952

18. AUDITORIUM BUILDING
LOUIS SULLIVAN
1887–1890

19. EASTON NESTON
NICHOLAS HAWKSMOOR
c. 1695–1710

20. HOMEWOOD
EDWIN LUTYENS
1901

21. SNELLMAN HOUSE
ERIK GUNNAR ASPLUND
1917–1918

22. UNITE D'HABITATION
LE CORBUSIER
1946–1952

23. LISTER COUNTY COURTHOUSE
ERIK GUNNAR ASPLUND
1917–1921

24. VANNA VENTURI HOUSE
ROBERT VENTURI
1962

1. **ST. PAUL'S CHURCH**
   LOUIS SULLIVAN
   1910–1914

2. **ANNEX TO OITA MEDICAL HALL**
   ARATA ISOZAKI
   1970–1972

3. **PAUL MELLON ARTS CENTER**
   I. M. PEI
   1970–1973

4. **OBSERVATORY IN BERLIN**
   KARL FRIEDRICH SCHINKEL
   1835

5. **REDENTORE CHURCH**
   ANDREA PALLADIO
   1576–1591

6. **SANTA MARTA CHURCH**
   COSTANZO MICHELA
   1746

7. **VOUKSENNISKA CHURCH, IMATRA**
   ALVAR AALTO
   1950–1952

8. **WOLFSBURG CULTURAL CENTER**
   ALVAR AALTO
   1958–1962

9. **TREDYFFRIN PUBLIC LIBRARY**
   ROMALDO GIURGOLA
   1976

10. **DOMUS AUREA**
    SEVERUS AND CELER
    c. 64

11. **S. MARIA DELLA PACE**
    DONATO BRAMANTE
    1478–1483

12. **ARCHITECTURAL SETTING**
    DONATO BRAMANTE
    1473

Balance by Geometry

Balance by geometry exists when components with two different form languages occur on opposite sides of a balance line. In St. Paul's (1), a wall separates the orthogonal support spaces from the semicircular worship space. Different simple geometries are balanced in the Oita Medical Hall (2) and the Mellon Center (3). In the Observatory (4) and Redentore Church (5), a single, subdivided form is balanced by a series of additive forms. Santa Marta (6) exemplifies two manifestations of a circle, while the church in Imatra (7) is an example of two varied form languages that meet at the main aisle to create perceptual tension. Tension also results from varied form languages in Aalto's Wolfsburg Cultural Center (8). At Tredyffrin Library (9), the curved geometry is balanced by the straight lines of the opposite side. Different geometric configurations balance about two perpendicular lines in the Domus Aurea (10). In S. Maria della Pace (11), differences in geometry and orientation establish the balance. Bramante's architectural setting (12) exemplifies the essence of the idea of balance by geometry with two complete and different geometric forms.

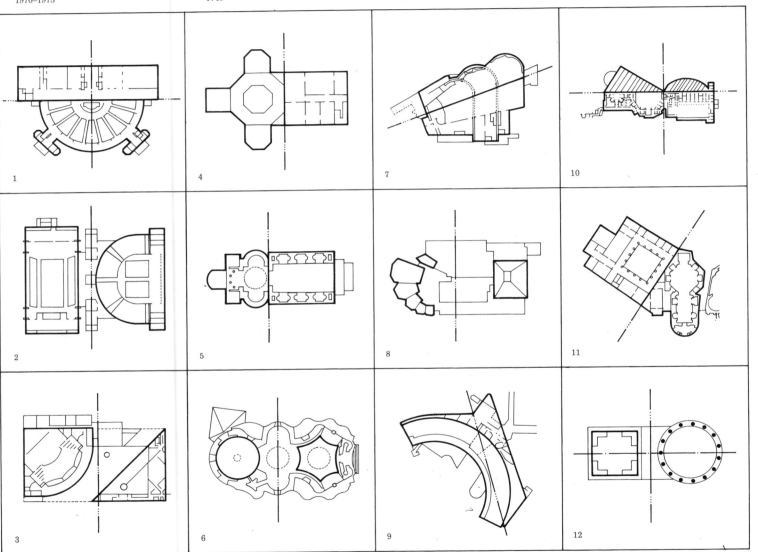

Balance by Positive and Negative

Balance by positive and negative occurs when equivalent components differ only in the manner in which they are made manifest, as solid or void. In the Smith House (1), the closed private area is balanced by the open public area. The two major use-spaces in Lang Music Building (2) are the enclosed auditorium and the open lobby. Balanced by configuration in one direction, the Wolfsburg Cultural Center (3) is balanced in the other direction by the largest special space and the defined court. The building is the positive form, and the entry forecourt its negative manifestation in the Hanselmann House (4), the Woodland Chapel (6), and the Crooks House (7). A similar condition exists at Power Center (5), where the building is the positive, and an adjacent park the negative. In the Ford Foundation Building (8), the volume of the interior greenhouse is the void, and the office spaces are the positive configuration. Differences between the interior and exterior living spaces establish the positive-negative balance line in Villa Savoye (9).

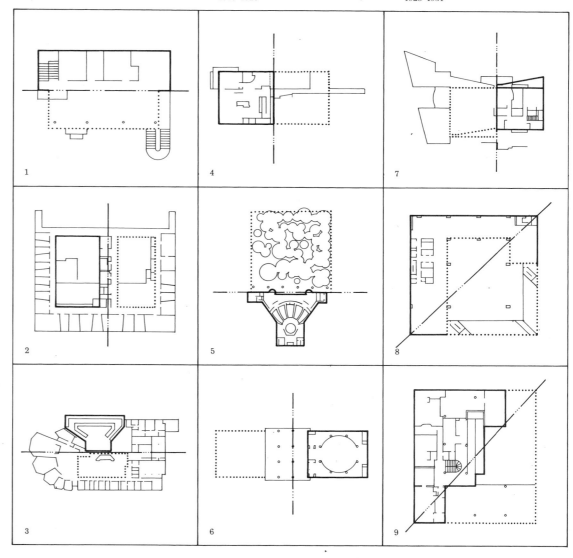

1. **MOORE HOUSE**
   CHARLES MOORE
   1962
2. **CARLL TUCKER III HOUSE**
   ROBERT VENTURI
   1962
3. **RUFER HOUSE**
   ADOLF LOOS
   1922

4. **SANT' ELIGIO DEGLI OREFICI**
   RAPHAEL
   1509
5. **ST. MARY WOOLNOTH**
   NICHOLAS HAWKSMOORE
   1716–1724
6. **VILLA SAVOYE**
   LE CORBUSIER
   1928–1931

7. **RESIDENCE IN RIVA SAN VITALE**
   MARIO BOTTA
   1972–1973
8. **BOSTON PUBLIC LIBRARY**
   McKIM, MEAD, AND WHITE
   1898
9. **NEW NATIONAL GALLERY**
   LUDWIG MIES VAN DER ROHE
   1968

GEOMETRY

Geometry is a formative idea in which the concepts of plane and solid geometry are used to determine built form. Besides examples of the basic geometries, illustrated are combinations, multiples, derivatives, and manipulations of geometries. Also included are examples of grids.

Basic Geometry

The basic geometric configurations used to determine a building's form include the square as used in the Moore House (1), the Tucker House (2), the Rufer House (3), and the churches of Sant' Eligio degli Orefici (4) and St. Mary Woolnoth (5). Squares were also used to design the Villa Savoye (6), a private residence in Switzerland (7), the Boston Public Library (8), and the New National Gallery (9) by Mies van der Rohe. The circle appears as the generator for the Tholos (10), the M.I.T. Chapel (11), St. Costanza (13), and the Pantheon in Rome (15). Thomas Jefferson used the circle in designing the Rotunda at the University of Virginia (14). Konstantin Melnikov used two circles in the design of his house (12), and the basic shape of the triangle in the Rusakov Club (16). Triangles also determined the Arena Building (17) and the Church and Parish Center in Hyvinkaa, Finland (18). The hexagon was used in designing the North Christian Church (19), a desert Synagogue (20), and Pfeiffer Chapel (21). Finally, the Baptistry at Ravenna (22), Poplar Forest (23), and San Maria degli Angeli (24) are developed from the octagon.

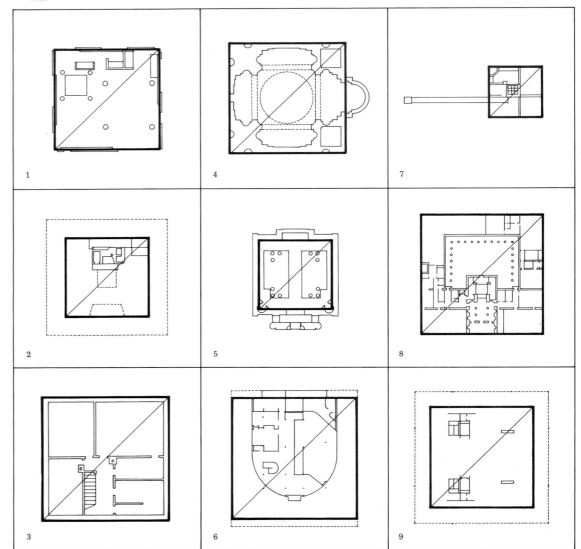

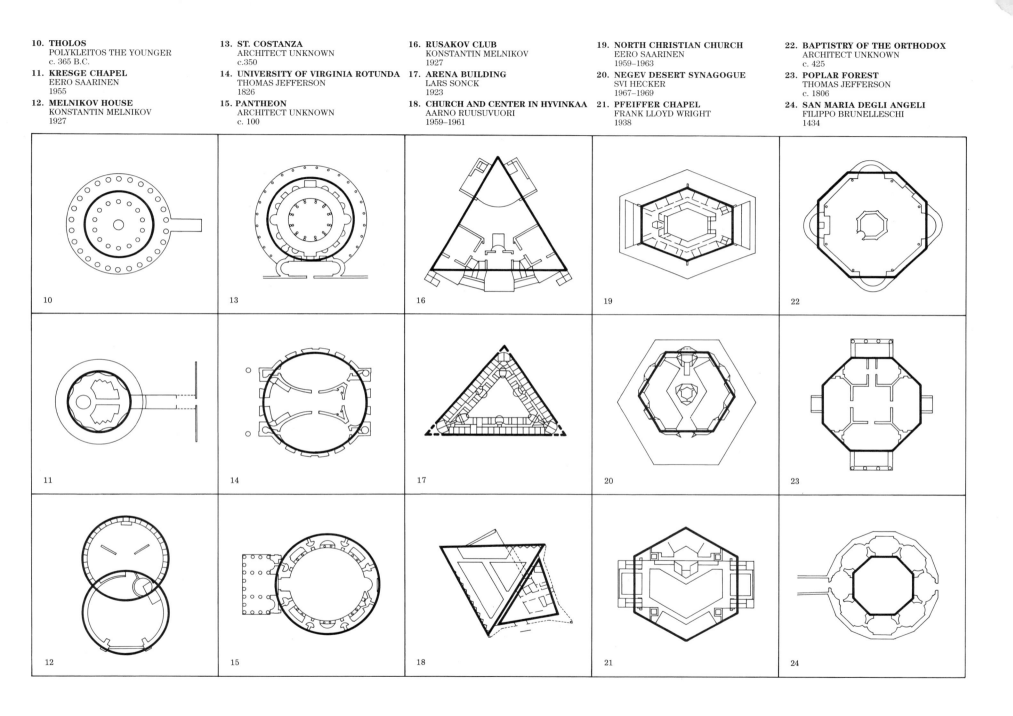

10. THOLOS
POLYKLEITOS THE YOUNGER
c. 365 B.C.

11. KRESGE CHAPEL
EERO SAARINEN
1955

12. MELNIKOV HOUSE
KONSTANTIN MELNIKOV
1927

13. ST. COSTANZA
ARCHITECT UNKNOWN
c. 350

14. UNIVERSITY OF VIRGINIA ROTUNDA
THOMAS JEFFERSON
1826

15. PANTHEON
ARCHITECT UNKNOWN
c. 100

16. RUSAKOV CLUB
KONSTANTIN MELNIKOV
1927

17. ARENA BUILDING
LARS SONCK
1923

18. CHURCH AND CENTER IN HYVINKAA
AARNO RUUSUVUORI
1959–1961

19. NORTH CHRISTIAN CHURCH
EERO SAARINEN
1959–1963

20. NEGEV DESERT SYNAGOGUE
SVI HECKER
1967–1969

21. PFEIFFER CHAPEL
FRANK LLOYD WRIGHT
1938

22. BAPTISTRY OF THE ORTHODOX
ARCHITECT UNKNOWN
c. 425

23. POPLAR FOREST
THOMAS JEFFERSON
c. 1806

24. SAN MARIA DEGLI ANGELI
FILIPPO BRUNELLESCHI
1434

1. **LA ROTONDA**
   ANDREA PALLADIO
   1566–1571
2. **OLD SACRISTY**
   FILIPPO BRUNELLESCHI
   1421–1440
3. **TEMPIETTO OF SAN PIETRO**
   DONATO BRAMANTE
   1502

4. **JOHNS HOPKINS UNIVERSITY HALL**
   JOHN RUSSELL POPE
   c. 1930
5. **STOCKHOLM PUBLIC LIBRARY**
   ERIK GUNNAR ASPLUND
   1920–1928
6. **WOODLAND CHAPEL**
   ERIK GUNNAR ASPLUND
   1918–1920

7. **PALACE OF CHARLES V**
   PEDRO MACHUCA
   1527
8. **TOMB OF CAECILIA METELLA**
   ARCHITECT UNKNOWN
   c. 25 B.C.
9. **EXETER LIBRARY**
   LOUIS I. KAHN
   1967–1972

Circle and Square

The most direct combination of circle and square, where both forms are whole or easily implied, and share a common center, occurs at Villa Rotonda (1), the Old Sacristy (2), the Tempietto (3), and University Hall (4). Woodland Chapel (6) contains whole figures, while Stockholm Library (5) consists of a strongly implied square and a complete circle. The circle is a court in the Palace of Charles V (7), a cone in the Tomb of Metella (8), and an interior elevation opening in Exeter Library (9). The square is embodied in a larger form in St. Peter's (10) and the Customshouse (11), and is adjacent to a circle in St. Mary's Cathedral (12). In the Museum of Art (13),

Stirling uses two circle and square forms. The square contains the circle in the Arnheim Pavilion (14) and the Palace of Assembly (15). In Knights of Columbus (16), four circles are added to the corners of a square, while at Montmorency (17) a square contains a circle and its transformation. The Olympic Arena (18) and the Tomb at Tarquinia (19) exemplify circles containing squares. Aalto's Studio (20) is derived from a shifted circle in a square, and Sforza Chapel (21) is an elaboration of a circle holding a square. The Cathedral (22), Tucker House (23), and Venturi House (24), are examples of the combination of circle, square, and triangle.

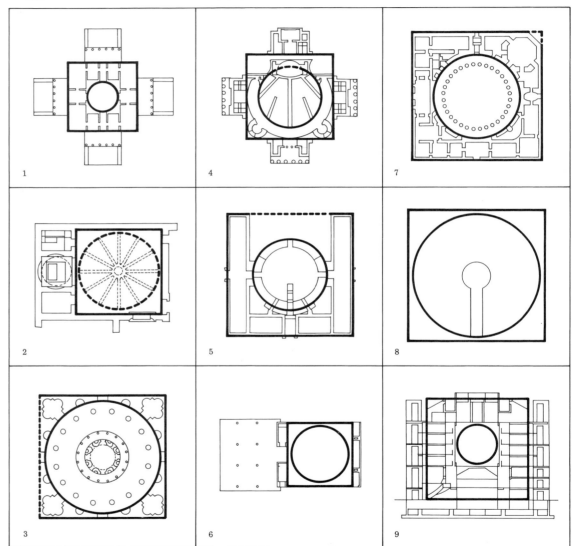

262

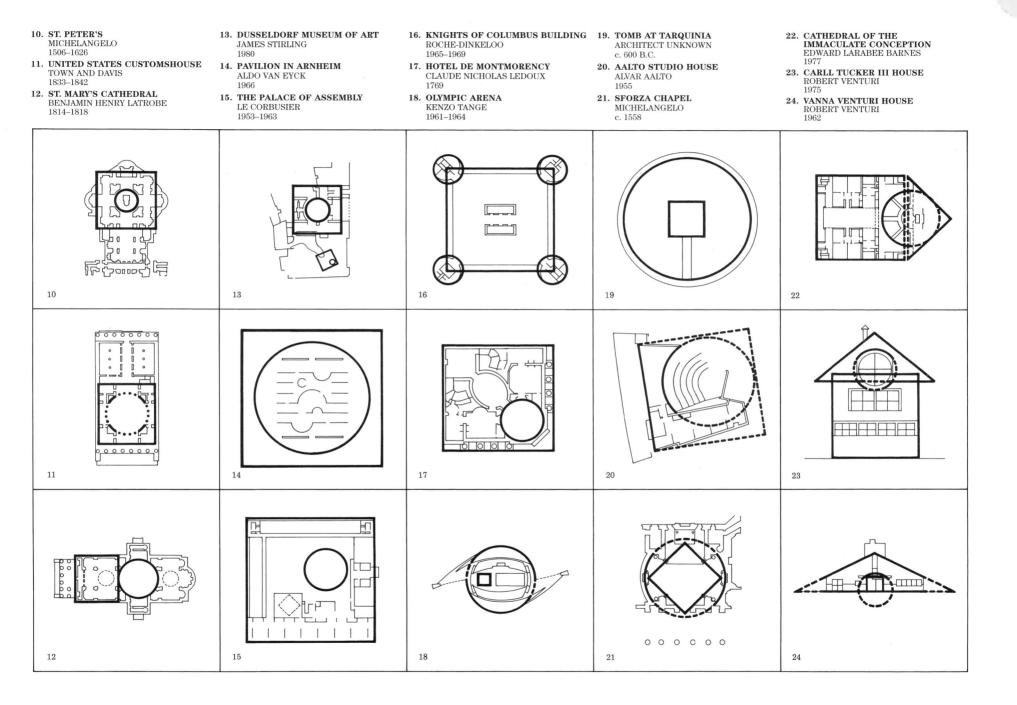

10. **ST. PETER'S**
MICHELANGELO
1506–1626

11. **UNITED STATES CUSTOMSHOUSE**
TOWN AND DAVIS
1833–1842

12. **ST. MARY'S CATHEDRAL**
BENJAMIN HENRY LATROBE
1814–1818

13. **DUSSELDORF MUSEUM OF ART**
JAMES STIRLING
1980

14. **PAVILION IN ARNHEIM**
ALDO VAN EYCK
1966

15. **THE PALACE OF ASSEMBLY**
LE CORBUSIER
1953–1963

16. **KNIGHTS OF COLUMBUS BUILDING**
ROCHE-DINKELOO
1965–1969

17. **HOTEL DE MONTMORENCY**
CLAUDE NICHOLAS LEDOUX
1769

18. **OLYMPIC ARENA**
KENZO TANGE
1961–1964

19. **TOMB AT TARQUINIA**
ARCHITECT UNKNOWN
c. 600 B.C.

20. **AALTO STUDIO HOUSE**
ALVAR AALTO
1955

21. **SFORZA CHAPEL**
MICHELANGELO
c. 1558

22. **CATHEDRAL OF THE IMMACULATE CONCEPTION**
EDWARD LARABEE BARNES
1977

23. **CARLL TUCKER III HOUSE**
ROBERT VENTURI
1975

24. **VANNA VENTURI HOUSE**
ROBERT VENTURI
1962

1. LISTER COUNTY COURTHOUSE ERIK GUNNAR ASPLUND 1917–1921	4. THERMAE OF CARACALLA ARCHITECT UNKNOWN 212–216	7. CASTLEGAR RICHARD MORRISON 1807	10. F. L. HIGGINSON HOUSE HENRY HOBSON RICHARDSON 1881–1883
2. GREEN PARK RANGER'S HOUSE ROBERT ADAMS 1768	5. JAMES SWAN HOUSE CHARLES BULFINCH 1796	8. TENDERING HALL JOHN SOANE 1784–1790	11. TATESHINA PLANETARIUM KISHO KUROKAWA 1976
3. CASINO IN ROME WILLIAM CHAMBERS 1754	6. RESIDENCE IN MASSAGNO MARIO BOTTA 1979	9. AUSTIN HALL HENRY HOBSON RICHARDSON 1881–1884	12. WHEELS OF HEAVEN CHURCH ALDO VAN EYCK 1966

Rectangle Overlapped by Circle

A specific geometric combination is a rectangle overlapped by a smaller circle. The Lister Courthouse (1), the Ranger Lodge (2), the Casino (3), the Thermae (4), and the Swan House (5) exemplify the circle as a major use-space half engaged on the centerline of the long side of a rectangle. The residence by Botta (6) has the same configuration with the circle, a stair, reduced in scale. In Castlegar (7), the rectangle is overlapped by an ellipse at the centerline, and in Tendering Hall (8), a circle and an ellipse overlap the rectangle. In Austin Hall (9), two rectangles are intersected by two circles with a third circle that overlaps at the entry. Richardson's Higginson House (10) has circles on opposite corners implying the diagonal, while in the Planetarium (11) two circles occur on the same side. Double major and minor circles overlap the rectangle in the Wheels of Heaven Church (12). In the castles, Rait (13) and Pitfichie (14), the circle overlaps the corner in two directions, and in Chateau de Chambord (15) multiple corners are overlapped by the circles.

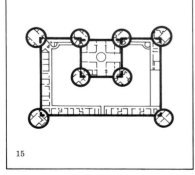

13

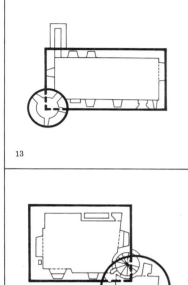

14

15

Two Squares

Two adjacent squares directly determine the limits of the plans of Sever Hall (1), Christ Church (2), and the Venturi House (3). In the Brant House (4), two adjacent squares have a common side that is the radius of the major circular form in plan, and the same two squares set the limits of the total plan configuration. Two squares can overlap to create a special condition of the common area. In Easton Neston (5), the shared part of the two squares denotes the central hall, and in the Allegheny Courthouse (6), the overlap locates the towers. Villa Trissino (7), by Palladio, and Drayton Hall (8) exemplify two overlapping squares which define a major central use-space and entry. In the Farnese Palace (9), two adjacent squares set the limits of the major elevation.

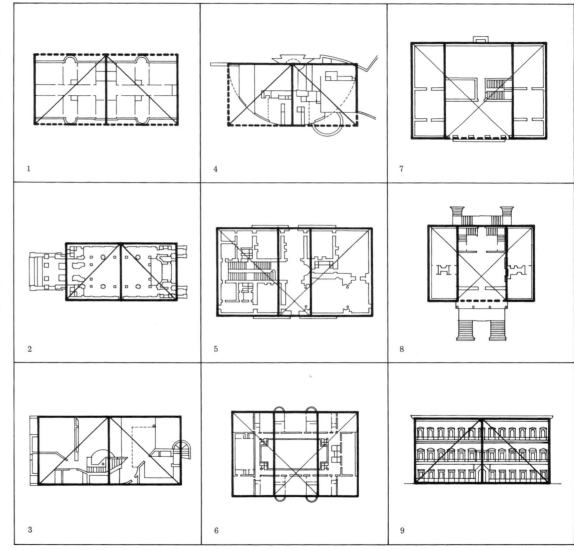

1

2

3

4

5

6

7

8

9

1. **LA ROTONDA**
ANDREA PALLADIO
1566–1571

2. **CHISWICK HOUSE**
LORD BURLINGTON
1729

3. **YORK HOUSE**
WILLIAM CHAMBERS
1759

4. **ST. LOUIS DES INVALIDES**
JULES HARDOUIN MANSART
1676

5. **SANTA MARIA DI CARIGNANO**
GALEAZZO ALESSI
1552

6. **HAGIA SOPHIA**
ANTEMIUS OF TRALLES
532

7. **HOTEL DE MONTMORENCY**
CLAUDE NICHOLAS LEDOUX
1769

8. **SAO FRUTUOSO DE MONTELIOS**
ARCHITECT UNKNOWN
665

9. **THE CAPITOL AT WILLIAMSBURG**
ARCHITECT UNKNOWN
1701

10. **UNITED STATES SUPREME COURT**
CASS GILBERT
1935

11. **WEEKEND HOUSE**
LE CORBUSIER
1935

12. **EXETER LIBRARY**
LOUIS I. KAHN
1967–1972

Nine-Square

Nine-square is a classic geometric form created by joining three sets of three adjacent squares each to form a larger square. It is the three cell by three cell arrangement that is most commonly referred to as a nine-square configuration, even though the shape of the cells may be other than squares. Villa Rotonda (1), Chiswick House (2), York House (3), St. Louis des Invalides (4), and Santa Maria di Carignano (5) are examples of this classic configuration. Hagia Sophia (6) and Hotel de Montmorency (7) demonstrate nine-square arrangements of rectangles. By combining select cells within the nine cell array, specific patterns can be created. Sao Frutuoso (8) is an example of the cross variation with the corners implied. Flanking the center cell with two rows of three cells creates the 'H' configuration, as in the Capitol at Williamsburg (9). An 'X' configuration is suggested in the Supreme Court Building (10), by the pattern of the major articulated courts and the center cell. The three, two, one stepped configuration is exhibited in Le Corbusier's Weekend House (11), and the square ring with the center void is seen in the Exeter Library (12).

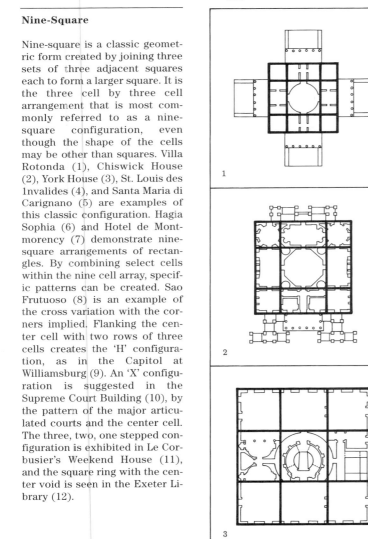

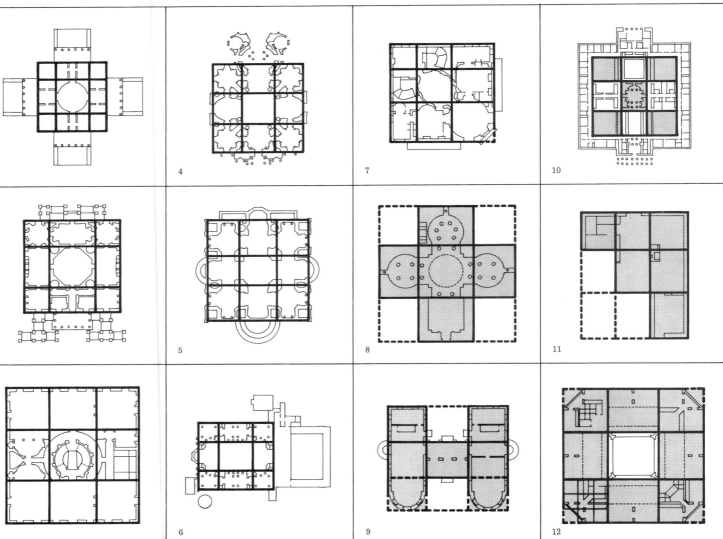

1. **THEATER IN BESANÇON FRANCE**
   CLAUDE NICHOLAS LEDOUX
   1775
2. **ST. GEORGE-IN-THE-EAST**
   NICHOLAS HAWKSMOOR
   1714–1729
3. **ADULT LEARNING LABORATORY**
   ROMALDO GIURGOLA
   1972

4. **VILLA SAVOYE**
   LE CORBUSIER
   1928–1931
5. **MUSEUM OF DECORATIVE ARTS**
   RICHARD MEIER
   1981
6. **TRUBEK HOUSE**
   ROBERT VENTURI
   1972

7. **ELIA-BASH HOUSE**
   GWATHMEY-SIEGEL
   1971–1973
8. **VILLA MAIREA**
   ALVAR AALTO
   1937–1939
9. **VIKING FORTRESS**
   ARCHITECT UNKNOWN
   c.1000

10. **YALE CENTER FOR BRITISH ART**
    LOUIS I. KAHN
    1969–1974
11. **SALK INSTITUTE**
    LOUIS I. KAHN
    1959–1965
12. **HOMEWOOD**
    EDWIN LUTYENS
    1901

Four-Square

A four-square is a geometric configuration that is two cells by two cells and has a common central point of contact. The most direct example is the Viking Fortress (9). Ledoux's theater (1) and Villa Savoye (4) have overall plans, and St. George-in-the-East (2) has an internal spatial organization developed from this construct. Four-squares are used in combination at Giurgola's Research Lab (3) and at the Frankfurt Museum (5) where the existing building becomes one quadrant of a four-square, which in turn becomes one quadrant of a larger four-square. It is not necessary to articulate the four cells equally, for instance, at the Trubek House (6) there are two sets of different sized cells. The Elia-Bash House (7) contains implied quadrants about a defined center, and Villa Mairea (8) has three cells as built form, with the fourth being a garden. In Kahn's British Art Center (10), the nine-square and four-square configurations are combined with the overall plan developed from overlapping nine-squares, each cell of which is subdivided into a four-square; while at the Salk Institute (11) the inverse occurs. In Homewood (12), a nine-square shares two edges with a four-square in a nested configuration.

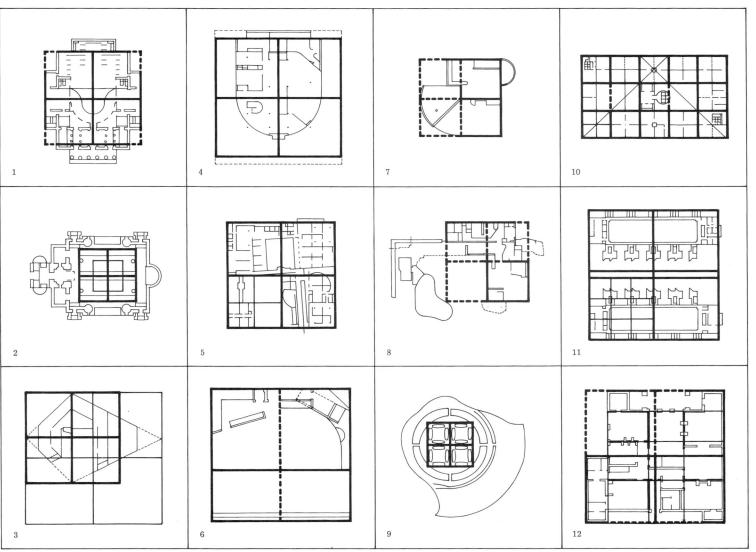

1. **SHAMBERG RESIDENCE**
   RICHARD MEIER
   1972–1974
2. **OLD SACRISTY**
   FILIPPO BRUNELLESCHI
   1421–1440
3. **LANG MUSIC BUILDING**
   ROMALDO GIURGOLA
   1973

4. **ST. JAMES**
   CHRISTOPHER WREN
   1674–1687
5. **LISTER COUNTY COURTHOUSE**
   ERIK GUNNAR ASPLUND
   1917–1921
6. **NASHDOM**
   EDWIN LUTYENS
   1905–1909

7. **ALTES MUSEUM**
   KARL FRIEDRICH SCHINKEL
   1824–1830
8. **SAN MIGUEL**
   ARCHITECT UNKNOWN
   913
9. **COUNCIL CHAMBER OF MILETOS**
   ARCHITECT UNKNOWN
   170 B.C.

10. **VILLA STEIN**
    LE CORBUSIER
    1927
11. **CONVENT OF LA TOURETTE**
    LE CORBUSIER
    1957–1960
12. **IL TEATRO DEL MONDO**
    ALDO ROSSI
    1979

1.4 and 1.6 Rectangles

The 1.4 rectangle is created by rotating the diagonal of a square 45 degrees to determine the length of the long side. This configuration sets the overall plan or internal spatial limits for the Shamberg House (1), the Old Sacristy (2), the Lang Music Center (3), and St. James Church (4). A square with both diagonals rotated creates a configuration which determines the plans for Lister County Courthouse (5) and Nashdom (6). The 1.6 rectangle, created by rotating the diagonal of one-half a square, sets the overall plan of Schinkel's museum (7), San Miguel (8), and the Council Chamber (9). With appendages excluded, Villa Stein (10) is developed within a 1.6 rectangle, and Le Corbusier also uses the 1.6 figure to set the limits of the court at La Tourette (11). The theater in Venice (12) has two concentric squares in plan with a 1 : 1.4 ratio relationship to each other. The larger square determines the overall form, less the stairs; the smaller square is the limit of the seating.

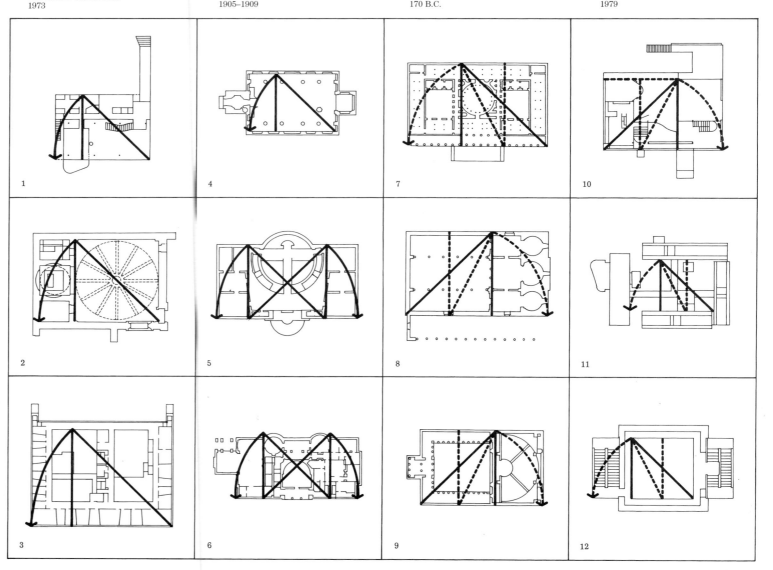

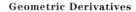

Geometric Derivatives

A multitude and variety of forms can be derived from basic geometries through combination, division, and the use of the parts. Three adjacent squares form the plan of the Snellman House (1), while two squares and four 1.4 rectangles set the limits of Hotel Guimard (2). The One-Half House (3) is designed by combining one-half a circle with an orthogonal half and a diagonal half of two squares. Where the Lutheran Church (4) and the Jacobs House (5) are derived from parts of two concentric circles, the Wies Church (6) is developed from two circles with different centers. The common area of overlap of two circles determines the plan of Orivesi Church (7). Borromini used an ellipse derived from parts of four circles to design San Carlo alle Quattro Fontane (8). A series of complex forms developed from multiple sphere segments is utilized at the Sydney Opera House (9). The Postal Savings Bank (10), the Guild House (11), and the Royal Chancellery (12) are derived from triangles. The triangles in the latter two are implied by a series of points at the corners of the building. The Chancellery design is also a composite of two triangles.

1. **SNELLMAN HOUSE**
   ERIK GUNNAR ASPLUND
   1917–1918
2. **HOTEL GUIMARD**
   CLAUDE NICHOLAS LEDOUX
   1770
3. **ONE-HALF HOUSE**
   JOHN HEJDUK
   1966

4. **NEW LUTHERAN CHURCH**
   ADRIEN DORTSMAN
   1668
5. **HERBERT JACOBS HOUSE**
   FRANK LLOYD WRIGHT
   1948
6. **WIES PILGRIMAGE CHURCH**
   JOHAN & DOMINIKUS ZIMMERMAN
   1754

7. **ORIVESI CHURCH**
   HEKKI SIREN
   1961
8. **SAN CARLO ALLE QUATTRO FONTANE**
   FRANCESCO BORROMINI
   1638–1641
9. **SYDNEY OPERA HOUSE**
   JØRN UTZON
   1957–1968

10. **POST OFFICE SAVINGS BANK**
    OTTO WAGNER
    1904–1906
11. **GUILD HOUSE**
    ROBERT VENTURI
    1961
12. **ROYAL CHANCELLERY**
    ERIK GUNNAR ASPLUND
    1922

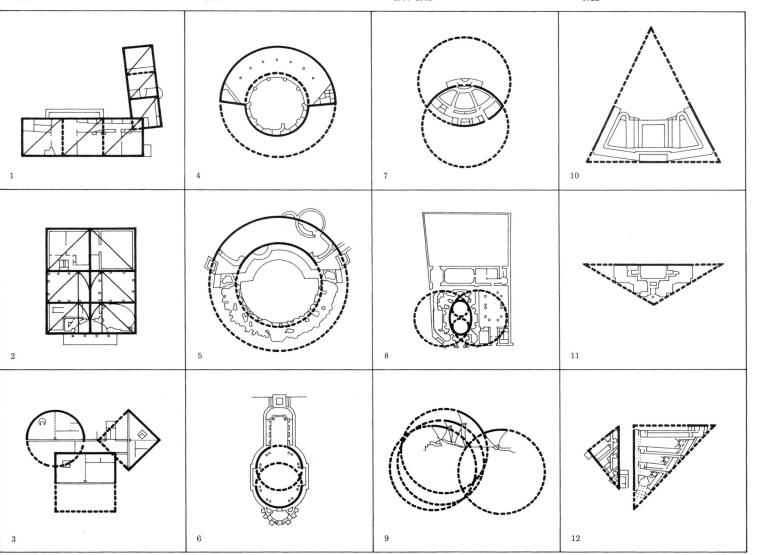

1. **SAN MARIA DEGLI ANGELI**
   FILIPPO BRUNELLESCHI
   1434–1436
2. **SAN SPIRITO**
   FILIPPO BRUNELLESCHI
   1434
3. **OCCUPATIONAL HEALTH CENTER**
   HARDY-HOLZMAN-PFIEFFER
   1973

4. **NORMAN FISHER HOUSE**
   LOUIS I. KAHN
   1960
5. **LANDERBANK**
   OTTO WAGNER
   1883–1884
6. **NEW YORK HERALD BUILDING**
   McKIM, MEAD, AND WHITE
   1894

7. **ST. ANDREWS DORMITORY**
   JAMES STIRLING
   1964
8. **CUNO HOUSE**
   PETER BEHRENS
   1906–1907
9. **SNELLMAN HOUSE**
   ERIK GUNNAR ASPLUND
   1917–1918

10. **DEERE WEST OFFICE BUILDING**
    ROCHE-DINKELOO
    1975–1976
11. **CARPENTER CENTER**
    LE CORBUSIER
    1961–1963
12. **CAMBRIDGE HISTORY FACULTY**
    JAMES STIRLING
    1964

Rotated, Shifted, and Overlapped

Rotating, shifting, and overlapping are manipulations applicable to basic geometries to create built form. Two equal squares with a common center are rotated 45 degrees in San Maria degli Angeli (1). In San Spirito (2), three sequential sets, each with two rotated squares, are used. Two different orthogonal configurations are rotated and overlapped in the Occupational Health Building (3), while minimum connection between similar, rotated forms establishes the plan of the Fisher House (4). A circular element becomes a pivot for rotation of two forms in the Landerbank (5). The Herald Building (6), St. Andrews Dormitory (7), the Cuno House (8), and the Snellman House (9) are examples of hinge configurations—linear elements rotated about some common point of overlap. The change in the circulation element strengthens the shift about a common space in Deere West (10). In Carpenter Center (11), similar forms are inverted and shifted about a circulation ramp. Through a diagonal shift and overlap, Stirling creates the major use-space in the Cambridge History Faculty (12). Other examples of overlapping geometries are the Melnikov House, Drayton Hall, Easton Neston, and the Yale Center for British Arts.

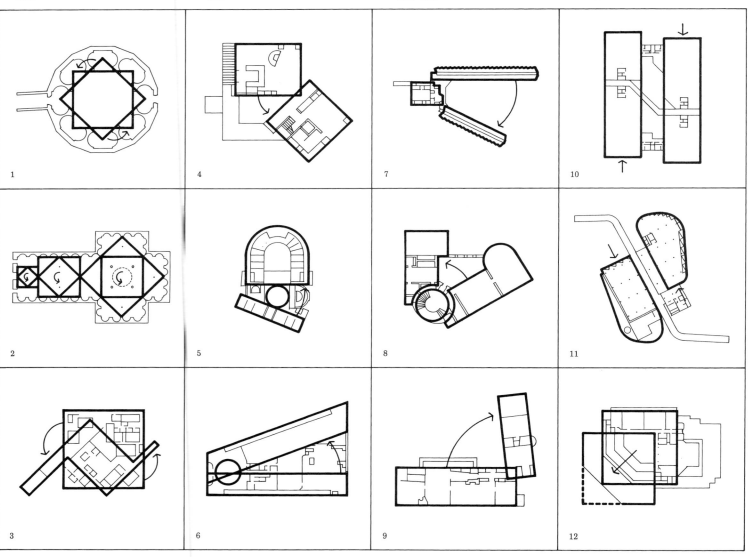

1. **WINGSPREAD**
FRANK LLOYD WRIGHT
1937
2. **GUGGENHEIM MUSEUM**
FRANK LLOYD WRIGHT
1956
3. **NEW PARK**
ARCHITECT UNKNOWN
c. 1775

4. **RICHARDS RESEARCH BUILDING**
LOUIS I. KAHN
1957–1961
5. **MUSEUM AT AHMEDABAD, INDIA**
LE CORBUSIER
1953–1957
6. **FLOREY BUILDING**
JAMES STIRLING
1966

7. **MAUSOLEUM OF AUGUSTUS**
ARCHITECT UNKNOWN
c. 25 B.C.
8. **WOLFSBURG PARISH CENTER CHURCH**
ALVAR AALTO
1960–1962
9. **NEUR VAHR APARTMENTS**
ALVAR AALTO
1958–1962

10. **SMALL OLYMPIC ARENA**
KENZO TANGE
1961–1964
11. **ST. ANTONIUS CHURCH**
JUSTUS DAHINDEN
1966–1969
12. **NEW ENGLAND AQUARIUM**
CAMBRIDGE SEVEN ASSOCIATES
1962

Pinwheel, Radial, and Spiral

Pinwheel, radial, and spiral are formal or spatial configurations which have in common a center of origin. A pinwheel is a uniform arrangement of linear elements about a defined core, as exemplified by Wingspread (1), or an implied core, as at the Guggenheim Museum (2). In Newpark (3), adjacent spaces pinwheel about a minor circulation core. Three complex units form a pinwheel about a service space in the Richards Medical Building (4). Two pinwheels, one within the main gallery, the second created by three built forms adjacent to the main building, are embodied in the Ahmedabad Museum (5). A radial configuration is denoted by a series of elements, defined or implied, which emanate from a center. The Florey Building (6) is developed from two centers, while the Mausoleum of Augustus (7) is a classic radial configuration. In the Wolfsburg Parish Center (8), the structure radiates from a single origin, and in the Neur Vahr Apartments (9) the walls radiate from multiple centers. The spiral form occurs in the Small Olympic Arena (10) and the St. Antonius Church (11). The New England Aquarium (12) is developed from two spirals: a central circular one and a rectilinear one at the perimeter.

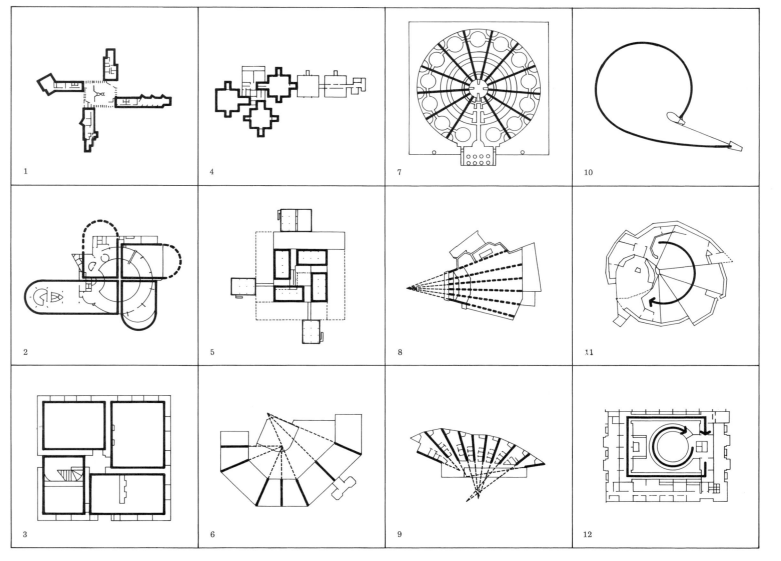

1. **VILLA FOSCARI**
   ANDREA PALLADIO
   c. 1549–1563
2. **SEA RANCH CONDOMINIUM I**
   CHARLES MOORE
   1964–1965
3. **CROWN HALL**
   LUDWIG MIES VAN DER ROHE
   1950–1956

4. **TEMPLE OF APOLLO**
   PAEONIUS AND DAPHNIS
   c. 310 B.C.
5. **FALLINGWATER**
   FRANK LLOYD WRIGHT
   1935
6. **ENSO-GUTZEIT HEADQUARTERS**
   ALVAR AALTO
   1959–1962

7. **CARSON PIRIE AND SCOTT STORE**
   LOUIS SULLIVAN
   1899–1903
8. **SAINTE GENEVIEVE LIBRARY**
   HENRI LABROUSTE
   1838–1850
9. **FARNSWORTH HOUSE**
   LUDWIG MIES VAN DER ROHE
   1945–1950

10. **LARKIN BUILDING**
    FRANK LLOYD WRIGHT
    1903
11. **A.E.G. HIGH TENSION FACTORY**
    PETER BEHRENS
    1910
12. **FOURTH TEMPLE OF HERA**
    RHOIKOS OF SAMOS
    575 B.C.–550 B.C.

Grid

Grids are developed from the repetition of the basic geometries. At Villa Foscari (1), Sea Ranch (2), Crown Hall (3), and the Temple of Apollo (4), the square grid is the generator. It is used with major and minor emphasis in Fallingwater (5) and in the elevation of Enso-Gutzeit (6). In Carson Pirie and Scott (7), Sainte Genevieve Library (8), and the Temple of Hera (12), a rectilinear grid, coincident with structure, occurs. Rectilinear grids occur in the Farnsworth House (9), the Larkin Building (10), and the A.E.G. Factory (11). Kimball Art Museum (13), the Bath House (14), and San Sebastiano (15) exemplify plaid grids. The Nebraska State Capital (16) develops from a three-unit plaid, as do Notre Dame Cathedral (17) and the Visser House (18). The Boomer Residence (19) and the Unitarian Church (21) have equilateral triangular grids, and the National Gallery (20) has an isosceles triangular grid. Leicester Engineering Labs (22), the Auditorium Building (23), and Turun Sanomat Offices (24) exemplify grid shifts that occur at junctures of major forms or spaces. Wells Library (25) developed from a plaid field created by grid rotation and overlap. The Anker Building (26) and the Gumma Museum (27) are examples of grids that are rotated.

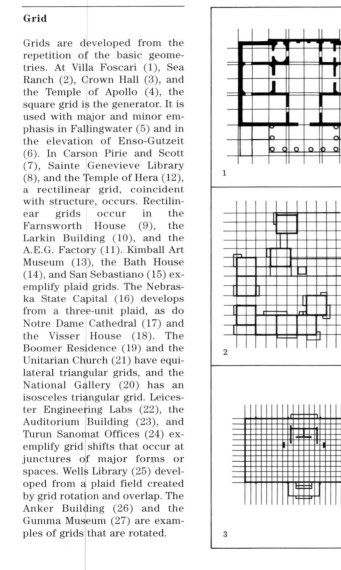

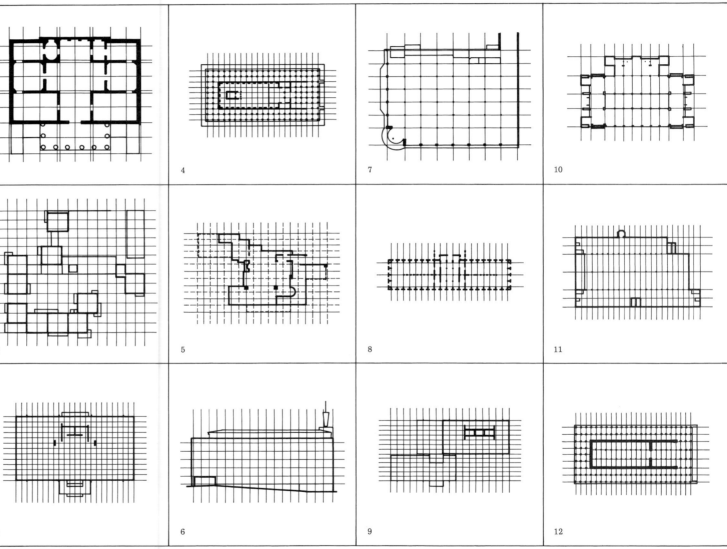

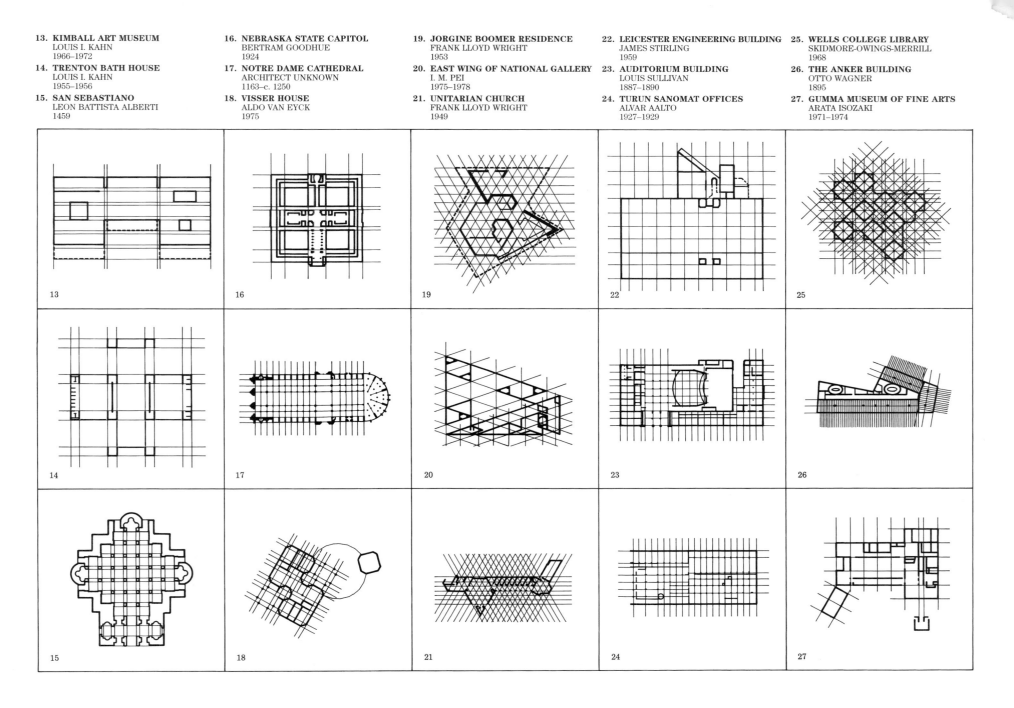

13. **KIMBALL ART MUSEUM**
LOUIS I. KAHN
1966–1972

14. **TRENTON BATH HOUSE**
LOUIS I. KAHN
1955–1956

15. **SAN SEBASTIANO**
LEON BATTISTA ALBERTI
1459

16. **NEBRASKA STATE CAPITOL**
BERTRAM GOODHUE
1924

17. **NOTRE DAME CATHEDRAL**
ARCHITECT UNKNOWN
1163–c. 1250

18. **VISSER HOUSE**
ALDO VAN EYCK
1975

19. **JORGINE BOOMER RESIDENCE**
FRANK LLOYD WRIGHT
1953

20. **EAST WING OF NATIONAL GALLERY**
I. M. PEI
1975–1978

21. **UNITARIAN CHURCH**
FRANK LLOYD WRIGHT
1949

22. **LEICESTER ENGINEERING BUILDING**
JAMES STIRLING
1959

23. **AUDITORIUM BUILDING**
LOUIS SULLIVAN
1887–1890

24. **TURUN SANOMAT OFFICES**
ALVAR AALTO
1927–1929

25. **WELLS COLLEGE LIBRARY**
SKIDMORE-OWINGS-MERRILL
1968

26. **THE ANKER BUILDING**
OTTO WAGNER
1895

27. **GUMMA MUSEUM OF FINE ARTS**
ARATA ISOZAKI
1971–1974

13   16   19   22   25

14   17   20   23   26

15   18   21   24   27

1. **TEMPLE AT TARXIEN, MALTA**
   ARCHITECT UNKNOWN
   2100 B.C.–1900 B.C.
2. **SOLOMON'S TEMPLE**
   ARCHITECT UNKNOWN
   1000 B.C.
3. **HOTEL DE MONTMORENCY**
   CLAUDE NICHOLAS LEDOUX
   1769

4. **TEMPLE OF HORUS**
   ARCHITECT UNKNOWN
   237 B.C.–57 B.C.
5. **TOMB OF SETNAKHT**
   ARCHITECT UNKNOWN
   13th CENTURY B.C.
6. **DULWICH GALLERY**
   JOHN SOANE
   1811–1814

7. **HOUSE IN CENTRAL PENNSYLVANIA**
   HUGH NEWELL JACOBSEN
   1980
8. **REDENTORE CHURCH**
   ANDREA PALLADIO
   1576–1591
9. **LAURENTIAN LIBRARY**
   MICHELANGELO
   1525

CONFIGURATION PATTERNS

Configuration patterns describe the relative disposition of parts, and are themes for designing space and organizing groups of spaces and forms. Illustrated are examples of linear, central, double-centered, clustered, nested, concentric, and binuclear configurations.

Linear: Use

There are two types of configurations in which path through use-spaces creates a linear organization. In the first, spaces are linked, and circulation is from space to space. In the second, one engages a singular space longitudinally. At the temple in Malta (1) the spaces are linked on the transverse axis, thus changing each longitudinal space into three implied spaces. The axial movement through a series of spaces places accent on the beginning and end of the path, and is exemplified at Solomon's Temple (2) and at the Temple of Horus, Edfu (4). At Ledoux's Hotel de Montmorency (3), the path doubles back on itself on the second floor so that beginning and end are above one another. The spaces in the linear configuration at the Tomb of Setnakht (5) are both longitudinal and transverse. The change provides accent. At Soane's Dulwich Gallery (6), the entrance is in the middle of the linearly linked spaces. In Jacobsen's house (7), the center between the linked spaces is solid, and the circulation is along the edges. Redentore (8) and the Laurentian Library (9) are examples of singular spaces that are organized linearly. At Redentore, as at the Tomb of Setnakht, there is an accent along the path.

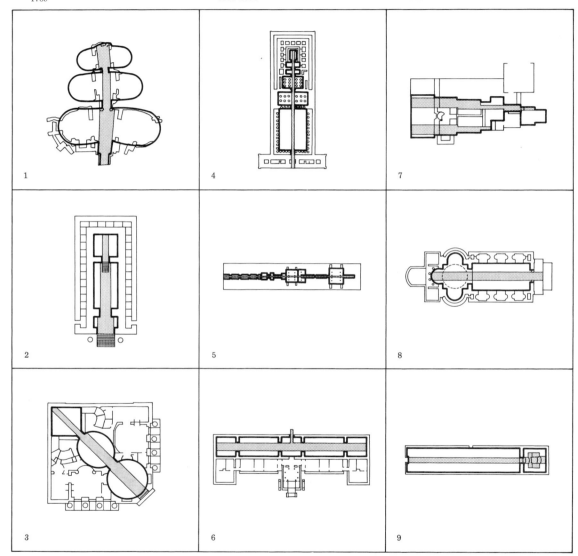

Linear: Circulation

Linear configurations in which the circulation is separated from the use-space are spine or corridor organizations. A Greek stoa (1) is the simplest form of this organization, while the gymnasium at Exeter (2) represents a typical spine scheme. In this case, the spine dominates the form. The spine in Utzon's church (3) embodies a repetitive form vocabulary that is deployed to create places for use-spaces. Examples of single-loaded corridors are the Irish Fort Shannon house (4) and the Snellman House (5). Aalto's dormitory (6) illustrates that the linear circulation need not be straight or symmetrical, while in Le Corbusier's Unite d'Habitation (7) circulation is significant in section. The circulation in the two buildings by Stirling (8 and 9) is visible externally and indicates the potential for the path to be not straight. It is also possible for two circulation spines to exist, as at Moore's Stern House (10), where they cross. At Centre Beaubourg (11), the two spines are parallel; one is for vertical circulation and the other for horizontal. Venturi's Pearson House (12) utilizes both types of linear configuration patterns. The private spaces are linked by a separate circulation path, while the public spaces have implied circulation through them.

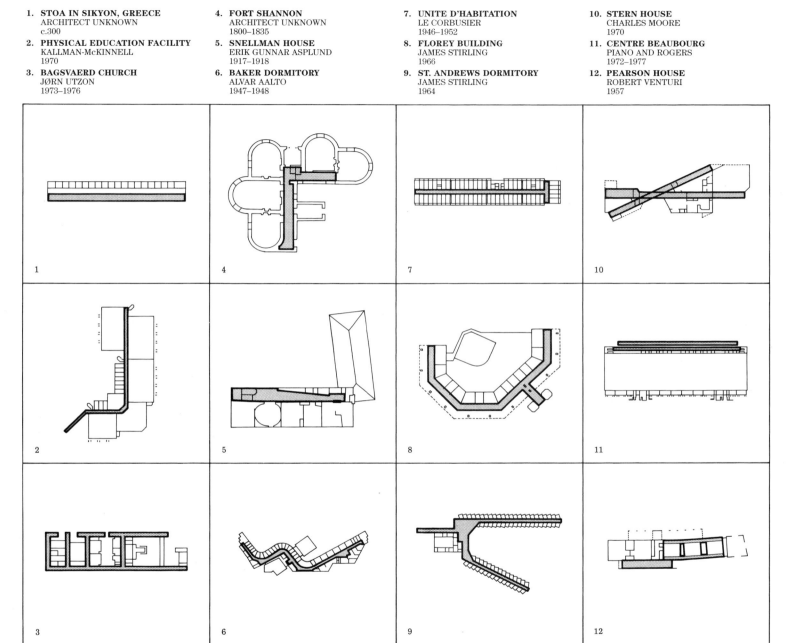

1. **FIRST UNITARIAN CHURCH**
   LOUIS I. KAHN
   1959–1967
2. **WOLLATON HALL**
   ROBERT SMYTHSON
   1580–1588
3. **SHAKER BARN**
   ARCHITECT UNKNOWN
   1865

4. **HUNTING LODGE**
   KARL FRIEDRICH SCHINKEL
   1822
5. **PALACE OF CHARLES V**
   PEDRO MACHUCA
   1527
6. **FARNESE PALACE**
   ANTONIO DA SANGALLO
   1534

7. **ST. COSTANZA**
   ARCHITECT UNKNOWN
   c. 350
8. **TRINITY CHURCH**
   HENRY HOBSON RICHARDSON
   1872–1877
9. **ST. MARY WOOLNOTH**
   NICHOLAS HAWKSMOOR
   1716–1724

10. **SECOND BANK OF THE U.S.**
    WILLIAM STRICKLAND
    1818–1824
11. **STOCKHOLM PUBLIC LIBRARY**
    ERIK GUNNAR ASPLUND
    1920–1928
12. **SAN MARIA DEGLI ANGELI**
    FILIPPO BRUNELLESCHI
    1434–I 436

Central: Use

Configurations that place the most important space in the central position are engaged by going to or around this space. At Kahn's Unitarian Church (1) and at Wollaton Hall (2), the central hall, which is lit from above and dominant in form, is surrounded by minor use-spaces and separate circulation. Circulation at the Shaker barn (3) is around a central haymow, which has symbolic, functional, and formal importance. The octagonal central hall in Schinkel's Hunting Lodge (4) has minor use-spaces on only four sides, with circulation at the perimeter. At the Palace of Charles V (5) and Farnese Palace (6), the central space is a court with a colonnade for circulation. At the center of St. Costanza (7) is the most sacred space, while at Trinity Church (8) and St. Mary Woolnoth (9) the center is located within a larger space. Strickland's Second Bank of the United States (10) has a dominant space that is central, with implied circulation and minor use-spaces on only two sides. Circulation at the Stockholm Library (11) is at the perimeter of the central space. Brunelleschi's San Maria degli Angeli (12) has a dominant central space that is surrounded by lesser spaces. Circulation is to and around the central space, but through the lesser spaces.

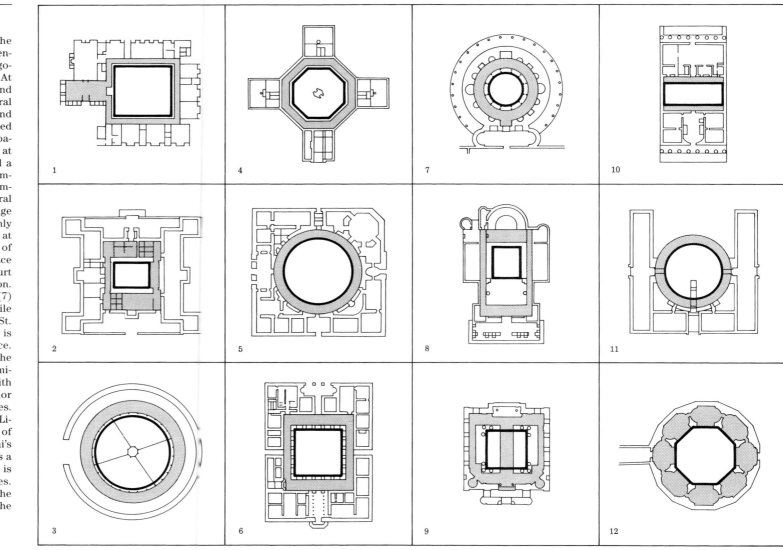

1. **LA ROTONDA**
   ANDREA PALLADIO
   1566–1571
2. **NORTH CAROLINA STATE CAPITOL**
   TOWN AND DAVIS
   1833–1840
3. **UNITED STATES CAPITOL**
   THORNTON-LATROBE-BULFINCH
   1793–1830

4. **HOUSE IN UR**
   ARCHITECT UNKNOWN
   2000 B.C.
5. **HOTEL DE BEAUVAIS**
   ANTOINE LE PAUTRE
   1656
6. **BLOEMENWERF HOUSE**
   HENRY VAN DE VELDE
   1895–1896

7. **BALTIMORE-OHIO RAILROAD DEPOT**
   FRANK FURNESS
   1886
8. **BURN HALL**
   JOHN SOANE
   c. 1785
9. **THE SALUTATION**
   EDWIN LUTYENS
   1911

10. **EXETER LIBRARY**
    LOUIS I. KAHN
    1967–1972
11. **CONVENT OF LA TOURETTE**
    LE CORBUSIER
    1957–1960
12. **STRATFORD HALL**
    ARCHITECT UNKNOWN
    1725

Central: Circulation

La Rotonda (1), the U.S. Capitol (2), and the North Carolina Capitol (3) are examples of classic rotundas. In these cases, the central space, though dominant on the exterior, is used for circulation and as an organizer of other spaces. The courtyards at the House in Ur (4) and the Hotel de Beauvais (5) are alternatives to the classic rotunda. In these two buildings, the courts are dominant plan forms and are used to organize circulation and lesser spaces, but they have no external expression. At the House by van de Velde (6), Furness's railroad station (7), Soane's Burn Hall (8), and Lutyens's Salutation (9), the central space is used for vertical circulation and organizes the building vertically. Kahn's library (10) has a central space that is a rotunda at the main level, while at the upper levels the circulation is around this space. In a somewhat similar fashion, the courtyard at La Tourette (11) incorporates the qualities of both types of central organizations. In some instances the circulation is around the court, as at a cloister, and at other times it is through the court. The central space at Stratford Hall (12) is the main use-space, and serves as a rotunda with circulation through it to lesser spaces.

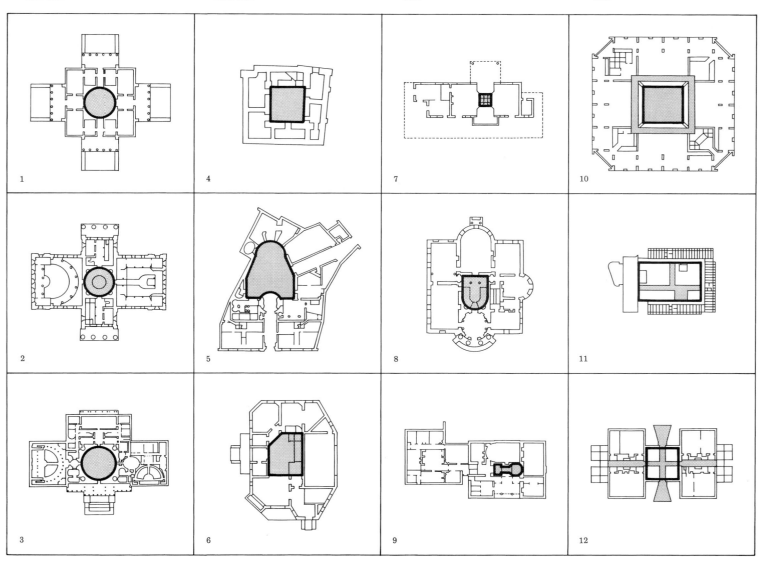

Double Center

Double centers are two equally important foci located within a precinct or field. The Temple of Venus and Rome (1) has two equal, primary rooms, oriented in opposite directions, within a field that is the remainder of the Temple. Each center is an object located within a precinct that is seen as a void. At the Horyu-Ji Temple (2) and the Market in Leptis Magna (3), the precinct is an outdoor court, whereas at Moore's Orinda House (4) and the Palace of Assembly (5), the precinct is a room and indoor space. The Cemetery by Scarpa (6) has one center as an object in an outdoor precinct, while the other center is a room inside the field of the building. If the precinct is solid, then the centers might be voids carved from that solid. At Dover Castle (7) the voids are major rooms, and at the Academy of Art (8) the voids are special places. The remainder of the building is poche. It is also possible that the voids as double centers might organize surrounding spaces and allow light to enter the interior of the building as at the Center for British Arts (9), the Ospedale (10), the Chancellery Palace (11), and Casa Milà (12).

278

1. **TOWER OF LONDON**
ARCHITECT UNKNOWN
1070–1090
2. **FORTRESS NEAR RUDESHEIM**
ARCHITECT UNKNOWN
1000–1050
3. **HOUSE OF VIZIER NAKHT**
ARCHITECT UNKNOWN
1372 B.C.–1350 B.C.

4. **W. WATTS SHERMAN HOUSE**
HENRY HOBSON RICHARDSON
1874
5. **D. L. JAMES HOUSE**
GREENE AND GREENE
1918
6. **OLAVINLINNA CASTLE, FINLAND**
ARCHITECT UNKNOWN
1475

7. **CASTLE IN SOBORG, DENMARK**
ARCHITECT UNKNOWN
c. 1150
8. **OCCUPATIONAL HEALTH CENTER**
HANDY-HOLZMAN-PFIEFFER
1973
9. **CONVENT FOR DOMINICAN SISTERS**
LOUIS I. KAHN
1965–1958

10. **HOUSE IN TUCKER TOWN, BERMUDA**
ROBERT VENTURI
1975
11. **OLIVETTI TRAINING SCHOOL**
JAMES STIRLING
1969
12. **FONTHILL-MERCER CASTLE**
HENRY MERCER
1908–1910

Cluster

Spaces or forms that are grouped without discernible pattern are considered clustered. The clustering of spaces often can determine the form, or at least, have impact on the form, as in the Tower of London (1) and the Watts Sherman House (4). However, spaces might also be clustered within a form whose exterior configuration is predetermined. The fortress in Germany (2) and the House of Vizier Nakht (3) exemplify this category of spatial cluster. Both types of spatial clusters are apparent in the James House (5), with the cluster-determining form variation dominant. The castles in Finland (6) and Denmark (7) are clusters of both forms and spaces. One criterion of clustering is the necessity for proximity between clustered elements. To a certain extent, the walls in the castles create that proximity, while in the Occupational Health Center (8) proximity is established by the large room in which the forms are gathered. Clustered forms may have spatial subdivisions within them as long as those subdivisions are minor. The Convent by Kahn (9), the Bermuda house by Venturi (10), the training center by Stirling (11), and Fonthill (12) are all examples of forms that are clustered.

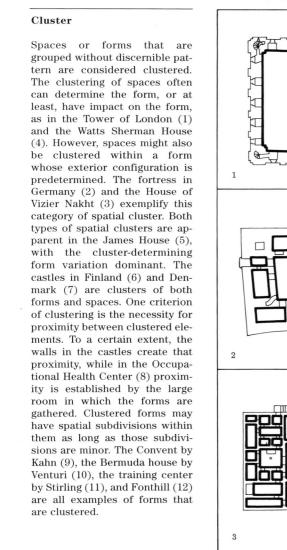

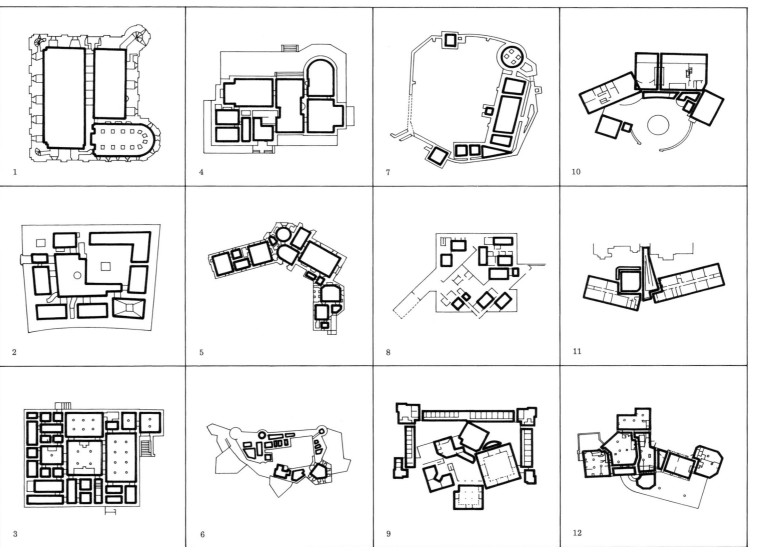

1. **TEMPLE OF APOLLO**
   ARCHITECT UNKNOWN
   c. 400 B.C.
2. **TEMPLE OF KOM OMBO**
   ARCHITECT UNKNOWN
   181 B.C.–30 A.D.
3. **THE PALACE OF ASSEMBLY**
   LE CORBUSIER
   1953–1963

4. **MOORE HOUSE**
   CHARLES MOORE
   1962
5. **ENSO-GUTZEIT HEADQUARTERS**
   ALVAR AALTO
   1959–1962
6. **CAMBRIDGE HISTORY FACULTY**
   JAMES STIRLING
   1964

7. **J. J. GLESSNER HOUSE**
   HENRY HOBSON RICHARDSON
   1885–1887
8. **CHANDLER HOUSE**
   BRUCE PRICE
   1885–1886
9. **HOMEWOOD**
   EDWIN LUTYENS
   1901

Nested

Nested configurations are patterns in which each unit in consecutive order is located inside the next larger unit so that each unit has a different center. At the Temple of Apollo (1) and the Temple of Kom Ombo (2) the units have a common centerline. The geometry change at the Palace of Assembly (3) illustrates that it is not necessary for the nested units to have the same form language. Charles Moore's house in Orinda (4) contains a double set of nested forms. Since nested units do not share a common center, they may have other parts of their configurations in common. This might entail having one side common to all units, as at Aalto's Enso-Gutzeit Headquarters (5). More commonly, though, two sides and a corner are shared by the nested units. The units, then, generally nest diagonally. Stirling's History Building (6), Richardson's Glessner House (7), Price's Chandler House (8), and Lutyens's Homewood (9) exemplify this kind of nesting.

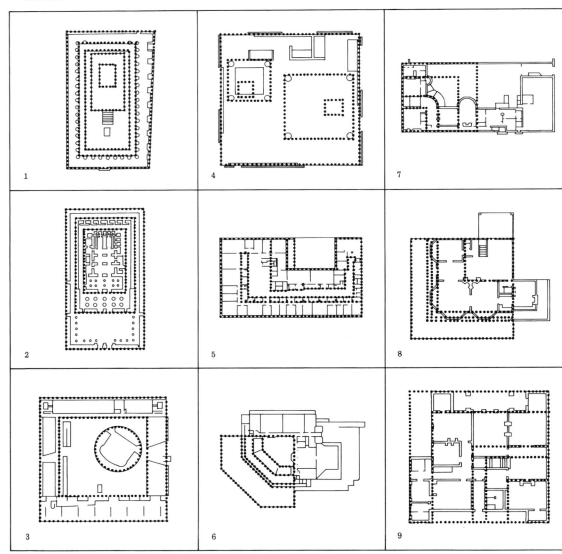

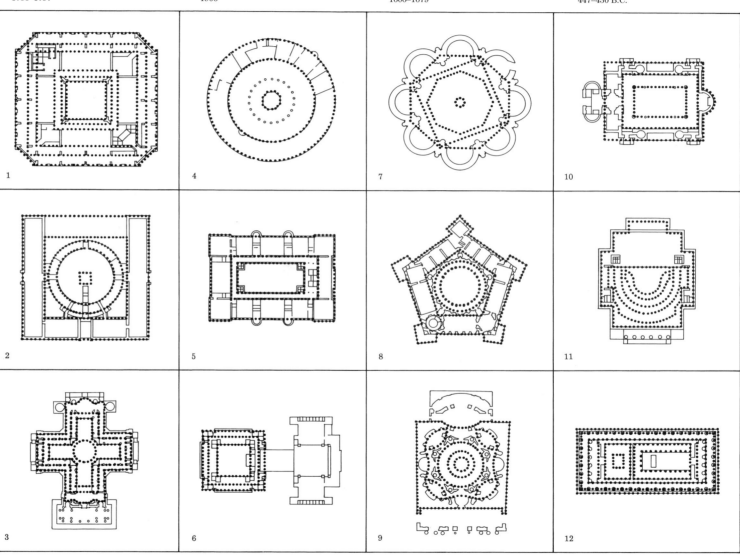

1. **EXETER LIBRARY**
   LOUIS I. KAHN
   1967–1972
2. **STOCKHOLM PUBLIC LIBRARY**
   ERIK GUNNAR ASPLUND
   1920–1928
3. **PANTHEON IN PARIS, FRANCE**
   JACQUES GERMAIN SOUFFLOT
   1756–1797

4. **SANTO STEFANO ROTONDO**
   ARCHITECT UNKNOWN
   468–483
5. **ALLEGHENY COUNTY COURTHOUSE**
   HENRY HOBSON RICHARDSON
   1883–1888
6. **UNITY TEMPLE**
   FRANK LLOYD WRIGHT
   1906

7. **FONTEVRAULT ABBEY**
   ARCHITECT UNKNOWN
   1115
8. **VILLA FARNESE**
   GIACOMO DA VIGNOLA
   1559–1564
9. **CHURCH OF SAN LORENZO**
   GUARINO GUARINI
   1666–1679

10. **ST. GEORGE-IN-THE-EAST**
    NICHOLAS HAWKSMOOR
    1714–1729
11. **THEATER IN BESANÇON, FRANCE**
    CLAUDE NICHOLAS LEDOUX
    1775
12. **PARTHENON**
    ICTINUS
    447–430 B.C.

Concentric

Concentric configurations are patterns in which each unit in consecutive order is located inside the next larger unit so that each unit has the same center. The Exeter Library (1) is an example of concentric configuration created with simple geometric forms. Simple forms of different languages are utilized by Asplund in the Stockholm Library (2). Somewhat more complex, but basically repetitive, units are used at the Pantheon in Paris (3). At Santo Stefano (4), simple geometric forms are repeated, but each ring is articulated in a different manner. The Allegheny Courthouse (5) illustrates a configuration in which each concentric unit is different in function. At Unity Temple (6), the concentric layering is in the major space only. Fontevrault Abbey (7), Villa Farnese (8), and San Lorenzo (9) exemplify the complexity that may result from changing geometries in each of the concentric units. Both nested and concentric configurations are employed by Hawksmoor at St. George (10). Ledoux's theater (11) is nested with half of the plan implied so that the total can be considered a concentric configuration. At the Parthenon (12), the pattern changes from concentric in the outer layers to nested at the inner units.

Binuclear

Binuclear is a configuration pattern with two equally dominant parts. The link between the binuclear components can be a built form which is an entrance space, as in the Robinson House (1), the Capitol at Williamsburg (2), and Unity Temple (4). The built link can also be the major use-space, as in Stratford (3), or a bridge, as in the Queen's House (5). Binuclear elements can be connected by a void or a space, which can be actual, as in the Salk Institute (9), or implied, as in the Postal Savings Bank (6), Olivetti (8), and Nashdom (7). Oita Medical Hall (10), Helsinki House of Culture (11), and the Mellon Arts Center (12) exemplify configurations with different

geometries which are separated. St. Paul's (13) and Dipoli Center (19) have two varied geometries united directly. The Observatory (14) and Redentore Church (15) bring complex and simple forms together. Binuclear elements as positive and negative forms occur in the Farnsworth House (16), the American Academy (17), and Power Center (18). Similar binuclear forms can have different orientations, as in the Carpenter Center (20) and Fisher House (21). Two elements can be similar in form and different in function, as in Lang Music Center (22) and the Robie House (23). Binuclear can also be made manifest in elevations like Le Corbusier's pavilion (24).

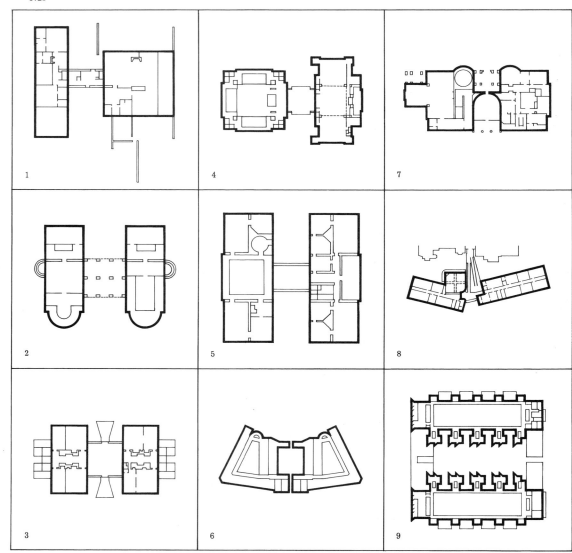

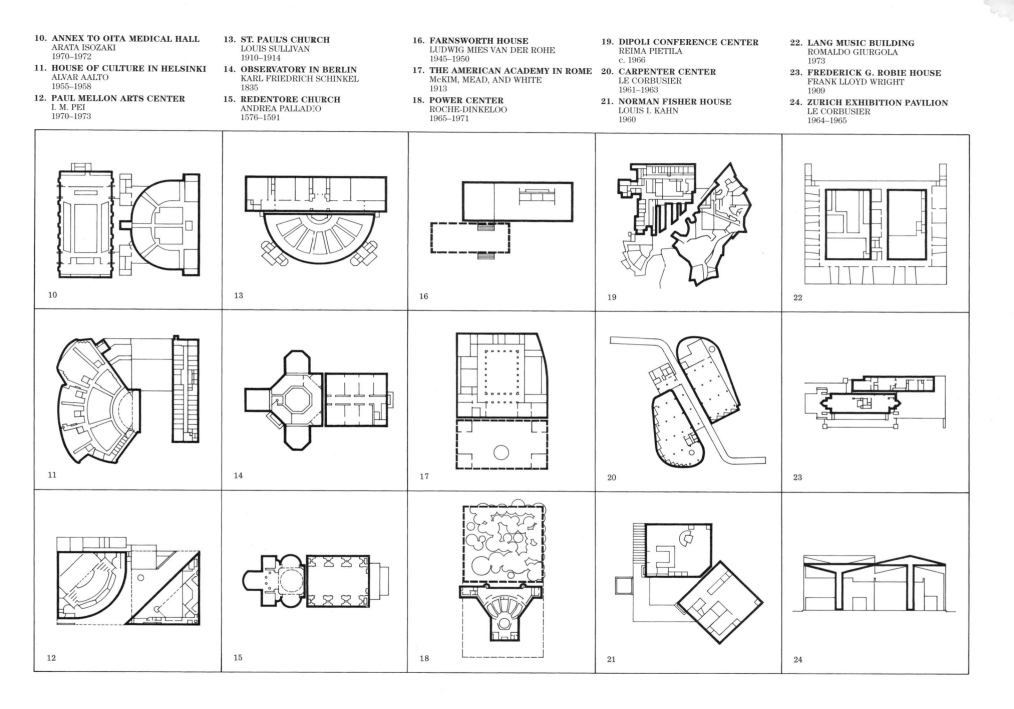

10. ANNEX TO OITA MEDICAL HALL
ARATA ISOZAKI
1970–1972

11. HOUSE OF CULTURE IN HELSINKI
ALVAR AALTO
1955–1958

12. PAUL MELLON ARTS CENTER
I. M. PEI
1970–1973

13. ST. PAUL'S CHURCH
LOUIS SULLIVAN
1910–1914

14. OBSERVATORY IN BERLIN
KARL FRIEDRICH SCHINKEL
1835

15. REDENTORE CHURCH
ANDREA PALLADIO
1576–1591

16. FARNSWORTH HOUSE
LUDWIG MIES VAN DER ROHE
1945–1950

17. THE AMERICAN ACADEMY IN ROME
McKIM, MEAD, AND WHITE
1913

18. POWER CENTER
ROCHE-DINKELOO
1965–1971

19. DIPOLI CONFERENCE CENTER
REIMA PIETILA
c. 1966

20. CARPENTER CENTER
LE CORBUSIER
1961–1963

21. NORMAN FISHER HOUSE
LOUIS I. KAHN
1960

22. LANG MUSIC BUILDING
ROMALDO GIURGOLA
1973

23. FREDERICK G. ROBIE HOUSE
FRANK LLOYD WRIGHT
1909

24. ZURICH EXHIBITION PAVILION
LE CORBUSIER
1964–1965

283

1. **OSTERLARS CHURCH**
   ARCHITECT UNKNOWN
   12th CENTURY
2. **DEAL CASTLE**
   ARCHITECT UNKNOWN
   c. 1540
3. **POLICE HEADQUARTERS**
   HACK KAMPMANN
   1918–1924

4. **EINSIEDELN ABBEY**
   KASPAR MOOSBRUGGER
   1719–1735
5. **TEMPLE OF HORUS**
   ARCHITECT UNKNOWN
   237 B.C.–57 B.C.
6. **RICHARDS RESEARCH BUILDING**
   LOUIS I. KAHN
   1957–1961

7. **DIRECTOR'S HOUSE**
   CLAUDE NICHOLAS LEDOUX
   1775–1779
8. **HEATHCOTE**
   EDWIN LUTYENS
   1906
9. **CHAPEL AT RONCHAMP**
   LE CORBUSIER
   1950–1955

PROGRESSIONS

Progressions are patterns of incremental change that imply movement from one condition or attribute to another. The nature of the change determines the type of progression. Illustrated are examples of hierarchy, transition, transformation, and mediation.

Hierarchy

Hierarchy is the rank ordering of elements relative to the range of an attribute, such that importance or value is ascribed according to the presence or absence of the attribute. The hierarchy in Osterlars Church (1) is determined by size of interior space. Deal Castle (2), an example of concentric configuration, exhibits a rank ordering of centrality: the closer to the center, the more important the space. The Police Headquarters (3) has a hierarchy that is determined by the size, integrity, and memorability of the forms and spaces, and it ranges from dominant figure to background or poche. Sacred to profane establishes the hierarchies in Einsiedeln Abbey (4), Edfu Temple (5), and the Director's House (7). The difference among the three is that the sacred space occurs in two locations in Einsiedeln Abbey, and terminates in a single direction at Edfu Temple and the Director's House. The last example also shows the hierarchy in section. In Richards Lab (6), the hierarchy progresses from collective servant to individual servant to nonservant spaces. Heathcote's (8) elevation exhibits a rank ordering based on proximity to center, and in the Chapel at Ronchamp (9), hierarchy is a function of height and complexity of opening.

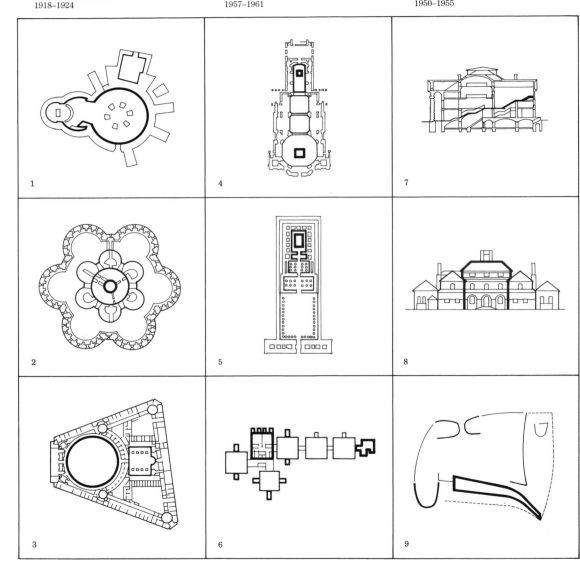

Transition

Transition is the incremental change of an attribute within a finite limit. In the Guild House (1), the configuration of the walls progresses from simple on one side of the building to complex on the other. The Malta Tombs (2), Boyer Hall (3), the House of the Faun (4), and the Jacobsen House in Pennsylvania (5) are examples of transitions of size. This is also the case at Holy Trinity Church (6), the Temple at Monte Alban (7), and the Moore House at Orinda (8). The Pazzi Chapel (9), the Woodland Chapel (10), the Palace of Assembly (11), and Frank Lloyd Wright's Fallingwater (12) exemplify progressions from open to closed.

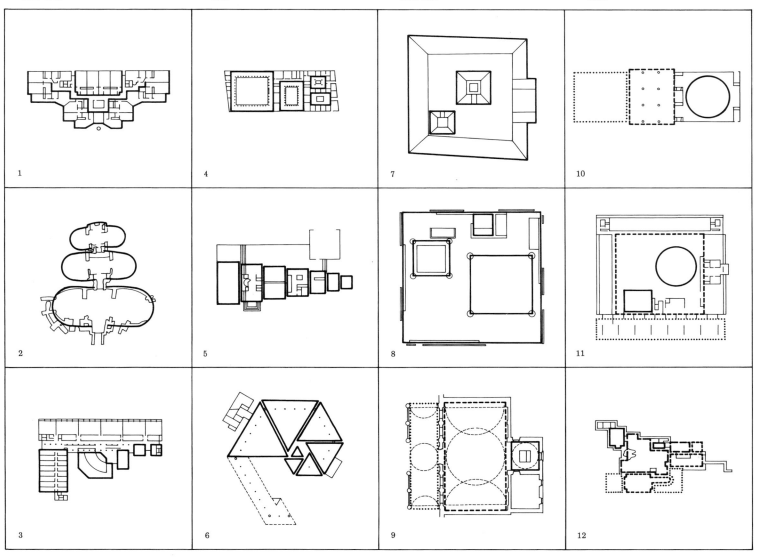

1. **CHURCH OF SAN LORENZO**
   GUARINO GUARINI
   1666–1679
2. **FONTEVRAULT ABBEY**
   ARCHITECT UNKNOWN
   1115
3. **HADRIAN'S MARITIME THEATER**
   ARCHITECT UNKNOWN
   125–135

4. **SAN MARIA DELLA CONSOLAZIONE**
   ARCHITECT UNKNOWN
   1508
5. **NATIONAL ASSEMBLY IN DACCA**
   LOUIS I. KAHN
   1962–1974
6. **ST. MARY'S CATHEDRAL**
   KENZO TANGE
   1963

7. **CHURCH AT FIRMINY-VERT**
   LE CORBUSIER
   1963
8. **LISTER COUNTY COURTHOUSE**
   ERIK GUNNAR ASPLUND
   1917–1921
9. **ADULT LEARNING LABORATORY**
   ROMALDO GIURGOLA
   1972

10. **KARLSKIRCHE**
    JOHAN FISCHER VON ERLACH
    1715–1737
11. **BATHS AT OSTIA, ITALY**
    ARCHITECT UNKNOWN
    c.150
12. **HOTEL DE MONTMORENCY**
    CLAUDE NICHOLAS LEDOUX
    1769

Transformation

Transformation is the incremental change from one form to a different form. San Lorenzo (1), Fontevrault Abbey (2), Hadrian's Villa (3), San Maria della Consolazione (4), and the National Assembly (5) are examples of concentric transformations. In these buildings the form at the center transforms, through a series of changes, to a different form at the perimeter. In St. Mary's Cathedral (6) and the Church at Firminy (7), the transformation occurs vertically from ground level to top. St. Mary's changes from a diamond to a cruciform, and at Firminy a square is transformed into a circular form. The Lister County Courthouse (8) and the Adult Learning Research Lab (9) exemplify form change, from outside to inside, of significant elements within the building. Transformation of direction and change of adjacent forms occur in Karlskirche (10). In the Baths at Ostia (11) and Hotel de Montmorency (12), a transformation of adjacent units occurs.

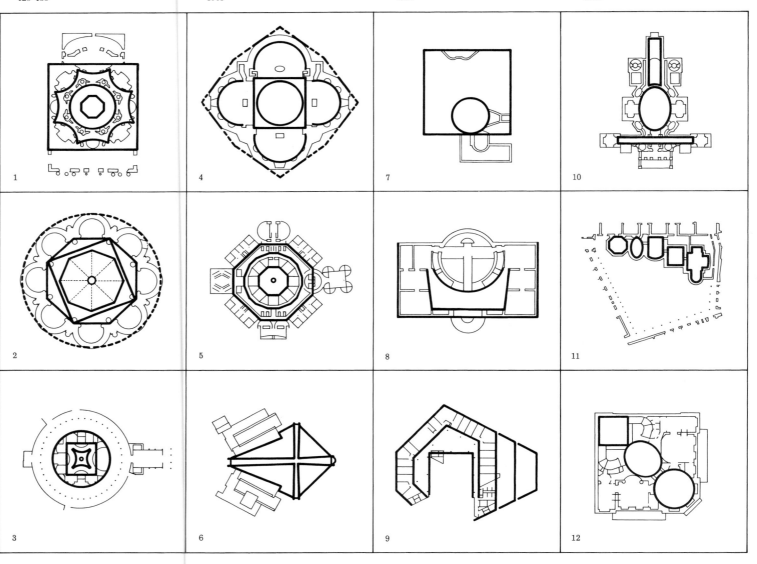

Mediation

Mediation is the insertion of some form of progression between two conditions which occur outside the limits of the building. It is common for mediation to occur between two natural conditions, an element in nature and a built form, or two built situations. The Royal Chancellery (1), the Euram Building (2), the Alajarvi Town Hall (3), the Allen Art Center (4), and the AIA Headquarters (5) are buildings designed to mediate between existing contextural conditions within a built environment. The weekend house (6) mediates between two natural situations: the horizontality of the water and the verticality of the woods. The Atheneum (7), Tredyffrin Library (8), and Aalto's Church at Imatra (9) mediate between a component in nature and a condition in built form. The Atheneum occurs between the curvilinear form of the river and the orthogonal grid of the town. At Tredyffrin, the mediation is between a special point marked by a tree and the orthogonal built environment. In Imatra the design is inserted between other buildings and the natural context of the woods.

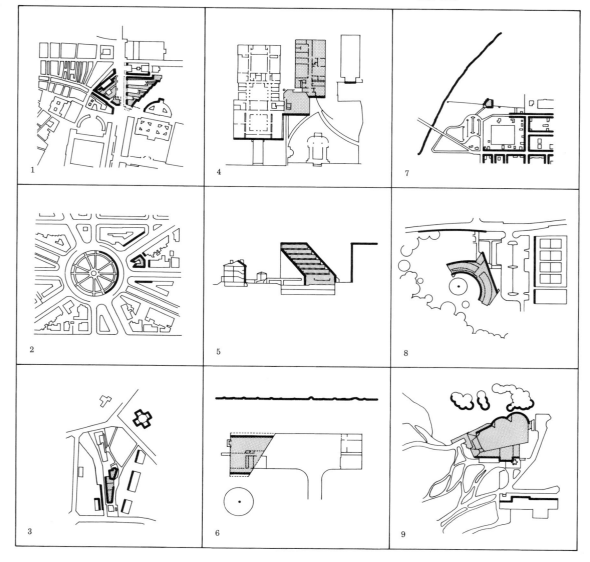

287

1. **THE SALUTATION**
   EDWIN LUTYENS
   1911
2. **VILLA SHODHAN**
   LE CORBUSIER
   1951

3. **SYDNEY OPERA HOUSE**
   JØRN UTZON
   1957–1968
4. **GOETHEANUM I**
   RUDOLF STEINER
   1913–1920

5. **SHUKOSHA BUILDING**
   ARATA ISOZAKI
   1974–1975
6. **SNELLMAN HOUSE**
   ERIK GUNNAR ASPLUND
   1917–1918

REDUCTION

Reduction is the miniaturization of the whole or a major part of a building. This scaled down component can be included as a part within the whole or as a secondary element added to the primary form.

Large Plus Small Reduction

It is common for the reduced form to be the servant element, as at Salutation (1), Villa Shodhan (2), Shukosha Building (5), Snellman House (6), Robie House (7), and Coonley House (8). Unity Temple (9) is similar in that the reduced form is also servant, but the reduction occurs in elevation. Scaled down forms for comparable use occur in the Sydney Opera House (3), the Goetheanum I (4), the Mummers Theater (11), the Woodland Crematory (12), the Van Buren House (13), and the Wolfsburg Parish Center (14). Large plus small reduction is not limited to one form at each scale. Castle del Monte (10) is an example of multiple smaller units added to the original form. Interesting uses of this reduction concept include the design of an addition that is a miniaturization of the existing Claghorn House (15), and the design of the Council Chamber, as a reduction of the entire building, in Aalto's Saynatsalo Town Hall (16).

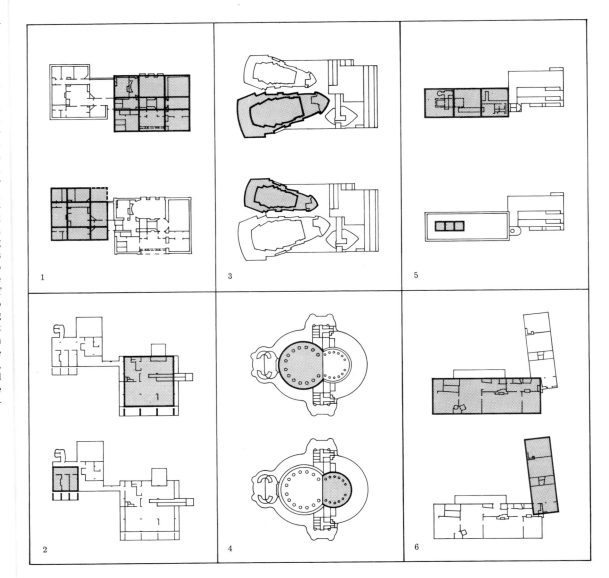

1

3

5

2

4

6

7. FREDERICK G. ROBIE HOUSE
FRANK LLOYD WRIGHT
1909

8. AVERY COONLEY HOUSE
FRANK LLOYD WRIGHT
1907

9. UNITY TEMPLE
FRANK LLOYD WRIGHT
1906

10. CASTLE DEL MONTE
ARCHITECT UNKNOWN
c. 1240

11. MUMMERS THEATER
JOHN M. JOHANSEN
1970

12. WOODLAND CREMATORIUM
ERIK GUNNAR ASPLUND
1935–1940

13. TRAVIS VAN BUREN HOUSE
BRUCE PRICE
1885

14. WOLFSBURG PARISH CENTER HALL
ALVAR AALTO
1960–1962

15. CLAGHORN HOUSE
MICHAEL GRAVES
1974

16. SAYNATSALO TOWN HALL
ALVAR AALTO
1950–1952

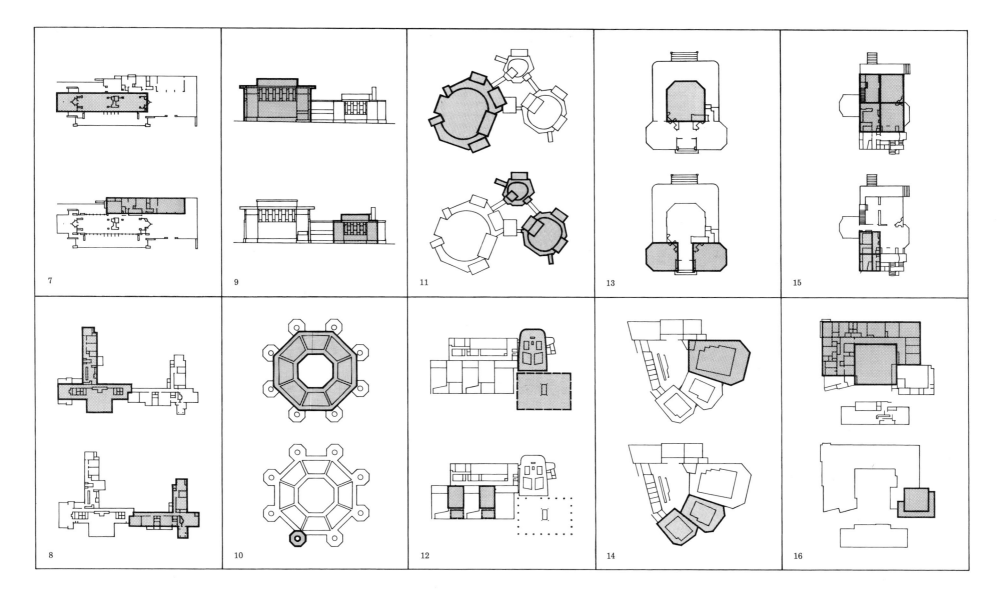

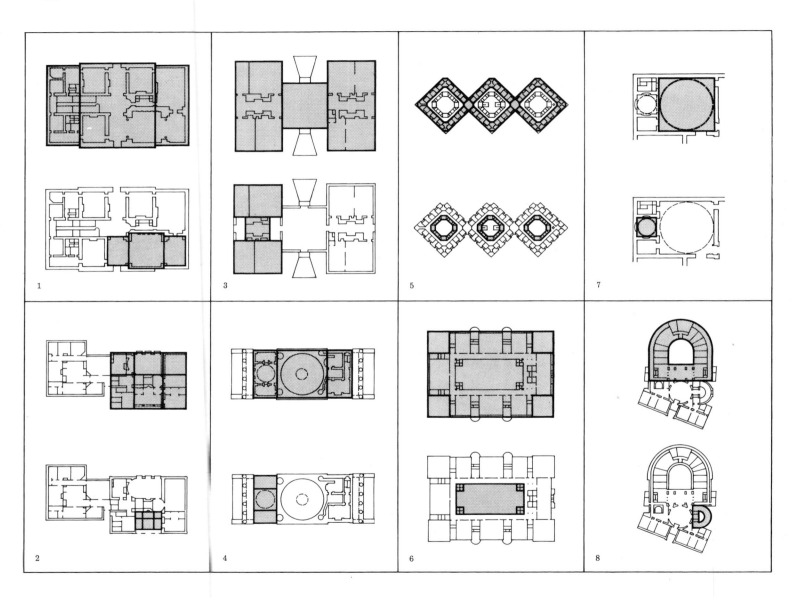

Part of Whole Reduction

Major rooms, spaces, or groupings of spaces form the reductions of the whole building in
Easton Neston (1), Salutation
(2), Stratford Hall (3), and the
Bank of Pennsylvania (4). This is
also the case in Bryn Mawr Dormitories (5), the Allegheny
County Building (6), and Guild
House (14). In the Old Sacristy
(7) and the Landerbank (8), the
part, an altar space and main
stair, respectively, is a reduction
of the dominant space or form of
the building. Christ Church (9)
and St. Clement Danes (10) are
similar in that adjacent spaces
defined by columns are the
buildings and towers reduced.
Two aedicula in the Moore
House (11) reflect the whole,
and in St. Mary's Cathedral (12)
the nave is reduced to a smaller
dome and adjacent space. At
Heathcote (13), the plan configuration of the garden side of the
house is reduced to form the entry side. In the Parthenon (15),
the reduction includes a reversal
in space definition by walls or
columns. The positive-negative
configuration of the Hanselmann
House (16), with its forecourt, is
reduced to create the main living
spaces. In the Yano House (17)
the plan is reduced to form part
of the section, and an elevation
reduction forms the fireplace in
the Tucker House. (18).

1. **EASTON NESTON**
   NICHOLAS HAWKSMOOR
   c. 1695–1710
2. **THE SALUTATION**
   EDWIN LUTYENS
   1911
3. **STRATFORD HALL**
   ARCHITECT UNKNOWN
   1725
4. **BANK OF PENNSYLVANIA**
   BENJAMIN HENRY LATROBE
   1798–1800
5. **ERDMAN HALL DORMITORIES**
   LOUIS I. KAHN
   1960–1965
6. **ALLEGHENY COUNTY COURTHOUSE**
   HENRY HOBSON RICHARDSON
   1883–1888
7. **OLD SACRISTY**
   FILIPPO BRUNELLESCHI
   1421–1440
8. **LANDERBANK**
   OTTO WAGNER
   1883–1884

290

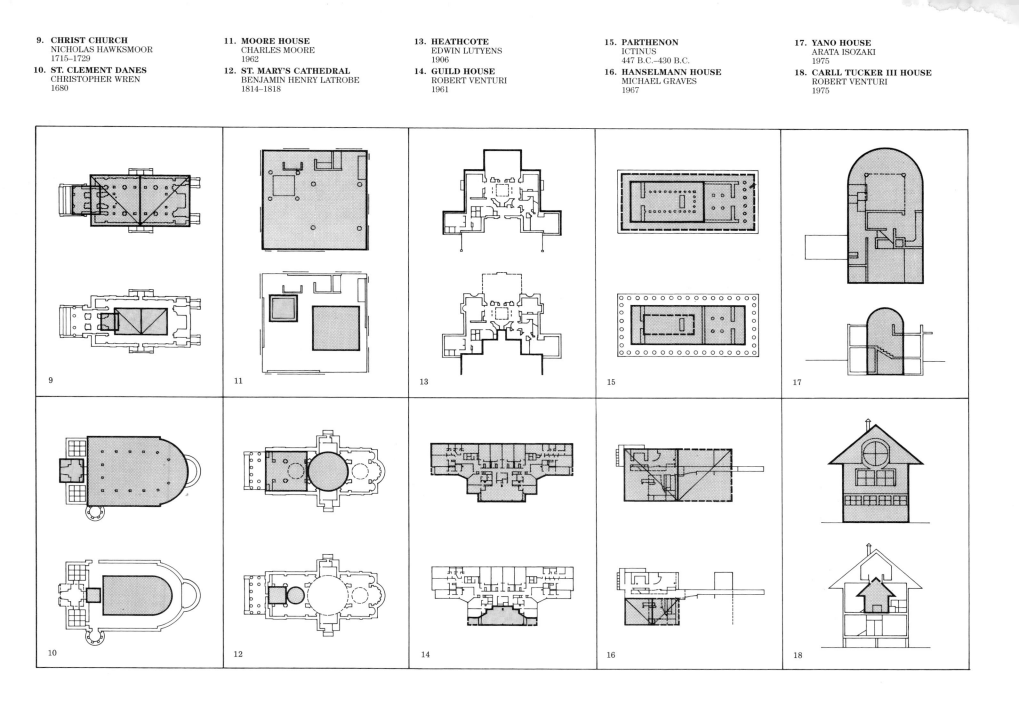

INDEX BY ARCHITECT

The information in this book has been indexed twice—by architect and by common building name. The index by architect includes the life dates of the person when known, the buildings by that architect that are included in this volume, and the dates of those buildings followed by the page number.

INDEX BY BUILDING